New Con

NEW
FOR YOUNG PEOPLE

New Connections 99

NEW PLAYS
FOR YOUNG PEOPLE

faber and faber

First published in 1999 by Faber and Faber Limited
3 Queen Square London WC1N 3AU
Published in the United States by Faber and Faber Inc.
a division of Farrar, Straus and Giroux Inc., New York

Typeset by Country Setting, Kingsdown, Kent CT14 8ES
Printed in England by Mackays of Chatham plc, Chatham, Kent

All rights reserved

A CIP record for this book is available from the British Library

ISBN 0-571-20196-2 (Faber edn)
ISBN 0-7487-5117-3 (Stanley Thornes edn)

2 4 6 8 10 9 7 5 3 1

Contents

Introduction vii

After Juliet by Sharman Macdonald 1
'Scratching the Itch' 85
Production Notes 89

Can You Keep a Secret? by Winsome Pinnock 93
'Something to be Reclaimed' 138
Production Notes 142

The Devil in Drag by Dario Fo
translated and adapted by Ed Emery 147
'Unleashing the Powers of Liberation' 225
Production Notes 229

Don't Eat Little Charlie
by Tankred Dorst with Ursula Ehler
translated by Ella Wildridge 233
'Write in the Morning and the Rest is Adventure' 275
Production Notes 279

Early Man by Hannah Vincent 285
'Reach Out across the Ages' 327
Production Notes 331

Friendly Fire by Peter Gill 337
'Young Men Sent to War as the Serpent Enters the Garden' 384
Production Notes 388

Gizmo by Alan Ayckbourn 393
'I Will Take the Boy for £3 a Week' 444
Production Notes 448

The King of the Castle by Christina Reid 453
'Secrets of a Five-Year Diary Unlocked' 506
Production Notes 510

The Pilgrimage by Paul Goetzee 515
'Held in the Hands Like a Butterfly' 551
Production Notes 555

Taking Breath by Sarah Daniels 561
'The Most Courageous Thing is to Keep Breathing' 602
Production Notes 605

Introduction

Now in its third cycle, Connections is the most imaginative, exciting and significant large-scale theatre project in the country. Throughout the UK and Ireland, more than a thousand young actors perform in several hundred premieres of ten specially commissioned new plays by top writers from England, Ireland, Scotland, Wales, Italy and Germany. This bumper volume includes new plays by Alan Ayckbourn, Sarah Daniels, Tankred Dorst with Ursula Ehler, Dario Fo, Peter Gill, Paul Goetzee, Sharman MacDonald, Winsome Pinnock, Christina Reid and Hannah Vincent.

Connections is chiefly about the writers and the actors. It aims to introduce the work of exceptional living play-wrights to today's young actors. Since repertory theatres largely ceased to commission or produce new work, and the touring circuit for new writing diminished drastically, young actors will probably not have had the chance to see and enjoy the sheer scope, variety and power of the new plays written over the last twenty years. The Connections project gives them the opportunity to create premieres by some of the best playwrights in the country in their own spaces.

In commissioning the plays we kept several things in mind. Firstly, we had to be great admirers of the writers' work. Next, their language, themes, stories, characters and obsessions – their dramatic and imaginative view of the world – needed to resonate strongly with that of young people. Also, we wanted to extend our range so that we could include contemporary playwrights from Europe. We needed a selection of plays which would work for the huge variety of companies involved in the project, with their various cast ages and sizes. And we wanted plays which would possess an instant universality – so a play written by an Italian would work immediately in, say Scotland.

Above all, we wanted imaginative power and ambition. When we commissioned the plays we set out the structure of the project, and discussed ideas and shards of ideas with the writers. But real plays get their inventive energy from the surprises and unexpected associations and discoveries made in the act of writing; what they are really about emerges this way, rather than by forward planning. So we wanted to be surprised by the plays. And we didn't want them to be safe options either: new writing is always a dramatic and imaginative challenge to the invention, skill and stamina of the company. Our conviction about this was confirmed during the last cycle of Connections plays, when we went to Cornwall to see Simon Armitage's *Eclipse*. A young cast had created a production of conviction, power and poetry. Talking to them afterwards they said at first they hadn't 'understood the play' – they weren't sure they liked it. But as they worked on it, they came under its spell and began to make discoveries and connections. In the end, they said, they were obsessed with its complexity, mystery and power; it was the most important thing they had ever done.

THE PLAYS

Alan Ayckbourn's *Gizmo* is a characteristically, inventive, dark and entertaining play. The Gizmo project is a cutting-edge scientific development in which a device like a watch worn on the wrist by a doctor, together with a tiny implant in the patient's brain, allows Ben, paralysed in a shoot-out in his bar, to walk again – in fact, to copy every tiny movement of the person wearing the 'watch'. However, when this technological marvel falls into the wrong hands things go seriously awry.

Sarah Daniels's play *Taking Breath* takes a fast and funny look at aspects of contemporary environmental protest; a group of determined teenagers attempt to save a row of ancient trees from demolition by building a platform and chaining themselves to it for a night. The play is a vivid ghost story in which the past and present meet and also a moving love story in which several of the characters, desperately in need of forgiveness and understanding, discover each other.

Friendly Fire by Peter Gill is a beautifully nuanced, detailed and moving study of a love triangle at the heart of a group of teenagers. Adie likes Gary, but Gary likes Shelley, who likes Adie . . . None of this is simple, as the three discover as they struggle to find out 'what they can put up with and what they can't'.

Paul Goetzee's *Pilgrimage* is an original and powerful fable about friendship and enmity, family and foe. Set in a fictitious East European country – a wild, remote land-scape that only supports sheep and goats – two tribes, the shepherds and goatherds, live in mutual animosity and fear, as they have done since time began. Nothing new is allowed to challenge or interrupt the time-honoured traditions of the two clans. But when Josef, a goatherd, happens upon the shepherd twins Mendel and Chaff, one of the twins wants to hear what he has to say, while the other believes any contact is blasphemous betrayal. From this moment on the family are divided, and only a miracle will break the cycle of hatred and revenge, and reunite the warring sides.

Sharman Macdonald's *After Juliet* is set during the tense aftermath of the deaths of Romeo and Juliet. The dead lovers' families and friends are commanded to respect a truce, but the younger Montagues and Capulets continue to feud. Benvolio, Romeo's best friend, loves Rosaline, Juliet's cousin. But Rosaline is still in love with Romeo and determined on revenge. As the stage directions indicate, the play is a dramatic, poetic and musical invention on the themes, characters and consequences of the old story of the famous lovers.

The Devil in Drag by Dario Fo is a riotous celebratory piece of theatre in which a corrupt church tries to trick a good judge into debauchery and corruption. Complicated by the involvement of two conniving devils, the stage is set for chaos and confusion. A classic piece of commedia dell'arte by a Nobel Laureate and one of the world's masters of the genre, adapted for the project by his translator Ed Emery.

Christina Reid's *The King of the Castle* is set on a Belfast housing estate and wasteground of the 1950s. Eileen, Rose and Billy spend their time playing pavement games and flying their kites as high as the wasteground pigeons, under the steady gaze of Arthur, a young man traumatised by what he witnessed in the Second World War, a child living inside a man's body. When Eileen's mother encourages her to be kind to him, she touches and awakens the horror of his experiences, the consequences of which will affect them all.

Early Man by Hannah Vincent takes place in a museum where the body of a young boy preserved for thousands of years in a peat bog is on display. Bog Boy is lonely, so when Sam and her class arrive for a week's field trip he tells her that everything people say about him is untrue, that he was murdered and has been separated in death from a precious brooch given to him by his girlfriend. Disbelieved by everyone, Sam decides to help Bog Boy and discovers what really matters to her. This surreal fable becomes a voyage of friendship and discovery.

Can You Keep a Secret? by Winsome Pinnock tackles the difficult and controversial issue of racial hatred and violence. When a young black boy Derek is brutally murdered by Sean, who is white, Derek's friends swear revenge while Sean's gang who witnessed the attack are sworn to secrecy. But this proves too big a burden for the young people, whose consciences are torn apart by what they have seen. When Sean's girlfriend Kate decides to tell the truth she meets a wall of complicity and silence which eventually shields the killer. She swears that she will devote the rest of her life to telling the truth.

Don't Eat Little Charlie by Tankred Dorst with Ursula Ehler is an original fairytale by one of Germany's leading playwrights. It has been translated by Ella Wildridge. Granmaha found Charlie, his brother Olmo and Pug at the station buffet where she works and brought them to live with her. Olmo has started to eat everything, and would eat Charlie if he could. He grows to such a size that he must live outside. When newcomer Fizzipizzi the electric girl arrives and their racist landlord threatens them all with eviction, their only hope lies in the arrival of the black King, his music and his golden crown.

THE PRODUCTIONS

Having chosen their play the directors were invited to start the rehearsal process in the best possible way – by workshopping it with the writer and a facilitating director from the National Theatre. The notes accompanying the scripts in this volume are based on the work carried out on a residential weekend in the Midlands. The workshops were led by Connol Orton and Jack Murphy (*Gizmo*), Gemma Bodinetz (*Taking Breath*), John Rettalack and Christian Daly (*Don't Eat Little Charlie*), Jonathan Lloyd (*The Devil in Drag*), Paul Miller (*Friendly Fire*), Ed Woodhall (*The Pilgrimage*), Chris Barton (*After Juliet*), John Burgess (*Can You Keep a Secret?*), Dominic Hill (*King of the Castle*), and Mary Peate (*Early Man*). Soutra Gilmour provided advice on set and costume design. The directors and their companies were then able to keep in touch with the writers and other companies in the project through the Connections Website. Here they were able to compare approaches to the same script throughout the rehearsal period.

As we write, the companies are about to produce their shows in their own venues, across the UK and Ireland. They will continue to be supported by the Connections producers at one of the ten flagship theatres: Sonia Rose at Eden Court (in collaboration with Annie Wood at MacRobert Arts Centre), Ian Wainwright at the Stephen Joseph Theatre, Tim Baker and Dave Greenhaulgh at Clwyd Theatr Cymru, Wade Kamaria at Nottingham Playhouse, Roberta Hammond at Cambridge Arts Theatre, Andy Brereton, Chichester Festival, Russ Tunney and Fiona Clark at Bath Theatre Royal, David McFeteridge at the Lyric, Belfast, Sue Emmas at the Young Vic and Clare Binden of Plymouth Theatre Royal. Most will go on to take part in one of the ten regional festivals created by these theatres in the spring of 1999.

Connections 99 will culminate in a summer festival in the Cottesloe and Olivier Theatres at the National Theatre where the most interesting production of each of the ten plays will be performed. But the effect of the project won't stop there. Plays from previous cycles are being translated and performed across the world from Bangkok to New Jersey, from Munich to Florence and Hong Kong. The National's own adult company will 'borrow' *Sparkleshark* by Philip Ridley (created for the last cycle of the project) and the production will join the repertoire and play in the Lyttelton Theatre in June 1999, directed by Terry Johnson. This will bring about an important role reversal because young people normally borrow from the adult canon of work. And plans are already under way to commission a new series of world class plays for young performers to take us creatively and confidently into the twenty-first century.

Nick Drake, Joanne Reardon, Suzy Graham-Adriani
February 1999

AFTER JULIET

Sharman Macdonald

*based on an original idea by Keira Knightley
with thanks to William Shakespeare*

Characters

Benvolio
A Montague. Sixteen. Romeo's best friend.

Valentine
A Montague. Sixteen. Mercutio's twin brother.

Rosaline
A Capulet. Fifteen. Juliet's cousin.

Bianca
A Capulet. Fourteen but younger than her years.
Suffers from *petit mal*. Juliet's cousin.

Helena
A Capulet. Sixteen. Bianca's sister. Juliet's cousin.

Rhona
A Capulet. Sixteen. A visitor from Glasgow.
Juliet's cousin. Plays the flute (or another silver
solo wind instrument. A tin whistle would do).

Alice
A Capulet. Sixteen. Juliet's cousin.

Livia
A Capulet. Fourteen. Rosaline's half sister.
Juliet's cousin.

Angelica
A Capulet servant. Juliet's nurse. Thirty.

Lorenzo
A Capulet. Sixteen.

Gianni
A Capulet. Sixteen.

Petruchio
A Capulet. Eighteen. Tybalt's brother.

Romeo
A Montague. Dead.

Juliet
A Capulet. Dead.

The Drummer
Ever present. Non-partisan. A slight threat.
A small sense that he's a puppeteer. At times he cues
the action. This should be subtle; there and gone in the
flutter of an eyelash. The sentences that describe the
action are long: the action itself should be short.

A Musician

*The music is original; written by Caleb Knightley and
Adrian Howgate for sampler, drums and flute.*

One set.

*The quotations in the text are adapted from
Brooke's Romeus and Juliet (1562) which was,
in turn, a translation from the Italian of Bandello's
Romeus and Juliet (1554).*

*The text should be played at speed.
Should 'fuck' be a pain and a trouble
please change it to 'feck' or a rhythmic equivalent.*

*** or * in the text indicates that two pieces
of dialogue run simultaneously.*

Silence.
   The drummer alone.
   Stands.
   Moves.
   Drums. Rolling soft and long.
   Rosaline's idly throwing dice. Again and again and
again.
   The drummer click click clicks. Benvolio edges into
the sunshine. Gazes up at Rosaline's balcony.

Livia
   He's looking at you.
Rosaline
   Let him.
Livia
   Romeo's dead, Rosaline
   And didn't even think of you.
   Forgot you as soon as he saw Juliet.
Rosaline
   I can't turn my love off like a tap.
Livia
   Forget Romeo.
   He didn't know you loved him.
   You wouldn't speak to him.
   You sent his letters back;
   Left his flowers without water to die
   And his poems in the rain.
   In what land do you call that love?
Rosaline
   I wanted him to see

5

I wasn't so easily won.
He was a Montague after all.
'Never trust a Montague.'
I sucked that in with mother's milk.

Livia

Your mother!

Rosaline

My mother loved my father
Then your mother came along
And my father treated my mother with scorn
And traded her in for
A somewhat younger woman.
Don't talk to me about caution with men.
I learnt from observation
That what's most hard come by is most valued.

Livia

If I were a man I'd look for a woman to keep me
If I were that way inclined
Or a man if no woman could be found.
There's no intrinsic honour in work
Only stress sweat and labour.
Whatever the gender.
Not to do it
That's what I'm after.
Marry. Marry money, Rosaline.
Hire a cook for the kitchen
A nanny for the children
And unless he's very talented in that direction
Hire a mistress for the bedroom.
** Time would never hang heavy on my hands.
For I can live quite happily with my female friends.

The drummer click, click, clicks and points at
*Rosaline. ***

Recorded words. An announcement. Coming from
afar. Coming close. Moving on. Moving away.

PA

'Both households straight are charged on payne of
  losing lyfe
Theyr bloudy weapons to lay aside; to cease the
  styrred stryfe.
The wiser sort Prince Escalus calls to councell streyt
That a trial may be held in front of the populace
And justice meted out to those elders of this place
Judged to blame for the deaths of Romeo and Juliet.
  Angelica the nurse stands accused
The servant Peter.
Fryr Lawrence.
The apothecary of Mantua.
  Both households straight are charged on payne of
  losing lyfe
Theyr bloudy weapons to lay aside; to cease the
  styrred stryfe.'

** Rosaline climbs down and moves swiftly through
the piazza.*
  *Valentine slides out of the shadows. Catches hold of
her. Holds her tightly by the wrist.*

Rosaline

Is this how you keep the truce? *
Valentine

There's no knife at your throat.
Rosaline

* Tybalt sported with your brother;
Cat and mouse.
Romeo killed Mercutio
Who stepped between.
Ask Benvolio.
All who were there say so.
I say it who loved Romeo.
Valentine

I see a spitting cat

7

In your eyes, Rosaline.
I don't see a truce.

Rosaline
You must like my sleeve very much
To hold on to it for so long.

Valentine
Benvolio watches you day and night.

Rosaline
So where is he now
When I need him?

Valentine
Leave him alone, Rosaline.
Don't smile at him.
Don't stop when you see him.
Don't, knowing he's watching
Wash in the sunlight
With the shutters open.
No girl's tricks.
I know them all.
Don't rouge your cheeks for him.
Nor wear perfume for him.
If you do any of these things
I will see.
I will know.
I will come for you.
With no Prince of Cats
Your rabble won't protect you.

Rosaline
We elect a new Prince tonight.
Keep clear, Valentine.
Lest you get scratched.

Valentine
Know what I want right now?

Rosaline
A dress like mine?

Valentine
Wash my hands of you
That's what I want. * *
Get the smell of you and all Capulets
Off my hands.

Rosaline
* * You want your Mammy, Valentine, like all the wee
bully boys.

Lorenzo and Gianni slide out of the shadows.
Begin to close on Valentine.

Go Valentine. Go.
Don't be a fool.
This is our territory.

He lets her go. Ostentatiously spits on his hands and
*wipes them on his tunic. * **
This could be Verona.
Or it could be Edinburgh, Dublin, New York or
Liverpool.
Narrow alleys. High buildings almost touching at
the top. A strip of blue sky shading into cloud far
away. Heat. The sudden space of a piazza.
** The boys slide away. Melt.*
Rosaline runs.
The girls on balconies. Like a thought murmuring.

Bianca
* * Clouds coming.

Alice
Rain on its way.

Livia
Thunder.

Rhona
Close.

Rosaline
August.

Helena

Muggy.

Bianca

Clouds coming in.

Distant thunder.
   *** The girls murmur continues round and round,
under Gianni and Lorenzo, accompanied by music.
Almost a song. Until it fades and dies.*
   *** Light hits the drummer and moves on to Gianni
and Lorenzo in the shadows.*

Gianni

D'you feel a breeze?

Lorenzo

Nah. You?

Gianni

Nah.

Lorenzo

The earth's holding its breath.

Gianni

What?

Lorenzo

Feels like.

Gianni

Feels like the earth's holding its breath?

Lorenzo

Feels like.

Gianni

Fuck off.

Lorenzo

Day like this. I made love.

Gianni

You did not.

Lorenzo

After the day. In the night. I did. I made love.

Gianni
  To a girl?
Lorenzo
  To a marmoset.
Gianni
  A marmoset?
Lorenzo
  To a girl. To a girl.
Gianni
  What girl? What fucking girl?
Lorenzo
  Juliet.
Gianni
  Fuck off.
Lorenzo
  Her name was Juliet.
Gianni
  You made love with Juliet! That's what you're telling
  me?
Lorenzo
  Juliet.
Gianni
  Juliet?
Lorenzo
  You're in my face, Gianni.
Gianni
  You made love with Juliet?
Lorenzo
  I made love with Juliet.
Gianni
  You had her.
Lorenzo
  I had her.
Gianni
  You did not.

Lorenzo

I know who I made love to.

Gianni

You're a big fuck-off liar, Lorenzo.

Lorenzo

You calling me a liar?

Gianni

A fuck-off, fucking liar.

Lorenzo gets his arm round Gianni's neck.

Lorenzo

Know what I call this? Do you know what I call this?
'Last Gasp' that's what I call this. Fucking last gasp.

I'm fucking sharing something with you man.
You're my friend, and I'm sharing it with you.
Capulet to Capulet. Lorenzo to Gianni. I'm sharing a
treasured moment with my friend.

I made love to Juliet. It was hot. I was thirteen. The
night before I was fourteen. She came to me.

First she was babying me
Like she was my mother
Then she's wrestling me
Like she was my friend.
Then . . .
She's my lover.

Gianni

Juliet?

The hold tightens.

Lorenzo

Juliet.

A beat. A thought.

Gianni

Juliet who?

A beat. A realisation.

Lorenzo
Shit, Gianni.
Shit, man.
Juliet!
Not that Juliet.
Juliet!
Gianni
Not that Juliet?
Lorenzo
Not that Juliet.
Gianni
Another Juliet?
Lorenzo
Another fucking Juliet.
Gianni
Common enough name.
Lorenzo
Common enough name.
Gianni
Easy fucking mistake.
Lorenzo
Easy fucking mistake.
Gianni
Not dead Juliet?
Lorenzo
Not dead fucking Juliet.

The hold's released.

Gianni
Too hot.
Lorenzo
Too fucking hot.
Gianni
You were thirteen?

Lorenzo
Thirteen.
Gianni
August you say?
Lorenzo
It was hot.
When we had our clothes off
Lying there.
The breeze cooled the sweat on her skin
Her skin like ice
Breeze like a kiss
Kiss like silk
Her skin was green in the moonlight.
Gianni
Green?
Lorenzo
Green.
Gianni
Green skin?
Lorenzo
Next day was August twelfth,
St Lorenzo's Day,
Open season.
We came at them from above.
They defended well.
I was fourteen.
Gianni
Good day.
Lorenzo
Sweet good day.
Gianni
Green skin?
Lorenzo
Like she came to me
From another world
Another fucking world.

A clash of a cymbal. Music.
   Rosaline alone. Running. Dodging. Running.
   A stone's thrown. And another. And another.
   One hits her.
   She cowers down.
Benvolio comes up quietly behind her.
   Startles her.
Takes her under the arcade.

Rosaline
   I'm not frightened.
Benvolio
   No need now.
Rosaline
   Now you're with me?
Benvolio
   I came to talk to you.
Rosaline
   And your shadow?
Benvolio
   I'm on my own, Rosaline.
Rosaline
   Someone's throwing the stones.
Benvolio
   Some kid that's all. Not one of ours.
Rosaline
   Hardly one of ours.
Benvolio
   The truce is holding.
Rosaline
   It's a fine peace.
   A bruising peace.
   Prince Escalus's peace.
Benvolio
   It'll settle when the trial's over.
   The day's hot with the sweat of it.

Rosaline
  When there's a new Prince of Cats.
  Then the days will breath again.
Benvolio
  You are frightened.
Rosaline
  I'll conquer it.

  Thunder rolls.

  That was a long one.

  Benvolio runs roaring at the shadows.
    Rosaline claps her hands over her ears. Laughing.

Benvolio
  See anyone?
Rosaline
  Was that entirely necessary?

  He smiles.

Benvolio
  You're safe.
Rosaline
  With a Montague?
Benvolio
  At your service.

  Benvolio comes towards her.

  You're shivering.
Rosaline
  A goose walked over my grave.
Benvolio
  Don't say that.

  She sits down on the cobbles. Takes out a rollie.
  Lights it.

These'll kill you.
Rosaline
A lot else in this world'll kill me faster.
Stones now.
Flung with a certain force
And on it's mark.
A stone'll kill you
Faster than tobacco.
Benvolio
Are you hurt?
Rosaline
What's a few bruises?

The sound of a flute.

I'm getting a crick in my neck.
Benvolio
Eh?
Rosaline
Sit down. I won't bite you.
Afraid I'll poison you if you get too close?

She looks at him.

Cat got your tongue?
Benvolio
What?
Rosaline
Don't look so sorrowful.

The flute haunts the shadows.
  Silence.

Pity.
Benvolio
What?
Rosaline
It's gone.

He grabs the rollie from her.

Hey.

He chucks it.

That's good tobacco.
I paid hard cash for that.
Doesn't grow on trees.
Not for me it doesn't.
    I bet you always wash your hands.
After.
Benvolio
    After?
Rosaline
    Touching a Capulet.
Benvolio
    Velvet your claws, Rosaline.
Rosaline
    Do you find it a strain?
Benvolio
    What?
Rosaline
    Being so decent?
Benvolio
    I love you.
Rosaline
    Good God, why?
Benvolio
    I always have.
Rosaline
    How can you love me?
    You don't know me.

She swirls up ready to leave him. He catches her hand.

Each day when I awoke
The sun shone

Because round a corner
I might see Romeo coming.
The days I didn't see him
Were lost days.
The surprise of him
Was what I lived for.
Who do you love, Benvolio?
Rosaline?
Don't you know?
Romeo took her away with him
When he crossed over
Into the far country.
Benvolio
Rosaline?

She hesitates a moment puzzled by his gentleness.
   The drummer clack clack clacks on the rim. Points
at Rosaline.
   She goes.
   Benvolio stares at the drummer.

Gianni
You see her again?
Lorenzo
Juliet?
Gianni
After that night?
Lorenzo
Never saw her again.
Gianni
That's sad man, Lorenzo.
Lorenzo
Love of my life.
Gianni
So fucking sad.

A cymbal's struck. Music.
   Blackout
   Shadow and light. Clouds and sun.
   Bianca alone watching.
   The vision.
   Frozen figures. Their clothes are punk Elizabethan.
Reds and greens. Their makeup, slightly stylised.
   The drummer cues these figures into movement.
   Tick tick ticks on the drum sticks.
   The figures move into slow life. Join hands.
   A minuet on a sampler. Live drums. Rhona's
playing a lonely flute.
   A line of dancers, partnering each other, moves in
unison. A sword comes from somewhere. It's thrown
and caught. Thrown and caught. Thrown. A girl
catches it. Draws it from its scabbard. Teases the
line leader into a fight. Draws blood from his cheek.
So that, provoked, he draws his sword in anger.
The greens line up behind the girl: the reds behind
the boy. Weapons are drawn.
   Bianca's whimpering.
   A cymbal.
   Blackout.
   Still figures in the shadows.

Bianca
Waking shadows come to visit me.

Bianca and Helena alone. Helena's basket's on the
ground.
   The sun's in and out of the clouds.
   Not till the drummer signals to her does she put her
arms round Bianca.

Helena
You're standing on your feet. Your eyes are wide open.

Bianca
  Come from sleep's country.
Helena
  What did they say?
Bianca
  Alice will wear her bridesmaid's dress
  At the election tonight.
Helena
  All the way from beyond
  They came to tell you that.
  They were fond.
Bianca
  I can't hear what else
  They came to say . . .
  They came . . .
  I can't hear . . .
Helena
  Blow. Blow them away. See.

She blows. The figures move and become just people
going to market. Meeting. Passing. Going home.
Disappearing.

  All gone, Bianca?
Bianca
  All gone.
Helena
  The clouds are gathering.

Helena picks up her empty basket. Takes Bianca's
hand.

Bianca
  I want to put a flower down.
Helena
  On the way back.
Bianca
  I want to put a flower down now.

Helena
I haven't got a flower.
Bianca
Give me a flower.
Helena
I haven't got one.

The drummer tick tick ticks with his drum sticks.

Bianca
I'm hot. Very, very hot.

Helena's watching the clouds.

Helena
The rain's coming.

She tugs at Bianca's hand. She's childlike, Bianca, but not a child.
    Benvolio's moving to get a better view. Careful not to come out of the shadows of the arcade.

Bianca
Feel me.
I'm sweating.

She takes Helena's hand. Puts it to her forehead. Helena pats her cheek.

Can I take this off?
Can I?
Can I take this off?
I need . . . I need . . .
Helena
I haven't got an umbrella, Bianca. Move.
Bianca
Ohhhhhhhhh.
I can't manage the buttons,

My fingers won't . . .
My finger's on the buttons.

Helena
Come here.

Helena undoes the buttons for her.

Bianca
I need . . .
I need . . .
I'm itchy.

Helena
Scratch.

Bianca
I'm itchy inside.
I need . . .
I need . . .

Helena
What?

Bianca
Do you love me?

Helena
Of course.

Bianca puts her hands on Helena's face.

Bianca
Cross. Lines here. Shadows here.

Helena
Smooth them away.

Helena shrugs Bianca's jacket free of her shoulders.
Tugs it down over her hands.

Promise not to take any more off.
No stripping in the market place
With all the folk there for the trial.
They won't like you stripping.

*Bianca pulls at Helena's forehead to smooth the lines
away.*

Bianca
I need . . .
Helena
What?
Bianca
Something.

Gently touching Helena's face.
    Thunder.
    Sudden dark. Sudden rain.
    A wail from Bianca.

Helena
I told you. I told you.

*Helena pulls her under the shelter of the arcades and
away.*
    *A song. Called and echoed quickly and lightly
among the Capulet girls on their balconies.*

Alice
Que sentimada.
Others
Que sentimada.
Rhona
Paina.
Others
Paina.
Livia
La Bellina.
Others
La Bellina.
Helena
In la casa.

Others
 In la casa.
Alice
 Dit.
Others
 Dit.
All
 Bertolina.

Suddenly harsh.

Laa laa laa
La la la la la
La la la
La la la
Laaaaa.

It could be 1500; 1900; 2000; or 3000.
 Scaffolding on three sides. An impression of height.
Two irregular levels.
 Rhona and Alice are on the second level.
 Percussion on the ground underneath the
scaffolding.
 Pots of trailing red geraniums on each level.
Opulent pots. Red and green and terracotta.
 Pieces of domestic modernity here and there.
A chrome toaster. A gleaming electric fan. A fridge.
 Here and there, fish bowls full of terrapins.
 In a corner on the ground, a heap of lilies. The
bottom ones dried out. The middle ones rotting. The
top ones fresh.
 Thunder and church bells.
 The rain's pouring down.
 Benvolio's watching from the shadows with
Valentine.
 In the distance, Rosaline.

Benvolio
She's coming back.
Valentine
There's better fish in the sea than ever came out of it.

Benvolio grabs him.

Benvolio
Do you call my love a fish, sir?
Valentine
Do I call your love a fish, sir?
Benvolio
Do you call my love a fish?
Valentine
I do call your love a fish.
Benvolio
Do you call her a fish, sir?
Valentine
I do call her a fish, sir.
I do not call her a trout.
Benvolio
You do not call her a trout, sir?
Valentine
I do not call her a trout, sir.
Do you crush my collar?
Benvolio
I do crush your collar, sir.
Valentine
Do you crush my new collar?
Benvolio
What kind of fish?
Valentine
What kind of fish?
Benvolio
What kind of fish, sir?
Valentine
A red snapper.

Benvolio
A red snapper?
Valentine
A red snapper.
Benvolio
That's a pretty kind of fish.
Valentine
It is a tasty fish.
Prettier than a pike.
Benvolio
Do you call my love a pike?
Valentine
I do call you a fool.
Throw your cat fish back in the pond.
And unhand my lace, Benvolio.

Misery provoked.

Benvolio
I haven't got her out of the pond yet.
She is a young carp.
Queen of fish, Valentine,
Who will not come to my hand
Though I tempt her with soft white bread.
And I tell her my hand is gentle.
Valentine
A carp?

Valentine pouches up his mouth and makes a fish face.

Benvolio
It was a metaphor.
Valentine
Fuck off.
Benvolio
I'm not asking you to love her.
Valentine
Don't go down this road, Benvolio.

Benvolio
   Will I lose your friendship?
Valentine
   For loving a Capulet?
Benvolio
   Well?
Valentine
   The Prince says hostilities are at an end.
Benvolio
   What do you say?
Valentine
   Can the Prince change the habits of a lifetime with
      a word?
   Did his 'word' bring my brother back to life?
   Do the dead live because an amnesty is called?
   And if they don't live how can there be peace?
      Where is Mercutio now?
   There is such a silence
   In the world
   Since he has left it.
   I was never alone
   Not even in the womb.
   For we were twin souls
   Mercutio and me.
   Now I am cut in half
   My good part's gone.
   His death sets my heart
   To beat a tattoo of hate.
   The Prince may speak his word.
   May speak and speak.
   He cannot change my heart beat.
      I'll watch the girl with you in friendship.
   Approach her and our friendship ends.
Benvolio
   At least it's wet.

Valentine
Why?
Benvolio
Hate cools in the rain.
Tears become invisible.

The drummer hits the rim: points at Valentine.

Valentine
And yet it's close.

He whirrs a small electric hand fan into life.
The shadows hide them.
The rain patters down.
The drum sticks click.
Rosaline walks up to a pile of flowers in the corner
of the piazza. She's holding a single lily. And an
umbrella.

Rosaline
Your spirit haunts me, Juliet.
I see more of you dead
Than I did when you were alive;

Valentine splutters with laughter.
The drummer whirls and points.
Benvolio puts his hand over his friend's mouth.

That's a joke.
'More of you dead.'

She stamps her foot hard down as if knocking on the
door of the grave.

Go on laugh.
And more of you alive
Than I wanted to.
Laugh. Laugh, go on.

Knocks again.

Come on, Juliet.

Benvolio pulls Valentine deep into the shadows.

We were hardly close as cousins.
You were too small, too pretty, too rich,
Too thin and too much loved for me to cope with.
'Spoilt' is the word that springs to mind
Though I don't want to speak ill of the dead.

*She touches the stamen of the lily. Yellow nicotine
pollen stains her fingers. She rubs it in.*

All a flower does is wither
It's the memories that stay for ever:
So they tell me.
So what do I recall of you?
Juliet, daddy's princess, rich,
Mummy's darling, quite a bitch.
You scratched my face once,
From here to here;
I have the scar. I have it yet.
You can see it quite clearly
In the sunlight;
A silver line.
You wanted my favourite doll.
And of course you got it.
For though I was scarred, you cried.
And your nurse swooped down
And took the moppet from me.
Spanked me hard for making you unhappy;
Gave my doll to you, her dearest baby.
Later you stole my best friend;
Wooed her with whispers;
Told her gossip's secrets;
Gave her trinkets, sweetmeats.
Later still, you took my love
And didn't know you'd done it;

Then having taken him
You let him die.
If you'd swallowed the friar's potion earlier
You would have wakened.
And my love would be alive.
None of this would have happened.
I know you, Juliet.
You hesitated, frightened.
Didn't take the stuff until the dawn.
Wakened too late in the tomb.
   In the night I dream of Romeo.
He's reaching his arms out from the vault.
The poison has him in its hold.
He fills my nights with his longing for life.
Until I am afraid to go to sleep.
For though I love him still
I cannot soothe his pain.
If I could, I would
But it is not me he's reaching for.
   So why, Juliet,
Should I spend my cash
On flowers for you?
Are you a saint
Simply because you were daft enough
To die for love?
Love?
A passing fancy,
No more nor less.
Tomorrow or tomorrow or tomorrow
You would have tired of him.
Like your fancy for the doll;
Once possessed, you left it in the rain;
Yesterday's fancy, mud in its hair,
Damp stained the dress I'd made for her.
   They think you brave to have taken your life
But you believed in immortality.

Daddy's princess could not die.
She would be there at her own funeral
To watch the tears flow
And hear her praises sung.
    So you haunt me.
Don't turn away.
Listen. Listen.
What is it that you've brought about?
What trail does your fancy drag behind?
What punishments lie in your fancy's wake?
Listen, Juliet.
Come here. Come close.
Press your ear to the earth
So I know you're listening.
There's a trial going on.
Even now. In all solemnity.
Four lives hang in the balance
Forced by your selfish suicide
To take their chance
Standing at the mercy of the court.
They wait to see whether life or death
Is granted them by what we call justice.
It's a strange justice. Law meted out by the rich
Who measure their wisdom
By the weight of their gold;
As if riches bear witness to virtue.
You and I know they don't.
So four poor people are brought before the Prince
To see whether they live or die.
You brought this on them.
No feud wrought their trials.
Their misery is tribute
To your precocity.
Married. And at thirteen!
    So. So. Sweet Coz.

Here. This is the last flower
You'll get from me.
Death flowers have the sweetest scent.

She casts the flower down. Shrugs.

That's that bit done.

She puts down the umbrella. Stands with her face up to the rain.

Benvolio
Some loves are for ever.
Valentine
Jealous of dead Juliet.
Oh Lord. Oh Lord.
These Capulets.
Love?
This is love.
A pile of rotting lilies.
Benvolio
They're still fresh on the top.
Valentine
Only you.
Benvolio
What?
Valentine
A pile of stinking lilies bathed in catpiss,
Only you would see the fresh ones on the top.
And love Rosaline whose heart's in the grave.
There are softer beds to lie on
Than fair Rosaline's nail strewn cot.
Benvolio
I love because I love.
I can't say why I love.
I would take her in my arms,
Confess my love,

33

Ask for her clemency.
Change her name.

Valentine

She'd have you for breakfast.
That girl is the enemy.
She'd eat you up, suck on the bits
And after, lick her chops.
She's a hurt animal.
A cat that would attack the hand
That gentles it.
And bite it hard.
Princess of Cats.
She's a better man
Than Tybalt ever was
Or Petruchio ever shall be.
Give her a sword
She'd show you no mercy.
Though she has no need of a sword.
What woman does?
While the Prince has taken our weapons
He's left them theirs.

Benvolio

What weapons?

Valentine

Have you no sisters?
A woman's weapon is her tongue.
See her. See.
Conjoin with her.
You'll fight the oldest feud of all.
Not Montagues and Capulets.
Men and women Benvolio.
Men and women. There's a war.
Will never end by any decree
Of man, or Prince, or God. Don't go near her.

Valentine mimes whipping out a sword. Mimes balancing it on the tips of his fingers by its point.

Benvolio
There's no sword there.
Valentine
I see a sword.
A Toledo steel.
My sword.
The hilt thirsty for my hand.
The blade starved of blood.
See it gleam in the light.
See it. See it.

He mimes throwing it up in the air, catching it again and sheathing it.

Now it's gone.
When the trial's over
And the guilty hung
I'll have my sword again.

The sun gleams out for a moment.
  Light everywhere.
  Below, Lorenzo leans against a pillar. Waiting. He has a little blue electric fan. It whirrs. He leans and fans himself. Lethargically. Leaning into the breeze from the fan. Trying and trying to click the fingers of the other hand.

Gianni
Tea. There is no point even trying to make it without first warming the pot. They do it. People do it. Lemon? Milk? They say, brandishing a cold tea pot. The question doesn't arise. Why? Why would you make tea if you hadn't warmed the pot. Once the pot's warmed, with boiling water mind. Once the tea's spooned in, dry and black and perfumed with

35

bergamot. Not blended, no shred of dust. I won't have
sweepings from the floor that some chap's relieved
himself upon. Once boiling water is added. While
waiting in that delicious pause when the tea is giving
of its essence. Then the question of lemon or milk can
be addressed. With Earl Grey lemon always. But in
the winter I would maintain it has to be lemon any
way. Whether Darjeeling or Assam; lemon and not
milk in the winter. Because. There is always a danger
that the milk is contaminated. Turnips. That's the
danger. In the winter time. There are those who feed
their cows turnips.

Lorenzo

I can't get a click out of my fingers.

Gianni

I can taste the turnip in the milk.

Lorenzo

I'm so hot I can't get my fingers to click. My hands
are damp. Slimy to touch. No woman will marry a
man with a damp hand.

Gianni

In the tea I can taste a turnip fed cow.
An abomination.
I hope there's no turnips in heaven.
    Suppose they hang them.
Suppose they do that?

Lorenzo

It's not our business.
We're here, Petruchio's men,
Waiting to be counted
To elect him Prince of Cats.

Gianni

Foregone conclusion
No man will stand against him.
    I wouldn't like to hang.
Dying in front of a crowd.

36

Dancing for their amusement.
Shitting myself. Piss rolling down my leg.
    We've all been to Mantua after all. Saturdays would
never have been Saturdays without his pinks and blues.
The apothecary only served us.

Lorenzo

We paid him, Gianni.

Gianni

We taught him to depend on us.
And we only paid him sometimes.
We kept him on a string.
Rich men have enough to eat.
His pills didn't make him fat.

Lorenzo

He didn't do it for charity.

Gianni

We kept him dangling.
He scraped a living.
Then Romeo comes along.
'You give me poison:
I'll give you forty ducats.'
Like that's a bloody fortune
Like he's going to say no.
Romeo seduced him with his ducats,
Why hang the apothecary?

Lorenzo

They can hardly hang Romeo.
He's saved them the price of the rope.
I'd turn out for that.
To see a Montague hang.

Gianni

The heat and waiting for a man you've known to die.

Lorenzo

It's not decided.

Gianni

Tell me it won't happen.

37

Tell me.
Even honourable men
Need a scapegoat.

Lorenzo sticks out his tongue. He brings the whirring fan towards it. Gianni watches terrapins. To and fro the fan goes until the tongue's held there on the whirring fan.

A girl standing on a table, Alice. Looking down at Rosaline. Rhona's pinning up her dress. Then tacking the hem.

Alice
My God. My God. What's she got on?
Standing there. Standing in the rain. **
Rhona
Turn.
Turn.
Alice
** I wouldn't wear that.
I wouldn't give that to my servant to wear.
I'd rip it off my mother's back, for God's sake,
If I saw she had it on.
And my mother is not known for her taste.
But that. That beats anything
My mother might buy in a flea market.
She won't come to the election tonight in that?
She'd hardly dare.
Vote Petruchio Prince of Cats?
Put her hand in the air in that?
There's holes in the armpits.

Benvolio pulls Valentine into the shadows as Rosaline goes past.

I know she's unhappy.
We're all unhappy.
I mean look at her. Look at her, Rhona.

She's letting the side down.
She should have more pride.
If she's got to mourn publicly
She could at least do it prettily.
What did she see in Romeo
That our boys don't have?
I wouldn't waste my time.
All this for a dead man.
What can you do with a dead man
When there are live ones waiting
Who can give you some return.

Below. Lorenzo takes the fan away from his tongue.
A couple of hideous sounds. Then tortured speech.

Lorenzo
My tongue is numb.

His words are indistinct.

My tongue is totally . . .
Gianni
Ever seen terrapins doing it?

Lorenzo's prodding his tongue. Squeezing it.

You listening to me?
Lorenzo?
I'm talking to you?
Lorenzo
My tongue's numb.
Gianni
Have you seen a terrapin on the job?

Very slurred.

Lorenzo
Tortoises.
Gianni
I've seen tortoises. They're always humping. Tortoises.

When they're awake they're humping. When they're
not eating. When they're not sleeping. Humping.
Course it's a slow business.

If I was stuck in a bowl and all I had was another
terrapin I'd be doing it. All day I'd be doing it. Every
day. In every way.

What did we used to talk about? In the old days?
Last week? We had plans last week.

Lorenzo

My tongue is numb. My tongue is numb.

Gianni

I'd kill for a cup of tea.

It's all I've got left to excite me.

They melt away.
    The drummer click click clicks his sticks. Points at
Rosaline.
    She walks away from the flowers.
    Alice is craning to see.

Alice

Coming home.

Rhona

Keep still.

You've got St Vitus dance.

Alice

That's a curse.

Take it back.

Say a thing

And you make it so.

Take it back, Rhona.

Rhona

You're a drama queen.

Alice

And you're from Glasgow.

It's a well known fact

Glaswegians
Don't know anything.

Rhona

They know how to kiss.

Alice

Are you threatening me?

Rhona

Keep this up
It'll be Christmas and this dress
Still won't be done.
Forget the election tonight.
Keep this up,
You'll be an old woman;
You'll be dead
And this won't be ready
To be your winding sheet.

Silence.
   Alice shrugs. Stands still.

Alice

One fresh flower, that's all.
Six yesterday.
Ten the day before.
It's falling off.

Rhona

They're all watching the trial.

Alice

I wish we'd gone.

A pin goes into her leg.

That hurt.
What's wrong with you?

Rhona

Gawping at those poor folk,
The crowd counting the tears,

Glorying in the thrill
Of watching folk who may be about to die
At the hand of the state.
Nurse calling on her Juliet.
The old man, the friar,
Aged ten years in a day.
Peter, who brought the ladder
Romeo used,
To climb to Juliet's room
Just did as he was told;
Hasn't got a mind of his own;
Hasn't ever had one.
And the apothecary?
I feel sorry for him.
I won't go to the court.
I don't want to pry.

Alice

There's only one life.
You have to find enjoyment where you can.

Silence.

You're such a prude.
Lighten up, Rhona.
What will be, will be
And we can't change a thing,
Cavil we at it ever so.
I've more important things
On my mind than a trial.
I need this dress for the evening's frolic.
I'll dance with our new Prince of Cats.
Later I will marry him.
Not that he knows that.
Nor will he till it's done.
Make the dress fine, Rhona.
I have plans.

Clouds and shadows sweep the alleys.
A call like a wolf howling. Echoing.
Another and another. Music.
Helena has a basket over her shoulder. Loaves and green leaves stick out of it. She has Bianca by the hand.
Bianca hangs back.
The drummer whacks a big stick against a scaffolding bar.
Bianca cowers.

Helena
Come on.
Bianca
Dark.
Helena
Move Bianca. Move. Move.

She tugs but Bianca doesn't move.
Shadows loom and threaten. Become people.
The howling closes in. No faces. Flashes of green here and there. Montague colours.
Helena shelters Bianca with her body.
Rosaline runs down. She has a stick in her hand. Livia follows her.
She clacks the stick round the scaffolding uprights. Livia following.
The Montagues melt away. One stops. Stares at Rosaline. His face caught in a glint of sunlight. Benvolio.
Valentine pulls him away.
Bianca whimpers softly.

Rosaline
What news from the trial?
Helena
'The nurse of Juliet, is banisht in her age,

43

Because that from the parents she dyd hyde the
  mariage.'

Livia
  Poor Angelica.

Rosaline
  And Peter?

Helena
  No news of him. Nor Friar Lawrence,
  Poor fond old man.

Livia
  The apothecary?

Helena
  Held till last tonight.

Rosaline
  So she lives, the nurse.

Helena
  Than any punishment the Prince could give her,
  The loss of Juliet is the worst.
  Angelica truly loved her.

Livia
  But to leave here and live with strangers.

Helena
  She's allowed till sunset to do her rounds
  And say good-bye.

  The drummer whacks the scaffolding with his stick.

Rosaline
  They haven't gone.
  Take her home,
  Take her home.

  Blackout.

Rhona
  Have you a purse I could have?

Alice
  My Spanish leather.

Rhona
  Where is it?
Alice
  In the drawer.

Alice twirls in her dress. And twirls.

Rhona
  It's not done yet.
Alice
  This was my bridesmaid's dress
  When Juliet was to wed Paris.
  Then it was the dress
  At her first funeral
  When she died the first time
  And all we bridesmaids attended her
  Supposed corpse.
  Then it was at her real funeral.
  This dress has a history.
  More history than it needs.

She wriggles.

And less décolletage.

On the other balcony.
    Helena puts a light cover round Bianca.
    Bianca holds her hand.

Bianca
  I dreamed.
Helena
  Gone now.
Bianca
  You left me.
Helena
  I'm here.
Bianca
  Not in my dream.

45

Helena
Who was in your dream?

Bianca
Juliet.

Helena
What was she doing?

Bianca
She was waiting.
'Do you want me?' I said.
I wasn't stupid in my dream.
Juliet didn't say anything.
Didn't move. Went on waiting.

Helena wipes tears from Bianca's face with the heel of her hand.

Helena
They've gone now. You're safe.
They won't touch you.
I won't let them.

Bianca
If you're stupid, Helena,
Why do you have to know it?
No man will ever love me.
I'll have no child to call my own.
Any man would feel demeaned
By my hand on his arm.
I was like you in my dream.
I liked me.

Helena
Do you still see her?

Bianca
When this day ends Juliet will go.
But she won't be alone.
The barriers are all coming down
Between her land and ours.
And I'm frightened.

You won't cross over, Helena?
Helena
I won't cross over.
Bianca
Promise.
Helena
I won't leave you.
Bianca
When will the day be done?
Helena
When we have a new Prince of Cats,
When Friar Lawrence knows his fate
And the apothecary.
Bianca
Will the rain ever stop?
Helena
I don't know.
Bianca
Sing me.
Helena
What?
Bianca
Sing me the hunchback song.
Helena
Aren't you hungry?
Bianca
Sing me.

Helena curls up with Bianca.

Helena
** Gobba la madre,
Gobbo il padre
Gobba la figlia di sua sorella. *
Bianca
His sister's daughter was a hunchback.

47

Helena
* Gobba anchi quella *

Bianca
They were all hunchbacks.

Helena
* Gobba anchi quella.
Gobba la madre,
Gobbo il padre,
Gobba la figlia di sua sorella
Gobba anchi quella.
La familla Gobbetin
Gobba anchi quella
La familla Gobbetin.

** *There's a load of stuff in the drawer. Rhona finds the purse.*

Rhona
We'll fill it.
She'll need money.

Alice
Who?

Rhona
The nurse, Alice.
For her journey.

Alice
Spanish leather
For Angelica.
Take the other.
Here.

Rhona
It's threadbare.

Alice
So much the better.
And don't give her too much money.
Over generous charity
Only encourages idleness.

48

For her own good
Limit your kindness.
Nurse was after all a little less
Than wise.

Rhona

She's punished then.

Alice

I would have had her hanged.

Rhona

You'd make heaven cold.
With your philosophy.

Alice

I'm not good like you;
I'm just marking time,
Idling in chatter gear,
Because the world's changed.
It's standing still;
The clouds in the sky unmoving.
The world's in shadow,
Before it was fraught with light.
Now there's a glooming chiaroscuro
Over all. And I feel evil inside.
Why did they do this thing
To my world?
I wanted it to stay as it was
Charged with energy
Till I grew up
And joined it;
Some man's mistress.
Some warrior's Queen.
So hang them all
Who broke the world
Where I was happy.
Why should they live?
Who raped my dream.
    Don't look at me like that.

Do you have to try to be good
Or does it come naturally?
You were always grown up.
Glasgow's a dark place
I've heard it said.
It grows dour people
Steeped in fear.
Statistically
There are far more suicides there
Than we have here.

Rhona

You look nice.

She puts thread and scissors in the drawer.
Alice shrugs the dress down to give herself more
of a cleavage. Pushes her breasts up.

Alice

When Petruchio is elected Prince of Cats
He'll not look past me.

Rhona

You'll have your nipples hanging out
Any minute now.

Alice

Some women tattoo round their nipples.
And their actual nipples
They tattoo those too.
I'd quite like blue nipples.
That would be
Decadent.
Something to show my
Grandchildren
When I'm old,
To bear witness to a wild youth.
Chance would be a fine thing.
I'm just waiting to grow old;
Standing here waiting to grow old;

I'm older with every breath I take.
Nothing ever happens
Any more.
I feel time passing,
Every second of it heavy.
I'll have blue tattoos on my nipples
So I've got something to show.

Drum sticks click.
  Alice looks at the drummer.
  Nods.

She can have my leather purse.
I'm not as mean
As you deem me.
I was born a bitch.
It'll take a lifetime
To overcome it.

Rosaline's at the mirror changing into boy's clothes.

Rosaline
What is love?
Answer me.
A couple of sighs in the night.
A rhythmic expiration.
Slightly voiced.
As in
Ah ah.
Or
Mmm mm mm.
A quick thrust of time
And it's over.
  Love is not carried on an evening's zephyr breeze.
Love is not in the pulsed scent of a woman's cologne.
Love is not in the turn of a man's head;
In his shadowed profile

In the laugh that you hear unawares;
In the gentle brush of his hand on your skin.
  Love is only the rut
A quick pant and it's gone. **

Alice
  Five times she's said love
  In five breaths.
  And you think I have a one-track mind.
Rona
  Where's the money?
Alice
  In the jar.

Rosaline
  ** If love maintains
  That's the desire
  To rut again.
Livia
  I liked you
  How you used to be.
Rosaline
  Something happened
  I grew up suddenly.
Livia
  Benvolio's looking for you.
Rosaline
  After what he's done?
Livia
  He was trying to stop them.
Rosaline
  It's never going to end, Livia.

  A beat.

Livia
> You could look back at him.
> It's only polite.

Rosaline
> Three of our family are killed by his family.
> It's never going to end.

She buckles on an empty scabbard.

Livia
> What are you doing?

The drummer click click clicks. Rosaline nods.

Rosaline
> The Gods want war.

Livia
> Where are you going?

Rosaline
> To even the score.

Livia
> Romeo's mother died the night of his banishment,
> Died of a broken heart.

Rosaline
> That doesn't count.
>   We need weapons, Livvy.
> Will you come?

Livia
> Where are you going?

Rosaline
> The tomb.

Livia
> Why?

Rosaline
> So the men can lend me their honour
> For the honour of all Capulets.

Livia
> You're as bad as they are.

Pause.

Rosaline
I'll go alone.

She climbs down.
   Benvolio stares from the shadows. Smiles.

Don't be nice to me.
I don't want you to be nice.
Benvolio
I'm sorry.
Rosaline
What for?

*As they're talking, Gianni and Lorenzo set up a trip
wire.*

Benvolio
What happened down there
With Bianca.
Before.
Won't happen again.
Rosaline
I know it won't.
I'll make sure it won't.
Benvolio
I'm sorry.
Rosaline
That's easy said.
Benvolio
It's not Bianca you care about.
Rosaline
Sorry's just a word.
Benvolio
Whatever you do
You're not doing it for Bianca.
Rosaline
Why else am I doing it?

Pause.

Benvolio
Romeo.
Rosaline
Alive
I could have fought to regain his love.
I could have fought
I would have won.
A heart that's fickle and can turn
Would be fickle still
And turn again.
Benvolio
As well he's dead then.
Rosaline
He was your cousin
And your friend.
Benvolio
As well he's dead for you.
If he'd been alive;
If you'd fought for his love;
If you'd won;
If you'd married then
Your whole long life
You would have spent
Wondering if this one
Or that one
Had taken his butterfly fancy.
I loved him as a brother.
But as well he's dead;
I wouldn't have that life for you,
Smelling his discarded clothes
For another woman's perfume.
What would he have driven you to?
I love you, Rosaline,
I'll not play around.

55

He touches her face so gently. And for a moment she lets him, responds even. Almost nuzzling her cheek into his palm.
   The drummer click, click, clicks. Rosaline backs off.

Rosaline
   You promise a whole lot more
   Than you can deliver.
Benvolio
   Test me.

She's about to speak.
   The drummer points.
   Rosaline runs.

Rosaline. Rosaline. Rosaline.

He begins to run after her.

Lorenzo
   Now.

The string's pulled. Benvolio falls.
   Gianni pinions his arms.

Gianni
   What have we here?
Lorenzo
   By his smell
   A Montague.
Benvolio
   Peace.
   Let me go.
Lorenzo
   'Let me go.'
Benvolio
   In the Prince's name.
Lorenzo
   'In the Prince's name.'

Benvolio

For the sake of the truce.

Lorenzo

He wants us to let him go.

Gianni

Make him ask nicely.

Lorenzo

What kind of nicely?

Benvolio

I have to . . .

Lorenzo

Quiet. Gianni's thinking;
Looking for a form of words
That would satisfy him
A Montague has some manners.

Benvolio struggles.

If I were you I would not struggle.
Gianni might think you were an agent
Come to spoil our ritual
When we make our Prince of Cats.
Then he would not be merciful.
** Escalus may have our swords,
There are other weapons,
A shard of glass
Will slice a throat.
* Handily
A stone may break a head.

* He picks up a stone. Raises it.
   ** The Nurse with all her bags rounds the side of the arcade.
   Takes in the scene. Dumps her bag. Runs at the boys.

Nurse

It is enough.

It is enough
Is it not enough?
Lorenzo, Gianni.
I want you here.
By me.
No more mischief.
Or I'll speak what I know of you.
Long tales of night fears and bed wetting,
To beguile the ears of a Montague.
Come now. Let him go.
And kiss your nurse.
Bid her farewell
Send her on her road.
I said my good-byes to your parents at the court.
Come down to me.
All the cousins of my Juliet
Who were to be her bridesmaids
But strewed wedding flowers round her tomb instead;
Come to me,
For I won't see you in this life again.
Not after this night.

The girls begin to climb down.
   Benvolio slides into the shadows. Runs after
Rosaline.

I don't see Rosaline.
Where is she, Livvy?
Alice that dress is much too low.
Rhona talk some sense into her,
She doesn't need to advertise her wares
So brazenly.
She can leave something to the imagination
And still hook Petruchio.
When do you go home?

Rhona
   When the trial's over

And life has settled down.
My aunt needs me to mind the house.
While she's at the court.
Please take this purse from Alice.

Nurse

My kind, sweet girl.

Alice

It's not just from me.
It's from Rhona too.

Nurse

Where's Helena?

Helena

Here. I've brought you a coat.
We had one to spare.

Nurse

Bring my Bianca to me.
My little love.

Helena pushes Bianca forward.
   The dream's in her eyes.
   She's far far away.

Livia

What news from the court?

Nurse

'Peter, for he did obey his master's hest
In wonted freedom has good leave to lead his lyfe
   in rest.'
One day he says. He may follow me.
I look forward to that day.
Petruchio's not here.
Nor Rosaline.
The sun sinks faster in this square than it would on
   a hill.

Silence.

Feel the quiet.
Smell it.
Time to go.

Petruchio runs in.

Petruchio
I thought I had missed you.
Nurse
Look after them.
You're a good man.
I charge you to keep to the peace.
I charge you, Petruchio.
Petruchio
I swear.
Nurse
Tell Rosaline.
Tell her I love her.
Say Angelica was here.

She picks up her bags.

Don't follow.
No more good-byes.
See the sun.
Glimmering out
From a low cloud.
See. See now –
The sun dies.

A moment.
And she's gone.

Lorenzo
I declare Petruchio
Prince of Cats in his brother's place.
Petruchio
Not yet.
We're not all here.

Gianni
    No man stands against you.
Petruchio
    Even so.
    We'll wait until we are all gathered.
    Alice that is a very fetching gown.
Alice
    An old thing
    It's hard to dress well
    When in mourning.
    I'm glad you like it,
    Petruchio.

The drummer clicks his sticks and points at Bianca.
Juliet and Bianca speak in chorus.

Bianca/Juliet
    'Don't touch him.'
Helena
    Bianca!
Bianca/Juliet
    'Don't let her.
    He's mine.'
Livia
    Juliet?

The drummer clicks.
    Light on Rosaline in the tomb.
    Taking Romeo's hand.

Bianca/Juliet
    'She takes his hand.
    Moves his cold fingers
    One by one,
    Makes him cup her warm cheek.
    His palm warms at her touch.
    And now she cradles him.'

Petruchio
>Hold her.

Bianca/Juliet
>'My one and only love.
>My night and day.
>In the moonlight I kissed his skin.
>His skin in the silver moonlight.
>Don't let her take the taste of my lips from his mouth.
>Please. Please. Please.'

Helena's trying to hold her.

Alice
>Who is she looking at? **
>What does she see?

Rhona
>** She sounds like Juliet.

Bianca/Juliet
>'Tell her no.
>Tell her don't.
>Tell her don't come near me.'

Drums.
>*Blackout.*
>*In the tomb.*
>*A single source of light. Not quite steady.*
>*A small voice of panic.*

Rosaline
>I thought they'd taken you.
>I thought they'd taken your bodies.
>I thought they'd taken you away.
>The Prince said . . .
>I wouldn't have come . . .
>The Prince said to take you from the vault,
>Lie you together in your own tomb
>Where we laid the flowers.

The Prince said . . .
'Lest that length of time might from our myndes
  remove,
The memory of so perfect, sound, and so approved
  love.'

Then she creeps close.

And is this love?
Her head on your shoulder.
Your arm around her.
And is this death?
Death it must be.
Sleep has a gentler air.
I watched my mother die.
But this is different.
Colder.
Sore.
  She washed your mind clean.
You didn't ever think of me.
Never once thought of me.
And I loved you so.
But being unloved
I am not allowed sorrow.
I am not allowed a widow's tears.
  You look like strangers.

A cymbal crash.
  Blackout.
  *A match is struck. Valentine holds it. A small glow
in the quite, quite dark. Rosaline's light moves to and
fro below.*
  Benvolio moves through the gloom. Trips. A curse.

Valentine
Shhhhh.

Another match struck on a tinder box. He lights a hurricane lamp.

Benvolio
Where have you been?
Valentine
Where are you going?
Benvolio
I asked you first.
Valentine
I've been at the court.
Benvolio
'What shall betide of the grey-bearded syre?
Of fryre Lawrence thus araynde, that good barefooted
    fryre?'
Valentine
'Because that many times he woorthely did serve
The common welth, and in his lyfe was never found
    to swerve,
He is discharged quyte, and no marke of defame
Must seeme to blot, or touch at all, the honor of
    his name.'
But he's taking himself to a hermitage.
To live quite alone.
In silence and contemplation.
He leaves his simples behind.
He takes no papers on which to write,
He takes no inks, no pens.
He will not mark down his knowledge.
For his knowledge killed.
He will communicate with no man.
The court having shown him mercy and respect
He has decreed his own punishment.
No wine will cross his lips.
No food but dry bread.

He will look at the world through a narrow aperture
  in a brick wall.
Benvolio
  A living death.
Valentine
  But for him, he says,
  Romeo and Juliet would be alive.
Benvolio
  So is it over?
Valentine
  But for the apothecary.
  They still sit in judgement.

  Valentine unsheathes his sword.
    Lays it on the earth.

Benvolio
  You have your sword.
Valentine
  Not mine. Still she is beautiful.
Benvolio
  It is like yours.
Valentine
  My brother's sword.
  I have one for you.
Benvolio
  How have you your brother's sword?
Valentine
  He lent it to me.
  I promised him I would give it back.
    The one yours came from
  Had lost his head;
  And having no lips
  Was reluctant to vouchsafe his name,
  Which though I asked most cordially,
  He didn't have the heart to answer.

Still it's a fine piece.
The donor was a little stiff.
He had no further need of it.
I promise you.

Benvolio

You spoke with your brother?

Valentine

I did most of the talking
In all honesty.
I promised him
A death
So he could rest easy.

Benvolio

You went down into the tomb?
This is madness, Valentine.

Valentine

I'm not the only one mad.

The light below them wavers and wavers.
    Rosaline climbs up onto a level with them. She's carrying a bundle.
    Valentine claps his hand over Benvolio's mouth. Shades the lantern.
    Rosaline turns. Sees nothing. Her light bobs away. Valentine lets the lamp glow again.

It seems we'll have some fun tonight.

A cymbal crash.
    Blackout.
    Bright candlelight.
    Rosaline unrolls her bundle. Swords clank out and lie gleaming dully in the night.

Petruchio

Illegal weapons?

Rosaline

What do you bring, Petruchio?

Petruchio

This is an election.

Rosaline

It precedes a war.

Petruchio

It precedes a peace.

Rosaline

So you say.

Petruchio

Your clothes don't make a man of you.

Rosaline

I wear the clothes to fight more easily.

I have no wish to be a man.

Petruchio

Are you challenging me?

Rosaline

There is nothing says a woman cannot be leader.

We've had women before.

Petruchio

A social role.

Rosaline

Our laws do not define the position by gender.

Prince or Princess they state.

Petruchio

Why, Rosaline?

Rosaline

Do the Montagues allow peace?

Helena tell him.

I don't want peace.

Petruchio

I do.

Rosaline

Why?

Why?

Look at us.

Without weapons
What will we become?

Petruchio

I'd like to see.

Rosaline

And when you've seen
When you've seen
And we are all ordinary
And we have no purpose.
What then? It'll be too late to turn back.
We'll be out of the fighting way.
What tales then will we tell our children?
We'll have no more heroes,
We'll die old and wrinkled in our beds.
Love will be less sharp.

Petruchio

It wasn't one of us you loved.

Rosaline

I don't want to see our race decline.
Where will our poetry come from,
Hate ironed out of our souls,
Our fighting days done?
Blossom is more sweet today
If death comes tomorrow.

Petruchio

I want to watch the blossom bud;
I want to watch it flower;
I want to watch it fall,
A snow shower of petals on the ground;
And see the buds break next year too.
And the next.
And the next.
And taste the wine
From vines yet to be planted.

I want that for all of us.
Capulets and Montagues.
Rosaline
You want to play boules in the sunshine
Old before your time?
Petruchio
I want to live:
You want to die
And join Romeo in the vault.
And you want to take us with you.
These weapons are chill, Rosaline,
The cold sweat of the grave is on them.

He throws a sword. She catches it.

In a May time. Blossom on the trees.
Perfume in the air. I put a sword in a girl's hand.
Watched her catch up her skirts and fight.
Teasing me. Laughing at me.
The immortal passado I taught her
The punto reverso, the hay.
Rosaline
You know I can fight then
Having taught me yourself.
You all know I can fight.
Petruchio
Can you govern?
Alice
You loved her then, Petruchio?

*She hits Petruchio. Hits him again and again so that
he has to catch her hands.*

You loved Rosaline?
You loved her?
Rosaline
Can you govern, Petruchio?

Laughter.

Petruchio
The Prince has decreed peace.
Rosaline
Peace? I don't know what to do with it.
Alice
Petruchio?
Rosaline
There will be killings anyway
To fill up the space in our minds
Wrought by this Prince-ordained peace.
They'll seem accidental.
But they won't be.
    Better to play by the old rules.
Control the foot soldiers.
Give them discipline.
Alice
Do you still love her?
Livia
Juliet will have died for nothing.
Rosaline
Do you think she had us on her mind
When she wakened in the tomb?
Or peace? You all knew Juliet.
She was a kitten who lived for pleasure.
Only the very fortunate die for something.
    We have a cause.
We still have that.
Petruchio
We don't like them,
They don't like us.
Should they die for it?
Should we?
Because they pierce their daughter's ears at birth
And that's not our practice

Should we die?
Should they?
Rosaline
A heart has only so many beats in it.
Livia
He's right, Rosaline.
You're wrong.
Rosaline
Then your vote goes to him.
Lorenzo?
Lorenzo
I prefer a plain scabbard
To a jewelled one.
A jewelled scabbard
Is good to look at
And promises a great deal
But it's doomed to disappoint.
Rhona
Just like a man.

Lorenzo picks at the pile of weapons.

Lorenzo
A plain scabbard
Is all discovery,
Is what you will,
A plain scabbard
Will last a lifetime.
The other is best at the beginning
Then loses its glitter
As the years go by.

He weighs a weapon in his hand.

Still a jewelled scabbard
Is better than an empty one.
I'll join Rosaline.

Rosaline

Gianni?

Rhona

He doesn't have a mind of his own,
He'll follow his friend.

She flings a sword. Gianni catches it.

Gianni

I don't want peace, Rhona.
I've seen old men.
They don't look happy to me.
I look better young than I would old.
And I want to be a pretty corpse
So the girls garnish me with rose petals
And bathe me in tears.

Petruchio

Tears and pathos, Gianni,
Is that your style?

Gianni

Pipe and slippers, Petruchio,
Is that yours?

Petruchio

You have two, Rosaline.
I have one.
Alice?

Alice

Petruchio?

Petruchio

Will you stand with me?

Alice

What do you think?

Petruchio

Your face is pale.

Alice

I wonder why.

Petruchio
    Stand with me, Alice.
Alice
    I don't like to see a man sitting around.
    Peace makes men fat. Slender, lean men
    Taut with excitement, that's how I like them.
        I never thought I'd follow a woman, Petruchio.
    See. I just want things back the way they were before.

She touches his face. And moves to Rosaline.

Petruchio
    Rhona?
Rosaline
    She has no vote
    Being a visitor here.
Rhona
    I'm still a Capulet.

A moment. Rosaline nods.

    At home in Glasgow
    We have ice-cream wars
    Amongst other things.
    It all seems stupid to me.

Rhona walks to Petruchio's side.

Rosaline
    Three to two, Petruchio.
Petruchio
    Helena?
Rosaline
    They came at you this afternoon.
Helena
    Boys calling names.

She walks to Petruchio's side.

    Three all.

Holds out her hand to Bianca.

Bianca?

Bianca sucks her thumb.

Come here. Come on.
Then Petruchio's won.
Livia
She's in a dream, Helena.
Helena
Bianca.

The drummer click click clicks.
  Rosaline calls and throws a sword.

Rosaline
Bianca?

A muffled drum roll.
  A reflex makes Bianca catch the sword.

Helena
Bianca.

Bianca turns to her sister.

Rosaline
That's my sword, Bianca.
Give it to me.

She holds out her hand.

Give it to me.
Helena
Bianca.

The drums stop.
  *In the silence the drummer takes Bianca by the
hand. Leads her to Rosaline. Bianca hands Rosaline
the sword.*

Rosaline
Sit by me.
Petruchio
Is this how your rule begins?
Suborning the innocent?
Rosaline
We were all innocent.
We were all suborned.
Petruchio
I say we can choose.
Rosaline
We've chosen, Petruchio.
As you see.
Petruchio
This feud began not in our father's time
But in our father's father's.
Some small difference began it. This ancient grudge.
In all the tales our mothers tell.
I never heard what was the root cause.
Was it some slight. Some preferment.
Even some small argument between women.

He shrugs.

And yet our young men die.
In the service of this fierce fate
Which Rosaline believes gives our lives meaning.

Rosaline stands.

Rosaline
I don't know where the beginning was.

She puts her hand on her sword hilt.

Here and now. I take the end on me.

*The drummer clicks his sticks. Points. Petruchio and
the others climb back up to the balconies.*

Rosaline waits.
Valentine enters with his sword drawn.
He sees a figure waiting. Only a tall shadow.
He can't tell that it's a girl at all.

Valentine
Will you fight Petruchio?

Rosaline draws her sword.
    She's light on her feet. A teasing swordswoman.
In and out of the shadows.
    She nicks Valentine's eyebrow.
    The blood runs into his eye.
    Scattered applause. Light as rain.
    Rosaline withdraws.

Rosaline
Wipe the blood from your eye.
Valentine
Rosaline?
Rosaline
I have a scarf here you can borrow.
Bind your head. Staunch the flow.

She holds out a scarf to him. He dabs at the wound.

I don't fight blind men.
Valentine
I don't fight women, Rosaline.
Rosaline
Afraid you might lose, Valentine?
Valentine
I challenge the Prince of Cats.
Rosaline
She salutes you.

Rosaline clashes her sword on his.
    He defends.

Valentine
I won't fight a woman.

She presses him hard.
He defends.
He has to cut her to save himself.
She falters slightly.

Valentine
Enough.
Rosaline
No.
Valentine
Enough, Rosaline.

She strikes his blade hard.

Rosaline
You didn't say 'please'.
Valentine
There's no honour in this.
Rosaline
There is for me.
Valentine
Stop this fight.

He appeals to the spectators.

Petruchio.

Petruchio moves.
The drummer points. Petruchio freezes.
Rosaline strikes Valentine's sword.

Rosaline
Dozy.

He has to fight.
Benvolio runs in.

77

Benvolio
Stop this.
One of you.
Livia?
Petruchio?

He walks round the spectators.
Again there is a small movement. Again the
drummer freezes it.

The world would be a better place
If it was peopled by cowards.

He puts himself in between Rosaline and Valentine.

Rosaline, the stars are in the sky,
The world is drenched
In the scent of orange blossom.
Put up your sword.
Valentine
The woman is a tigress,
She will never stop.

Rosaline's at him again.

Rosaline
I'll hurt you, Benvolio,
If you come between us.
Benvolio
Would you hurt me?
Would you hurt me?
Valentine, I'll take your place.
You require a death.
I'll be your champion.
Rosaline, you require a death,
I'll be your opponent.
I'll fight you.
Stand back, Valentine.

Benvolio strikes Valentine's sword.

Valentine. Stand away.

Takes his place.
   Benvolio and Rosaline fight.
   With one hand Benvolio unfastens his jacket.

Rosaline
What are you doing?

They're both breathless.

Benvolio
Making it easy for you.
Giving you clear sight of the target.
Rosaline
Don't patronise me.

He drops his guard deliberately.

Benvolio
Come on, Rosaline. Come on.
   I first saw you in the street
In a green dress,
Pale, pale green.
You laughed, Rosaline,
Before the colour was forbidden, yes.
And I turned my head smiling
At the music of your laugh
And the light in your eyes.
You were happy.
   Do you still have the dress?
I'd like to see you in that dress.
It was springtime.
Rosaline
You said you'd fight me.
You said you'd fight.
Put up your guard.
Put it up.

79

He opens his arms wide.

Do you think I won't cut you.
Do you think I won't.

He takes her sword tip and puts it against his skin.

Benvolio
Cut me, then.

A long moment.

Cut me, Rosaline.

Quietly.

Rosaline
No.

She lets the sword tip drop.

You win.

Sheathes it.

Benvolio
Did you love him so much?

They're close. He touches her cheek.
A moment.
She turns away.

Rosaline
Have your cats, Petruchio,
I hope they purr for you.

Pause.

Benvolio
That's it.
Valentine
Is it?

Benvolio

Put your weapon down.

A beat.
  Valentine sheathes his sword.
  Rhona's flute.
  The people on the balconies fade into the shadows.

Do you still have the dress?

Rosaline

Yes.

Benvolio

Will you put it on for me?

The moon is bright. Shadows flutter across it. Chase and chase again.

One day?

He takes her hand. Twines his fingers in hers.

Rosaline

In the spring.

But she doesn't smile at him.

Benvolio

Is that a promise?

Rosaline

Maybe.

She isn't close to him. Though she doesn't take her hand away.
  The drummer makes the high hat kiss-kiss.

Alice

So you like a woman who fights.

Petruchio

I never betrayed you.

Alice
What was there to betray?
We made no promises,
You and me,
Save a look here
A touch there.
Petruchio
As long as we have things clear between us.
Alice
Things are clear. Very, very clear
To me at least.
You like a woman who fights.

She hits him on the arm. Hits and hits again. A wind-mill of hitting.

So fight. Come on fight.
Fight, fight, fight.

He holds her arms tight against her.

That's not fair.
Petruchio
Shhh. Sh. Sh.

He kisses her.
  Rhona's flute lilts and haunts.

Lorenzo
That's a sad sound.
Gianni
Sad enough.
Lorenzo
A man could dance his last to that tune.
Gianni
The night's uneasy.
Lorenzo
What do we do now?

Gianni
  I don't know. What do we do?
Lorenzo
  I asked you first.
Gianni
  I asked you second.
Lorenzo
  What now though?
Gianni
  I don't know what now.

Lorenzo stares into a bowl of terrapins. Speaks on a long, long sigh.

Lorenzo
  Terrapins.

Gianni stares down into the night.
  Helena has her arms round Bianca.

Bianca
  'The apothecary high is hanged by the throte,
  And for the paynes he took with him, the hangman
    had his cote.'
    The trial is over
  Night has come.
    Juliet waited and waited.
  Now she's gone.
  The barriers are up again.
  The dream is done.

The drummer tick ticks with his drum sticks.
  The flute plays.
  Two Capulets, one Montague are left on stage.
  Valentine's leaning. Looking up at Gianni looking down. Catches his eye.
  Gianni tugs on Lorenzo's sleeve. They both fix on Valentine.

Valentine pats his sword hilt. Raises an eyebrow in question. Slightly lifts the sword out of the scabbard.

Gianni nods. Accepts the challenge.

He and Lorenzo jump down.

Valentine unsheathes his sword. Wipes it on his jacket.

Waits.

The drummer points.

Lorenzo and Gianni draw their swords.

The flute trills and falls silent.

Blackout.

Scratching the Itch

Sharman Macdonald interviewed by Jim Mulligan

Baz Luhrman's film of *Romeo and Juliet* with Clare Danes and Leonardo Di Caprio prompted Sharman Macdonald's thirteen-year-old daughter Keira Knightley to tell her to write a play about Rosaline. Undoubtedly Rosaline appears on stage in *Romeo and Juliet* at the Capulets' party but she is not in the cast list and, although Romeo is besotted with her in Act 1 Scene 1, she is only mentioned twice. Her daughter's demand together with the film's electrifying music and the tough sinewy style that made the Shakespearean language a dialect that young people could use, led Sharman Macdonald to speculate on how she could explore what happened in the days immediately after the deaths of Romeo and Juliet.

> I decided to use the text by Brooke that Shakespeare used as his source. *After Juliet* is written in a kind of doggerel because it has vitality and there is the potential for mischief in it. It's allowed to make a fool of itself occasionally. It gave me the freedom to leap off from the play and the film. Increasingly I want to write with music and an integral part of *After Juliet* is the music composed by Caleb Knightley and Adrian Howgate.

In *After Juliet* the embargo on weapons is being enforced but the feud between the young Capulets and Montagues is simmering. Rosaline, convinced that there should be fighting, raids the tomb to get the only swords available. Implacable Valentine does the same so that, when the new Prince of Cats is elected, 'the days will breathe again'. Rosaline forces the Capulets to choose between peace and war. After she is elected Princess of Cats, she fights Valentine with total conviction. However, she is unable to sustain her animosity when Benvolio takes up the fight and simply challenges her to kill him. She is not exactly enthusiastic in her response to Benvolio's passion but at least she takes his hand and promises that, in the spring, she will wear that special green dress that he liked, pale, pale green.

Rosaline is eaten up by unrequited love for Romeo and the conviction that Juliet was responsible for all the deaths and for the fate of the four people who are on trial for their lives. She is down a long way and has a journey to go but she is always fighting. She is a very feisty lady. There is hope that she is going to come through that deep despair of adolescence to a place where there is light and life. In the end she is redeemed by Benvolio's innocent love.

After-shocks rock this society which could be in Verona or in Edinburgh, Dublin, New York or Liverpool. Wherever it is, there is a deliberate tension created between the clear references to the original story and such things as hand-rolled cigarettes, chrome toasters, a gleaming electric fan and a fridge. In this setting *After Juliet* looks at how justice is meted out in the trial of those held responsible for the deaths of Romeo and Juliet. The friar goes into self-imposed solitude and contemplation; Angelica, the nurse, is spared but exiled; Peter, because he simply obeyed orders, is set free; but the apothecary is hanged by the throat. This is strange justice, 'law meted out by the rich as if riches bear witness to virtue'. In this timeless society even honourable men need a scapegoat and, although the young people can see that the apothecary was only supplying their needs and was seduced by Romeo's ducats, he still has to hang.

Despite convincing characterisations and some excellent exchanges between Benvolio and Valentine, the women dominate this play. Rosaline is scorned, vindictive, assertive and single-minded but she is also a fighter with a lightness and a sense of humour. Bianca, on the other hand is a visionary, other worldly, magical, holding the balance of the piece in her hands. Helena is the carer, the surrogate mother who expresses some of the frustration that a carer feels while Rhona, the outsider from Glasgow, is also seen as a threat.

Because this is a short piece, many issues are touched on but not fully explored. The death penalty, the shadow of Northern Ireland and the death of Princess Diana are there for the discerning. However, love, death and revenge are central and come together in the feud that persists despite the decrees of the authorities and the emotional involvement of the characters. The stage directions indicate that Rosaline is not close to Benvolio though she does not take her hand away from his. Alice attacks Petruchio and is subdued when he kisses her. The drummer tick-ticks with his drum sticks. The flute plays and two Capulets and one Montague are left on stage. Valentine unsheathes his sword, Gianni accepts the challenge. The drummer points. The flute trills and falls silent. The men prepare to scratch the itch once more.

West Side Story, which I love, and *Romeo and Juliet* end on a note of sad optimism. The impression given is that things will change. If only it were that easy. Things don't change because two people have died. There is no death that puts a full stop to anything. If the mind is emptied of the preoccupation that has been its obsession, what does the mind turn to? Where does it go? My conclusion is that the itch is still there and, because you can scratch it, you do.

There are themes in *After Juliet* that are germane to
how we live today and there is something for
performers to bite on. I was profoundly changed by
seeing *West Side Story* when I was young and now
I never write without wanting to affect people in some
way. I hope that *After Juliet* opens up discussion.
I hope the roughness and rawness of the play will
keep people talking, and maybe even laughing, for
at least a couple of minutes after the curtain comes
down.

Production Notes

After Juliet is the story of what happens immediately
after the tragic end of *Romeo and Juliet*. It is a powerful
and vivid play with a contemporary take on love and
death, war and peace, and can be set anywhere in an
imaginative way: 'This could be Verona. Or it could be
Edinburgh, Dublin, New York or Liverpool. It could
be 1500, 1900, 2000 or 3000.'

. There needs to be three irregular playing levels which
open out onto a piazza. These might be achieved with
scaffolding and zip-up towers. Two separate balconies
need to be suggested, perhaps with drapes. The scaffolding might be dressed very simply to give a mock-Tudor
feel to the set. You will gain clues to the environment as
the play progresses and the picture builds. Splashes of
colour are added with the introduction of trailing red
geraniums in pots and bowls of terrapins (which could
be projected). Symbols of domestic modernity such as a
chrome toaster, a gleaming electric fire and a fridge may
be added. You could experiment with setting the action
in a gym using the apparatus to create different heights.
This is the Capulet district and in one corner of the
piazza is a pile of lilies in varying degrees of decay, a
shrine to Juliet. The Capulet family coat of arms/family
emblem might be present. The two Montague men stand
out as outsiders by wearing green while the drummer
and musician may appear to be neutral. Costumes are
punk-Elizabethan. This effect might be created by adding
a ruff or some other Tudor features to modern dress. The
families are in mourning, it's up to you to decide how
this can be made apparent.

The tomb, narrow alleyways and high buildings can be suggested by lighting, which will also need to suggest heat and the changing elements. As night falls a hurricane light appears, the moon is bright and shadows flutter across it repeatedly. There is a sword fight towards the end of the play. On no account use swords with untrained actors without the specialist help of a trained combat director, even if the blades are tipped and made for theatrical purposes. You might seek alternative solutions to a stylised fight sequence using clawed gauntlets, for example, and cat imagery.

SOUND

will need to provide rain, thunder and church bells and to take into account the drummer and the music. The drum used needs to be portable to enable the drummer to move easily through the action. A specially created score to accompany *After Juliet* by Caleb Knightley and Adrian Howgate is available on CD with cue sheet. It combines instruments and effects such as acoustic piano, cello and guitar, samples of vacuum cleaners, fire extinguishers, answerphones and telephones to create a timeless quality. Or you could create your own mood music. There are also two songs.

CASTING

After Juliet is for a central cast of eleven actors aged approximately from fourteen to eighteen, as well as a drummer and a musician whose percussion and sound-track provide the score and sometimes influence the direction of the action. The nurse appears briefly and is the only adult character. There is scope for non-speaking roles in some scenes.

EXERCISES

You don't necessarily have to be familiar with Shakespeare's *Romeo and Juliet* in order to direct *After Juliet* because the play stands up in its own right. However, there are so many references to characters in Shakespeare's piece that it would be useful to have at least a passing acquaintance with it.

- Having looked at the plot of *Romeo and Juliet* identify the characters that appear in both plays. Look at the characters' journey through the play and create a back history for them.
- Create a tableau with Romeo and Juliet at the centre, position the other characters around them so that it is clear from their body language, facial expression and distance from them what their relationship is.
- Have the actors step out of the tableau one by one to observe the picture and adjust the positioning of the other actors if they feel it is inaccurate.
- Remove Romeo and Juliet from the picture. Have all the actors adjust their positioning so that it is clear how the relationships of those remaining have changed since the death of the two teenagers.

After Juliet is set a very short time after the death of Romeo and his lover, yet we learn that a lot has happened in the intervening period. Improvise some of the scenes outside the play that are referred to in it – for instance, the arrest of the apothecary, the nurse and the friar, the death of Lady Capulet etc.

Look at Rosaline's monologue where she walks towards the pile of lilies in the piazza and begins:

> Your spirit haunts me Juliet
> I see more of you dead
> Than I did when you were alive.

Improvise some of the scenes Rosaline refers to. What does the speech tell us about Rosaline and her relationship with Juliet?

Look at one of the sections involving the drummer. It might be the one before Rosaline enters the tomb. Decide how the drummer can best control the action . . . what sort of persona might he have? Is he grotesque? godlike? Young/old? – is he fate personified? What sort of relationship does he have with the audience – can he see them or are they a third wall? How about the characters, is he invisible or are there times when Bianca, or any of them, are aware of his influence? Try different approaches. Hot seat the drummer, ask him what he makes of the action in the play and what he hopes to achieve with the characters.

Frequently we hear the characters talk about what they want. Rosaline says she wants revenge, Petruchio wants peace, etc. Look at how these 'wants' inform the actions of the characters.

Suzy Graham-Adriani
February 1999

CAN YOU KEEP A SECRET?

Winsome Pinnock

Characters

in order of speaking

Kate
Aleysha
Candy
Sean
Derek
Fog (female)
Dilys (male)
Chunky
Mrs Lewis, Derek's Mum
Mr Lewis, Derek's Dad
Ben
Weirdboy
Johnson, Chief Inspector
Michael
Trish
Doctor
Father, Kate's Dad
Mother, Kate's Mum
Sally
Gary

SCENE ONE

Two young women – Kate, seventeen, and Aleysha, also
seventeen – are waiting outside a cinema where others
are waiting in a queue. They are both dressed up. They
eye each other up, neither letting the other know that she
is looking at her. Aleysha catches Kate looking at her.
This forces Kate to say something.

Kate I like your shoes. Red or dead?

Aleysha Yeah. I like your trousers.

Kate Got to make the effort, haven't you? I hate waiting.

Aleysha I told my boyfriend that if he was late again I'm
giving him the sack.

Kate Are you?

Aleysha We ain't a married couple. It's too soon for us
to be taking each other for granted.

Kate How long you been going out with him?

Aleysha Four years.

Kate You might as well be married.

Aleysha We got engaged a month ago. (*Shows Kate the*
ring. Kate admires it.) It ain't real – cubic zirconium
or something.

Kate Me and Sean's only been together three weeks.
I been waiting for him to ask me out for the longest
time.

Aleysha Why didn't you ask him out yourself?

Kate I did. I had to make it look like it all come from
him, though, didn't I? You're at sixth form college
aren't you? I seen you with your mates. I work in the
market. On the handbag stall?

Aleysha Is that you?

95

Kate Yeah.

Aleysha Cool. Me mum bought a bag off you the other week.

Kate (*smiles*) Yeah?

Aleysha Strap broke.

Kate Oh. Is he always late then?

Aleysha He's usually here before I am.

Kate Treat 'em mean, to keep 'em keen, eh?

Aleysha When you've been together three years you don't have to play games like that any more.

Kate Which film you going to see?

Aleysha He wants to see *Lost in Space* and I want to see *Armageddon*. We'll fight it out when he gets here.

Kate We might see you in there then.

Candy runs on shouting for Kate.

Candy Kate. Kate. (*panting*) I been looking for you everywhere.

Kate Where's the fire, Candy?

Candy It's Sean, Kate.

Kate What's wrong with him?

Candy (*panting. Taking Kate aside so that Aleysah can't hear them*) He's . . . he's . . .

Kate Get it out, Cand, he's what?

Candy (*panting*) He's . . . he's . . .

Kate You're scaring me, Candy. For God's sake what? Has he had an accident?

Candy Sort of.

Kate What sort of accident? For fuck's sake, Candy. Where is he?

Candy Not an accident exactly, but he's in trouble, Kate. You got to come with me. He might listen to you.

Kate What do you mean by that?

Candy He's lost it, Kate. You know what he's like when he gets started. Maybe you can calm him down.

Kate Oh no, not again!

Candy You know what he's like, Kate. He won't back
down, not even if it was Mike Tyson.
Kate Where is he?
Candy Follow me.

Candy runs off.

Kate (*to Aleysha*) Blokes. You can't leave them alone for
two minutes can you?
Aleysha Your bloke in trouble is he?
Kate Just mucking around. He's a real joker. Got to run.
See you around.
Aleysha Yeah. See you around.

*Kate leaves, running. Aleysha looks at her watch,
continues to wait.*

SCENE TWO

An alleyway behind the shopping centre.
Derek and Sean are fighting. Others in the group –
*Chunky, Dilys (male) and Fog (female) – are egging them
on. Sean has the upper hand.*

Sean Take it back.
Derek If the cap fits.
Sean I said take it back.
Fog Smash him, Sean. Show him what's what.
Dilys Give it to him good, Sean. He deserves it.
Chunky No one speaks to one of us like that. Fuckin'
do him.
Sean Take it back, black boy. Apologise.
Derek All right. All right. Let go of me. I can't speak.
You're choking me.

*Sean lets go of Derek who stands up and rubs his
throat.*

Sean Now. Apologise.

Derek Alright. Alright. I'm sorry I called you a div. Anybody looking at you can see that you're nowhere near a div. Anybody looking at you can see that you are in fact, a fine, upstanding, genuine homo.

Fog Uh-oh.

Sean What did you call me?

Derek You heard.

Sean I want you to say it again, just to make sure I heard it straight.

Derek Straight? No fear of that, is there, Batty Boy?

Sean You black cunt.

Derek Ooh, I've got him all angry now.

Sean Wog.

Derek See, you can call me what you like, but it's like I'm wearing a bullet-proof vest. It won't touch me 'cos I'm straight with myself, see?

Sean Jungle Bunny.

Derek You, on the other hand, you're all confused, aren't you? You haven't come to terms with who you are so every name I call you cuts like a knife because you don't want to see the truth of it.

Sean Nigger.

Derek And now you've come to the end. You've had the last word. What else you gonna pull out of your armoury now?

Sean Nigger. Nigger. Nigger. Nigger.

Derek And if you say it enough times it loses its power, becomes just a sound. (*very fast*) Nigger. Nigger. Nigger. Nigger. See what I mean?

Sean You black nigger cunt.

Derek That's right. Change the words round, recombine them. They still ain't got any power. And you know why? Because there's a new world order. Look at you, Nancy Boy, hair cut to the scalp. Who you trying to look like? Like a black felon on death row, that's what. New world order: The Niggers Rule OK and you, my dear Nancy Boy, are the new victim. That's why my name calling carries more weight.

As he calls Sean names he follows him around the stage.

Shit stabber. Shirt lifter. Queen. Raver. Batty boy.
Fog He can't treat you like that, show him.
Sean You coon.

Sean pushes Derek to the ground and punches him. Candy and Kate arrive followed by Weirdboy who stands in the shadows watching.

Kate (*trying to pull Sean off Derek*) What you doing? Stop it.
Sean (*pushes Kate away*) Get off me.

One of the others throws him an iron bar. The others egg him on, making noises every time he hits with the iron bar. Soon Derek is still. Sean stands up and throws down the bar. Kate goes to Derek.

Kate He's not breathing. He's not breathing, Sean. You've . . .
Sean We've nothing. Understand? Are you my friend Fog?
Fog You know I am.
Sean Chunky?
Chunky We been friends since primary school. We're mates, do everything together. We're like Siamese twins. If one of us gets hurt the others feel it.
Sean Do everything together. We're all going to a club tonight, have a laugh. Nothing happened, right? You're my best friends. We all stick together and I want you to swear. On my blood, I want you to swear that you'll stand by me. Promise me nothing happened.

As Sean goes round the group he takes blood from his cheek and marks their foreheads with it.

Fog?

Fog I ain't seen nothing.

Sean Chunky?

Chunky We went to a club and had a great time.

Sean Dilys, Candy, Kate.

Candy We went to a club. Had a few drinks. Fog popped an E and made us all laugh with her craziness, just like she always does.

Dilys I got in at two in the morning and my mum brought me breakfast in bed the next day. Ask her.

Sean Kate?

Kate Me? (*Kate steps forward.*) Me and Sean split from the others around midnight. We went back to his parents' house. We talked and talked. He couldn't stop talking. It was like he wanted to tell me everything about himself all in one go. I've never talked with any boy like that. Then the talking stopped and we got into bed. He started to shake. He was trembling all over. I held him in my arms and felt the fear running through him. We made love for the first time. It was incredible.

SCENE THREE

A few days after the killing. The sound of loud crying. Mr and Mrs Lewis, Aleysha, and Ben, Derek's friend, all come on wheeling a coffin.

Mrs Lewis I had a dream that I answered a knock on the door. And it was him, standing there as though nothing had happened.

Mr Lewis My son is dead. Why did my son have to die?

Aleysha I loved him, Mr Lewis. He loved me. I been with him since we was thirteen. We were going to get married after college.

Ben He was my best friend. A true friend, Mrs Lewis. He never let me down.

Aleysha He had a mischievous sense of humour. He'd tease everybody.

Ben He always took the piss out of me. He made me laugh at myself.

Mr Lewis He was no angel. Once he took money from my pocket. He thought I wouldn't notice. I made sure he paid.

Aleysha I knew things about him, things that he wouldn't ever tell anybody else. And he knew my secrets too. Nobody else will ever know me in the way that he did.

Mrs Lewis My son is dead. Why did my son have to die?

Ben I hate to think of him dying like he did on his own in some back alley. He would never have let me die like that. He was always there for me.

Mrs Lewis When a mother says that she is proud of her son, what she means is that she loves him in undescribable ways because his life has made hers better. It made me happy just to look at him, just to see his smiling face.

Ben He liked his books, but he knew how to have a good time as well.

Mrs Lewis Other women's children get into trouble. I thought that I was one of the lucky ones.

Ben Whoever did this, Mrs Lewis, I swear that they will not get away with it.

Mr Lewis It isn't easy to be a good father. Not in this day and age when there are so many temptations to drag a boy onto the wrong path. But I was proud of myself for the job I'd done with Derek. His success

was my success. All my hard work was worth it.
Someone is going to have to pay for taking him away
from me.

Aleysha I feel all my love being sucked down a black
hole. It isn't fair. How can someone get away with
something like this?

Ben I swear, Mr Lewis, that I won't rest till I've had my
revenge.

Mr and Mrs Lewis Our son is dead. Why did our son
have to die?

SCENE FOUR

Weirdboy and Kate enter.

Weirdboy I can read your mind.

Kate Go away, weird boy.

Weirdboy Weirdboy, yes. That's what they call me, isn't
it? I prefer Danny, which is my real name. Been
shopping?

Kate What's it to you?

Weirdboy What did you buy, Katie?

Kate My name isn't Katie.

Weirdboy That's all that's left to us these days, isn't it?
Buy buy buy. Spend spend spend. Where do they get
the money from? That's what everybody's asking
themselves. Young people today. Well I never. Still,
what does it matter? Makes us feel good about
ourselves, doesn't it?

Kate You are so weird.

Weirdboy And that makes you feel good too, doesn't it,
Katie? That you're not me? That you're not the one
who doesn't belong to any gang? Who everybody can
laugh at. What you have to remember, Katie, is that
you need me.

Kate I don't need you, Weirdboy.

Weirdboy But you do, Katie. You all do. How else would you know how 'in' and trendy you were if you didn't have me around to compare yourselves with? What did you buy, Katie? So what did you buy?

Kate That's none of your business.

Weirdboy You don't have to tell me. I know anyway. You bought an Alaia jacket and two Karen Millen dresses. After all, the labels are important, aren't they, Katie? How would we know who we were if we didn't have labels? Katie, Weirdboy.

Kate How did you know what I bought? Have you been following me?

Weirdboy I told you, Katie, I can read your mind. And just then you were imagining yourself in the Alaia jacket and you were seeing the expression on your boyfriend's face when you meet him tonight all dressed up. What's this? You've got a secret, haven't you, Katie?

Kate Fuck off.

Weirdboy A big dark secret. You've put up a wall. There's something you don't want me to know, isn't there?

Sean enters.

Weirdboy Must dash. Got loads to do.

Sean What you talking to him for?

Kate I wasn't. He's weird.

Sean Exactly. I want you to do me a big favour, Kate. I want you to get rid of this.

Hands her the plastic carrier bag.

Kate What is it?

Sean A jacket. The jacket I was wearing . . . The night . . . you know.

Kate What do you want me to do with it?

Sean Get rid of it. Burn it. Throw it away. Anything.

Kate Why didn't you get rid of it?

Sean Someone might see me.

Kate What if they see me?

Sean They won't. You could burn it in the garden when your parents are out. I can't do it meself, Kate. Can you imagine? Will you? (*angry*) I thought you loved me.

Kate I do.

Sean Then why won't you help me? I thought I could trust you but you're just like everybody else.

Kate Don't be angry with me, Sean. Please. Please don't turn away from me.

Sean I'm on my own again. Just like I always am.

Kate I'll do it, Sean. I'll get rid of the jacket.

Sean Thank you, Kate. I knew I could rely on you. Be careful. You don't want anybody to see you.

Kate No.

Sean What do you want to do today? It's up to you. Anything you want we'll do it.

Kate Brighton.

Sean Eh?

Kate I want to walk along the pier and look at the sea.

Sean All right then. Brighton it is.

SCENE FIVE

Three weeks after the killing. The Lewis's house. The grieving parents are with Chief Inspector Johnson.

Johnson Had there been any trouble before that night?

Mrs Lewis Trouble?

Johnson With your son.

Mr Lewis What kind of trouble?

Johnson Friends of his. Well, I say friends . . .

Mr Lewis What do you mean?

Johnson Had anybody been round here, threatening?

Mrs Lewis I don't understand what you mean. What does he mean?

Johnson If you'll let me finish. Threatening your son. Troublemakers.

Mr Lewis My son didn't know any troublemakers.

Mrs Lewis He was a very quiet boy.

Johnson Quiet? Excuse me but that's not what I've heard. I've heard that he was quite a lively sort, life and soul of every party – nobody said he was quiet.

Mrs Lewis He was a boy. A regular boy.

Mr Lewis He knew how to enjoy himself. Yes.

Johnson It's so easy to get involved with the wrong crowd. If you could only see some of the things I've seen. And some of the kids involved are much younger than your son. And their parents knew nothing whatsoever about what their children were up to.

Mrs Lewis My son did not get involved with the wrong crowd.

Johnson Frightening. I'm a father myself. You can't keep your eye on them all the time, can you? Certainly not when they're seventeen. So how do you know what they get up to?

Mr Lewis My son had no secrets. We talked about everything.

Johnson They don't tell us everything do they? It wouldn't be right. It would take away the fun of being a teenager.

Mrs Lewis We knew all his friends. (*pointedly*) He was not involved with drug dealers, pimps or criminals.

Mr Lewis My son had no secrets.

Johnson I'm sorry to have to ask you these questions, but you do understand my position, don't you? I have to make sure that no stone is left unturned. I have to investigate every possibility before I can eliminate it.

Mr Lewis Have you found my son's killers?

Johnson You know we haven't.

Mrs Lewis Have you pursued any of the clues?

Johnson There is very little concrete evidence.

Mrs Lewis Everybody has heard the rumours.

Johnson My work cannot proceed by rumours, Mrs Lewis.

Mr Lewis But it can by guesswork?

Johnson I have to follow my nose, Mr Lewis. My aim isn't to alienate you, but, as I say, I have been involved in so many 'incidents' of this nature that I've built up a knowledge, shall we say, about these things. You're not the first parents I've met who have been shocked to learn about their child's involvement in the darker side of life.

Mrs Lewis My son was not involved with drugs or with violence of any sort.

Mr Lewis The night that he was killed he was on his way to meet his girlfriend. That's how he liked to spend his time. They were inseparable.

Johnson What was he doing in that alleyway? Perhaps he had a meeting with somebody else before meeting her?

Mrs Lewis Somebody knows what happened.

Johnson Well if they do they haven't told me yet. We have very little evidence.

Mr Lewis Maybe you're not listening.

Mrs Lewis Maybe you're not looking hard enough.

Johnson I'm only human, Mrs Lewis. People these days think that we are more powerful than we are. They think that we're clairvoyants. I blame the television. Every crime solved in sixty minutes flat. It isn't like that in real life, Mr and Mrs Lewis, one clue leading neatly to another. In real life it is often far messier and unclear.

Mrs Lewis I should investigate myself. If I were investigating myself I wouldn't waste a minute standing here talking about television. I would be out there searching for the vital clues.

Mr Lewis With every minute that you're standing here vital evidence is being lost. Since my son died it has rained three times. All the evidence washed away.

Johnson Please, Mr and Mrs Lewis. I am on your side.

Mr Lewis Really? You could have fooled me.

Johnson Do you think I haven't got a heart, Mr Lewis? Like I said, I am a father myself. I can only imagine what it would be like to lose a son like that. I do have a heart and to prove it I'll make you a promise. I will not rest. I will not let this case go until I find the people that killed your son.

SCENE SIX

Sean and his gang enter, shouting, laughing, etc. They have cans of drink with them. Weirdboy sits apart from them, watching.

Candy (*distraught*) I can't believe they made him die.

Fog Shut up, Candy.

Candy I mean, he's so handsome.

Dilys What a load of rubbish. They're playing with us, aren't they? A load of sentimental crap.

Candy He must feel cold, so cold. And all alone.

Chunky Rubbish. He's living it large in Hollywood, isn't he? Did you see how many birds he had on his arm at that night club the other night? I saw it in the newspaper.

Fog He's a lucky bastard.

Kate It's just a film, Candy.

Candy I know it's just a film, I'm not stupid, but when you're watching it it's for real, isn't it? I'm not some cold-hearted bitch.

Kate I know you're not Cand.

Candy If I was some cold-hearted bitch then I could walk out of that cinema with dry eyes like you lot.

Chunky Leo, Leo, wherefore art thou, Leo? Glug. Glug.

Sean Good special effects though.

Dilys My dad reckons he's going to take us on a holiday to the *Titanic*.

Fog You can't go on the *Titanic*. It's sunk.

Dilys You can visit the ruins, can't you? Scuba diving and that.

Fog They won't let you visit the ruins.

Dilys Why not?

Fog They're still excavating them.

Dilys You can't excavate in the sea.

Fog Whatever.

Chunky They're building a theme park ent they? You can experience what it was like for those on board the *Titanic* when it was sinking.

Dilys That is so sick. Who wants to experience drowning?

Chunky I don't know. There's a certain thrill to it. All theme parks work on the same principle don't they? Face the fear.

Candy Poor Kate Winslet.

Sean For God's sake, Candy.

Candy Her one true love gone. How will she cope?

Chunky What would you do with all her millions?

Fog Buy a Maserati.

Dilys You'd have to pass your driving test first.

Fog Don't you worry, I'll pass.

Dilys Her driving instructor won't enter her for her test, will she, Fog? Last lesson she had she drove through a shop window.

Fog I couldn't see, could I? It was foggy.

Dilys It's always foggy for you ennit, Fog?

Kate Why don't you wear your glasses, Fog?

Fog Because I don't need them.

Sean All right. How many fingers am I holding up, Fog? Come on.

Fog Forget it.

The others laugh.

(*insistent*) I don't need glasses.

Candy Kate Winslet wears specs.

Dilys Let's have a fag, Sean.

Sean passes cigarettes around. They pass the cans around too.

Fog Kate Winslet can afford Calvin Klein. I have to settle for NHS specials.

Dilys NHS specials are groovy these days.

Fog I'm telling you, Dilys, it may look like it but Mel B is not wearing NHS specials.

Sean How many fingers, Fog?

Dilys Maybe she can't count.

Fog Fuck off.

Dilys She used to do them special classes, remember?

Fog Only 'cos I lost a year when I was in hospital.

Candy He didn't even have time to sit his 'A' levels.

Sean Who?

Candy Leonardo Di Caprio.

Kate She's still on about that stupid film. I told you we should have gone to see something else.

Sean But you been wanting to see that for ages.

Kate No I haven't.

Sean What's up with you, Candy? It's just a film.

Candy Yeah. It's just a film. But why did they let him die? They aim those films at young people like us because they know what we're afraid of, what we

have on our minds. They knew that it would upset us
and that we'd never get it out of our heads about a
young boy dying.

They knew that it would give us bad dreams and
I haven't had bad dreams since I was a little girl.
But now I go to bed and as soon as I close my eyes
I see his face and hear the sound of him dying and
that's a terrible thing to hear a young man dying.
A young boy who could have been any one of us.
That's a thing that could haunt you for the rest of
your life.

*There is an awkward silence as the group take in the
implications of what she has just said. Sean starts to
sing (a rap song about dying young or something.
Groups who perform the play may want to create
their own song). His tone is defiant. Candy opens her
mouth to speak but the others take up the song and
drown her out.*

*The group have now completely drowned out the
thoughts aroused by Candy's speech. They all – apart
from Kate who is watching – sing the song and dance
around to it. When they finish there is a pause, it is as
though they are defying Candy to go any further.*

Sean Who wants to come to my house? My parents are
out for the evening.

Fog You lucky bastard. My parents never go out.

Dilys That means we can raid the drinks bar.

Sean Unfortunately, they've locked the drinks bar.

Chunky Spoilsports.

Sean But fortunately I know where they've hidden the
key.

The others cheer.

Come on, let's go.

They all go off, leaving Kate and Candy on the stage together.

Candy I've seen that film five times and every time I go I hope that it'll turn out different and that he doesn't fall into the sea this time.

Kate But you know that it won't turn out different, don't you, Candy? You know that every time you see it, it'll always end the same way.

Candy Every time I watch it I'm hoping that he'll hang on tight to that piece of wood. I can't bear the thought of him drowning, Kate.

Kate So stop seeing it. You can block anything out of your mind if you really want to.

Candy Is that what you've done?

Kate Yes.

Candy But how? How do you do that?

Kate Every time the thought comes into your mind you think about something else, something completely different, and before you know it, you've forgotten.

Candy Think about something else.

Kate That's right.

Candy And you promise that I'll forget?

Kate I promise.

Candy So what do you think about when the bad memories come into your mind?

Kate A day out in Brighton with Mum and Dad when I was seven. It was a perfect day, Candy. That's how I remember it – blazing hot sun and the sea so perfect. And Mum and Dad laughing all day.

Candy (*repeating the phrase*) Think about something else.

Kate Dad kept making me laugh even more and Mum told him off 'cos I was hysterical and that made me laugh again.

Candy I like the sound of you laughing.

Kate So, now, shall we go and get drunk with the others or do you want to stay here?

Candy Let's go with the others. It's when I'm on my own that I remember what happened and, like you say, I don't want to remember. Let's go, Kate. I want to be with the others. I can't stand to be alone.

SCENE SEVEN

Aleysha, Ben, and other friends of Derek's – Michael and Trish – come on stage. Again Weirdboy is on stage watching.

Michael I can't believe it, man. One minute I'm standing here talking to him, the next they're telling me that I'll never see him again.

Trish It ain't fair. It ain't bloody fair.

Ben He always watched my back. Remember at primary school when the others used to pick on me? He always stood up for me, remember? Now I'm going to stand up for him.

Michael There's rumours flying, Ben, about a group of kids running up that alleyway the night of the killing.

Ben Anyone know who they were?

Michael It was Calvin what told me. But it was too dark and too fast to see their faces.

Trish You can't jump to conclusions, Michael. They may have gone up the alley, seen him dead and run off to get the police or something.

Michael That's why he wasn't discovered till the next day then is it? They must have been the ones.

Aleysha Kids? How old?

Michael I don't know. Our age I suppose.

Aleysha Kids like us.

Ben The police don't care, do they? Why should they? It isn't their friend, their son? If the police don't care who will? We can't rely on the police, can we? We bring them evidence and they don't believe us.

Michael My cousin's friend died in police custody.

Ben See what I mean.

Michael He was asthmatic, yeah, and he was calling out for his medication, because they'd locked him up and everything, but they thought that he was making trouble. Being aggressive because of the shouting and everything so they didn't take any notice of him. Next thing he collapsed and they still didn't take any notice. Next day they found him dead.

Ben Exactly what I'm talking about. If we're going to get anywhere we're going to have to take things into our own hands, aren't we? We're going to have to find out who did this and make sure that they pay for it.

Aleysha Why was he in prison? Your cousin's friend.

Michael Dunno. Theft or something. I can't remember.

Aleysha That's a high price to pay.

Trish You're telling me. His mum still ain't got over it.

Ben Are you all with me?

Michael Take matters into our own hands?

Ben What other choice have we got? Derek was a good friend to all of us. Don't we owe him this?

Aleysha I for one would do anything to get hold of the bastards that killed him.

Trish Me too.

Michael But when we find them, what will we do with them? If we're not going to the police.

Ben We'll cross that bridge when we come to it.

Michael Because I don't want to be involved in any violence. I don't believe in violence.

Ben Let's find them first, shall we? We ought to make a promise to Derek. We ought to promise that we'll all avenge his death for him.

Aleysha I promise. And even that doesn't feel good enough. Not while I'm alive to do even that and he isn't.

Trish I swear. He didn't deserve what happened to him.

Michael No one deserves that. I swear. Except if it involves violence. I won't hurt anybody. No violence.

Ben We won't rely on what the police tell us. If they say that they can't find any witnesses, then we'll make sure that we go all out to find them ourselves. If they say that people aren't speaking then we'll make them speak. Our parents are always talking about how hard our grandparents had it and how they went through all that crap just to make things easier for their kids. And, now, our parents, they go through crap to make things better for us. And us – just when we were beginning to take things for granted, now we can see that things are going to be just as tough for us and that we're going to have to fight just as hard as they did. And that's when we have to ask ourselves whether or not we're up to it. And you got to think long and hard when you answer that question because you have to understand that we can't rely on anybody but ourselves.

SCENE EIGHT

Kate's bedroom. Night. A figure appears in the window. He opens the window and steps into the room. It is Derek, dressed exactly as he was when he died. He looks around the room and then perches on the end of Kate's bed, looking at her. She wakes up startled and stares at him. He smiles at her.

Kate Oh my God.
Derek Don't be frightened.

Kate This is a dream right?

Derek Why don't you try thinking about something else, see if I'll go away. Close your eyes, why don't you?

Kate closes her eyes for a long moment. She opens them again.

I'm still here Kate.

Kate This is a joke. Someone set you up to do this.

Derek Why would I do that? Why would I want to frighten you after everything you've already been through?

Kate Go away.

Derek You're the only one I can talk to. I tried Aleysha and my parents, but they're all in too much pain. If I speak to them it could throw them over the edge.

Kate Please leave me alone. I'm trying to forget you.

Derek You can't think me away, Kate. I'll never go away. You'll never forget me.

Kate I will. I already have. I know this isn't real. I know that you're just my dream and soon I'll wake up and everything will be back to normal.

Derek Why haven't you thrown away the jacket, Kate?

Kate Which jacket?

Derek The jacket that Sean gave you. Why are you keeping it?

Kate I did throw it away.

Derek I know that's what you told him, but you're talking to me, remember? And I know everything. Why didn't you throw it away? Are you thinking that you might have to show it to somebody one day?

Kate No. I'll never show it to anybody. I made a promise.

Derek A promise sealed in blood. I know. But that still doesn't answer my question. You've kept the jacket under your bed. Whether you know it yet or not, you're thinking that you should show it to somebody.

Kate That's a lie.

Derek Ever since it happened you've been feeling less in love with Sean, but you don't want to own it to yourself. He isn't at all like you thought he was, is he? From afar, when he used to come and buy stuff from your stall, all you saw was the way he looked. You liked the way he ruffled his hair with his fingers. You thought he seemed so cool and self-assured and you thought that he could give those things to you because you think that you haven't got them. And now you're not so sure, are you? Now you realise that he isn't anything like you imagined he would be but you can't own up to it yet because you still need to believe in the fantasy.

Kate Don't tell me you can read my mind. You're just like Weirdboy.

Derek Don't forget, Katie, I've been with you ever since that night. I've been a real guardian angel to you. Every night when you go to sleep I've climbed in here and watched over you. I can almost read your mind because all your dreams are on your face, Kate.

Kate Piss off and leave me alone. Why won't you let me sleep?

Derek You're the only one I can talk to.

Kate What do you want from me?

Derek You know what I want.

Kate I made a promise.

Derek My 'A' level results came last week, Kate. My dad saw the envelope drop on the floor and he picked it up and hid it. He didn't tell my mum they'd come and he still hasn't opened the envelope. He's terrified that I might have failed, see. If I've failed then that will be a big blow to him, as though fate had it in for him. But if I've passed, then that'll be even worse because he'll be devastated thinking about what I might have been. I needed three 'C's to get on the Art course. I want

you to speak for me, Kate. I want you to tell them
what happened to me that night.

Kate No.

Derek Then my life will have been worthless. My death
would be worth absolutely nothing.

Kate I'm trying to put all this behind me.

Derek You'll never put it behind you. You'll never forget
me, Kate. I can see you now – a grandmother. You've
lived quite a life and you are respected and loved by
everybody who knows you. But despite all the things
you've done with your life – all the good and bad
things that you've been through – you still can't forget
me. You'll go to your grave with my image on your
memory. You'll never forget me.

Kate I have. I've forgotten you already. I know this is
just a dream. I'm going to close my eyes and think
about something else and when I open them you're
going to be gone.

She does so.

Derek I'm still here, Kate.

Kate You bastard. You're spoiling everything. You're
ruining my whole life. You just don't understand, do
you? You don't understand.

Derek Understand what?

Kate That I can't speak. I won't.

Derek You have to. Who else will speak for me?

Kate I'm in love with Sean. I can't let him down.

Derek And what about me? My dad doesn't have to
open the envelope for me to know what the results
are: 'B' and two 'C's. Not brilliant, I know, but it
would have been enough, Kate. It would have been
enough.

SCENE NINE

A few weeks later. Aleysha is waiting in the same spot as in Scene One. Kate enters. She is waiting too. She recognises Aleysha and tries to hide her face from her so that she can't see her.

Aleysha I know you, don't I?

Kate I don't know. Do you?

Aleysha You work up the market, don't you? You're the girl on the handbag stall.

Kate That's me.

Aleysha Waiting for your boyfriend?

Kate Yeah.

Aleysha Me too. What you going to see?

Kate Dunno.

Aleysha Decide when you get in there. That's what we do.

Silence.

Kate Waiting for your boyfriend, yeah?

Aleysha Yeah. He's coming straight over from college.

Kate Oh.

Silence. The women wait. Kate would rather not be here. Suddenly Aleysha starts to cry. Kate doesn't know what to do. At first she tries to ignore it but Aleysha is racked by huge sobs. Kate goes to her and gives her her handkerchief.

Aleysha He's not coming. He's dead. Derek's dead.

Kate I'm so sorry.

Aleysha And every day I come here, sometimes twice a day. I come here and I wait because I think that he's going to turn up. Every day I come here and I think that he's suddenly going to appear in front of me, saying that they got the wrong guy and that he's sorry he's late. Then I'll go into a sulk telling him that he's always late. I'll be sulking on the outside but inside I'll be happy because I'll be glad that he isn't dead. And I feel so ashamed standing here waiting like this. I mean, I went to a funeral and everything. I was the first person to throw earth on the coffin. And I still come and stand out here every day waiting for him. It's stupid.

Kate It isn't stupid. I'd be the same.

Aleysha I should be getting on with my life, shouldn't I? Isn't that what they say?

Kate You can't get over something like that overnight, can you?

Aleysha We were going to get married but now I never will. I'll always be faithful to Derek.

Kate You'll be faithful to him whatever you do.

Aleysha Maybe. I'd better go home. He's not going to turn up now, is he?

Kate No. I don't suppose he will.

Aleysha Maybe I'll meet you here again. I'll clean your hanky and give it back to you.

Kate Don't worry about it. I've got plenty of hankies.

SCENE TEN

Kate is with Sean. They are kissing. He breaks away.

Sean When a bloke kisses you, Kate, you should try to show some emotion. Even if you are just faking it. It might make him feel as though he's having some effect on you.

Kate I'm just not in the mood today.

Sean You're never in the mood these days. What's the matter?

Kate Can't you guess?

Sean No I can't. Tell me.

Kate Sex is the last thing on my mind these days.

Sean Tell me what is on your mind, Kate.

Kate Nothing. You made us promise not to talk about it but it won't go away, Sean. It's more real now than it was that night.

Sean What is?

Kate You know.

Sean I want you to tell me.

Kate I promised not to talk about it.

Sean Good. And you just remember that. You made a promise, Kate. You're not supposed to tell on a friend. You tell anything and you'd have to move out. No one round here would ever speak to you again.

Kate He comes to my bedroom at night, Sean.

Sean Who does?

Kate The boy. The dead boy. Every single night. He won't let me sleep. He just sits on the bed and talks to me. He tells me things that I don't want to hear. Last night he was telling me about what he missed and the night before he was telling me what his life would have been like if he hadn't been killed. He was going to be an artist, Sean. A good one too.

Sean Have you gone completely mad?

Kate He won't leave me alone. He needs to talk to somebody. He goes over and over it. He won't let me rest. Why don't you tell someone, Sean?

Sean What?

Kate Tell them what you did. I know you didn't mean it. It was a sort of accident, wasn't it?

Sean You have gone completely mad, haven't you?

Kate Look at Candy. She's seen *Titanic* a million times. She's obsessed with dying. All you have to do is tell somebody what you did and then you'll release all of us.

Sean I'm not telling anybody. We promised. I'm not going to break that promise.

Kate You're the one who made that promise. If you free yourself from it then we'll all be free.

Sean If I tell someone then they'll blame me. I'd be saying that I'd done something wrong and if you ask me I did nothing wrong. The bastard deserved it.

Kate But why? What did he do to you to deserve that?

Sean I don't have to justify myself.

Kate You don't know why you did it, do you? It doesn't make any sense.

Sean Leave it, Kate. It's over.

Kate If you can't tell them yourself, then let me tell them for you. Would that make it easier?

Sean You say you love me but it's all just words, isn't it?

Kate I do love you.

Sean Get the fuck off me. I thought you were my friend, Kate, but now I know I can't trust you, can I? It's always the same. Nobody cares. I'm always on my own, en I?

Sean turns on Kate and holds her by the neck.

You bitch.

Kate I won't tell anybody. Not if you don't want me to.

Sean I'll make you another promise, Kate, and this one I'm gonna keep. You tell anybody and, I swear, I'll cut your fucking tongue out.

Sean goes off leaving Kate alone, rubbing her neck. She tries to call out but can't.

SCENE ELEVEN

Katie. Her parents and Doctor come on.

Doctor Come on, Katie, try to say a few words.

Kate tries to speak but can't.

Father What's wrong with her doctor? She hasn't spoken for days.

Mother Three days ago we couldn't shut her up. Please give us something to help her.

Father It's a game, is it, Katie? You're having a joke on your mum and dad. All right, Kate, you've had a laugh, now snap out of it. For fuck's sake speak to us, Katie.

Kate starts to cry. Her parents hug her.

I'm sorry, Kate. I didn't mean to shout. I just got carried away. I'm so worried about you, darling.

Mother We love you, Katie.

Doctor Can I speak to you both alone?

Mother Go upstairs, Katie. Don't you worry about anything. Everything will be all right.

Kate goes.

Doctor The symptoms would suggest that she'd suffered some kind of shock.

Father What kind of shock? She'd have told us if anything bad had happened to her, wouldn't she?

Mother She tells us everything.

Doctor Trauma is very complex. It might even be that she's suddenly remembered something that happened to her as a child.

Father Are you saying it's our fault? We're good parents. We've always given her everything we could.

Mother We've always tried to shelter her from the world.
Father Just tell us what we can do to help her.
Doctor I'm afraid there's nothing you can do. Obviously, there's a very good reason why she can't speak at the moment. When she's ready her voice will return. I'm very sorry but in a case like this there's nothing we can do. Except wait.

SCENE TWELVE

Cemetery. Aleysha is kneeling beside Derek's grave.
He watches her on one side and Weirdboy watches her
on another. A young girl, Sally, enters carrying a few
flowers.

Sally Would you like some flowers?
Aleysha No thank you.
Sally I notice you never leave any flowers.
Aleysha He was an artist. He loved colours. What's the point of flowers? He'll never see colours again.
Sally You don't know that he won't appreciate them.
Aleysha Why should I buy flowers he can't see?
Sally I'm Sally. (*pointing to grave*) This is my brother Terry. You've been here every time I've come to see him.
Aleysha I've got nothing better to do.
Sally Graveyards are for the living, not the dead. I want to be cremated. My friend Gary will be along in a minute. I'll introduce you to him.
Aleysha (*bitter*) Some sort of club is it?
Sally Sort of. (*Points to Derek's grave.*) Killed was he?
Aleysha How did you know?
Sally They put all the kids who were killed here. I used to come here every day and I noticed that a lot of the other people visiting graves here were young people

too and then we got talking and we just started going for coffee and confiding in each other.

Aleysha Sounds very cosy.

Sally It really helped me. There was no one else who knew how I was feeling.

Gary enters.

Gary Sorry I'm late. I couldn't get away.

Sally This is Aleysha. Gary.

Sally (*points to grave*) Gary's best friend.

Gary You don't think of someone that young dying.

Sally Aleysha's new.

Gary Still pretty raw then? Don't worry, it will pass.

Aleysha Will it?

Sally We've all been there.

Aleysha Listen, I come here to be alone. Yes, I feel raw. I feel like shit. I hate every fucking white bastard in the world because they all killed Derek. And I tell you something, I don't want to stop feeling like that. I don't want to get over it. I don't want to be part of no cosy death club.

Gary When I say get over it . . .

Sally You never get over it.

Gary You never forget them. They're always with you and every time you think about them it will always be raw. That never goes. But the pain does get duller.

Sally And what's left of it becomes part of you.

Gary When it happened to us, we had no one who had been through the same thing to help us out.

Sally But if you need someone to talk to, we'll be there for you.

Aleysha And why should I talk to you two? Why should I trust you? How do I know that you won't turn around and kick me where I'm most vulnerable? No, I'd rather keep it to myself.

Sally Whatever you want.

Aleysha I'll never trust again.
Sally If you change your mind . . .
Gary You know where to find us.

SCENE THIRTEEN

Kate enters followed by Weirdboy. Kate still isn't speaking.

Weirdboy I'm so chuffed that we've become friends, Kate. It's what I've always wanted. I've been on my own for such a long time. You don't know how lonely I've been. And you're such a good listener. What shall we do today? What do you fancy? A walk along the river? Pictures? There's a couple of good films on I'd like to see. What about you? We could eat something. I'll treat you. Anything you want. Not that I've got much money on me. Or we could go shopping. You haven't been shopping for a while. Haven't bought yourself a new outfit for ages. Go on, Katie – you don't mind me calling you Katie, do you? – treat yourself. You mustn't let yourself go. What will Sean think if you don't look good for him? I'll help you choose, shall I?

Do you ever wonder what it would be like to be old, Katie? I do sometimes. My aunt says I have an old soul. Which means that I'll probably be happier when I'm older because by then I'll have caught up with meself. Then it won't matter so much to belong to a group. Have you noticed that about older people, Katie? They don't seem to want to go around in packs. The older you get, the more you want to hide away inside. That's why people marry I suppose. Do you think you and Sean will marry?

Katie. I hope you don't mind me saying this but

I don't think he's right for you. When you're with him
I get this sense that you're trying too hard, do you
know what I mean? That you're trying to be someone
else. It's no good if you can't be yourself with a man,
Katie. One day the game'll be up and the whole trick
will fall apart, won't it? Maybe it already has. I mean,
look at you, Katie. I have to say it's something that's
always puzzled me: why is it that women love guys
like Sean? What is it? My aunt says it's the challenge
of the chase.

Did you know that I live with my aunt, Katie?
It was either that or go into a home. You didn't know
that did you? There's a lot about me that you probably
don't know, isn't there? But now that we're friends,
maybe we'll get to know each other better.

I've told her all about you. I told her that you didn't
want to have anything to do with me and she said
that I should just give it time, that you'd come round.
And you have, haven't you?

Kate yawns.

Tired, Kate? Why don't you just lie down and relax in
the sun. You should relax more, Katie. You always
seem to be rushing off somewhere. What's the hurry?
We've got all the time in the world.

*Kate lies back on the grass. Weirdboy gazes at her.
He tentatively reaches out a hand to stroke her face.
He pulls it back quickly. He bends down slowly and
kisses her cheek. She sits up and hurriedly puts her
shoes on.*

What's the matter, Katie? I'm not that repulsive am I?
What, can't I even touch you?

Kate stands.

You're not too good for me, Katie. Do you think I don't
know that? Remember, I know you, Katie. I know
everything that you are, everything you've done. You
forget that I can read your mind. No, you can't put a
wall up against me now. I can see everything and you
know what I see, Katie? I see blood. I see death, Katie,
a young man dying, and you killed him. You think
you can hide in your silence, Katie, but you can't hide
from me. I know what you are. You're a murderer,
Katie. A murderer.

*Weirdboy runs off. Kate stands, at a loss. She stands
and screams. At first nothing comes out of her and it's
a silent scream but then it comes, loud and terrible, a
howl of pain.*

SCENE FOURTEEN

*Weirdboy comes on pursued by Ben, Michael, Trish and
Aleysha. He has come to a dead end and they have him
cornered.*

Ben So. It's you. You're not what I imagined. But I guess
you wouldn't be. Not when you're on your own. Not
such a big figure without your friends, are you?

Weirdboy What are you talking about?

Ben If I gave you a knife would you be a big man then?

Weirdboy Why were you chasing me? What have I ever
done to you?

Ben Don't you know?

Weirdboy 'Course not. I don't know you.

Ben That's right. You don't know me. To you I'm just
another black guy, ain't I? We're all the same as far as
you're concerned, aren't we? That suits you, doesn't it,
lump us all together. What is it? Coons are taking all

the jobs? Coons are spoiling the country with their weird spicy food and their music.

Weirdboy You've got the wrong person. I'm not like that.

Michael He would say that, wouldn't he, now that he's on his own. You make me sick. At least you could stand up for yourself.

Weirdboy Honestly, you're making a big mistake. A lot of my friends are black.

Ben (*laughing*) Hear that, Michael? A lot of his friends are black. Well done. Good for you.

Weirdboy I've never been racist in my life. Never even had a racist thought. Never heard anybody in my family say anything.

Ben Gold star. So if you're not a racist why did you kill my friend?

Weirdboy Kill? Me? Do I look like a killer?

Ben You tell me what a killer looks like. And while you're at it, you tell me how you could kill somebody you don't know just because you don't like the way he looks.

Weirdboy I'm telling you it wasn't me.

Ben So who was it? All of a sudden there are no racists round here. Are you asking me to ignore what I can see with my own eyes?

Weirdboy I'm sorry about your friend. I really am. It's terrible what happened to him. Nobody should have to face what he did. And I'm sorry that you've had to go through what you've been through but you've got to believe that it's not my fault.

Ben Someone did this. Someone has to pay.

Michael It's him, Ben, I'm telling you. He's just trying to wriggle out of it.

Ben All right. Even if you had nothing to do with it, why should I let you go? My friend was chosen at random, wasn't he? Why shouldn't I just pick on you at random?

Weirdboy Yes, why don't you pick on me? Everybody else does.

Michael Aaah. I feel sorry for him, don't you, Ben?

Weirdboy What are you going to do with me? Why don't you get it over with? I don't care what you do to me. I know the truth and whatever you do you can't take that away from me. I know how you're feeling, I'm not stupid. You're guilty, aren't you?

Ben Guilty? Me?

Weirdboy Because you weren't there to help him the night he died. You feel guilty and because of that you're blocking out all reason. Deep in your heart you know that I'm the wrong person. You can tell that just by looking at me, can't you? But you won't accept what you know. It doesn't matter who you take as long as you take somebody. What are you going to do with me?

Ben I'm going to give you what you deserve.

Weirdboy You'd like to kill me, wouldn't you? You'll tell your friends that you did it for revenge, to pay back for having lost your friend. But it wouldn't be true, would it? If you killed me you'd be doing it for yourself, wouldn't you? You'd be doing it to make yourself feel better. To take away the guilt that keeps you awake at night. Isn't that right?

Ben Shut up. I don't want to hear any more of your rubbish.

Weirdboy (*to Michael*) And as for you. You're afraid aren't you? Ben is running out of control and you haven't got a clue what he's going to do next. But you hate violence. You're not going to let him hurt me, are you?

Ben I told you to shut up.

Trish enters with Aleysha. Silence.
She looks Weirdboy up and down.

Aleysha But you're just a boy. Just another boy.

Aleysha is about to walk away. She is suddenly seized
by anger and all she can do with it is to spit in
Weirdboy's face. She goes. Ben approaches Weirdboy.

Ben See what you've done? You've broken her heart.
She used to be a really happy lively girl and you've
broken her spirit. Well, she might not stand to touch
you but me . . .

Ben raises his fist as if to strike Weirdboy.

SCENE FIFTEEN

Detective Inspector Johnson and Kate. Kate is holding a
carrier bag.

Johnson (*pleased to see her*) Kate. Haven't seen you for
a while. When was the last time I saw you?
Kate You passed me in the street last week.
Johnson Oh yes. Had to virtually chase you to get a
hello out of you. You're not frightened of me are you,
Kate?
Kate No, Mr Johnson.
Johnson Because the way you ran away from me anybody
would think that you thought I was going to arrest
you.
Kate I had a lot on my mind, that's all.
Johnson You shouldn't be worrying about life at your
age, Kate. Plenty of time for that when you get to be
old like me. You're supposed to be enjoying yourself.
Raving. Isn't that what you lot do these days? Not
that I'm saying you should drop E's or anything like

that. I wouldn't want to encourage you. Of course
not. Still, I don't have to tell you, do I? You've always
had an older head on you, haven't you? How are your
parents?

Kate They're all right, Mr Johnson.

Johnson Tell your father that we ought to meet up,
go out for a pint. I haven't seen him for ages either.
You know, Kate, I'm beginning to feel as though
people are deliberately avoiding me. Especially the
'youth'.

Kate Dad's been really busy, Mr Johnson. He's been
working really hard so that he can get rid of the stall
and open a shop.

Johnson Don't humour me, Kate, I know that I'm a
social pariah. Ever since I've been on the Lewis case
nobody wants to know. So why have you come to see
me? Taking me out to lunch are you?

Kate I need to talk to you, Mr Johnson.

Johnson Yes, Katie.

Kate It's about the killing, Mr Johnson. Of the Lewis
boy. You've been saying for weeks that there must
have been at least one witness. You've been saying
how you've been coming up against a wall of silence
and that those who are keeping that silence are as
guilty as those who did the killing.

Johnson That's right, Kate. Anyone who has knowledge
and maintains silence is an accessory to the crime.

Kate Then I'm a murderer, Mr Johnson.

Johnson Do you know something, Kate? Tell me what
you know.

Kate I don't know what I'm supposed to do, Mr
Johnson. I promised I wouldn't tell. You're supposed
to keep a promise, aren't you?

Johnson But a secret like this, Kate, that's a heavy
burden. You've been carrying that since it happened.
You don't have to carry it any more, Kate.

Kate But no one will ever trust me again.

Johnson Anyone who makes you keep a secret like that doesn't deserve your loyalty. Tell me what you know, Kate.

Kate reaches into the carrier bag and takes out the jacket. She gives it to Johnson.

I assume this is evidence. You've held on to it all that time?

Kate nods.

Kate I was supposed to throw it away. (*almost in tears*) I'm sorry, Mr Johnson.

Johnson Kate. You've done the right thing. The good thing. You're a very brave girl.

Kate I'm not brave. I should have come here weeks ago but I cared more about fitting in than I did about doing the right thing.

Johnson That doesn't matter. What matters is that in the end you did what you felt you had to. Of course, by now, all the evidence might have disappeared.

Kate What do you mean?

Johnson On the jacket. Because you kept it so long.

Kate But there's blood on it.

Johnson (*lying*) It's dried in. We may find that this is a useless piece of information.

Kate But even if it is, I'm still a witness, aren't I?

Johnson Of course you are. (*He puts the jacket back into the carrier bag.*) We'll have a cup of tea shall we, and then I'll take your statement.

Kate I thought I'd feel free once I'd told you, but I don't feel free at all.

Johnson That's because this is just the beginning. You give me a statement, Kate, and you've got to be prepared to go all the way – there'll be a court case. You'll have to be prepared for some tough questioning. They'll try to tear you to pieces, Kate. Think about it before you tell me anything. You can always walk out now. Walk away and I won't say anything about it.

Kate Are you saying you'd let me walk out of here after I've told you that I know something?

Johnson I don't want to see you torn apart, Kate.

Kate I'm already in pieces, Mr Johnson.

Johnson Good for you. You stick with it and I promise you that when it's all over you'll feel as free as a bird. Now, Katie, you go into that room there and I'll be in in a minute to take your statement.

Kate goes. Johnson takes the jacket out of the carrier bag again. He holds it tenderly as though it were a baby.

SCENE SIXTEEN

Sean and Detective Inspector Johnson.

Sean Sometimes I'll have the odd kick about with some of my friends but I must say that I prefer to watch a good game than play one.

Johnson You've always been a lazy little sod.

Sean I know which side my bread's buttered on.

Johnson At one time I thought you were going to turn professional.

Sean That was Dad blabbing on to everybody when I joined the youth team, how his son had turned professional. Honestly.

Johnson Don't be modest, son. You were good. Very good. A little application and you might have been exceptional.

Sean It wasn't for me. I knew that.

133

Johnson I can't see how anybody could turn their nose up at the prospect of millions of pounds a year, fans cheering on their every move, not to mention the birds.

Sean I wasn't that good. I know that.

Johnson As long as you're not going to turn out like one of those saddos who's always sitting around crying about how it could have been them.

Sean (*laughing*) Like old Dizzy Thomas. He's still carrying on about how Bob Monkhouse stole all his old jokes when he stopped in the pub for a drink on his way to the Palladium. Every time he comes on the telly Thomas goes mad saying that Monkhouse is still telling his old jokes.

Johnson (*laughing*) They are pretty old.

Sean (*laughing*) Old? They're bloody ancient.

Johnson So what is for you? What do you want to do with your life?

Sean Did Dad ask you to have a word with me? Is he worried about my future, is he? He should have said he wanted to start up a job club for me.

Johnson He didn't ask me to talk to you. I'm interested, that's all.

Sean Always take an interest in your friends' sons, do you? Though Dad isn't a friend of yours, is he? Not officially, anyway. I'd have thought that you wouldn't be seen dead talking to Ryan Nugent's son.

Johnson Your father and me go back a long way.

Sean And now you've gone even further in the opposite direction, haven't you?

Johnson We were good friends once. Our lives took us on different paths, that's all. He went one way, I went another. Once we'd both made those choices there was no going back.

Sean And don't we know it.

Johnson (*angry but managing to hold it*) I've looked out for your father, made sure he didn't get into too much trouble. And you. I've always kept an eye out for you.

Sean I don't need you keeping an eye out.

Johnson I know what it's like to be young, you know, Sean. Me and your dad did some pretty stupid things when we were kids.

Sean And then you found religion in a blue uniform.

Johnson We did some bad things but we never went too far.

Sean What do you mean go too far?

Johnson Don't you know?

Sean No.

Johnson (*slight pause*) All I'm saying is that you've got your whole life ahead of you. Use it wisely, Sean.

Sean What's got into you? It's the football isn't it? Dad's asked you to try to get me to get back into it, hasn't he? Well, it's no use. I'm not fit enough.

Johnson I'll never forget that last game you played. When you ran across the pitch, dodging all the other side's attackers and finished it off by tucking the ball in the corner of the net.

Sean I had determination then. That was a different person.

Johnson And what I'm saying is that that person is still there inside you.

Sean Here endeth the first lesson. Listen, Lenny, I know you all had a lot of faith in me, wanted me to succeed but believe me, I was never that good.

SCENE SEVENTEEN

Kate's bedroom. Kate enters wearing a suit. She sits on the edge of the bed. Derek appears in the window.

Derek I'm still here, Kate.

Kate Derek.

Derek It can't have been easy for you, standing up in that witness stand all by yourself.

Kate The hardest thing I've ever done.

Derek Speaking up like that when they all closed ranks against you.

Kate I should have known they'd all turn their backs on me.

Derek I thought for a moment that you were going to back down.

Kate I very nearly did. It was so much easier when I was in the group. It's so hard to be alone. And now I've let you down. I'm sorry, Derek.

Derek It wasn't your fault, Kate. You tried your best.

Kate But it wasn't good enough. They still threw the case out. Not enough evidence. What more evidence did they need?

Derek You're not going to leave it there are you, Kate? You're not going to give up now, are you?

Kate Your parents, your friends, they're not going to give up. You don't need my help.

Derek I need all the help I can get. This is just the beginning, Kate. You're not going to give up now, are you? Are you? Kate?

Kate I'm listening, Derek.

Derek Your old friends may have turned against you but you've got me now. You're not going to let me do this on my own, are you? You were so brave in that stand, Kate.

Kate You're the brave one.

Derek I was with you in the court room. You knew that, didn't you?

Kate (*nods*) I was nervous, so nervous. But once I started to speak I felt all the words come rushing out of me and I couldn't stop. It was like they had a life of their own. I won't let you down, Derek. I'm going to speak and keep on speaking and I'm not going to shut up until we win. Yes, Derek, from now on I'm going to speak. Just you let anybody try and stop me.

There is a knock on the door. Derek stands aside. Kate goes to the door. It's Aleysha. She enters. They stand looking at each other for a short while until Aleysha reaches out to Kate. They embrace. As Derek watches them, the lights go down.
Ends.

Something to Be Reclaimed

Winsome Pinnock interviewed by Jim Mulligan

Winsome Pinnock has always written from conviction and will take on political issues not because she wants to shock or provoke but because that is the kind of writing that interests her. Inevitably, a play about a racial killing and a conspiracy to prevent the murderers from being sentenced brings to mind the death of Stephen Lawrence, but Winsome Pinnock based her play on a different incident.

> *Can You Keep a Secret?* is based on the killing of an Asian man a few years ago. The girlfriend of one of the killers found out about it and her dilemma was whether or not to tell the police. If she did, she knew she would be ostracised. She was an ordinary young Londoner and I thought it was incredibly brave of her to give evidence knowing that, in her community, that was something you simply did not do. I was very struck by her heroism and it's been on my mind for a long time.

Can You Keep a Secret? opens with the casual meeting of Kate and Aleysha followed by a fight between Derek and Sean. Without doubt Derek is provocative. He taunts Sean who is unable to cope verbally and resorts to the only strategy he knows, beating his opponent into silence. Sean is undoubtedly out of control and Derek appears to be asking for trouble. The language here is shocking, the violence explicit, the emotions raw. All except Weirdboy, an outsider and an observer, are drawn into complicity to protect Sean.

This is raw emotion but I think young people will handle it because they are honest. The language is not provocative or inflammatory. It is the language of young people, the language I hear as I am walking in the street. The language is at times racist, foul, and homophobic but it is the language of the characters I have created. You don't clean up the language because the play is coming to the National Theatre. Some people will find the killing of a black youth on stage shocking. When I am writing there are conscious choices and instinctive ones. On one level I am thinking of the best possible way of telling the story and there is an instinctive level. I didn't feel it was right for this death to happen off-stage where the audience could either imagine it or choose to block it out. Some things are unimaginable and this is one of them. In writing I had to confront the death and other people have to face it as well.

Derek is young and intelligent. He is not a tight-lipped person who will walk away from trouble. He is volatile and has his own prejudices. He is brave but like any young person he does not contemplate his mortality or envisage any fatal consequences.

Derek is much more articulate than Sean and he allows his clever exuberance to get out of hand. He manipulates Sean and pushes him over the edge. He goads him in the way that young people do when they are having an argument and want to win. He doesn't know what the consequences are. He simply defends himself. You can relate this character to real life but you have to remember that in the end he is a character in a play.

Kate is in love with Sean, thinks that she needs him and will keep silent to protect him, but there is a part of her which knows that it is wrong to keep silent. Although she promises to destroy Sean's bloodstained jacket, she keeps it and later gives it to the police. Derek reappears in the play to talk to Kate.

> Some people will see Derek as the personification of Kate's guilt and grief but for me he is real. In the world of the play you can believe that he comes back and pleads for someone to speak on his behalf. With cases like this in the real world the victim disappears and his side of things ends. Somehow there is something to be reclaimed. There are deep myths and stories about the dead returning to seek justice and the theatre is the place where you can explore these ideas.

Winsome Pinnock sees *Can You Keep a Secret?* as being about friendship, loyalty and making a stand. Looked at as a whole the society portrayed in this play is dark and depressing. A young black man is killed, the murderer's friends conspire to protect him, the police suppress evidence and the community closes ranks, allowing Sean to get off. Looked at from Kate's point of view the play is optimistic. She moves from seeing the world in one way to a radically different view. She comes close to a dark experience and is able to do something very positive and to redefine her place in the world.

> Kate loves Sean and for this reason is willing to keep his secret. But there is an underlying conflict within her and, to a lesser extent, within the other characters as well. Deep in her heart she knows what the right thing to do is but at first she is unable to act because of her loyalty to Sean and his friends. She and Aleysha have little in common but they come together at the end and Kate is drawn closer into Aleysha and Derek's world.

Winsome Pinnock is convinced that drama can affect people in the way that she has been changed by seeing and reading plays.

> I have had some real emotional experiences and if drama can affect me it can affect others. It is not a passionless medium. It is one of the last areas where you can have a public debate. It's good if a play invites young people to ask questions. For me this play says Derek's life is not something that was insignificant but it is worth everything to his family and they will not let it rest until justice has been served.

Production Notes

STAGING AND SETTING

The play is set in a number of locations – outside a
cinema, the alleyway behind a shopping centre, Kate's
bedroom, Derek's home and a graveyard. The settings
for Scene Six and Scene Seven aren't specified but might
be a point where the young people congregate – perhaps
a concrete playground, a basketball court or a local park.
The locations should be suggested as simply as possible
in order for the actions to move fluidly between them.
Outside the cinema might be indicated by a slide or gobo
with an Odeon sign or a hoarding advertising the film
Titanic, which is referred to further into the play. The alley
might be suggested by industrial bins, the graveyard by
simply placing flowers centre stage etc. Blackouts should
be avoided and the lighting should suggest the moves
from indoor to outdoor locations as simply as possible.
Think carefully about use of colour. The sobriety of
black and white in Scene Three, for instance, could be
interrupted by the bright colours of Kate's bags in Scene
Four, when she has gone out shopping in an effort to
blank out the murder that has just taken place. Derek
returns as a ghost but this shouldn't affect anything and
he certainly shouldn't go in for 'ghost acting'.

CASTING

There are seven major speaking roles – three female and
four male – plus ten other smaller speaking roles for
members of Derek's family and the two rival gangs.
Other than the central characters, the race of the cast is

open to interpretation as long as the play itself isn't altered.

EXERCISES

This is an entirely fictional story but there is wide scope for discussion and debate around this controversial subject matter. Research some of the cases of teenage murder that the British judicial system has failed to solve in recent years.

Find ways of allowing the transition from scene to scene to happen as fluidly as possible. Rehearse from the middle of one scene to the middle of the next as opposed to scene by scene. Overlap scenes so that images merge and clash. Work at the ending of Scene Three, for instance, and merge it with the beginning of Scene Four – have Kate look at Derek's coffin as it moves off. Have the rival gangs in Scenes Six and Seven occupy the same location unaware of who has just vacated it. Have Johnson step straight from Scene Fifteen to Sixteen.

Be aware of the rhythm and shape of the play. Work at unpacking the beginning carefully so that the audience are unaware of the seriousness to come. Play Scene One as a warm-up scene. Here we have the calm before the storm. The opening scene between Kate and Aylesha is warm and comic. We want the audience to be drawn into their dialogue and recognise their predicament instantly.

- Have Kate and Aylesha play the scene as strangers without a queue.
- Let them play the scene knowing each other slightly with a small and impassive queue up until Candy's entrance.

- Play the scene so that the actors playing Kate and Ayesha really bring out the comic opening exchange.
- Have Candy enter and see how slowly you can get away with Ayesha realising the seriousness of the situation.
- Have the people in the queue react as minimally as possible, find a way of transforming the queue into the fight of the next scene.

Take the fight sequence in Scene Two. Work out what happens moment by moment by producing a series of freeze frames. Use a dummy bar which looks heavy and metallic but can cause no injury. Activate the freeze frames and add dialogue but keep the action as slow as possible. Play it against the dialogue so that Sean is completely laid back and Derek is aggressive. Speed up the action and now have Sean wired throughout the scene and the focus of attention. Kate's dialogue at the end needs to be full of energy so that it doesn't jar with the rest of the scene. Try introducing a silence after it and discover how it emphasises the shock.

Follow Sean's journey through the play. His status is challenged by Johnson in Scene Sixteen. Have the actors work in pairs. Hand A a high playing (say a nine or ten) card and B a low card of two or three. The aim of this exercise is to watch a pair improvise a situation where A starts with high status and through the interaction with B descends to low status while B has the opposite experience. Now have the actors play Scene Sixteen and decide what cards Johnson and Sean might be holding. Play the scene with Johnson's back to the audience so they only see Sean's reactions. Decide whether he is defiant or shifty, still or restless at any given moment.

Improvise a 'missing' scene. What does Derek see when he visits his family but dare not disturb them?

Imagine the last two scenes are the first scenes in the play. See how you can create an upbeat ending and avoid a drop in energy at the end.

Suzy Graham-Adriani
February 1999

THE DEVIL IN DRAG
(*Il Diavolo con le zinne*)

Dario Fo

translated and adapted by Ed Emery

Characters

As indicated below, if necessary the characters in this play can all be performed by a total of twelve actors.

The Judge
Alfonso Ferdinando de Tristano

Pizzocca Ganassa
housekeeper to Judge Alfonso de Tristano

Cardinal Ambone and **Intruder** / **Father Mirone** / **Crewman** on Galley

Francipante, a master Devil / **Prosecuting Lawyer** / **Follower** of Father Mirone / **Helmsman** of Galley

Barlocco, an apprentice Devil / **Prosecuting Lawyer** / **Follower** of Father Mirone / **Devil** (in Act Two) / **Prisoner** on Galley

Jacoba Stareffa, lover of the Captain of the Guard / **Townswoman** / **Follower** of Father Mirone / **She-Devil** (in Act Two)

Zoanna, a young serving girl / **Operator** of the puppet of the Devil Barlocco / **Woman** possessed by Devil / **Townswoman** / **She-Devil**

Clarissa, a young serving girl / **Operator** of the puppet of the Devil Barlocco / **Townswoman** / **Follower** of Father Mirone / **She-Devil**

**Young Servant / Townswoman /
Follower** of Father Mirone / **Devil** (in Act Two)

Geron de le Noci, a thief / **Inquisitor /
Francipante's Double / Follower** of Father Mirone /
Devil (in Act Two) / **Prisoner** on Galley

Acrobat Stand-in for Judge / **Musician / Operator** of the
puppet of the Devil Barlocco / **Man of the Town /
Follower** of Father Mirone / **Devil** (in Act Two) /
Prisoner on Galley

First Guard / Blacksmith / Devil / Follower of Father
Mirone / **Devil** (in Act Two) / **Prisoner** on Galley

Second Guard / Follower of Father Mirone /
Devil (in Act Two) / **Prisoner** on Galley

The action takes place in a city in Central Northern Italy
at the end of the sixteenth century.

First performed on 7 August 1997
at the Teatro Vittorio Emanuele in Messina, Sicily.

Act One

The stage setting represents a classic Renaissance stage. Where possible it will have five levels of wings moving back in perspective, and two traversing arcades emerging from the second and fourth wings. As the curtains open we find ourselves on a terrace at the top of a stately building. At each side of the proscenium are two small balustrades to indicate the limits of the terrace.

As the lights come up, or the curtain opens, we find a musician on-stage playing a lute. Three girls, Zoanna, Clarissa and Simona, bring in a step-ladder and a large basket. They take out sheets and linen which they hang at the back of the stage, to dry in a slight breeze. As they do this, they sing quietly, and their song provides a gentle background to Pizzocca's opening speech.

From between the hanging sheets, enter Pizzocca, serving maid and housekeeper to Judge Alfonso de Tristano. She is as dry as a stick, and walks with strange movements like an ostrich. She adjusts her costume as she comes.

Pizzocca (*noticing the audience*) Oh lord – the ladies and gentlemen are here already! (*to the wings*) Why didn't you warn me? (*to the audience*) Good evening, welcome, welcome ladies and gentlemen . . . It looks like it falls to me to open the proceedings, so first allow me to present myself. My name is Pizzocca

151

Ganassa, and I am the ruler, that's to say the housekeeper, in the house of his Honour the Judge, one of the most notable men in this city . . . who lives right here . . . in this palace . . . his Honour Alfonso Ferdinando de Tristano! You should know that my master is a terribly serious man. Not that he hasn't got a sense of humour – I myself have seen him laugh – once. But more to the point, he's terrifically intelligent! He's got a brain . . . such a brain . . . that when he thinks . . . (*Raising her hands she mimes wheels going round in her head.*) Brrrr brrrrr . . . it makes a noise!

Zoanna Yes, yes . . . (*making a similar gesture*) Brrrrrrrr! The house even shakes!

Pizzocca Don't make fun of me, you! (*to the audience*) As I was saying, he's really intelligent! And he's also terribly brave and honest! He bows to nobody. But as you know, in this city, intelligent, brave and honest judges have a hard time of it . . . Just as they're on the point of uncovering the misdeeds of wrongdoers and murderers, the first thing that happens is that out come the gossip-mongers . . . who scurry about . . . spreading rumours and slander. And then they blow them up! They kill them! But my Judge stops for nothing and nobody! I'll give you an example . . . You will have heard of the fire at the city's Cathedral, which happened the other week . . .

Exit one of the three serving girls.

Zoanna (*interrupting her*) Oh yes! What a disaster . . . A huge blaze, and the Captain of the Guard was burned alive!

Clarissa Yes, the Captain of the Guard . . . Imagine it! Up in the sacristy, in the sacristan's bedroom, making love with a woman, and her running off with the flames coming out of her backside!

Pizzocca Oh yes? Ran off with flames coming out of her bum? Imagine how many men running behind her to put out the fire!

She chuckles amusedly. The two serving girls sit down to listen, one on the trunk and the other on the floor.

That's enough laughing! A man is dead, here! Anyway, this Judge of ours calls an inquiry . . . and listen to the intelligence of the man: in order to find out who started the fire, he has his guards going round the streets by the Cathedral picking up horse-shit!

Zoanna Why on earth would he do that?

Pizzocca Because he's a mathematical genius, that's why. In the course of his investigation he discovered that a big statue had disappeared from the cathedral – the statue of St George on horseback killing the dragon, which is covered in gold-leaf and worth a fortune . . . But in the ashes of the burned cathedral there was no sign of any gold . . . Not a bit! So the Judge concluded: 'They've stolen it!' But *who had stolen it?* What kind of cart would have been needed to carry away a statue as big as that? And what kind of horse would have pulled the cart? As the proverb says: 'When a horse is straining with a big cart, it shits mountains!' So what does he do? He tells the city guards to gather up all the horse dung they can find in the streets around the cathedral, and bring it to the courtroom immediately! Such a scene, you'd die laughing . . .

Zoanna So what was he going to do with all this dung?

Pizzocca I'll tell you . . . In the courtroom, he had all the dung spread out on a big table, all labelled to say where it came from. The stink was deadly! The Judge sent for a blacksmith, and he told him:

Voices off.

Judge I want you to examine all this dung. Sniff it, feel it, even eat a bit if you have to . . . But tell me which of them was dropped by a heavy-duty horse.

Blacksmith This one, for sure. This comes from a big draught-horse. You can tell by the consistency – strong-smelling and rich! If this shite was found . . .

Judge Would you mind calling it dung?

Blacksmith Yes, sir. If this shite-dung was found on the road to Santa Margherita, then I've an idea where you might find the horse!

Pizzocca No sooner said than done. The guards went off with the blacksmith, and they found the horse at the Grande Cascina dei Biss. And there, in the hay barn, lo and behold, a big cart, and on it the statue of St George and the Dragon!

Zoanna Oh, the intelligence of the man!

Clarissa What an amazing mind!

The two serving girls pull on the clothes line and raise the sheets to reveal the next scene. Then they move to one side of the stage. Trumpets sound.

SCENE THREE

We find ourselves in the main courtroom.
On stage are the Judge, a Prosecuting Lawyer, the Prison Warder, Guards, Witnesses and Members of the Public.

Judge Silence! What is this, a henhouse or a court of law? Bring in the farmer, the owner of the shire horse.

Enter Geron de le Noci, between two Guards. He is limping visibly.

First Guard (*cuffing him from behind*) And you can stop the play-acting with the limping. Walk properly!

Judge What has happened to you?

Second Guard (*matter-of-fact*) We stretched him on the rack, sir. And then we had to singe him a bit . . . as per usual.

Judge As per usual?

Second Guard Yes, and then, quick as a flash, he confessed!

A murmuring among the crowd.

Judge (*indignantly*) I will not have torture in any court of mine! Next time you'll be under arrest yourselves. (*to the prisoner*) What's your name?

Geron de le Noci Geron de le Noci.

Judge (*leaning forward in his seat to look into his face*) Did they hurt you a lot, stretching you on the rack?

Geron de le Noci Yes, your Honour, hurt me terribly . . . All cracked up!

Judge And did they use fire?

Geron de le Noci Burned me right up my back, your Honour!

Judge Hmmm. The court needs to know, was it you who stole the golden statue of St George?

Geron de le Noci No, sir . . . I swear it, by all that is holy!

Judge Listen to me, Geron de le Noci . . . as you will have noticed, I will not tolerate in my jurisdiction the disgrace of people torturing Christians. But don't you go forcing me to hand you over to these brutes. I want you to tell me the truth. Now, repeat after me: 'It was me who stole the statue!'

Geron de le Noci (*with emphasis*) It was me who stole the statue!

Judge (*leaning back*) Oh well done! Now, did you steal it on your own account, or did someone else put you up to it?

Geron de le Noci It wasn't for me . . . I stole it for a gentleman . . . he gave me a purse of two hundred florins in advance.

Judge And what was his name? Who is this gentleman . . .?

Geron de le Noci I don't know his name.

Judge I suppose he appeared to you in a dream . . .

Geron de le Noci No . . . He turned up at my hut with the horse . . . and with his face masked.

Judge And did he also pay you to set fire to the Cathedral?

Geron de le Noci No, nobody said anything about fire, and I swear, it wasn't me who did it!

A Guard hands the Judge a 'bautta' mask.

Judge The mask that the gentleman was wearing, was it perhaps a *bautta*, like this?

A dressmaker's dummy is brought on-stage. The various items are placed on it one by one.

Geron de le Noci Yes, the very one!

Judge (*as above*) And was he wearing this kind of hat?

Geron de le Noci Exactly!

The Guard passes a cloak, which the Judge waves under the nose of Geron de le Noci.

Judge And maybe a big cloak of this colour and style?

Geron de le Noci Yes, exactly the same!

Judge You're very lucky that we found them.

Geron de le Noci What d'you mean, 'found' them?

Judge They were found in the house of the late lamented and supposedly incinerated Captain!

Geron de le Noci So then, your Honour, it was actually the Captain who ordered me to steal the statue?

Judge Yes, but he was acting on orders too. He was acting on behalf of a group of leading citizens of this city, who had their reasons for wanting the Cathedral burned down. This was a deliberate ploy to mislead us by making it look as if the fire had been started in order to cover the theft of the golden statue. And that way, a big stupid-brain ends up taking the blame for the fire. In other words, you!

Geron de le Noci Oh! The bastards! They wanted to blame me for everything!

Judge Exactly!

Geron de le Noci Well fancy that – so it was the Captain himself who started the fire, and then he ends up getting burned alive . . .

Judge That is a possible interpretation.

Geron de le Noci So I'm free to go!

Judge Certainly. Free to go as regards starting the fire. But you stay in jail on account of stealing the statue . . . Even if it was on commission . . . Take him away!

Geron de le Noci (*despondently*) This isn't my day!

He is led off by the two Guards.

Judge Good, we've finished for today. We start again tomorrow. (*general applause*) No, no applause! We're not in a theatre, here . . .

Everyone heads for the exit, but then they stop in their tracks and turn to look at the Judge. A pause.

Or are we?

Everyone except Pizzocca exits. The two young serving girls lower the sheets and then also exit.

SCENE FOUR

Pizzocca (*directly to the audience*) You have seen, you have watched, and now you must agree: this Judge is

157

a real hawk! Oh, what a story! I can't wait for
tomorrow's session, to find out what happens next!
So, you've already met the main characters of our
comedy.

*The characters pass in front of the sheets as they are
cited, and they bow as they go (Note 1).*

The Judge. The Thief. The Blacksmith . . . The two
girls . . . who are beautiful, but a bit of a handful!
Then there's another girl that you've not met yet . . .
(*She indicates breasts, hips and backside.*) . . . narrow
at the waist like a wasp, with two thighs as plump as
hams. What happens then? Somebody arrives who
likes ham! The Cardinal! And that leaves who? Oh
Lord, how silly! There's me . . . Such a modest soul
that I was forgetting myself. My name is Pizzocca
Ganassa . . . As I told you before. But what I haven't
told you yet (*She raises her hands as a megaphone in
front of her mouth, and lowers her voice.*) because if
the others hear me, they'll get jealous . . . is that I'm
far and away the most important character in this
play, and without me this show goes nowhere! Now,
I'm going up on the terrace to put my feet up for a
bit. I'll be back to see you later . . . I don't think you'll
find our little play hard to follow. But don't go
nodding off. Pay attention. It's got allegories, and you
should listen out for them . . . Don't forget! Theatre
isn't like reading a book. If you miss something, you
can't turn back the page and read it again. No. Theatre
is like life: what's done is done, and there's no turning
back!

*She blows a kiss to the audience and exits, stage left,
to the strains of a tarantella. A curtain is lowered,
depicting the facade of the palace.*

SCENE FIVE

*Stage left, two Devils appear, if possible with a flash.
They are lit by spotlights. Maestro Francipante and his
apprentice devil Barlocco.*

Barlocco-Devil (*shouting after Pizzocca*) Just a moment
. . . Hey, I say, Mrs Lady Leading Actress, you forgot
to introduce *us*!

Francipante (*peremptorily*) Barlocco! (*pointing to a lady
in the audience*) You gave that poor lady a fright!
Barlocco, forget it . . . The Pizzocca woman doesn't
even know we're here. (*to the audience near him*)
Sorry about this, he's just a learner.

Barlocco What d'you mean, doesn't know we're here?
The woman stands up here, spewing out prologues,
and she names every dog and pig in the place, and
says nothing about us? I presume you're joking! You
mean we don't even get a mention?

Francipante Barlocco, you are being very silly. Will you
please hold your noise!

Barlocco (*indicating the audience around him*) Maestro!
Oh, what a lot of Christians here! Whoever of you is
without sin, let him throw the first stone!

*They cower slightly, covering their heads with their
arms to ward off an expected shower of stones, which
does not come.*

Haha! Maestro, is it really true what you say, that
Pizzocca didn't introduce us because she doesn't know
we're here?

Francipante Indeed, sir. For the reason being that this
comedy which we are about to perform is an improvised comedy . . . We make it up as we go along . . .

Barlocco Improvised?

Francipante Yes. In other words, everything that happens on this stage happens as if by chance, and cannot be predicted . . . Especially the sudden appearance of unscripted characters such as ourselves!

Barlocco You mean we're not even in the script? But aren't you the master devil? And am I not your demon apprentice?

Francipante (*worried*) Shush! Stop your stupid prattle! You'll get these spectators into terrible trouble. Don't you know that these days they take Christians who believe in the Devil and they burn them at the stake?

Barlocco And what about if they *don't* believe in the Devil?

Francipante They burn them too!

Francipante wanders off into the wings.

Barlocco But wait a minute, Maestro . . . If Pizzocca doesn't know we're here, then maybe the audience doesn't know either . . .

A stand-in for Francipante pops back in, stage right, but the next line is in Francipante's voice.

Francipante Wrong again! Christian *spectators* can see us and hear us . . . But Christian actors, no! Understand?

The stand-in for Francipante disappears, stage right.

Barlocco (*looking into the wings, stage right*) Maestro, don't keep running away like that! Where are you?

With a leap, Francipante appears at stage left, accompanied by a flash, a small cloud of smoke and maybe a loud raspberry on a trombone.

Francipante (*as if in a fanfare*) Taraaa!

Barlocco Ha! That's amazing! Brilliant! (*to the audience*) Did you see that? One second he's here, the next he's over there! A miracle? How did you do that?

Francipante's Double (*wandering back on-stage*) What d'you mean, idiot – we tricked you. I'm his double! (*to the audience*) Goodbye!

He disappears with a snigger.

Francipante Hang on, I need a minute to get my breath back!

Barlocco So, tell me, Maestro . . . You have brought me here to see this Judge Alfonso de Tristano doing his business in the courthouse. But why?

Francipante Because you, my son, are destined for a great mission! Historic, even.

Barlocco A mission?

Francipante Your mission is . . . to take possession of his Honour the Judge!

Barlocco How d'you mean, possession?

Francipante Of his body, his brain, his limbs, his voice, his thoughts and actions, and his every wish and fancy!

Barlocco Hell's cancer – all in one go? And what do I do then?

Francipante Ruin him! Corrupt him! He is a holy man. Chaste and inviolate! Never even had a woman. It seems he can't be corrupted. Imagine it! A saint! It also seems that his intention is to start a public inquiry, in order to bring down the government of this city, which is run by crooks and swindlers. Your job is to drag him down, turn him into a seething sex-pot, a swindling hypocrite!

Barlocco But that's hard, Maestro. What if I fail?

Francipante In that case you know what the punishment is: you will be dissolved in the seething shite of Hell's inferno!

Barlocco Well spike me up my grunge-pipe, what a
terrible way to go!

Francipante And we won't be having vulgar language!
Because you're going to infiltrate the body of a very
proper Christian!

Barlocco Infiltrate him? Don't tell me – he's going to
swallow me like a communion wafer . . .

Francipante No, you won't be going in through the
mouth.

Barlocco So how, then?

Francipante Through the best and most fundamental of
orifices: his bumhole! (*Note 2.*)

Barlocco Tell me that you're joking, Maestro!

Francipante Not at all. It's the easiest way in . . . A little
devil like you should go up there easy-peasy. Think of
yourself as a suppository.

Barlocco Do I *really* have to become a suppository for
this man's bumhole?

*Enter a Devil with a saw, which he hands to
Francipante.*

Francipante Yes! Now, let's have your head!

Barlocco No, no, you're not going to saw my head off!

Francipante (*sawing off his horns*) No . . . Just these two
pointy bits . . . Because a suppository with horns on
presents . . . certain problems . . .

Barlocco Oh God, a suppository! Don't let my mum get
to hear of it!

Francipante Oh do stop complaining! And remember
that going up the back passage of a magistrate is an
honour without equal in this world . . . One up on the
camel through the eye of a needle . . .!

*They exit, dancing to the strains of the tarantella
heard previously. The lights dim.*

SCENE SIX

Enter Pizzocca. She makes the briefest of entries to say her line.

Pizzocca Right? Ready? Wait for it . . .

> *Pizzocca exits.In the half-light we hear a loud bang, followed by another.*

SCENE SEVEN

The facade of the palace rises, and we find ourselves in the drawing room of the Judge's apartments. The entry door is stage left. Stage right is another door which gives access to other rooms. Stage right there is a hint of a staircase leading to an upper gallery. The following items are on-stage: in the centre is a large table; there may be various chairs and armchairs. At the back of the stage is a classic Renaissance sideboard, on which sits a large covered vase full of balls of horse dung. There are also plates, drinking vessels of pewter and silver, and various bottles. At the back of the stage is also a dressmaker's dummy on which clothes can be hung. We hear knocking at the door, stage left.

> *Pizzocca re-enters, dusting herself down and brushing bits of plaster out of her hair.*

Pizzocca I'm coming! (*She is obviously in a state. She crosses the stage with her curious ostrich-like walk.*) I'm coming! God, what a state I'm in! You see? You see? Now they've started chucking bombs at him! Demolished half the verandah! I knew it would come to this. And you know why? Because he has this mania for going out on his balcony and waving to

Brother Michele da Lentini and his pathetic band of
heretics every time they come by in procession.
Heretics are no good. Heretics mean trouble. And the
Master is like a moth to a candle when it comes to
trouble! (*further violent knocking at the door*) I'm
cooooming! Who is it?

*She opens the door. Enter a young woman, rather
haughtily. She is dressed fairly showily, and wears a
large shawl and a veil to hide her face.*

Hey – stop right there! Where do you think you're going,
all covered up like that?

Jacoba I have to speak with the Judge!

Pizzocca No, dear. If you have to speak with the Judge,
go to the courtroom with your face uncovered, and
there you can prattle away to your heart's content . . .

Jacoba I can't go to the courtroom. I'm in terrible
danger! They'll kill me!

Pizzocca Kill you? What d'you mean, kill you?

Jacoba You should know that I am the woman who was
in bed with the Captain of the Guard when the
Cathedral caught fire.

Pizzocca Oh! By Saint Gertrude violated by the Turks . . .
So you were the one who went running off naked
with the fire coming out of your backside? Ha, ha!
(*She bows obsequiously.*) Pleased to meet you! Highly
honoured . . . Do sit down, make yourself at home.
(*She almost forces her to sit down.*) So now let's take
a look at you! (*She attempts to raise Jacoba's veil.*)

Jacoba (*leaping to her feet to prevent her*) No, I dare not!
What I have to say can only be revealed to the Judge!

Pizzocca (*sitting down with a sigh*) Sorry to tell you this,
but first you have to reveal it to *me*!

Jacoba And why might that be?

Pizzocca For the legally cast-iron fact that I am the
Judge's sole collaborator. I'm his secretary! And either

you confide in me . . . Or there's the door, and off you
go, *fuori dai coglioni*! (*Note 2.*)

Jacoba (*She sighs*) Oh, alright then . . . (*She raises her
veil.*)

Pizzocca Well, well, well, the Captain's moll! (*to Jacoba*)
I told you, dear, sit down, make yourself comfortable.
Now tell me – so the Captain and you were up in
your little love-nest, and while you were enjoying a bit
of slap and tickle, he had arranged for a thief to come
and carry off the statue . . .?

Jacoba No, we only started making love afterwards . . .

Pizzocca Afterwards . . . After he started the fire?

Jacoba No, he had nothing to do with it!

Pizzocca But *you* had something to do with it . . .

Jacoba No, what d'you mean . . .? If you must know, he
was actually killed before the fire started.

Pizzocca Killed?

Jacoba Yes. Stabbed! (*She gestures as if plunging a
dagger into her breast.*) Like that!

Pizzocca Just like that . . . While he was in bed with you?

Jacoba Yes. And that was the reason why he couldn't
save himself from the fire . . . Because he'd been
stabbed . . . like a Saint Sebastian . . . And the blow of
the knife cut me too! (*She opens her bodice, copiously
revealing a breast with an obvious wound.*)

Pizzocca Oh Saint Agatha of the transfixed tits! It's a
miracle. They stuck a knife in your tit and it didn't go
pop? (*She changes tone.*) Is that a real wound? Let me
feel.

Jacoba No!

Pizzocca Let me touch it, I said!

*She grabs her by one arm and either swings her or
flicks her over in such a way as to make her do a
somersault. Jacoba ends up front-stage.*

And where d'you think you're going? Into the arms of
the audience? (*She points to a lady in the first row.*)
You see the fright you gave to that poor lady there . . .

SCENE EIGHT

Enter the Judge.

Judge Pizzocca, why are you looking at that girl? Who
is she?

Jacoba covers her breasts and face.

Pizzocca She is someone who has . . . tragic news, your
Honour!

Judge And she keeps this news hidden between her
breasts?

Jacoba Oh sir, sir, are you his Honour the Judge? (*She
removes the veil from her face.*) I was telling your
secretary here –

*Pizzocca gives her a kick or somehow tries to shut her
up.*

– about my lover the Captain . . . who was killed while
he lay at my breast! (*She reveals her breasts again.*)
Look, you may see the wound!

Judge (*stopping her, in embarrassment*) Not necessary,
thank you.

Jacoba You can even touch it, if you want!

Judge (*embarrassed*) Thank you, but I don't touch a thing
when I'm fasting. (*He changes tone.*) Anyway, what
d'you mean, 'secretary'? I don't have a secretary . . .

Jacoba (*amazed, pointing to Pizzocca*) But the lady
said . . .

Pizzocca Some mad woman who was hanging round
here . . . I sent her away with a kick in the pants!

Judge (*furious*) Pizzocca . . . You're going to have to stop interfering and sticking your nose into the business of the Tribunal . . .! One of these days it's going to end up with me kicking you out . . . (*to the girl*) And you, daughter . . . If you really do have something to reveal . . . apart from your female attributes, that is . . . follow me to the courtroom . . . And if I were you, I'd cover that fruit from the sun . . . because it's ripe enough already! (*He turns back to Pizzocca.*) And you . . . next time . . . you'll be out on your neck!

Exit the Judge and Jacoba. Pizzocca exits by another door.

SCENE NINE

The two Devils enter through the main door and look around.

Francipante Watch out they don't discover us! You can bet your life that Pizzocca's round here somewhere, spying on us . . .

Barlocco (*peering into the other rooms*) It's alright, there's no one here.

From the room next door we hear the scream of a woman. The Devils hide under the big table, while the Judge appears, holding in his arms a young woman. It is Jacoba, who has fainted.

Judge Oh that's all we need! She's passed out! (*He calls out.*) Pizzocca . . . Quick, bring some water and smelling salts! Pizzocca . . .! Pizzocca, quick! This is a disaster. The girl's passed out on me. Hurry up and do something, we've got to get her out of here.

Pizzocca Has she fainted, or what?

Judge I don't know. Look, she's got a sort of froth coming out of her mouth.

Pizzocca (*sniffing*) Oh, by all the saints in heaven! She's poisoned herself! It's deadly nightshade! But why? Why would she have done that?

Judge I think I can guess the reason.

Pizzocca Would you mind telling me too, so's I can get some sleep tonight?

Judge Oh Lord . . . I think I'm going to be sick!

Pizzocca Tummy upset, your Honour?

Judge Er, yes.

Pizzocca Just go and relax in the toilet, and let yourself go, your Honour . . . I'll see to the girl.

Judge She can't stay in here! Pizzocca, for goodness' sake, do whatever you have to, but save her . . . If she dies here in my apartments, my reputation will be shot to pieces.

He exits, groaning and clutching his belly.

Pizzocca Relax, your Honour, if she's going to die, I'll make sure it's somewhere else! (*to the audience*) Poor man, he's got a terrible problem . . . No sooner does he see a pair of tits than . . . he gets all cranked up inside . . . (*She points to her stomach.*) . . . so bad that he can be stuck in the toilet for five hours at a stretch. (*She calls the two serving girls loudly.*) Zoanna! Clarissa! Where are you? (*She goes to the sideboard and rummages among various pots, jars and bottles for the antidote.*)

Zoanna and Clarissa (*from off-stage*) Coming!

Pizzocca Get a move on, you wretches. Come and give me a hand!

SCENE TEN

*Enter the two young serving girls, holding the Judge's
ceremonial robe and hat, which they place on the
dressmaker's dummy.*

Clarissa You called?

Zoanna We were preparing his Excellency's ceremonial
  robe!

Pizzocca Oh yes, I forgot, he's invited to supper with the
  Duke after the theatre tonight. (*She points to Jacoba.*)
  I need your help to get this girl sorted out.

Zoanna She's so pale! Who is she?

Clarissa And what's that stuff coming out of her mouth?

Pizzocca Seems like she tried to poison herself, that's
  what. (*She continues rummaging.*) Oh Lord, and I've
  still got all this shite here. It's the master's fault for
  rushing me: 'Hurry up . . . I want these pickled in
  alcohol, to use them as evidence . . .' And then he
  forgets to take them and they just end up making the
  house stink! (*She sniffs them.*) God they smell weird!
  Right, girls, this should be pretty simple. (*She
  produces a bucket.*) First of all, shawl off. (*She
  removes the shawl.*) Now you two, hold her over the
  bucket.

The girls do as she says.

Hold her steady. And now two fingers down the
throat . . .

Jacoba vomits into the bucket.

Clarissa Oh God, that's revolting . . .!

Zoanna It stinks . . .!

Pizzocca Now, lay her out on the table.

The girls do as she says. Jacoba's womanly attributes are somewhat revealed. Meanwhile there is a violent banging at the door.

Who's that now? This place is a madhouse! (*She shouts.*) I'm coming! (*She leaves the bucket and goes over to the entry door in the wings.*) Who is it . . . I don't care who you are . . . If you want to put in a statement, go down to the Courthouse!

Zoanna and Clarissa exit hastily.

SCENE ELEVEN

The intruder enters, pushing Pizzocca out of the way. He wears a Venetian bautta *mask and a broad-brimmed hat, and is wrapped in a large cloak.*

Intruder Out of my way! I have to confer with the Judge. At once! (*With large strides he goes straight past Jacoba on the table.*) Inform the Judge that I am . . . (*Faced with the sight of Jacoba's womanly attributes, he is stopped in his tracks. He backs up a bit to get a better sight of her.*) Er . . . here . . . um . . . yes . . . here . . .

Pizzocca (*grabbing a long stick*) Oh no you don't! Wallop!

She fetches him a mighty blow on the back. The intruder falls heavily to the ground.

Show's over!
Intruder Help!

He makes as if reaching for something under his cloak.

Pizzocca Drawing your sword, eh?

She thumps him again. As if doing fancy sword-work.

Intruder It's not a sword, it's my purse!

He produces a small velvet bag containing money, and throws it to her.

Pizzocca A purse! With money. To corrupt his Honour the Judge, I presume!

A further series of blows.

Intruder What's got into you? Calm down! (*He tries to escape the woman's blows.*) Stop it, you wretch! I am Cardinal Ambone!
Pizzocca Yes . . . (*more blows*) Oh yes, the Cardinal goes round with a big sword and bags of money to corrupt his Honour the Judge, eh? I *don't* think!
Cardinal Help! She's killing me!

SCENE TWELVE

Enter the Judge.

Judge Pizzocca, for God's sake, what on earth are you up to now? Why are you hitting that poor man?
Pizzocca For sure he's a murderer . . . He's come to kill the girl, so's she can't turn up as a witness at the trial, and he wants to bribe you with money . . .

She hands him the money and aims another blow at the man, but it ends up hitting the Judge's foot.

Judge Ouuuch!
Pizzocca Sorry, Master, I was getting carried away! Look, *and* he's got a *bautta* mask!
Judge Cardinal, is that you?

Pizzocca is alarmed, and moves away.

Cardinal Get me out of the hands of that lunatic before she kills me!

Judge Get out of here, you stupid woman! And get that girl out of here too!

The two serving girls re-enter, and help Jacoba off the stage.

Forgive me, your Eminence . . . Get out, you halfwit!

Pizzocca exits, in a huff.

Forgive me . . . I suppose she meant well . . . (*He points to the sideboard dresser.*) There's some brandy, your Eminence, please do help yourself . . . I'll be back in a minute . . .

Exit.

Cardinal Brandy, eh? Now there's a treat . . . just what I was needing . . . (*He picks up a bottle, removes the stopper and sniffs the contents.*) Hmmm . . . excellent bouquet! (*He pours himself a glassful and tastes it.*) Excellent! Now, if only there was something to get my teeth into . . . (*He picks up the jar with the horse droppings pickled in alcohol and sniffs it.*) Must be pickled faggots or something . . . strange smell, though . . . (*He takes out a piece, tastes it and puts the jar back onto the table.*) Nice! Delicate! . . . Tastes like shite, in fact, but then all the best foods have a touch of *ripeness* about them . . .

From behind, one of the Devils snatches the morsel from the Cardinal's hand. Having tried it, the Devil spits it out over the Cardinal in disgust.

Where did it go? What on earth was that? Oh dear . . . now, where's that bottle gone? (*He pours himself a drink, takes a plate, puts a piece of horse dropping on it, sits at the table and begins to eat. He takes a bite*

out of the horse dropping.) Mmmm, this is exquisite!
(*He drinks contentedly.*)

SCENE THIRTEEN

The Judge re-enters.

Judge Ah. Glad to see you've helped yourself. Good
brandy, eh? Now tell me, if you don't mind my
asking, what on earth put it into your head to come
visiting me here, all masked up like that?

Cardinal I have something very important to tell you.
But first of all, who was that girl on the table there?
I found her very . . . disturbing . . .

Judge *You* found her disturbing, your Excellence . . .
Imagine how I felt.

Cardinal What d'you mean?

Judge Not ten minutes since, I found myself with that
woman in tears all over me . . .

Cardinal What d'you mean, 'all over you' . . .?

Judge I mean with her breasts half bared, and clinging
to me, and breathing warmth and fragrance all over
me, and holding me like she would never let me go . . .

Cardinal (*pulls out a handkerchief and mops his brow*)
And then? What happened then?

Judge I felt these hot, seething passions rising up inside
me.

Cardinal And then what?

Judge Then nothing.

Cardinal Nothing?

Judge Not exactly nothing. Sennapods.

Cardinal Sennapods?

Judge Yes, because a man must protect himself from the
Devil's works. The Devil may tempt me, but I am
prepared! (*He shows him a small bottle, takes a pill*

from it, and waves it under the Cardinal's nose.) Six at
a time!

Cardinal But it's a laxative . . . you'll blow your insides
out with a dose like that!

Judge Exactly! Every time this demon passion of mine
begins to rise, straight away I swallow a handful of
these, and they have me rushing to the toilet, and that
way I'm saved from the Devil.

Cardinal Seems a terrible waste . . . I mean, a shame . . .
I suppose that's what drove the poor girl to poison
herself. There she was, offering herself to you, and the
best you can manage is to run off and lock yourself in
the bog.

Judge No. The swallowing of the poison was for a quite
other reason. Which may become apparent later but
which I am not yet in a position to reveal to you.

Two Guards enter through the main door.

What do you want?

First Guard We are here to accompany you to his
Excellency the Duke.

Enter the serving girls.

Judge Oh yes, I'd forgotten about that. And we're late
too.

Cardinal I've been invited as well.

Judge Let's get out now, before the front of the palace
comes down on our heads.

*As the backdrop for the facade of the palace drops
down, the Judge and the Cardinal move to the front
of the stage, followed by the two Guards, who help
them to put on their respective cloaks. The Devils
watch the scene, spying through the centre door.*

But to get back to what we were talking about . . . why
did you arrive here wearing a mask?

Cardinal I had to come in secret. To give you a piece of advice.

Judge What advice?

Cardinal Bear in mind that I am taking a risk here, and it is only because I hold you in the greatest regard . . .

Judge I thank you for that, but I repeat, what advice?

Cardinal Let's start with the business of the cannon shots, which came close to leaving you like Bolognese sauce.

Judge So you heard about that? If you happen to know the gunner, convey my compliments to the man . . . he has a terrific aim.

Cardinal Don't joke about it. It was a warning to you.

Judge And what comes after the warning?

Cardinal The warning says: stop following that gang of crazies who go round after Brother Michele da Lentini. And stop going up onto your balcony and waving to these fanatics every time they pass, it only encourages them.

Judge And why do you call them fanatics?

Cardinal Please, don't play the innocent with me! Haven't you heard the way they preach against the Church and the gentry?

Judge But they're just being satirical; anyway, some of what they say is pretty spot-on.

Cardinal Spot-on, you say? Like the stuff comparing the Church of Rome with Sodom and Gomorrah?

Judge That was just a figure of speech.

Cardinal And I suppose when they talk about burning all paintings with naked women in, that was a figure of speech too? And perhaps it is reasonable to suspect that people who begin by burning naked women end up burning cathedrals and suchlike . . .

Judge Aha! So now we know the rogues we should be arresting! Heretics and idiots, they always come in useful, don't they! But you gentlemen should be careful not to end up like the lion when he overloaded the ass.

Cardinal Overloading the ass . . . What are you talking about?

Judge It's an ancient Greek fable. Would you like to hear?

Cardinal Why not, why not . . .

Judge Right. Here we go. *Mia fora' kai ena kairo, enas meghalos leona* . . .

Cardinal (*interrupting*) Wait a minute – you're surely not telling it in Greek?

Judge Of course. It's a lot funnier in the original.

Cardinal If you don't mind, I'd be just as happy in the common tongue.

Judge I couldn't possibly tell it in the vulgar tongue wearing fancy robes like this.

The Guards remove his cloak.

Cardinal (*removing his own cloak, with the assistance of the serving girls*) Me too. Out of solidarity.

Judge Well anyway, one year, as every year, all the beasts of the valley were invited up to the sanctuary on the top of the mountain for the blessing of the animals. The lion chose the donkey as his travelling companion, because he thought: 'This journey is going to be long and wearisome, and when the going starts to get steep I can get up on the donkey's back. He can carry me. And then, if I happen to get hungry, I can eat him too!' So he suggests to the donkey that they travel together, and the donkey agrees. But the donkey proposes a deal: 'We'll take turns in carrying each other. Alright? Two miles each.' So off they go. When the road starts to get steeper, up speaks the lion: 'Time for me to get up on your back!' 'Alright, up you go . . .?' And with a leap the lion is up there on the donkey's back. 'Hey, go easy with those claws sticking into my ribs,' says the donkey. 'You scratch me like that and I bleed to death!' 'I can't help it. I have to hold on as best I can with what I've got . . .! Giddy-up! Giddy-up! Away you go!' So the donkey reaches the top of the mountain, and by this time he's got blood pouring down from his scratches. 'Well,' he says, 'now at least for the journey down it's my turn to ride on your back!' 'True enough, fair's fair,' says the lion. 'You did the work on the way up, I do it on the way down. Away you go!' And the donkey jumps up onto the lion's back . . . But he has a terrible time keeping his balance. He slithers here and there, because he's got hooves, you see, and he can't get a proper grip. Then all of a sudden our donkey jockey has an idea – a thrust of his loins, stiff as a ramrod, and straight up the lion's backside. Held in place. Good and solid. 'Hey, ho, ouch!' shouts the lion. 'What is that blooming great truncheon that you've stuck up my rear?' 'Forgive me, your majesty . . .' says the donkey. 'I can't help it – each of us has to hold on as best he can with what he's got . . .! Giddy-up! Giddy-up! And away you go!'

Song

Giddy-up, giddy-up, giddy-up
And away you go, and don't even stop.
Giddy-up, giddy-up, giddy-up, and go
And imagine that you're flying.

The two serving girls and the two Guards help the Judge and Cardinal with their cloaks and hats. Singing and dancing, and followed by the Devils, they all exit.

Musical interlude.

SCENE FOURTEEN

*The canvas traverse depicting the front of the palace
is raised and we find ourselves in the Judge's bedroom.
It has a large canopied bed on the right and a chest of
drawers with a mirror on the left. On the left there is
also a fireplace with a large hooded chimneypiece. At the
back of the stage stands a large picture frame on wheels,
its bottom edge just clear of the ground. Also a low table
and two chairs. Draped across a chair are two gowns of
identical colour (the ones which the Judge wears during
trials) and a hat to accompany each of them.*

*Enter Pizzocca, in a nightdress, holding a lighted
candle, and wrapped in a large shawl.*

Pizzocca Ye gods, it's freezing in here! (*She sneezes
violently. She looks at the empty bed.*) And his
honour's not back yet! What time is it?

A bell sounds the hour with four strokes.

Four o'clock already . . . He's never been this late before!
(*She puts the candle on one of the chairs and goes to
the fireplace.*) I don't believe it, the fire's out again!
(*She tries to light it, using bellows to get the flames
going. A cloud of smoke billows out of the chimney,
right in her face, and makes her sneeze.*) Atchoo! Oh
to hell with it. Damned chimney, won't draw! I bet
he went for a natter with the Duke after the theatre!
(*She sneezes.*) Atchoo! Oh bother, I'm all shivers! My
teeth are chattering with the cold! (*She picks up one
of the Judge's two gowns, and puts it on.*) This ought
to warm me up . . . You know, if I was born again,
I'd be a judge, and I'd put all the big bad wrongdoers
on the bonfire! And the lawyers who defend them too!
To the stake with the lot of them! Let's have the hat

too . . . (*Pizzocca takes the Judge's hat and puts it on her head.*) I'll get into bed . . . That way, when his Honour comes back he'll find it nice and warm, and that way I get a nap too.

She lies down, draws the curtains of the bed, and goes to sleep.

SCENE FIFTEEN

Francipante, the master Devil, enters via the chimney-piece, followed by Barlocco. As they shake the soot off them, they both sneeze. Pizzocca sneezes too, in her sleep. We have a brief concert of sneezes.

Bartocco Maestro, why is it that, every time, out of all the ways in . . . atchoo . . . we have to pick the . . . atchoo . . . dirtiest?

Francipante Oh do stop moaning . . . atchoo . . .

Pizzocca Atchoo!

The violence of Pizzocca's sneeze makes Bartocco jump.

Francipante Look, see, he's back . . . (*He pulls aside the canopy of the bed.*) All tucked up in beddy-byes.

Barlocco (*sneezing in turn*) Takes his job a bit seriously, doesn't he – going to bed in his ceremonial robes!

Francipante Shush, I told you . . . you'll wake him! Right, are you ready? Your big moment has come!

Barlocco To be honest, Maestro, I'm a bit nervous . . .

Francipante Calm down. Relax. Now, sit here, because I've got to get you down to the right size.

Barlocco Eh? Won't I do the way I am?

Francipante You're joking! That big you'd be a suppository for an elephant! No, I need to make you smaller . . . Turn you teeny-weeny.

He gets Barlocco to squat down. Then, like a magician, he pulls a cloth out of his bag and waves it in the air.

Are you ready? Now just relax. (*He holds the cloth in front of Barlocco in order to hide him from the audience, and chants a spell.*)

Izzio-wizzio, let's get busy-oh
With a one two three and a Hey Prest-O!

There you are! (*He whips away the cloth. Barlocco has not disappeared. Addressing the audience:*) Oh damn! I can never get that wretched spell to work!
(*to Barlocco*) I told you, you've got to be calm and relaxed, otherwise the spell won't work! (*He places the cloth in front of Barlocco again, and repeats the spell.*)

Izzio-wizzio, let's get busy-oh
With a one two three and a Hey Prest-O!

Again he removes the cloth. This time Barlocco has disappeared. In his place we see a tiny moving puppet, a perfect model of him.)

Barlocco, where are you?
Barlocco I'm here!
Francipante (*deliriously happy*) It worked! It worked! Ha, ha!
Barlocco Oh God, what's happened? You've reduced me to a midget!
Francipante Ha, you look brilliant, all little like that.
Barlocco (*shouting*) A mirror! A mirror so's I can see myself!
Francipante No point. You know devils can't be reflected in mirrors. You're perfect! Now, before you take possession of this body (*He points to where Pizzocca is lying.*) I need to give you a little something for your journey.

He hands him a tiny watch with a little chain attached.

Barlocco (*taking the watch*) What is it?

Francipante It's a wind-up watch . . . dummy!

Barlocco I've never seen one that small.

Francipante It's a masterpiece . . . It strikes the hour, and it plays tunes too. Listen!

The watch chimes a jolly tune. The puppet does a few dance steps.

Barlocco That's wonderful, Maestro!

Francipante Now get ready. And remember, every time the clock chimes, you gain power and total possession of this person's body. But when it strikes again . . . at that very moment you stop, you fall asleep, you go into a kind of hibernation. And at the same time the Judge regains possession of his body and his faculties.

Barlocco Why would he want to do that?

Francipante For the simple fact that you can't just move in and take him over lock, stock and barrel. You need to take it one step at a time . . . Otherwise he goes mad, and his brain explodes like a melon!

Barlocco I understand . . .

Francipante Good! Now, concentrate . . . (*He picks up the Barlocco puppet and slips him under the sheet.*) Take a good deep breath, get your head down, find the hole and get stuck in, boy! Good luck!

Barlocco Ooo-er – it's dark, Maestro . . . I can't see a thing in here!

Francipante Just take the plunge!

Barlocco Ooo . . . aah . . . I can't breathe . . .

Pizzocca (*leaping about and waving her legs, she shouts*) Huh . . . huh . . . What's happening? Help! Oh mamma, the Turks, the Turks . . .!

Francipante You're in there, son! Congratulations!

*He pulls the curtains of the bed across, and,
sniggering, exits via the fireplace.*

SCENE SIXTEEN

*We are still in the Judge's bedroom. Noises off. A door
flies open. Enter two Guards, supporting the Judge, who
is visibly drunk.*

Judge Leave me . . . I can stand up on my own . . .

First Guard Your Honour, be careful . . . That's the third
time you've . . . fallen over . . . on your own!

Second Guard You should watch out, your Honour,
you're extremely drunk!

Judge Take note, young man, that only peasants and
poor people get drunk . . . Gentlemen and people
of learning become spiritually inebriated. Leave me,
I said! I can manage perfectly well . . .

*The Judge takes hold of the frame of the big picture.
The Guards try to stop it falling over. With one rip, he
ends up with the picture in his hands. The Judge
moves round the stage, supported only by the picture
frame on wheels. He thinks that it's a mirror.*

I really must have imbibed too much of those spiritual
spirits . . . I warned the Duke that I'm not a drinker.
'Oh no, just a glass or two, won't do you any harm.'
And now look at me, I don't know if I'm coming or
going . . .

He is about to remove his cloak.

Second Guard Be careful taking your cloak off, your
Honour . . . It's very cold in this room . . .

Judge Away with this robe . . . makes me look like an
imperial peacock!

He removes his robe.

First Guard (*he helps him put on the gown which is on the chair; it is identical to the one that Pizzocca is wearing*) At least put this robe on . . . because the fire's gone out!

Judge And why didn't Pizzocca keep it going?

Second Guard I've no idea.

Judge Where is she? Where's the wretch hiding? (*He wobbles.*) Go and find her at once! (*He wobbles again.*) Oh, my head's spinning!

Second Guard I'll go and look for her now.

He exits.

Judge If she's asleep, wake her up! (*to the audience*) Who are you? What is this, party time? What a lot of drunk people! Lord, it's an invasion of drunks!

Re-enter the Second Guard.

That was quick!

Second Guard She's nowhere to be found, your Honour, not even in her room.

Judge She must have gone out looking for me.

Second Guard Could be, sir . . .

Judge So what are you doing, just standing there? Go out and find her.

First Guard Yes, your Honour, at once, your Honour . . . But are you sure that . . .?

Judge Shut up and go! (*The two Guards head determinedly for the fireplace.*) No, not through the fireplace!

Guards (*in unison*) Yes, your Honour!

Judge Through the door!

Guards Sir!

The Guards exit. We hear a great crash.

First Guard (*re-entering*) It was shut! (*He exits.*)

Judge Presumably explains why soldiers always wear helmets! Oof, I'm going to bed . . . (*He pulls aside the canopy, only to discover Pizzocca lying there, wearing his clothes and his hat.*) Oh dear! I'm already in bed! So how do I go to bed now? God, I'm the image of myself! (*in desperation*) I never imagined that getting drunk would mean there'd be two of me! That's it, I swear I'll never touch another drop!

At this moment the clock in Pizzocca's belly chimes.

And where's that strange sound coming from . . .? Oh dear, I must be hearing things!

Barlocco-Pizzocca gets up and stands on the bed. She starts moving her belly and hips in time with the chimes.

Barlocco-Pizzocca (*speaking with the voice of Barlocco: Note 3*) What's happening . . .? Where am I . . .?

She gets off the bed, and finds herself in front of the picture-frame-cum-mirror, behind which the Judge stands, looking at her dumbfoundedly.

How can this be . . .? I'm inside the Judge, but at the same time I'm outside? And how come I can see myself in the mirror . . .? I thought devils couldn't do that. It must be because I'm in a new body.

Judge Who on earth are you? (*The Judge takes the candlestick and peers as if to look at her more closely.*)

Barlocco-Pizzocca Not a very good mirror this . . . Can't really see a thing . . .!

Using one edge of her robe, Barlocco-Pizzocca polishes the non-existent glass between them. The Judge moves towards Barlocco-Pizzocca.

What on earth are you doing? Reflections aren't supposed to come out of mirrors!

Very agitated, Barlocco-Pizzocca attempts to snatch the candlestick from the Judge and jostles him.

Judge Get your hands off me, and take my robe off!

Finally Barlocco-Pizzocca succeeds in taking the candlestick from him, and whacks him violently over the head. The Judge passes out, and sprawls across the bed.

Barlocco-Pizzocca That'll teach you! Reflections should know their place! (*He puts down the candlestick and feels his body.*) Sacripante . . .! What on earth have I turned into? What's happened to me? I've got a horrible feeling something's gone terribly wrong! (*shouting towards the fireplace*) Francipante . . .! Maestro, help! What's happened? Come here! Help!

He disappears from the room for a moment, in search of Francipante.

SCENE SEVENTEEN

Francipante comes tumbling down the chimney. He leaps through the frame of the non-existent mirror and moves it to the back of the stage.

Francipante I'm here! What's the problem? Where are you?

Barlocco-Pizzocca I'm here. (*So saying, she removes her robe.*) In this body . . . Actually, to tell the truth, I don't know where I am!

Francipante You idiot! You've gone and stuck yourself in the body of Pizzocca, his monkey-faced housekeeper! You were supposed to go up the Judge, you fool!

Barlocco-Pizzocca Oh no . . . (*She feels her face, breasts and thighs, and when she reaches her sex she shrieks.*)

It's true! I'm in a woman!! I've been switched! Waaah –
how did that happen? You were there . . . you saw
me . . . I went up the Judge!

Francipante Well, will you look at this disastrous idiot,
who goes up people's backsides like he's blind, or
something!

Barlocco-Pizzocca You've got to rescue me! Get me out
of this big turkey . . . Please . . .!

Francipante No can do, son! You know the laws of the
Nether Regions. 'Any devil taking possession of the
body of a Christian has to stay there until he has
completed his mission.' So you're going to have to
stay with her. Change of plan. You reshape this lump
of female from the inside. Like she's pizza-dough. You
got that?

Barlocco-Pizzocca Yes, Maestro. Change her from the
inside. Change her into what, though?

Francipante Your job is no different to what it was.
You're going to have to ruin this Judge. Corrupt him.
Make him fall passionately in love with you!

Barlocco-Pizzocca But I don't know how to make people
fall in love!

Francipante Improvise! Turn her into a brawling
strumpet. Teach her how to walk with a wiggle and
a wave. But first of all, learn to talk like a woman,
not with that voice of a drunken ox. Repeat after me:
'I will become a sensual female!'

Barlocco-Pizzocca 'I will become a sensual female!'

Francipante Can't we have it a bit more . . . luscious?

Barlocco-Pizzocca I shall become a terribly talented
female . . .

Francipante Well done! Bravo . . .! Try again! A bit
more of the *femme fatale* . . .

Barlocco-Pizzocca (*beginning with a guttural voice,
gradually she improves, until in the end she's speaking
with Pizzocca's normal voice*) I shall become a wicked,

wicked temptress . . . Oh so languid . . . (*increasingly convinced of herself*) And I shall make this Judge drunk with passion, make him mad with love. From this wrinkled old prune of a body I shall create a queen of lust!

Francipante Bravo – just carry on like that! Right. Now I'm afraid I have to leave you, Barlocco. I have another job to attend to . . .

Barlocco-Pizzocca Oh no, don't leave me, Maestro! Help! Who's going to help me now?

Francipante You're on your own now, boy! Goodbye . . . And good luck!

Exit Francipante.

Barlocco-Pizzocca Alas, poor me, poor innocent Devil, left all alone in this wicked world! (*At this moment the watch chimes sound in his belly.*) Oh dear, oh no, the bells, it's time for the personality change . . . I'm feeling terribly sleepy!

Barlocco-Pizzocca moves her body convulsively, gives a little twitch, goes rigid and passes out on the bed, next to the Judge, who is still out for the count.

SCENE EIGHTEEN

Enter Francipante, accompanied by She-Devils and He-Devils.

Francipante Oh look, now, isn't that sweet! Barlocco's off to sleep and Pizzocca's in charge of herself again. Look at the two of them. Like peas in a pod. Haha! Come to think of it, we could have a bit of fun, here. Why don't we improvise a bit? Rearrange them a bit? Lying like that, they could almost be lovers . . . Except that they've got too many clothes on.

So saying, Francipante and the Devils sing and dance,
and quickly undress both the Judge and Pizzocca.
They move them as if they are puppets, throwing their
clothes in the air. They mark the rhythm by stamping
and clapping, and letting out strange shouts. The whole
scene becomes a kind of 'tammurriata' (Note 4).

You must be all naked!
As your mother made you.
All naked you must be!
To be naked is not a sin.
Take it off, remove it!

Take it off, remove it!
That blouse.
That petticoat.
And that bodice, hat and hood,
Trousers and cloak,
Culottes and corset,
Ahiha!
Take them off! Undo . . .
All naked you must be!
Aaahaaa!

A general cackling and sniggering of Devils. The
Devils contrive to re-arrange the Judge and Pizzocca
into an embrace, with their arms and legs wrapped
round each other. They cover them with the sheet.
Then they close the curtains of the bed. They pick up
the clothes from the floor, and then, still singing and
leaping about, they exit.

SCENE NINETEEN

The two Guards re-enter by the main door. They peer
round looking for the Judge.

First Guard (*in a hushed voice*) Hello . . . Your Honour . . . We couldn't find Pizzocca . . .

Second Guard Maybe he's in bed already . . . Gone to sleep. (*They pull aside the canopy of the bed, and are amazed at what they see.*) Oh my God! Look, it's Pizzocca, all lovey-dovey with his nibs!

First Guard Maybe it's true what they say – rub two old sticks together and you get fire!

Enter the Cardinal, through the door, which was left open. Behind the Cardinal enter a couple of Devils, who amuse themselves doing silly tricks during the dialogue.

Cardinal May I come in?

The two Guards swiftly close the curtains of the bed and rush to the door, pulling out their swords.

First Guard Halt, who goes there!

Cardinal (*he backs off, and pulls back his cloak to reveal his religious habit*) Don't be alarmed! Put up your weapons, I am Cardinal Ambone!

First Guard Oh, forgive me, your Eminence . . .

Second Guard (*with a slight bow*) At your service, sir!

Cardinal I've come hurrying over to find out about the Judge . . . I gather he was a bit drunk, coming back from the Duke's . . .

Second Guard Could say that, your Eminence . . . Fell off his horse . . . Rolled down into a ditch.

Cardinal And was he badly hurt?

Second Guard I don't think so . . . In fact . . . you *could* say he was up and riding again pretty quickly. Look.

He pulls aside the curtains to reveal the two of them in bed.

Cardinal Oh Lord God, look at that! Not with his creepy old housekeeper!?

Second Guard Maybe he uses her for a hot water bottle.

Cardinal He must be pretty desperate . . . Depraved, I'd call it.

He lifts one edge of the sheet and peers under with morbid curiosity.

 The First Guard pulls across a chair and offers it to the Cardinal.

Second Guard Do sit down, your Eminence.

The Cardinal goes to sit down, still holding up the edge of the sheet. One of the Devils snatches the chair away from under him and scampers off with it. The Cardinal goes down with a tumble, and takes the two Guards with him. All three contrive to end up under the sheet, which covers them completely. The noise of all this wakes the Judge. He sits up in bed and suddenly realises that he is holding Pizzocca in his arms.

Judge Eh? What's this? Pizzocca! What on earth are you doing in my bed?

Pizzocca Er . . . Are you ready for lunch, sir?

Cardinal (*peering out from under the sheet*) O dear, hello . . . Do please excuse me . . .!

Judge Cardinal Ambone! What on earth are *you* doing in my bed? Have you been there long?

Cardinal No, I arrived just a moment ago . . . Unfortunately!

Judge Oh, please . . . I know what you must be thinking. But it's not like that!

Cardinal I'm sure it's not!

Judge And who's that under the sheet with you?

Guards (*peering out from under the sheet. In unison*) We just happened to be passing!

Judge Pizzocca, I think you owe us an explanation.

Pizzocca Oh, your Honour . . . I don't know what's come over me! Oh God . . . I've got no clothes on! (*She snatches the sheet to her.*)

Judge And I've got no clothes on either! (*He does the same.*) Oh, the shame of it! Your Eminence . . . I have to admit, I was drunk!

Guards (*in unison*) Yes, we can vouch for that. He was drunk!

Judge And I have my suspicions that you were drunk too, Pizzocca . . . On account of you were speaking with the voice of a man.

Pizzocca Me, with the voice of a man? But I couldn't . . . I am a lady!

Judge Oh Lord, this is scandalous! You mustn't let word of this get around!

Guards (*ponderously*) No, we won't say a word to anyone!

Cardinal You need have no fear . . . No one will ever know. Because this is a country where people mind their own business.

Lively musical interlude to end the scene.

Act Two

SCENE ONE

On a barely-lit stage, we see flickering candlelight and swinging incense burners. As the lights come up, we see a kind of holy man. This is Father Mirone. He is performing a massage on a girl afflicted with a hysterical crisis.

Enter Pizzocca. She gestures vigorously to Father Mirone.

Pizzocca Father Mirone, quick, I need you! You're the only one I can talk to.

Father Mirone You'll have to wait . . . I have a problem with this girl. She's hysterical.

Pizzocca I can assure you, I'm more hysterical than her . . . I'm about to burst!

Mirone (*he continues massaging the girl*) What's happened, what's the matter?

Pizzocca Somebody's put the evil eye on me!

Mirone Evil eye? Oh dear . . . Very nasty . . . Tell me more!

Pizzocca I found myself in bed . . . with the Judge . . . Imagine it . . . Naked! I did have a hat on, though!

Mirone Well hallelujah!

Pizzocca And he was naked too . . . No clothes . . . And no hat, either!

A few young men and women filter on from back-stage. Mirone leaves the hysterical girl to their attentions. As the dialogue continues, they continue the massage.

Mirone (*he changes tone*) But were you making love?

Pizzocca I don't know . . . I was asleep.

Mirone Shame!

Pizzocca Under the sheet there was me, the Judge, two
guards, and the Cardinal!

Mirone Fascinating! Do tell. What were you all doing?

*The hysterical girl is unobtrusively ushered off-stage.
As the dialogue continues, the Chorus gathers around
Mirone and Pizzocca.*

Pizzocca They say I started talking with a man's voice . . .
in Neapolitan! I've never even been to Naples!
(*Note 5.*)

Mirone In Neapolitan?

Pizzocca No, it's true. I actually heard myself.

Mirone I don't believe it! When did this happen?

Pizzocca I was just ringing a little bell. Like this . . . (*She
pulls from her pocket a small ritual bell.*) I was calling
his Honour the Judge down for lunch . . . Like so.

*She rings the bell, and we hear the voice of a sleepy
Barlocco from inside Pizzocca.*

Barlocco-Pizzocca Oh no . . . don't start waking me
with that wretched bell again!

Pizzocca returns to speaking in her own voice.

Pizzocca You hear that? A voice in my belly! D'you think
I've been possessed by the devil?

Mirone Are you out of your mind? Don't even think
it . . . In times like these, they'll have you straight on
the bonfire. Burned at the stake. Roasted! Without
even peeling you first!

Pizzocca Yes, I mean to say . . . But something worse has
happened . . . I haven't even told you the worst . . .

Mirone And what would this worst be?

Pizzocca I'll die of shame!

Mirone Forget the shame, just tell me. (*He changes tone. Severely*) Have you ended up pregnant?

Pizzocca Worse! I've sprouted tits!

The Chorus move in and form a circle round the two in order to facilitate the gag of inflating her breasts. They seem both shocked and amused.

Mirone Tits, now? At your age!

Pizzocca Yes!

Mirone Why, didn't you get tits when you were a girl?

Pizzocca Yes, but they were small . . . Squashed . . . They went in instead of out. But now they're growing like crazy . . .! Look! Look, right now . . . Aaargh! My tits are swelling! (*She begins undoing her bodice. Realising that nothing is happening, she stops, and repeats the line more loudly.*) My tits are swelling! (*a second's wait, and then, in the previous tone*) My tits are not swelling! (*She turns to a girl behind her, and steps out of character.*) What's happening?

Girl from the Chorus (*whispering*) I can't find the tube!

Pizzocca You can't find the tube . . .? (*Her breasts suddenly begin to inflate.*) My breasts are . . . swelling! (*She undoes her bodice to reveal two breasts, swelling visibly.*)

Mirone Oof . . . Miraculous melons!

Chorus Gloria in excelsis deo!

Two members of the Chorus sound a fanfare from two trumpets.

Mirone And you're not happy?

Pizzocca But it's terrible, Father! I feel as if I've got someone under me, pumping me up. Look: they move! And when somebody comes in the room, they turn round and look. I've got inquisitive tits! And d'you know what's even more strange?

Mirone What?

Pizzocca I'm getting round bits round the back too. Look!

She turns round and lifts up her dress to reveal two visibly enlarged buttocks.

Mirone And are they afflicted with curiosity too?
Pizzocca (*looking alarmed*) Oh God . . . *now* what's happening to me?
Mirone I tell you what, this might help.

Father Mirone summons a girl from the Chorus. She places a small crown of flowers on Pizzocca's head.

Pizzocca What's that for?
Mirone Flowers. To ward off the evil eye. Does that feel any better?
Pizzocca No sir . . .! I'm getting the shakes again!
Mirone What d'you mean, 'the shakes'?
Pizzocca I've been getting them for three days . . . It just takes me over . . . My legs, my knees, my sides, my arms . . . they all start moving of their own accord . . . It's as if I've got someone inside me moving me like a puppet . . . Look . . . My foot's tapping, my foot, my foot (*She moves one leg repeatedly.*) and the other foot, (*as above*) and my arm . . . (*She raises one arm, and in so doing she cuffs Father Mirone.*) And look at my belly . . .

Her belly moves in time with her thighs. Everyone on-stage begins to copy her, creating a musical rhythm.

What is all this? Oh, goodness, it's wonderful!
Mirone (*he calls out to his acolytes*) Here, everyone! It's the tarantella! Come on, let's dance! One, two three.

The girls of the Chorus put on shawls to cover their heads. A profusion of ribbons, leaves and flowers. The dance begins. Everyone on stage takes part, and they

*may also play percussion instruments, wind instruments
and viols. Fireworks go off. Pizzocca dances wildly in
their midst. In a half-turn towards the wings, she may
be substituted by a stand-in, who does double
somersaults, one after the other. Everyone sings.*

*As the songs, shouting and music continue, the
lights dim as everyone falls to the ground, exhausted.
In the half-light they get up again and rearrange the
stage for the courthouse, in full view of the audience.*

SCENE TWO

*A trumpet sounds. The lights come up. The public take
their place in the courtroom. A guard beats on the floor
with a long staff.*

Guard Be upstanding for the Judge!

Enter Judge de Tristano, followed by the Inquisitor.

Judge Let's begin! Call the first witness.
Guard She is a woman, your Honour. Her name is
  Jacoba Stareffa, and she says she was born in Crotone
  in Calabria.
Judge We know her well. She comes of her own free
  will, so she has the right to testify from behind the
  screen.

*The girl enters, behind a screen, but emerges from
behind it almost at once.*

Jacoba I don't need that. I have nothing to hide . . . I am
  a woman of virtue, not like you, Judge, who promised
  not to haul me into the courtroom, and now here
  I am!
Judge I promised you on condition that you would tell
  the truth, but you have lied to me.

Jacoba What lie, your Honour? I have given you visible
   proof . . . I have even bared my . . .
Judge Your wounds . . . Yes, we have already seen
   them . . .
Inquisitor And what might these wounds be?
Jacoba These breasts of mine! (*She makes as if to bare
   her breast.*)
Judge Cover yourself!
Voice of the People (*in chorus*) No, don't cover yourself!
   We want to see the wounds too!

*Enter the Cardinal. He is ushered to a seat by one of
the Guards.*

Judge Silence, or I'll have you thrown out! (*to Jacoba*)
   Jacoba Stareffa, you are a liar! For a start, you swore
   to me that the Captain of the Guard was dead, killed
   in your arms . . .
Jacoba But it's true!
Judge And you also told me that his body was burned in
   the fire at the Cathedral . . .
Jacoba And so it was!
Judge Silence! Well perhaps you can explain how, this
   very morning, the guards of this court found him, isn't
   this strange, in Crotone, in your home town, and very
   much alive and kicking!
Chorus Alive?
Jacoba Alive? Have you really found him? Oh no, that's
   impossible! It's a lie, a trap, to trick me!
Judge Silence, or I really will trick you: into prison!
   Now, my girl, you're going to have to tell me the
   truth, because anyway this Captain, this resurrected
   lover of yours, has already told us everything we need
   to know. For instance, we now know that this whole
   charade, from the stolen statue of St George, to your
   making love in the sacristan's bed, right through to
   the alleged killing of the Captain, was an elaborate

trick, to divert our attention from the real nature of the machinations behind the Cathedral fire.

Inquisitor Might one know more about the nature of these machinations?

Judge Since you ask, sir, we are talking about the large profits which certain groups of people are going to reap from the rebuilding of the Cathedral, which they deliberately arranged to have set on fire!

Inquisitor Can you name names?

Judge As of this moment, I can reveal to you that the shameful confraternity of these criminals is to be found among the city's building contractors and in the person of the Archbishop himself.

Chorus The Archbishop?

Cardinal (*rising to his feet*) Sir, you should be careful in your allegations.

Judge We are familiar with the old proverb, your Eminence: 'Blaspheme against Christ,' they say, 'and you will be forgiven. But accuse his Bishop, and you will be hanged!'

A murmuring among the bystanders in the Court.

Cardinal Listen to him, the blasphemer!

Judge I am risking my neck here, but before you succeed in silencing me, I'll give you something to think about! In the evidence that I have sent to the Grand Council, I show how the leading lights of this city have been sitting down at a feast. The banks served the portions, and you, your Eminence, were the cook!

Voice among the Public He's very brave!

Voice among the Public If you ask me, he's done for!

Voice among the Public Nobody can save you now!

Cardinal No! This is unacceptable! This is a vile slander! What proof do you have? If it's all like the fairy tale that you were telling, about the Captain of the Guard suddenly coming back to life . . .

Judge (*to the guards*) Very well . . . Bring in the Captain.

The two guards lead the Captain to the witness bench, closely guarded.

Behold, the man!

Jacoba Antonio . . .! My sweet love, you are alive! Oh, life of mine! A miracle! Let me embrace you!

Judge Alright, you can spare us the play-acting.

Woman Let me touch this Lazarus!

Guard (*stopping the woman in her tracks*) Go back to your place!

Second Guard (*to Jacoba, who is screaming and trying to free herself*) Stop pushing!

The prisoner takes advantage of the kerfuffle to make his escape. He goes up the steps leading into the wings.

Judge Look out . . . He's running up into the rafters!

Voice of a Man Catch him!

Voice of a Woman Where can he go, though? That leads to the roof.

Other Voice of a Man If he gets up on the roof, they'll never catch him.

A Guard points an arquebus up at the skylight.

Judge No, don't shoot! He's the only witness I have!

Voice from the Public Look, he's walking on the beams!

Guard Stay where you are!

The Guard fires at the fugitive Captain. From the skylight we hear a scream, then the Captain falls from above and crashes to the ground with a thud. Obviously this is a puppet, made up to look like the Captain.

Judge Damn you, you've taken away my only evidence!

Guard I only wanted to give him a warning, to stop . . .

Judge Well, you stopped him a bit too damn much . . .
Completely, in fact!

*The Guards lift the Captain and carry him off stage,
among the mourning laments of Jacoba and other
women following the corpse.*

Chorus (*singing*)
My son, my breath . . .
My son, my breath . . .
You left me!
My breath . . .
My breath . . . My breath . . .
Jacoba Aaaah . . . Murderers! You killed him on
purpose . . .! Oh, the pain . . .!

SCENE THREE

The bystanders come back into the courtroom.

Inquisitor (*in stentorian voice*) Silence! I demand that
the proceedings be adjourned, in order that we can all
recover from the shock of this incident, and also
evaluate the very serious allegations that Judge de
Tristano has advanced.
First Woman Who *is* that man?
Other Woman The head of the Inquisition!
Cardinal Just a moment . . . I don't see any reason for
adjourning . . . I and my office have been cast under
the gravest of accusations by the lies of this
hypocritical Judge, who masquerades as a saintly man,
free of all corruption, yet has been found naked and
in flagrante fornicating with his serving woman,
before the very eyes of his guards . . .

A murmuring among the crowd.

... who has other lovers all over the place, and who has even raped one of the witnesses!

Chorus No!

Judge And who is this witness that I'm supposed to have violated?

Cardinal This young girl who now stands before you . . .

The Public (*these lines are spoken more or less in unison*)
Can it be true?
It wouldn't surprise me!
I always suspected something.
Reckon he's the one!
The usual filth!
Where will it ever stop?

Re-enter Jacoba, like a fury.

Jacoba Oh no! Don't think you're going to get away with this . . . You have killed my man . . . And now I'm going to give you the names of those who paid me to go to the Judge and show him my breasts in order to ensnare him!

Chorus Well said! That's it . . . You tell 'em, girl!

Judge Oh Lord, I thank you, for giving me a new witness to my advantage!

All the audience in the courtroom surround the girl and hide her from the view of the audience.

First Woman Tell us, say what you know!

Other Woman Bravo! Speak out, girl!

Guard (*calling out*) Your Honour, this girl has lost her head!

Inquisitor In what sense has she lost it?

First Woman Lost her head through love . . .

Judge No. Through the knife!

From among the crowd, Francipante tosses Jacoba's head to the Judge. At that same instant, the circle

*around the girl opens; we see the body of the woman,
beheaded. The public scream in horror. The Judge
displays the head of the decapitated woman in his
hands, which is obviously a dummy head made up to
look like Jacoba.*

It's true, Justice, like Fortune, is blind . . . But when it
comes to chopping the heads off inconvenient witnesses,
it sees, and it sees very well!

*Blackout. The traverse depicting the Judge's palace is
lowered.*

SCENE FOUR

Lights come up. Enter Francipante.

Francipante (*to the wings*) Barlocco, hurry up! This is
the moment. This is where you seduce the Judge . . .
Hey, you look gorgeous! He'll be putty in your hands!

*Enter Barlocco-Pizzocca, wearing an elegant bodice
and lace bloomers. She wears a dazzling blonde wig.*

Barlocco-Pizzocca I have to tell you, I feel like a
Carnival queen!
Francipante I told you, you're magnificent!

*Enter two She-Devils with a gown, which they put on
Barlocco. Around his shoulders they place a long silk
shawl, and then they put a fan in his hands.*

Ladies and gentlemen, behold the marvel! The caterpillar
transforms into a butterfly! But Barlocco, mind that
you don't go becoming a woman for real! Because,
don't forget, we devils can only play-act languors and
sighs. If we do it for real, we're cursed for all eternity.

Take this fan, and wave it – not too much wind,
though!

Barlocco-Pizzocca I really can't see what's the point of
going through with this charade. This Judge is
completely done for anyway . . . They've completely
discredited him . . . they've even chopped the heads
off his witnesses . . . why are we even bothering?

Francipante You're right, he is pretty well done for.
But he's still got a lot of people helping him, and
supporting him, and that might end up saving him.
So the time has come to deal the final blow! Look out,
here he comes!

Barlocco-Pizzocca (*looking towards the wings*) Oh well,
wish me luck.

Francipante (*to the Little Devils*) You lot, vanish! (*to
Barlocco-Pizzocca*) And remember, your whole
reputation is at stake here!

Barlocco-Pizzocca I'm ready!

SCENE FIVE

*Enter the Judge. He turns to the windows of the Palace,
and calls loudly for Pizzocca.*

Judge Pizzocca! (*He crosses paths with Barlocco-Pizzocca,
but does not recognise her. He has a moment of
uncertainty, and then crosses back to her.*) Good day,
madam . . . (*to the windows again*) Pizzocca, come
down and open the door, I've forgotten my key.
Pizzocca, where have you vanished to?

Barlocco-Pizzocca I haven't vanished anywhere . . . I'm
here!

Judge Madam, I do not know you . . . Who are you?

Barlocco-Pizzocca I am Pizzocca!

Judge What do you mean, Pizzocca? She's my house-keeper. You look nothing like her!

Barlocco-Pizzocca Of course . . . because I have always sacrificed myself for you, and disguised myself as an old bat! I have never shown myself as I really am. But now I've had enough!

Judge And what about the Lombard dialect that you have always used?

Barlocco-Pizzocca That was the dialect of my grandfather, a saintly man, from Lodi, who reared me and also educated me.

Judge I don't believe this! You mean to say, for all this time those stuffy old clothes have just been a disguise?

Barlocco-Pizzocca Yes!

They walk towards the entrance to the palace, and the traverse depicting the front of the palace is raised. We find ourselves in the drawing room from previously. On-stage are Devils, who watch the proceedings.

Judge Why, though? Why would you do that?

Barlocco-Pizzocca So as not to provoke disturbances in you, Master. We all know that you live in mortal fear of the perils of the flesh.

Judge That's no business of yours! And anyway, when and how could *you* have provoked 'disturbances' in me?

Barlocco-Pizzocca (*she flings open her cloak, and reveals two swelling breasts overflowing the daring décolleté of her dress*) With these, Master!

Judge Ye gods!

Barlocco-Pizzocca You like them? Eh? Do you really think that I could have waved them before you, this feast of breasts and buttocks? And how many laxatives would you have had to take then? You would have squittered yourself away down the toilet pan! Pardon the vulgarity!

Judge Cover yourself up, please . . . And stop it . . . You won't trap me: this is all carnival trickery. It's a trick: those are balloons, blown up . . . with air!

Barlocco-Pizzocca Sir, in that case it remains only to touch them with your hand! (*She grasps his wrists and pulls him to her.*) Touch me, sir, at your pleasure. If they are trickery, take them in your hands! Make the most of it, this show is for free!

Judge (*tears himself furiously from the woman's embrace, and moves abruptly away from her*) No! No! Stop that!

Barlocco-Pizzocca (*going over to him*) Don't be frightened, Sir! There is nobody here.

Judge These are mad times that we're living in! Everything's falling on my head! On one side they're coming down on me because I'm a threat to the rich and powerful . . . And on the other I'm accused of being a fornicator, because you climbed into my bed naked! But I don't remember ever seeing these breasts of yours! Now, tell me . . . Enough playing about! Who are you really?

Barlocco-Pizzocca I am a deeply sensual woman!

Judge Have you gone out of your mind?

Barlocco-Pizzocca Yes, a deeply sensual woman. And the things I have done for you! Mortified myself, cancelled myself out, just to be close to you, and preserve your reputation intact!

Judge My reputation? What do you mean?

Barlocco-Pizzocca Yes . . . During the daytime, in order not to give you disturbances, I disguised myself. I bound up my overflowing breasts, I pulled in my backside with murderous corsets . . . For thirty years I've hardly been able to breathe! I spoke with a Lombard dialect . . . I ate garlic and onions, in order to give myself dog's breath. But the more ugly I made myself, the more my unbounded love for you grew!

Judge Love for me?

Barlocco-Pizzocca I am hugely, deeply passionate about you, Master . . . And in order to give rip to this passion . . . to give vent to the desires of my body . . . at night, while you were asleep I unleashed my bounden breasts and my abundant buttocks, and I went off, to the taverns, and I went with men, and I gave myself over to SIN . . .!

Judge With men? This is incredible! I'm all topsy-turvy! But how were you able to descend so far into lasciviousness and still continue living in my house?

Barlocco-Pizzocca What do you mean? What are you saying? Lasciviousness? For thirty years I have remained in your service . . . kneeling before you . . . disguised as the old, ignorant Pizzocca, just so as to stay close to you . . . And now that I am no longer capable of hiding my huge love for you, I reveal myself for what I am . . . I cry aloud my passion, and instead of taking me in your arms and drowning me in kisses you insult me! Offend me! Humiliate me!

Is that all the Christian charity that you have? I admit I have gone with men, and I weep in repentance, but you, hypocrite and so-called gentle-man that you are, you condemn me . . . You stand with the Pharisees, Master. You were with Pontius Pilate, and you too washed your hands! Now I no longer love you, Judge . . .! Now I despise you . . . I hate you . . .! And I spit on you too! Pah!

She spits in his face, and leaves the stage.

The lights dim. Music. Enter other Devils, who rearrange the stage in full view of the audience.

SCENE SIX

*Enter the Cardinal and the Inquisitor. They kneel
together as if to pray. At the back of the stage we see
Francipante, who listens to everything with some
amusement. Gregorian chant is heard in the background.*

Inquisitor Your Eminence, I believe that this time, with
the Captain coming down from the rafters, and the
girl decapitated, we have perhaps gone a bit far! We
should ease up.

Cardinal Perhaps. Maybe we should do like the bear
did. It caught the rabbit, and the poor rabbit was
terrified. So the bear began dancing on its feet like a
clown, and then, when the rabbit relaxed and began
falling about laughing, the bear, between one laugh
and the next – gulp – swallowed it whole.

Inquisitor Good idea. But where's the bear who's going
to do the dancing?

Cardinal A female bear. Pizzocca. She is coming to court
to testify against de Tristano.

Inquisitor Pizzocca? His servant?

Cardinal The very one . . . The woman came to me . . .
and offered her services . . . I hardly recognised her,
she seems like a woman who has been liberated . . .
She even speaks in Neapolitan.

Inquisitor Neapolitan? She *must* be liberated! So, Pizzocca
the betrayer, comes to ruin her master! And I suppose
this cost you a few gold coins?

Cardinal Of course . . . I told her that as of this moment
she is a free woman. And she made me promise a
passport for her, so that she can flee as soon as de
Tristano has been found guilty.

Inquisitor Betrayed and abandoned even by his servant! And then they say that the judge's profession is the best of all!

Cardinal Indeed . . . What patent nonsense!

Chuckling with delight they exit, in a gentle crescendo of Gregorian chant.

SCENE SEVEN

From an upper arch, stage left, Francipante calls Barlocco-Pizzocca in a loud voice. He arrives wearing Pizzocca's nightdress. During the dialogue between the two of them, the serving girls prepare the Judge's bedroom.

Francipante Hurry up, because in a minute the clock will strike, and you're going to have to pass the body back to Pizzocca!

Barlocco-Pizzocca All right . . . I'm going as fast as I can, but all these costume changes are getting a bit much.

Francipante Right. Let's have a look at you – check the details.

Barlocco-Pizzocca Why?

Francipante When Pizzocca wakes up, she needs to find that she's back at the start.

Barlocco-Pizzocca What do you mean, the start?

Francipante Doesn't matter if you don't understand . . .

The clock chimes.

That's it – bye-byes time . . . Enjoy the snooze!

The clock strikes. Pizzocca gives a shudder, kicks her legs about, and falls on the bed, sound asleep.

SCENE EIGHT

We hear the ringing of a bell. Pizzocca wakes up.

Pizzocca (*she looks around, in a daze*) Oh goodness . . .
what a sleep I've had! Where am I? Oh no – in the
master's bed again! Why do I always seem to wake up
in the Judge's bed? God, and what a dream I had . . .!
I had two tits . . . Oh, what tits, oh, what a tittery . . .
(*She feels her breasts.*) I sprouted tits! I've still got
them! All nice and round! Oh, a miracle!! Oh, Saint
Agatha of the big tits, I thank you! (*She realises that
she still has the necklaces from the previous scene.*)
The necklaces . . . I don't know if they're a miracle of
St Agatha, or if I just didn't manage to get them off
during the scene-change, 'cos it was so quick . . .
So maybe it wasn't a dream . . . The dancing, for
instance, I'm sure that was real . . . And what a lot
of dancing . . .! (*She makes a dance step or two.*)
I wonder if my evil eye has gone. And I wonder if I've
still got a nice round bum!

*She lifts up her nightshirt, revealing her backside, and
twists herself round in a strange pantomime trying to
look at her reflection in the mirror on top of the chest
of drawers.*
    *Enter the Judge. Ogling the woman from behind
the mirror, he falls into a passionate frenzy.*

Judge Oh, my sweet Pizzocca . . .
Pizzocca (*she is alarmed, covers herself up, and as she
turns round she sees the Judge*) Oh, your Honour . . .!
You gave me such a fright! I thought it was my
bottom talking to me!

Judge (*going over to her*) My sweet Pizzocca . . . How lucky that you are here! I was scared that you had run away for ever!

Pizzocca Me, run away, your Honour?

Judge Oh, I pray you . . . Enough of this pretending, and hurting each other!

Pizzocca We have hurt each other?

Judge Yes, dear, sweet Pizzocca!

Pizzocca Oh, sir, you are losing your mind!

Judge You called me Pontius Pilate . . .

Pizzocca I called you a conscious pirate?

Judge And it's true . . . I am Pontius, a Pilate and a hypocritical Pharisee, but I will put all that behind me. I will stop taking laxatives and enemas . . . Now I open my heart to you . . . I declare myself. I am in love with you . . .

Pizzocca Your Honour, just lie down on the bed, relax . . . I'll bring you a nice cup of tea . . .

Judge No, Pizzocca . . . Let me embrace you!

Pizzocca What are you saying, illustrious sir?

Judge (*he seizes her and tries to embrace her*) And enough of that crude dialect, like a Lombard peasant woman! Go back to speaking in that Neapolitan that so consumes me with pleasure.

Pizzocca I have to speak in Neapolitan? That's it – I hand in my notice now!

The Judge tries to embrace her.

Don't squeeze me like that, your Honour . . .! I'm sweating all over!

Judge Yes, that's right, sweat, sweat, and let me sniff you. Let me get drunk on the smell!

He is literally on top of her. He flings open her nightdress and handles her inflated breasts. Pizzocca

*looks as if she is about to faint, but she puts up a
desperate resistance.*

Lovely, these palpitating breasts of yours, which you
kept hidden! They're mine! They're mine! All of them!
(*He tries to seize her breasts.*) Oh look at them . . .
swelling to the touch . . . let me hold them!

Pizzocca (*stopping him*) Stop that! Get your hands off
my new tits!

The Judge hauls her across towards the bed.

No! Not on the bed! It's a sin! Your Honour . . .
(*coming out of character*) I've got my backside half
hanging off the bed . . . You're crucifying me!

*She refers to the inconvenient position in which she
finds herself.*

Judge I'll pull you up! (*He does as he says.*)
Pizzocca Thank you!

*Now she sits on the bed. The Judge attempts to
handle her breasts again.*

That's enough, your Honour!

Judge That's enough 'your Honour' . . . Call me
Alfonso!

Pizzocca At once, sir. (*She calls into the wings.*) Alfonso,
the Judge wants you!

Judge Who are you calling? *I'm* Alfonso!

Pizzocca Oh yes . . . You're Alfonso . . . (*as above*) It's
alright, forget Alfonso, we've found him . . . He was
here all the time!

Judge That's enough! You're making fun of me, you
cruel whore!

Pizzocca What did you say?

Judge A little while ago, didn't you tell me that you're a
deeply sensual woman?

Pizzocca Sensual?

Judge And didn't you tell me that you went with men?

Pizzocca Did I?

Judge Howling at the moon like a she-wolf, you said. Let me hear you howling.

Pizzocca What, like a wolf?

Judge Yes!

Pizzocca I'm not sure if I can do it very well . . . I'm a bit out of practice . . . (*She howls like a wolf, positioning her neck and body in the manner of a wolf howling at the moon.*) Ooooooooooh!

Judge Sublime! Oh, Pizzocca, you drive me wild! Come to me, vile she-wolf of the crossroads!

He pulls across the curtains of the bed. From his grunts and her protests we gather that they are doing naughty things together There is music, and the bed exits slowly from the stage, in a paroxysm of musical crescendo.

Blackout.

SCENE NINE

A large arras is brought on-stage, to act as the backdrop for the courtroom. Enter the Inquisitor, followed by the guards, the crowd, Francipante and Judge de Tristano, who is in chains and wearing a prisoner's outfit. Trumpets sound.

Inquisitor Silence in court! (*to Judge de Tristano*) The Council of the Inquisition accuses you of having cast vile slanders upon the leading figures and honest men of this city, inducing the grave suspicion that they conjoined in a conspiracy to burn down the Cathedral in order to extract from it ignoble profits by speculation.

Judge But I showed you the written evidence for all that!

Murmuring among the crowd.

Inquisitor Silence! Furthermore, the aforementioned
Judge is accused of demeaning his high office through
fornication and the violation of female witnesses.

Judge That is a blatant and premeditated lie!

Murmuring among the crowd.

Inquisitor We shall begin with hearing the witnesses!
Call Pizzocca Ganassa, servant of the accused.

*Enter Barlocco-Pizzocca. She crosses the courtroom
with the bearing of a grand lady, wearing the fancy
clothes that we saw previously. She is accompanied by
a guard. She winks at the Judge, blows him a kiss, and
goes to sit on the witness bench. A ferment and
chattering among the public.*

Barlocco-Pizzocca Yoo-hoo!

Judge (*dumbfounded*) Pizzocca, what on earth are you
up to?

Barlocco-Pizzocca Relax, sugar-plum!

First Woman God, she's looking tasty. She looks like
another woman!

Second Woman Surely it can't be her . . . It must be her
younger sister.

First Woman A bit of a trollop, if you ask me.

Guard Order! Silence in court!

Inquisitor Tell us, Pizzocca, do you and the Judge enjoy
relations of intimacy?

Barlocco-Pizzocca Yes, your Honour, I have had a
passion for him for quite a while, and I think I can
say that he feels the same about me.

Murmuring among the crowd.

Inquisitor And would these sentiments also be carnal in nature?

Barlocco-Pizzocca (*coming down from the witness bench*) I wouldn't know, Sir. You wish to know if we have embraced in intimacy, with quiet passions . . .

Inquisitor Yes.

Barlocco-Pizzocca (*going over to where the Judge stands in his chains*) No sir, we did not.

Chorus Aaaah!

Barlocco-Pizzocca We romped all over each other, in a frenzy of passion, and we gave each other such satisfaction that even the bed on which we performed our sin . . . was creaking with passion and wanting more.

Shouting, laughter, a bustle of movement and applause. Francipante also applauds.

Chorus Hooray!

Man Will you listen to her!

Other Man I'd like to have been the bed!

Woman Bravo, Pizzocca!

Judge Damn you! You'll get me burned at the stake!

Barlocco-Pizzocca Relax, sugar-plum!

Inquisitor Silence, or I'll have you all thrown out! (*to Pizzocca*) And are you also aware of the fact that your employer has attempted to violate a female witness?

Barlocco-Pizzocca Violate a girl, sir? Yes, they gave me the full story of that.

Inquisitor Who told you the story? We want names!

Barlocco-Pizzocca Er – the Cardinal, sir.

Chorus The Cardinal?

Barlocco-Pizzocca He told me all the details. And then he paid me lots of money!

Man That's disgraceful!

Other Man Hardly surprising, though!

First Woman Quite normal!

Barlocco-Pizzocca He paid me to come here and tell the whole story before the court!

Cardinal You liar! It's a lie! You're under arrest, I'll have you flogged! (*to Pizzocca*) Whore!

Barlocco-Pizzocca A whore repented, sir!

Cardinal Show me the proof that I paid you!

Inquisitor This is hardly the language for a Cardinal!

Barlocco-Pizzocca (*showing a small chest of money*) There's the money!

Inquisitor And how is one to recognise the provenance of this money? Is the name of its donor perhaps written all over it?

Barlocco-Pizzocca Your Honour, what you say is true . . . The money provides no evidence of its source. However, there are these earrings . . . and necklaces . . . rings and bracelets, which the Cardinal gave me in addition . . . and on each of those one can easily discover the donor. For instance, the engraving on this ring: (*She reads.*) 'To Clarissa, with all my love, Giovanni Piccolo.'

First Woman That came from me! That's my ring! I gave it to the Cardinal, for the Cathedral building fund!

Barlocco-Pizzocca And then there's this very distinctive necklace with the dark green gems.

Man That looks like the one I donated.

Judge Oh, Pizzocca, you have saved me!

Shouting, applause, insults and laughter among the crowd. Barlocco-Pizzocca wraps herself up, covering herself from head to toe in a large cloak.

First Woman The usual bunch of swindlers!

Second Woman The Judge is not guilty! Lock up the Cardinal!

Chorus Now the lid's off the sewer! Let the swindlers and liars be put in chains! Lock them away and throw away the key!

Inquisitor Silence, or you'll all be out! Be quiet!

The noise slowly subsides, and the voice of the Inquisitor rises above it.

Pay attention and listen! By judgement of this Tribunal, it is ordered that Judge Alfonso Ferdinando de Tristano be absolved of all the charges.

Chorus Hooray for justice!

Inquisitor And a new Inquiry shall be opened into these crimes.

All the participants in the trial surround Pizzocca, hiding her from the audience's view.

Chorus Well done . . . At last . . . A woman who'll stand up for herself!

Inquisitor You, Pizzocca, are under arrest for having made a mockery of the high office of magistrate. Put her in irons! Lock her away!

Barlocco-Pizzocca Don't touch me! Leave me alone. I have a safe-conduct!

The circle around Pizzocca opens. As the guard comes towards her to put her in chains, the shawl falls open, and instead of Pizzocca we find a small Devil, who leaps here and there, giving mocking cries and then escapes. There is laughter among the crowd, and then everyone, including the arras and except Francipante and Barlocco-Pizzocca, exits. Music.

SCENE TEN

The Master Devil Francipante grabs Barlocco-Pizzocca as he tries to escape by hiding behind the arras as it is carried off-stage. A new arras is now brought on stage by various Devils. It portrays scenes of hell. From

*behind it, out pop the heads of various other Devils,
who watch the trial of Barlocco.*

Francipante You, bastard, traitor, worse than Judas,
where do you think you're running off to? Come here!

Barlocco-Pizzocca Leave me alone, Maestro! Let me go!

Francipante Stop right there! You may think you're very
clever, but let me tell you, you're done for. You just
wait . . .

Barlocco-Pizzocca I admit it, Maestro, I failed in my
mission.

Francipante Your orders were to ruin and corrupt this
Judge, but you went and did the opposite. You saved
him!

Chorus of Devils Ha, ha, ha, ha, ha!

Barlocco-Pizzocca But I never expected to end up stuck
in a woman's body.

Chorus of Devils He never expected . . .!

Francipante Stuck? Don't put the blame on the body.
You wretch. You had a lovely time in that woman, a
whale of a time!

Chorus of Devils A lovely time! A lovely time!

Barlocco-Pizzocca And I still remain possessed!

Chorus of Devils (*disappointed*) Ooooh hoooo!

Francipante Don't tell me I didn't warn you of the
dangers!

Barlocco-Pizzocca Oh yes, you warned me . . . But tell
me, Maestro, have you ever lived in a woman's body?

Francipante No, never.

Barlocco-Pizzocca Do you not know that anyone who
takes on a woman's body also wears her heart . . . her
emotions . . . her passions?

Francipante No, that I did not know.

Barlocco-Pizzocca So you're not such a good Master
Devil after all . . . Really you're just a poor devil like
the rest of us!

Chorus of Devils (*mockingly*) A poor devil! Hee, hee!

Barlocco-Pizzocca And since you are just a poor devil . . . who are *you* to judge and condemn *me*? You trapped me in this woman's love . . . and now you are surprised that I was swept away by it! Well fair enough, I understand. This is like the justice of men. Whichever way you turn, you always end up guilty! So now go ahead and dissolve me in the infernal shite, and let's have an end to it!

Francipante Oh no! That would be too easy – too convenient! Shall I tell you what your real punishment is going to be? You are going to remain locked in the body of that woman for ever!

Chorus of Devils (*tremendous general laughter*) Ha, ha, ha, ha!

Barlocco-Pizzocca But is that a sentence, Maestro, or is it a gift?

Chorus of Devils (*as above*) Ha, ha, ha, ha, ha, ha!

Everyone exits, taking the arras with them.

SCENE ELEVEN

Enter Judge de Tristano.

Judge (*addressing the audience directly*) Well, what a hurly-burly! Now I suppose you'll be curious to find out how it went with my trial . . . Actually, it went very well! And so, here I am, found not guilty of all the accusations, including having sullied the honour of the 'good' men of this city. But then the Tribunal of the Inquisition opened a new Inquiry . . . Into what? Into whom? Guess . . . Into the crime of the Cathedral fire? Into corruption in the builders' corporation? Into the archbishopric? No. Into me . . .! And in particular into my suspected affiliation with the religious sect of

Michele da Lentini. They dragged me through four
trials, together with the heretics . . . In the end,
Michele and three of his followers were sentenced to
burn at the stake . . . which is a regular event, to
celebrate the burning of Savonarola. But not me! Out
of respect for my past profession as a judge, I was
sentenced only to be hanged. Aha! But then a miracle
happened.

*Trumpets sound. Enter the Inquisitor, from stage
right.*

Inquisitor (*to a roll of drums*) Silence in court. Hear ye,
hear ye. By intervention of His Magnificence the Duke
in person, who has granted him a pardon of his life,
this sentence is to be commuted to five years in the
galleys. This means that de Tristano will be shipped
aboard a galley or ship of the dukedom as an
oarsman, for the duration of his sentence!

Judge Well, see how well it's all turned out! Today's my
lucky day!

*Enter the two guards, the oarsmen, and the Prison
Warder, who is helmsman of the galley.*

First Guard Take this oar, and prepare to row!
Helmsman Raise your oars, and prepare to row!
Judge Just a moment, this is the point where we do the
envoi!
Chorus of Oarsmen The what?
Judge That's French. It's the speech that closes the show
. . . The summing-up, if you like.
Chorus of Oarsmen Oh alright, fair enough.

*The guards, oarsmen, etc, leave the stage. Only the
Judge remains.*

Judge (*To the audience*) It's alright, don't panic! Don't
think that I'm about to serve up a sermon on the

impossibility of extracting men from their endless games of wickedness . . . And then conclude with the hoary old chestnut that 'well, what do you want, there's nothing to be done . . . that's the way the world is!'

No! I want to finish by talking of you, the audience, of those who have followed our show, and enjoyed it, laughing where appropriate, and in order to let it be understood that they are more than usually intelligent, they grasp and immediately understand every joke and allusion . . . They don't even let us finish the sentence . . . 'Ha, ha!' So that all the rest who are a bit slow are mortified, and laugh without knowing why.

Then there's the person who, in order not to be shown up, laughs at the beginning of *every* sentence, even the most tragic. (*He pauses.*) Then there's the one with his wife next to him explaining all the jokes . . . And there's the one who only laughs as he's on his way out of the theatre, because he's finally understood the joke! Then there's the jolly fellow who claps away, and his wife hisses at him: 'What are you doing? It's *you* that the actor's making fun of!' And he, in order not to let anyone see, pretends to be dusting off his face and sleeves, and doesn't laugh again for the whole evening.

No, I would most like to make a dedication to those who aren't here this evening . . . or, if they are here, are well disguised and hidden. I refer to those members of the audience who laugh only if they are very sure that the joke is at someone else's expense, and never mind who it is. As long as the joke is about those who have a different way of speaking, or who come from another country, who are different, who have another smell, another colour . . . of their face, or feet, and who enjoy blowing raspberries at them and shouting: 'Go back to your own country!' . . . 'Go home!' And if there happens to follow some throwing of stones, or a good kicking, it's really a lot better. I'm talking about those people who at every opportunity spout: 'We are the master race, we are the best! We are the brainiest, the smartest, the cleverest, and the most in-tune . . . And we've got the biggest . . . ' understandings, of course . . .

In short, I am speaking of imbeciles, which is a race apart! The imbeciles who at every opportunity wave flags and sing national anthems . . . and who seem to think that they're making history! Those that launch themselves against anyone who comes from the other side of the river. The imbeciles who are incapable of listening to any point of view other than their own. The imbeciles who applaud any act of theft, and who say: 'This new leader may be a thief, but if he steals for himself, he may allow us to steal a bit too!' The imbeciles who contrive to produce tremendous disasters, but never notice a thing! (*He pauses.*) And I would conclude that I, personally, I far prefer professional criminals to run-of-the-mill imbeciles. Yes, because criminals take a break every once in a while . . . but imbeciles, never!

He exits.

SCENE TWELVE

Enter the Prisoners, including the Judge. Each of them holds a long oar. The proscenium is occupied for its entire width by oarsmen, standing about a metre apart. The Chief Helmsman orders them to sit to their oars.

Helmsman Let's have you! Get your oars in the water. Prepare to row. Anyone who doesn't row properly or who's out of time gets a whipping! Right, rooooow!

All the oarsmen extend their oars towards the audience and begin to row. We hear the rowers' song, growing in intensity.

Chorus
The wind goes through the plains.
It comes down from the mountain to the valley,
And loses itself in the sea.
The weather changes with the moons,
The storm changes the river,
Only the sun never changes.
A sad thing is the man who does not change.

A sad thing is the man who does not change,
Who does not live the seasons,
Who remains forever static.
No amount of killing makes him angry.
He doesn't leave himself open, nor does he lament,
And when he dies, nobody weeps,
It is as if he had never been born.

The procession of oarsmen moves across the proscenium and disappears into the wings. Meanwhile, at the back of the stage, men and women, some of whom may be puppets, wave them farewell. Enter a small rowing boat, following the galley at speed. On board the boat is Pizzocca.

Pizzocca Alfonso, wait for me . . . Alfonso, I love you! Alfonsooooo!

As the rowing boat disappears into the wings, the lights slowly dim.
     The End.

Translator's Notes

1. In the original play, the sheets were used for a shadow-theatre effect, so that the characters paraded behind the sheets, illuminated from behind. This effect was also used elsewhere in the original.

2. Here you may feel free to change the terminology if you find it excessively (or indeed not sufficiently) vulgar.

3. It is my opinion that a lot of fun could be had by having Pizzocca (and hence Barlocco-Pizzocca) played throughout by a male.

4. The *tammurriata* is a wild drumming-singing kind of thing, to be found in Southern Italy. I can provide recorded examples of such a thing, should they be required.

5. You may prefer to change some of the place-name references – for example, the recurring joke about Pizzocca speaking Neapolitan.

6. The original of *Il Diavolo* . . . was performed in North Italian dialect. I have translated it into standard English. However, we would welcome dialect or local regional versions.

7. There's nothing worse than English productions of Italian plays with the names mispronounced. If you are in doubt, write the names on a piece of paper and take them to your local pizza parlour, where somebody should be able to help you.

8. The scenery and stage settings for this play can be as simple or as complicated as you care to make them. In some places a painted traverse is called for (e.g., end of Act One Scene Four), as in English pantomime. This can be elaborate, or a simple canvas on poles carried by two people. The courtroom and the Judge's apartments may also be elaborate – period furnishings – or simple – imaginative use of boxes, steps etc. The important thing is to achieve a sense of a Renaissance stage-setting.

9. My brief in translating *Il Diavolo con le zinne* in this version for the National Theatre has been to remain as close as possible to a literal rendering of Fo's play, but to cut its running time by half. No mean undertaking! Some of the ruder bits have also been cleaned up.

10. If you have any comments or queries regarding the text, songs, music, etc, I can be contacted at: ed.emery@mcmail.com

Ed Emery,
Levanto,
September 1998

Unleashing the Powers of Liberation

Ed Emery interviewed by Jim Mulligan

With over 70 plays and a lifetime of political activity behind him, Dario Fo was awarded the 1997 Nobel Prize for Literature. The citation reads, 'With a blend of laughter and gravity he opens our eyes to abuses and injustices in society and also the wider historical perspective in which they can be placed.' Dario Fo is a great writer but he is also an outstanding actor, mime artist and musician. As well as his scripted work, he is an improviser of sketches about current political events. In addition to theatres, his performance spaces have included factories, football stadiums and public spaces.

The citation also makes reference to Fo's translator, Ed Emery, who works 'by staying close to the original text and retaining Dario Fo's allusions.'

Ed Emery reckons to spend most of his time working for the revolutionary communist transformation of society. He studied Greek and Latin at school, and then at Cambridge. Those being the years of hot protest, he stood for president of the nascent Cambridge Student Union and tore up his finals papers as part of a protest against the exam system. He has done his fair share of factory-gate leafletting and shares Fo's taste for anti-clericalism and scatology, having once been arrested for 'obscene behaviour in an ecclesiastical precinct' (a protest at St Paul's cathedral, for Chilean political prisoners), and having produced the only human turd ever to be thrown in the House of Commons (in support of Irish political prisoners). Ed Emery translates from a multitude of languages, and is slowly working through a project of translating the entire collected works of Dario Fo and Franca Rame.

I have a stormy relationship with my bosses – Dario and Franca, I mean. Periodically they sack me and cast me into outer darkness, but then we argue and shout, and now I have been appointed their more or less official translator in England. I love *The Devil in Drag*. It's a terrific piece for kids, really – devils going up people's bumholes, cardinals eating horse-shite and ladies on stage with inflating tits. Dario has a great reputation as a Leftist political playwright, and when you look at his work as a whole, it's a truly amazing, wonderful, funny, humane outpouring of stuff. He's thoroughly educational too – a mine of historical information and understandings about theatre.

At the start of *The Devil in Drag* there has been a fire in the cathedral of a Renaissance Italian city. The Judge is determined to nail the culprits. His inquiries lead straight back to the church hierarchy and big power interests represented by the Cardinal. The Judge appears to be incorruptible. He is also so repressed sexually that he is able to resist the advances of the girl Jacoba, sent by the Cardinal to seduce him. The Cardinal is as corrupt as he wishes the Judge to be. In order to ruin the Judge he gets him blind drunk, so that he ends up naked in bed with Pizzocca. The plan to ruin the reputation of the Judge is to be helped along by infiltrating a tiny devil up his backside, but this goes farcically wrong when the devil enters by mistake the body of Pizzocca, the Judge's elderly housekeeper. Pizzocca then fluctuates between wanton depravity and horror at her actions. Working with the Inquisition, the Cardinal contrives the death of witnesses who know the true story and the Judge is put on trial for fornication. Finally, as the Judge is removed from office and sentenced to be a galley slave, he casts off his inhibitions and declares his passion for Pizzocca.

For Ed Emery the story of the Lion and the Donkey is a key moment of the play's meaning. On a journey to the top of a mountain, the powerful lion persuades the donkey to carry him, saying they'll take turns. He reckons if he gets hungry, he can always eat the donkey. When it comes to the donkey's turn to ride he keeps slipping off, but then he finds a way to stay in place, good and solid. Stiff as a ramrod he gives a thrust of his loins, and jams himself up the lion's backside. When the lion protests he justifies himself: 'Forgive me your majesty, I can't help it – each of us has to hold on as best he can with what he's got . . .' Here we have the familiar elements of Dario Fo's work: oppressive religion, ruling class exploitation and the triumph of the oppressed masked in deference. To add to the zest, the Judge tells the story in the style of a pub joke.

The characters in *The Devil in Drag* are effectively stereotypes with their origins in the Commedia dell' Arte. So, for example we have the Learned Man, the Judge and the Pretty Girl. Despite this, a figure such as the Cardinal is meant to summon up images of corruption today – the corruption not just of churchmen but of all those in power who preach a moral code for others and ignore it in their own lives.

People have asked me, is *The Devil in Drag* a political play? In a curious sort of way, it is not. Not politics with a big P. Not like earlier Fo texts such as *Accidental Death of an Anarchist* and *Can't Pay? Won't Pay!* Here the politics are far more subdued. Take the Judge's final speech, for instance. At first sight it's downright wishy-washy – derived in fact from a passage in Aristophanes. On the other hand, when played in the right key it becomes a powerful plea for humanity and tolerance. And that, I suppose, is the real politics of Fo – an abiding concern for the ordinary people. Unleashing the powers of liberation, against the powers of oppression. For him, theatre can be a way of attacking those who have money and power, and having a fun time while you're doing it. And that, as much as anything, is why I translate him.

(For more information visit the Dario Fo and Franca Rame research page at http://www.emery.archive.mcmail.com)

Production Notes

STAGING AND SETTING

The scenery and setting for the play can be as simple or complicated as you like, but might have a Renaissance feel or be transported to other settings – Prohibition era America, for instance. If you can create wing space, so much the better, but the play will work if you can provide as many entrances and exits as possible. A trap door would be an added bonus providing the possibility of some great visual gags. There are a number of scene changes as the action moves from Judge Alfonso's residence to a court of law, a palace facade, the judge's apartments and bedroom etc. These changes should be made by the actors, whether it is the girls at the start of the play drawing back the washing hung out to dry to reveal the next scene or the devils in full view of the audience. In places a painted traverse is called for – this can easily be suggested by a simple canvas on poles carried on by actors. The settings should feel temporary, the tackier the better. You might like to give the impression that they can be packed up easily by a travelling troupe and toured to the next venue.

Make the *design* as big and bold as possible. You might like to borrow *costume* ideas from Commedia dell'Arte characters and adapt them accordingly. The furnishings in the courtroom and Judge's apartments need not be lavish. The curtained bed, however, is essential for the comedy to work. Stairs can be suggested by ladders which will also provide additional entrances and exits.

There is great scope for *puppetry*. The devil Barlocco shrinks to suppository size and the Captain falls from a great height. The script suggests a glove puppet and a dummy can be used. Originally the sheets were used for a shadow theatre effect so that the characters paraded behind the sheets and were illuminated from behind. You might want to reintroduce this idea and use a mixture of actors and shadow puppets to tell the story.

Music is very important to Fo's work. You might want to search out some of the folk music which has the strong political overtones he often uses. The actors sing and might also carry instruments to provide the odd fanfare, raspberry on trombone, drum roll and percussion, street call, where appropriate (or at inappropriate moments where someone needs bringing down to size). The tarantella and Gregorian chants might be prerecorded or specially composed and played live and irreverently by the chorus of devils.

Lighting might take into account the sixteenth-century Renaissance stage setting to create an impression of yellow-ish oil or candlelights. The devils need a spotlight and it would be great if they could appear in a flash of smoke.

CASTING

The Devil in Drag can be performed by as few as twelve and as many as fifty actors. The script offers clear guidance on how this can be achieved. Several of the female parts can be played by men and vice versa, in fact any combination is possible in keeping with the spirit of the piece. The play is suitable for a bold cast with a good sense of comedy and is not a piece for the faint-hearted. It can work brilliantly with a wide age-range of actors with dramatically different body shapes.

EXERCISES

Find out what special talents the group have such as an ability to juggle, handstand, walk on stilts, cartwheel, form a human mountain etc. Have them teach one another these skills throughout the rehearsal period. See how they can be incorporated in the piece.

Have the group walk around the space leading in turn from the nose, chin, bottom, groin or chest. Sustain one of these points as a centre, move into pairs and interact.

• Now have the group take on the character of the judge, Pizzocca or Barlocco. Have them imagine what the centre of that character is and how it would affect their mannerisms.

We know that Pizzocca is as dry as a stick and walks like an ostrich. Look at the other central characters and decide how they might be described and what animal they most resemble.

Take the transformation scene where Pizzocca is occupied by the devil Barlocco:

• Experiment with one actor using their own voice, which might start in a dialect and end up as received pronunciation, performing the transformation.
• Play the scene with Pizzocca as a woman and Barlocco a man.
• Take the same scene with both Barlocco and Pizzocca played by women and finally with both played by men.

Have the scene where Pizzocca/Barlocco declares love for the judge played by a man and then a woman in turn. Experiment with trying this combination with actors of different builds and ages – the judge might be aged eleven, female and tiny while Pizzocca/Barlocco is chunky, male and older.

Look at some of the visual gags, as when Jacoba loses her head/exposes her breast. See if Jacoba works well being played by a male member of the company. Find ways of revealing her breast to cause laughter and not shock. Her severed head might simply be a cabbage or a turnip. Find other instances where the play does not have to be treated realistically and you can fit in a gag instead.

Have the group develop their choral/storytelling skills by having them collectively tell the story of the donkey and the lion. One passes an object to another, whoever has the object – something associated with the play like the jar of dung balls for instance – picks up and continues the story. Make sure that the actors include the audience in the narrative and are aware at all times of their presence. Have the whole group enrich the storytelling experience with a mixture of animal noises, wailing drums, castanets, Jesus harp, drum rolls and percussion etc.

Suzy Graham-Adriani
February 1999

DON'T EAT LITTLE CHARLIE

Tankred Dorst

with Ursula Ehler
translated and adapted by
Ella Wildridge

Characters

Charlie

Olmo
his greedy-guts of a brother

Tana Schanzara, known as
Granmaha
waitress in the station buffet

Antunes o Rei
king of musicians, a black Brasilian

Pug

Fizzipizzi
the electrified girl

Man
with the huge carbuncle on his head,
the house-owner

Place: a rather chaotic room, half kitchen,
half living-room.

SCENE ONE

The radio's blaring away, noise and crackling. On the TV loud advertisements.

Olmo and Charlie are at the table. Pug sits quietly nearby. Olmo is stuffing his face with bread, cornflakes, cake. Charlie is chewing away slowly, stops, looks up. Granmaha, with a crown on her head, goes backward and forward, sweeping busily.

Granmaha (*irritatedly to Charlie*) Why aren't you eating?

Olmo (*with his mouth full*) I'm eating.

Charlie (*giggling*) My spoon's gone.

Granmaha And where might your spoon be?

Charlie (*giggling*) Olmo's gone and swallowed it.

Granmaha Your brother's a great eater, but even he wouldn't swallow your spoon.

Charlie But the spoon's gone.

Granmaha The things you make up!

Olmo I'm eating.

Granmaha There's no finding anything in this mess. TV's making a terrible racket! You could at least turn off the radio.

No one moves.

Pug (*calmly*) There's the spoon there, under the table.

Granmaha There, you see, there it is. (*She lifts it up.*) It's a good thing we've got you, Pug.

Pug That's what I say too.

Olmo That mutt stinks. He's got to go!

Pug I smell ever so sweet.

235

Olmo He stinks.

Pug If I didn't smell, I wouldn't be real.

Granmaha What a racket! What a racket! (*Angrily, she switches off the radio and the TV.*)

Pug Do you mind, that was the news.

Granmaha Don't care. What do I want with the news.

Olmo I want something else to eat.

Granmaha If only I didn't have you lot around, my life would be ten times better. I'd make myself a cup of nescaf, smoke a fag, put my feet up.

Olmo That mutt stinks!

Granmaha If only I had just left you sitting there, on the bench by the door to Platform One. No one wanted you. A really stupid move.

Charlie I like it here.

Olmo But that beast stinks!

Granmaha And what was I meant to do with him, at half past twelve at night in the empty bar, all the tables cleared, customers all gone with the last train. I'd washed up all the glasses already and I had to close up – and the dog's still sitting there, next to the chair, and *on* the chair not a soul. Just poor pug still sitting there.

Olmo Stinking!

Granmaha It's a scandal what people leave behind in our place. Brollies and keys of course. But a funeral wreath! Imagine someone walking forward to the grave to lay his wreath all solemn-like, then he notices he doesn't have one! He's forgotten it. (*Points to the wreath on the wall.*)

Charlie (*giggling*) And the false teeth.

Granmaha Yes, and the false teeth under the table! (*She sings.*)

So many things are left behind.
There's no accounting what you'll find.

DON'T EAT LITTLE CHARLIE

At close of day you shut up shop,
You've cleared away, you're fit to drop

And the buffet's full of things
From smart straw hats to water-wings.

Fine plum jam, a pair of flippers,
Plus a crutch and carpet slippers.

Biros, diaries, leather-bound,
And even once an ancient hound.

Pills galore and nebulisers,
Herbal teas and tranquillisers.

Dolls and comics, old back issues,
Sticks of rock and paper tissues.

It's hard, it's hard, you can't believe
The things the careless people leave.

One day I found abandoned there
Two brothers – yes, a right fine pair!

Charlie (*cheerfully*) Yes, Olmo and me!
Granmaha Come on and eat now, Charlie! You've got
the spoon in your hand and you're staring into space.
Charlie (*surprised*) Oh yes.
Granmaha A vest! A medal even ! What's to be done
with all these things we haven't got any use for!
Pug I'd like to have a medal!
Granmaha I've earned one, simply by putting up with
you lot.
Olmo And someone left the crown behind.
Granmaha (*hurt*) Steady on! That's quite another story!
Charlie (*to Olmo*) That was quite different!
Granmaha No one simply left that lying on the counter!
It was a king gave that to me!
Charlie (*to Olmo*) It was a king gave that to her.
Granmaha Yes, at the very counter of the station buffet!

Olmo There are no kings at the station!

Granmaha He gave me the crown and said he'd return in a year.

Olmo A king travels by car.

Granmaha And all the customers in the bar burst into applause

Olmo The king always sits in the back and the chauffeur in the front.

Pug A medal on a beautiful piece of corded ribbon – I'd look good with that.

Granmaha There was joy and jubilation, and my king even missed his train – and the next one too.

Charlie And the next after that?

Granmaha That too!

Charlie And what did you do then?

Granmaha That was five years ago! Don't ask.

Pug My life is full of reasons why I deserve a medal. For example, a medal for strategic research. One for major contributions to cultural exchange. Peace studies, but I'd be entitled to a medal for close combat as well or at least a lovely plaque awarded for tolerance, tolerance when dealing with the human race.

Charlie (*spluttering with laughter*) Now Olmo's started biting the edge of the table.

Granmaha Olmo! (*She strikes out with her cup at him. The handle breaks off.*) Nothing stays intact. It all gets broken!

Pug Table edges are bad for your teeth!

Granmaha You really can't be left on your own, can you, but I've got to go. (*She is about to leave.*)

Charlie You're still wearing the crown, Granmaha.

Granmaha (*shocked*) Oh God, imagine if I'd gone out into the street with the crown on! You know how jealous people can be. (*She takes the crown off.*)

Olmo I want something to eat! I want something to eat!

Pug A medal for frugality – Most befitting!

Granmaha (*holding up the crown in front of her*) Oh
golden crown, you're my one and only treasure. How
my heart leaps with joy whenever I look at you. I want
to delight in you my whole life long. You sparkle so.
(*She puts the crown into the fridge.*) I can still see you
gleaming even when the door is closed. Even if my
king never returned . . . unfortunately . . .

Charlie You could have sent him a postcard.

Granmaha I don't have his address.

Olmo I want something else to eat!

Granmaha Do give over! You eat and eat and you're
growing bigger and fatter by the day.

Pug *Comme c'est degoutant.*

Olmo Something to eat! Something to eat!

Charlie (*laughs*) You could eat the sofa cushions.

Granmaha Yes, and the sofa as well, and the piano too.
Eat what you like. Just don't eat my little Charlie.
(*She makes a hasty exit.*)

SCENE TWO

Charlie (*spluttering with laughter*) 'Just don't eat my
little Charlie!'

Olmo You've still got something on your plate.

Charlie Yes, I'm saving it for tonight. It's delicious.

*Olmo takes away Charlie's plate without Charlie
noticing.*

Olmo Give me the spoon.

Charlie But I still need the spoon.

Olmo No you don't.

Charlie I want to eat my cornflakes . . .

Olmo You don't have any any longer.

Charlie (*now notices that his plate's missing*) Oh, right. Pity. I can give you the spoon then. (*Gives Olmo the spoon.*)

Pug Outrageous!

Olmo (*to mock Charlie*) De-licious! (*He eats up the cornflakes, then he eats the spoon.*)

Charlie That was mine!

Olmo Oh yes, I did feel something hard as it all went down.

Pug (*gloating*) That's bound to give you stomach-ache.

Olmo I'm ready for more. Give it here.

Charlie There's nothing left on the table.

Olmo Yes there is. There's still the plate! (*He eats up the plate.*)

Pug You're not meant to eat plates. A plate should be licked. Once it's empty you should leave it at that.

Olmo I want to go on eating.

Charlie All of a sudden you seem so much bigger!

Pug It's an illusion. He's just stretching and flailing around.

Olmo (*to Charlie*) I'm much bigger than you.

Pug We could measure that.

Charlie (*fetches the measuring tape*) Here's the measuring tape.

Olmo Hand it over! (*Grabs it off him and eats it.*)

Pug You can't measure size like that! You have to hold it up against your body and then read the figure at the top.

Olmo I eat everything!

Pug It's not right at all. It's not done!

Olmo Listen to the brute, yap, yap, yap.

Charlie Pug is very wise.

Olmo I'll eat everything and I'll grow.

Charlie Perhaps you'll eat the tablecloth then?

Olmo Yes, I'll eat it.

Charlie Chopped up into little bits with sugar and
cinnamon.

Olmo Yes, I'll eat and I'll grow.

Charlie Will you chew off the chair legs?

Olmo Yes, I'll eat and I'll grow.

Charlie And then the clock?

Olmo Yes, I'll eat and I'll grow.

Charlie Then tick-tock it'll start in your tummy. We'll be
able to put our ears to you and listen.

Olmo chases him off.

Anyway, I'm sure that even you can't eat the cupboard.

Olmo Just you wait. Oh – I've already grown so big.

Pug (*cunningly*) Before crunching on all these hard
things, I'm sure you could find something far tastier
outside. Cabbages from the vegetable patch, cucumbers
and pumpkins and the delicious fruit off the plum
tree.

Charlie They're still quite green.

Pug (*brushing it aside*) Better than chair legs anyway!

Olmo I'll go and see. (*to Pug*) You're not as stupid as
I thought.

Charlie Enjoy your meal! (*Splutters with laughter.*)

Olmo (*as he goes out*) I'm going to eat *you* up!

Pug Quick, shut the door and barricade it really well.

Charlie But then Olmo can't get back in.

Pug Get the cupboard in front of it. (*He pushes the
cupboard.*)

Charlie But he's my brother. We can't lock him out.

Pug I lured him out by cunning, and I'm proud of my
success. At least you could give me the credit for that.

Charlie (*goes to the window and shouts out*) Olmo,
we've barricaded the door, but you can climb in
through the window.

Pug Shut the window at once.

Charlie (*looks out*) I can see him now. He's got bigger again.

Pug Bigger and bigger. He'll come back and he'll eat little Charlie up just like a scrawny little chicken.

Charlie I'm not a little chicken.

Pug Crunch!

Charlie (*frightened*) And that'll be the end of me.

Pug The end of you – for ever. Such stupidity. Why's it have to happen to me, I have to put up with such stupidity.

Charlie I'd look a right Charlie, if I wasn't here any more. I can't imagine that at all.

Pug It's a good thing you've got me.

Charlie Yes, you're right.

Pug No need to be scared. I'll keep an eye out, so that no unwanted guests can get into the room.

SCENE THREE

Suddenly Fizzipizzi appears and sings, emitting sparks and with tongues of lightning licking around her.

Fizzipizzi (*sings*) Fizzipizzikizzihizzi glow!

Charlie (*astonished*) Where have you come from all of a sudden?

Fizzipizzi Beamed in.

Charlie How come? Everything's locked and bolted.

Fizzipizzi Haven't you ever seen it on TV? Zap – and there I am.

Pug I don't watch TV.

Fizzipizzi Zap – and there I am. You can touch me if you want.

Charlie (*touches her*) Oh, it makes my skin crawl.

Fizzipizzi Of course, I've got a fair amount of electricity around.

Charlie I can't even let go! (*He holds her hand, quivering.*)

Fizzipizzi Isn't that a mega-feeling!

Charlie My skin's crawling all over. Even up my nose. (*He sneezes so hard, he is torn away from Fizzipizzi.*) It's stopped now.

Fizzipizzi Not a bit of it! It's just beginning.

Pug I'd like to put the question again: where did you come from all of a sudden? We closed up all the doors and the windows tight.

Fizzipizzi I can see that.

Pug We are actually in a state of siege.

Fizzipizzi Phew, that's exciting!

Pug This is quite a dangerous place to be.

Charlie (*to Pug*) She's just beamed herself in, you don't need a door for that.

Pug May I ask where you got our address?

Fizzipizzi From the waitress at the station.

Charlie Granmaha!

Pug (*sighing and casting his eyes up*) Yet another piece of lost property!

Fizzipizzi She said, you can't stay here at the station. Okay, I say. I'll go and take a look at your place. Chop, chop and I'm off.

Pug We're not exactly geared up for visitors.

Fizzipizzi It doesn't matter. I'm staying.

Charlie May I touch you again? I got such a lovely tingling feeling.

Fizzipizzi You were shaking all over. (*full of enthusiasm*) Little Charlie, I'm going to marry you!

Pug But I would like to . . .

Fizzipizzi Lots of people don't notice a thing, and lots of people get frightfully scared.

Charlie I'm not a bit scared.

Pug Please, please – it's just not that simple. On my frequent visits to the Ritz Hotel in Paris, the director would always say . . .

Charlie Pity I had to sneeze.

Fizzipizzi It doesn't matter. The main thing is you love me.

Charlie (*hesitating*) Y . . . y . . . ees. That's true.

Fizzipizzi (*full of enthusiasm*) Charlie! I'm totally in love with you!

Charlie Marriage would be nice. But how do we go about it?

Fizzipizzi I'm going to kiss you now.

Charlie (*confused*) Please, not yet.

Fizzipizzi Why not?

Charlie Please wait a bit.

Fizzipizzi What a disappointment you are. A huge disappointment! I'm so disappointed. I'll just beam myself off.

Charlie No, stay there. Much better to marry me.

Pug It's all got to be thought through carefully. By all means go home to your parents and think about everything. I'll inch the cupboard to the side, I'll open the door a crack, then you can slip out smartly, my dear lady.

Fizzipizzi (*shrieks and emits sparks*) He called me 'dear lady'.

Pug (*shrinks back in fear*) I was only making a suggestion.

Fizzipizzi (*shouts*) I'll marry you. Yes, at once!

Charlie Yes, at once!

Pug Charlie's glowing bright red.

Fizzipizzi Of course, he's the light bulb and I'm the electricity. I'm going to stand in front of you. (*She does.*)

Charlie Yes, well?

Fizzipizzi I'm going to hitch up my blouse. (*She hitches up her blouse.*)

Charlie Yes, well . . . I can't see your face any longer.

Fizzipizzi You can see something else.

Charlie Oh yes.

Fizzipizzi You can see my breasts.

Charlie keeps his eyes shut, he's so embarrassed, and doesn't reply.

What are you doing? They're quite big, you know. You can look at them.

Charlie (*looks*) Oh yes. Is that us married now?

Fizzipizzi No, not yet. You've got to take them in your hands!

Charlie (*does so*) Oh, yes!

Fizzipizzi You're not saying anything.

Charlie There goes the electric current again. (*He starts shaking.*)

Fizzipizzi It's ten thousand volts.

Pug Probably an exaggeration, I'd say.

Fizzipizzi Charlie, I'm totally in love with you.

Charlie Time for the wedding.

Pug You've got to invite your parents.

Fizzipizzi Nonsense. They'll be glad to be rid of me. There was nothing but aggro with them, me being so electric. Light bulbs kept exploding, whenever I came in. And then the car would break down – I'd caused a short-circuit!

Pug What a catastrophe!

Fizzipizzi Yes. I'm not going to stay with a family like that. That's me left.

Pug You'll spend the first night of your honeymoon in a stylish hotel.

Fizzipizzi Yes. Then there'll be just the two of us and no one can gawp at us. Not even an old pug like him.

Pug (*feeling hurt*) Discretion is one of my best qualities.

Charlie and Fizzipizzi tip the table up, so that they can hide behind it.

Charlie (*happily*) Pug – it's good-bye till tomorrow.

The two of them dive down behind the table. Giggling and chattering can be heard.

Pug (*after a long silence*) One of these days I must write a full account of all the vicissitudes of my life. You see my biography is unusually interesting and I could make a great contribution to the increase of knowledge when it comes to both the canine and the human heart.

Fizzipizzi (*appears from behind the table*) Pug, you must sing us a jolly song.

Pug I'm not feeling jolly.

Fizzipizzi A pug's called a pug, because he's plum – puggled – happy, so I heard.

Pug That was in my youth, a long time ago.

Fizzipizzi What did you used to sing?

Pug I can't remember.

Fizzipizzi Was it 'Rum and Coca Cola'?

Pug Never.

Fizzipizzi Was it 'There's a hole in my bucket'?

Pug Not that either. Wait a moment, it's coming back to me. (*in a funereal voice*)

> I'm so glad, I'm so happy
> I'm the pug in clothes so snappy.

I had great successes with that.

Fizzipizzi Then you can sing it now and dance along with it.

Pug I'd feel silly.

Fizzipizzi No, it'll be fun. I'll just brush you with my finger-tips, then you'll get some electricity.

Pug Don't, for goodness' sake. I'd fall down dead.

Fizzipizzi No, it just feels tickly.

She touches him lightly, he begins to quiver agreeably and to giggle, then finally he does a few dance steps. Fizzipizzi leaves go of him, returns to Charlie behind the table and disappears.

Pug Pity that's it.

He stands with his eyes closed, moves about a little, does some dance steps and sings wistfully.

I'm so glad, I'm so happy
I'm the pug in clothes so snappy
I'm so glad, I'm so happy
I'm the pug, that's hippy happy – so
Oh, you know.

Whilst behind the table Fizzipizzi and Charlie are probably lying in one another's arms.

SCENE FOUR

Suddenly the cupboard in front of the door crashes over. The door bursts open. Olmo, who's become gigantic, stands hunched over in the doorway.

Olmo Where's Charlie?
Charlie (*out of sight*) Here.
Olmo I can't see you.
Pug (*signals to Charlie to keep quiet behind the table.*) He's gone.
Olmo But I heard his voice.
Pug Yes. In his absence.
Olmo That's impossible. Charlie, where are you?
Charlie (*behind the table*) I'm not telling.
Olmo You're hiding behind the table.
Charlie I'm away on a trip, to a hotel.

Olmo I need something for my great empty belly. I want to guzzle you up. I need nourishment, so I can keep on growing.

Charlie (*appears from behind the table*) I'm getting married! (*He disappears again.*)

Olmo What? You're getting married, you little toad, you miserable worm – you, you wee timorous beastie, you midge, you louse, you little piece of fly-shit! Who's your bride then, is she blind?

Fizzipizzi (*appears from behind the table*) Me.

Pug (*to Olmo*) Careful, she's got an electric charge!

Olmo She looks quite delectable! I'll have her for pudding.

Fizzipizzi Who's the monster?

Pug (*mediating*) You mustn't say monster. He's Charlie's big brother.

Olmo You're a beautifully spiky creature. You deserve something much bigger than him.

Fizzipizzi Size doesn't impress me.

Olmo (*with pride*) I'm fifty-two . . .

Fizzipizzi So what?

Olmo What if I grow to fifty-three?

Pug (*with hypocritical admiration*) That is an imperial size! One can only bow down in wonder before it. (*He bows to Olmo.*)

Fizzipizzi Watch out, pug. You'll topple over.

Pug (*topples over as he bows and fibs*) I've not felt such respect for a long, long time. (*He struggles to his feet.*)

Olmo I'll get to four meters easy-peasy. Five even.

Pug (*lying, exaggerating his enthusiasm*) Magnificent, magnificent. A new Goliath! (*applauds*) A veritable Superman. One should kneel down before him. (*He kneels to Olmo.*) You must be ingesting extraordinary amounts of powerful nutriments. Grab this, grab that.

Olmo Come here, little Charlie, or I'll come over and scrape you out of that frying pan, where you and your bride are all snuggled up nice and deliciously.

Pug Powerful amounts. (*Conspiratorially he sidles up to Olmo.*) If I may say . . . I am a diplomat by profession and by inclination.

Olmo (*pushes him away*) Stay away from me!

Pug I know, I don't smell very pleasant. I wouldn't expect you to like my smell. I smell of dog.

Olmo You stink!

Pug A little dog with such a strong smell has to be a diplomat. He needs a great master. Being so small myself . . .

Olmo Make it snappy.

Pug Just between ourselves: you won't get much nutrition from such small mouthfuls. (*He points conspiratorially to the table.*) He's still far too puny. That'll never fill you up. Better wait for a bit.

Olmo I am not a patient man.

Pug (*conspiratorially*) What are a few days, if you consider the advantages. (*quietly*) I'll feed him up on a new brand of wonder-food.

Olmo A new wonder-food! Hand it over!

Pug Oh no. It makes you very drowsy. You don't want that. A human being of your imperial size – drowsy.

Olmo Okay. But I'll get him tomorrow.

Pug Very well. (*conspiratorially*) I'll make sure that the door isn't locked.

Olmo (*flying into a rage*) You fool. No point. I'll just kick in the door.

Pug Oh yes, of course.

Exit Olmo.

SCENE FIVE

Fizzipizzi (*attacking Pug*) I heard you. You traitor! You'd just let him in so he can gobble up my little Charlie.

Pug Diplomacy.

Charlie (*reappearing*) Has he gone?

Fizzipizzi (*fizzing with anger*) Fizzipizzikizzihizzi, glow!

Pug You're wrong, you know, you're so naive.

Fizzipizzi Tomorrow he's going to come for Charlie – and you'll just open the door to him and let him in.

Pug Yes, that is what I said I'd do, but just to be diplomatic.

Charlie I'm going to grow and I'm going to get big too!

Pug You're quite wrong. (*to Fizzipizzi*) Let me explain, you hopping, fizzing sparkler, you. The reason I told him that I would make sure the door was open for him is that by tomorrow Olmo will have grown so big, he won't even be able to squeeze into this room. And then Charlie's safe.

Charlie That's a stroke of genius. Do you understand, Fizzipizzi?

Suddenly there's a great crash outside. Cursing and swearing.

Pug (*listening*) That's got to be Olmo!

Charlie I'll take a look out.

Fizzipizzi But not on your own.

Pug I'll come too.

All three stare out of the window.

Fizzipizzi Can you see anything, Charlie?

Charlie Not a thing.

Fizzipizzi Nor me.

Pug, Charlie and Fizzipizzi (*sing*)
  I only see what's always there,
  No change however hard we stare.

SCENE SIX

Whilst all three are looking out of the window, the man with the carbuncle on his head appears in the doorway.

Man (*stretches out his hands*) And what do you think these might be? (*Feathers fall from his hands.*)
Charlie Feathers.
Man Quite right.
Pug Nothing but.
Man Quite right. Once upon a time that was my goose.
Fizzipizzi And you cooked it?
Man No such luck. (*to Fizzipizzi*) Who might *you* be?
Fizzipizzi I'm not obliged to give that information.
Man I own this house.
Fizzipizzi Okay. I live here.
Man That's news to me.
Charlie She beamed herself here. We're glad.
Man I'm not. And where is that dear brother of yours?
Pug It's hard to say. Sometimes he's here, sometimes he's there.
Man It was him ate my goose. And here are the feathers to prove it.
Pug That's a shame.
Man And this here door's broken. Someone's kicked it in.
Pug Hasn't there been a storm? A fierce storm.
Man And as for the racket that's always going on in this house.
Pug I'm not saying a word.

Charlie Oh, there's been all kinds of things going on. We've had lots of fun and I think we'll . . .

Fizzipizzi (*swiftly interrupting, in case Charlie puts his foot in it*) Hey, man, you've got a great, fat lump on your head. What's inside?

Man That's where I keep my grey matter, because I've got more grey matter than most people, it won't all fit into my head, so the carbuncle acts as a reserve.

Fizzipizzi That's a lie!

Man (*taps the carbuncle*) Well, carbuncle, what should I do with this pimply pea?

Fizzipizzi (*immediately assumes a defensive position*) You be careful! I'll not stand for any nonsense.

Man Take it by the scruff of the neck and chuck it in the rubbish, that's what it says.

Fizzipizzi Who?

Man My carbuncle.

Fizzipizzi I don't believe you. Can I feel it?

Man (*taps the carbuncle again*) What do you say, carbuncle? (*to Fizzipizzi*) It's disgraceful, she says. Send her to a reform school for fallen children.

Fizzipizzi Can't! I'm married.

Man To whom? That midget there?

Pug And I sang at the ceremony.

Man What a rabble! I've got rabble in my house, just because I was good-hearted for five minutes. (*He taps his carbuncle.*) Throw them out, my carbuncle cries. Good idea, thanks, carbuncle. That's what I say too. (*Shouts.*) Throw them out.

Pug I can sing you a lovely song. That'll restore you to a good mood.

Man You break everything and you can't even pay for the damage. You're nothing but a lousy load of loafers and down and outs!

Pug Let me sing the song . . .

Man Stop that yappety yap, Pug.

Pug Just as you like.

Man Anyone who can't pay goes to jail!

Charlie We're not down and outs.

Pug On the contrary. We have valuable objects here, quite beyond your wildest dreams.

Charlie For instance, we've got the crutch.

Man You trying to make a fool of me, midget?

Fizzipizzi (*flaming*) Just because you've got two legs. What about people with only one leg?

Charlie And if you knew what we've got in the fridge and never show to anyone.

Fizzipizzi Don't act as though there are no people with just one leg. I've seen them on the tele – whole hordes of one-legged people from all the corners of the earth. There are people with only one leg everywhere. Whole congresses of one-legged people. There's even a whole nation of one-legged people. They're born with only one leg, and it never occurs to them that anyone might have two, they move around on one leg and even run one-legged races.

Charlie (*beckons to the man with the carbuncle*) You can have a look in, you'll see something shiny.

Man I'm not budging. You bring it over to me.

Charlie I don't want to take it out.

Man Then I don't want to see it.

Pug The sight of it will astound you.

Man I'm astounded by the chaos and complete mess around here, aren't you, carbuncle?

Charlie Well, then I'll show you. (*He takes the crown and shows it off to the man with the carbuncle.*)

Man (*astounded*) A crown!

Fizzipizzi (*shouting*) Seeing as we're rich, you'd better shut up!

Man I'd like to run my fingers over it, they'll soon tell me whether it's genuine gold or just a piece of tin.

Charlie It's genuine gold.

Man What do my fingers tell me?

Pug Granmaha wouldn't keep anything that wasn't genuine.

Man In the fridge! Valuable gold. You're joking, aren't you?

Pug Haven't you ever heard of something being in an unusual place? A black man at the North Pole? A child in the well? A lady's stocking on the flagpole? A mouse in a tiger trap? An elephant in a shoe shop? A woman in the gents' toilet?

Man And a pug in snappy clothes.

Pug Almost everything in the world's in the wrong place.

Man If that piece is genuine, it's a case for the police.

Charlie (*proudly demonstrating*) Here, these are precious jewels.

Man Even more suspicious.

Pug I would like to point out: this crown was a personal gift to Mrs Granmaha.

Man (*sarcastically*) Oh yes. May I ask, from whom?

Pug From a high-ranking personage.

Man Just listen to that, carbuncle. This place is frequented by kings and princes.

Charlie Not here, the station.

Man And all this time the king's gone around towns and villages without his crown.

Charlie Yes, and he will return. And fetch the crown.

Man Should I believe this, carbuncle? No, she says, there's a rampant imagination at work here. The crown was stolen.

Charlie (*angrily*) It's *not* stolen.

Man Probably nicked from the folk-museum. There are a few nations that still have kings. They're on exhibit. So the visitors have something to laugh at!

Fizzipizzi (*emitting sparks*) We're rich – and you should keep your mouth shut.

Outside there's a great crashing and splintering of wood and glass.

Man (*listens*) There he is again. It's all going on the bill, you tell your old woman that. (*He goes out, comes back again.*) If you don't pay up, I'm going to the police and I've certainly got something to tell them.

Man exits.

SCENE SEVEN

Charlie If only Olmo were back and was satisfied with cornflakes.

Fizzipizzi Boy, oh boy – that carbuncle is mad! It's too much!

Pug The crown should go back in the fridge. I was afraid he might take it with him. (*He puts the crown in the fridge.*)

Fizzipizzi I should have given him a few electric shocks and reduced him to a pile of ashes.

Charlie Can you do that?

Fizzipizzi I haven't tried it out yet. (*whisper*) I don't think so.

Pug Watch out! He's coming back.

Fizzipizzi (*shouts*) Don't you come in! Don't you come in!

All three take up a defensive position, ready to fight.

SCENE EIGHT

Granmaha arrives, she's got a watering can with her, she stands in the doorway, amazed.

Granmaha What *do* you look like!

Pug (*embarrassed*) We're very glad you're back.

Granmaha When I'm away, I always think to myself, what a lovely sweet family I've got. Then when I come home what do I find – CHAOS!

Pug We've had visitors.

Granmaha (*to Fizzipizzi*) What are *you* doing here?

Fizzipizzi You told me to come.

Granmaha I simply told you to leave the station and I told you the house number.

Charlie (*happily*) We've got married.

Granmaha Fine. All fine and dandy and thick as two bricks.

Pug You've come back with a watering can?

Granmaha Yes, for the flowers.

Pug We don't have any flowers.

Granmaha Then I can water Charlie then, to make him start growing.

Pug No way! No way! That's much too dangerous.

Charlie Small is beautiful too!

Granmaha Where's your brother Olmo?

Pug Outside.

Charlie This is how it was: we were sitting peacefully, eating our cornflakes and then he ate the spoon, then he ate the plate as well, and then . . .

Granmaha I haven't got time for long stories.

Pug He ate and he ate . . .

Fizzipizzi And then he wanted to devour my little Charlie.

Granmaha Don't exaggerate.

Charlie Now he's outside and nothing will satisfy his appetite.

Granmaha Och, if only all you lot weren't here, I could make myself a cup of nescaf, smoke a fag in peace and put my feet up. What visitors?

Pug hums and haws a bit, Fizzipizzi acts as though she hadn't heard anything. Finally Charlie bursts out . . .

Charlie Carbuncle was here!

Granmaha Was he after money again?

Fizzipizzi I wanted to give him an electric shock and reduce him to ashes.

Pug The bill was rather high.

Granmaha I shouldn't put up with it. You think you've got a Happy Family – and next thing you know the table's upended, the cupboard's on its side, the door's been kicked in and everything's yelling – pay up, pay up.

Fizzipizzi (*emitting sparks*) It's super here!

Pug I'm nice natured and devoted, I can prove that.

Charlie Och, Granmaha, you can't just send us away all because of the money.

Pug Whilst you were away there was a mini-disturbance, but it soon passed.

Granmaha Be quiet! I'm the one who'll have to cough up for it. It's my money they're after.

Charlie And the king is sure to return.

Granmaha (*angrily*) Which king is this?

Charlie The one who gave you the crown.

Granmaha The crown! The crown! Don't mention the crown!

Charlie But it's very beautiful!

Pug And valuable.

Charlie It was all because of your beautiful singing that he gave it to you, until he should return.

Granmaha I can't sing any more.

Pug I could sing. And if the king were . . .

Granmaha Be quiet about the king. He's not going to return.

Charlie Yes he is. You often told us he would.

Granmaha So – I told you? That was really stupid of me.

Fizzipizzi That's a shame. I'd like to have met a king.

Granmaha (*shouting suddenly*) I must get rid of the crown. I'll throw it away. I'll chuck it in the rubbish.

Pug That would be unwise. We need the money.

Granmaha Fine, then give it me! I'll go and sell it. (*She takes the crown out of the fridge and sticks it in a plastic bag.*)

Charlie (*in despair*) The crown's the most beautiful thing we've ever had!

Pug And we could pay all our debts with it.

Granmaha I'll buy a trampoline as well – just like I've always dreamed of. Then we can hit the heights. (*She hurries off.*)

Pug Wait! Wait! Something else is about to happen!

And in front of the window Olmo appears. He's become so big in the meantime that you can only see his legs. He bends down to look in and only then can his face be seen.

SCENE NINE

Night. Outside, bright moonshine. It's dark in the room. Charlie, Fizzipizzi and Pug. They're all asleep.

Olmo's Voice (*from outside*) Little Charlie, heeee! How big are you now?

Charlie (*in his sleep*) It's so dark.

Olmo's Voice (*from outside*) Come to the window. It's light out here.

Charlie (*in sleep*) I'm coming. (*He stays lying down.*)

Olmo's Voice (*from outside*) Coming? Don't see any sign of you.

Charlie (*in sleep*) But I am little Charlie.

Olmo's Voice (*from outside*) I don't recognise you.

Charlie (*in sleep*) Wait a bit longer.

Olmo's Voice (*from outside*) How big are you now?
I don't want to wait any longer.

Charlie (*in sleep*) Oh, I'm very big.

Olmo's Voice (*from outside*) That's good. As big as the
kitchen cupboard?

Charlie (*in sleep*) Yes, almost. Just a little bit smaller.

Olmo's Voice (*from outside*) But you're at least as big as
the table?

Charlie (*in sleep*) Yes, almost. Just a little bit smaller.

Olmo's Voice (*from outside*) You're lying!

Charlie (*in sleep*) Yes, I'm afraid I'm much smaller. I'm
only the size of the coffee pot.

Olmo's Voice (*from outside*) Only the size of the coffee
pot?

Charlie (*in sleep*) No, only the size of the milk carton.

Olmo's Voice (*from outside*) The milk carton?

Charlie (*in sleep*) Perhaps only a sugar lump.

Olmo's Voice (*from outside*) Sugar lump?

Charlie (*in sleep*) Um, a bit of exaggeration. Really just
the size of a pea.

Olmo's Voice (*from outside*) A pea?

Charlie (*in sleep*) Well, more like a grain of corn. I'll
have to watch the sparrows don't peck me up.

Olmo's Voice (*from outside*) Just a blasted grain of corn.
You're lying. I want to see you.

Olmo's giant fist silently smashes in the window pane.

Charlie (*in sleep*) Oh, my specs are smashed to
smithereens. I can't see any more.

Olmo's Voice (*from outside*) But I can see you full-size!

*His arm pushes in gigantically through the window.
The hand makes to grab Charlie. Charlie is still*

*asleep. Suddenly Pug gives a loud snore. Charlie
wakes with a start and saves himself right at the last
moment.*

Fizzipizzi (*starts up*) Who's that with the terrible snore?

Pug (*proudly*) Why me, of course.

Charlie Oh, I was having a horrible dream, and Pug
saved me.

Fizzipizzi (*excitedly*) Look, the window's broken. Has
there been a storm?

Charlie (*to Pug*) Thanks for snoring.

Pug No need to thank me, it's in my nature. If I didn't
snore, I wouldn't be real.

Fizzipizzi (*impatiently*) Look at the window!

Charlie Yes, my brother smashed the window open and
wanted to get his hands on me – that was all in my
dream.

Fizzipizzi It wasn't a dream, Charlie. The window's
broken!

Pug There's a draught.

Charlie He'd grown gi-normous, my brother! I feel sorry
for him.

Pug I'm not sorry for him.

Charlie I'm sorry for him, for he doesn't fit into the
room any more.

Fizzipizzi That's all we need. That guzzle-gob in the
room.

Pug (*indignantly*) That selfish brute.

Charlie (*shouts out the window*) Olmo! Olmo!

Pug (*angrily*) That trouble-maker.

Charlie (*at the window*) It's light outside already , but
I still can't see him anywhere.

Pug (*unperturbed*) What I need now is a good cigar to
smoke and time to calmly contemplate all the
vicissitudes of my life.

Fizzipizzi (*starts vibrating and emitting sparks*) I'm
    starting to charge up.

Charlie Shame you can't get a cigar, Pug. I would like to
    see the way you smoke a cigar. Pug with cigar – that
    must look funny.

Pug (*hurt*) Not in the least funny.

Charlie I didn't mean to hurt your feelings.

Pug Lots of people do find me funny. But why?

Fizzipizzi I do too.

Pug (*hurt*) I've scrutinised myself in the mirror to see
    what effect my appearance has. I didn't find anything
    to laugh about. So why do people laugh? I've sat at
    the knees of important people. In my younger years
    I was chauffeur-driven from Geneva to Paris, many,
    many times. I spent elegant weeks in the Ritz Hotel.
    I've seen important monuments and historic sites.
    Those smells. How different the Boulevard des Anglais
    is from the corner of Rue St Honoré at the Louvre.
    How exciting the trail of smells left by the dukes'
    Great Danes at the Place d'Etoile. The iron lamp posts
    I used to sniff along, post by post – and the plinths.

Fizzipizzi How boring! I can't stand sight-seeing.

Pug That, you fizzing sparkler, is all a question of life-
    style. And so it might have gone on. But after the
    great stock-market crash, they had to dispose of me.
    I am an object of value, you know – not just anyone
    can afford to buy me. So I went to the coloratura
    soprano. Distinct possibilities, I thought at the start.
    Interesting. How does singing work, I wondered. To
    sing is to breathe. You breathe not only from the
    thorax, you breathe right from your buttocks.
    Breathing – it's like a column inside your body. And
    up on top of this column notes can balance, like little
    balls on the jets of a fountain. Very interesting.

Fizzipizzi Don't understand a word.

Pug The whole milieu – highly interesting. The atmosphere of the theatre! Dressing-room! Make-up! First-night fever! An artist of note. But unfortunately the relationship turned out to be too full of stress. She couldn't endure my snoring, nor I the hours and hours of her warm-up before every performance. I had to yowl along whether I wanted to or not. And so we decided to part. It was all downhill from then on. The boredom of middle-class family life. Finally – to cut a long story short, I was abandoned by an au-pair at the station buffet.

Charlie Thank goodness. Otherwise Granmaha would never have brought you home to us.

Pug (*sighs*) New experiences.

Fizzipizzi Anywhere else is not half as interesting as here, admit it.

Pug There's a bit too much going on for an old stager like me.

Fizzipizzi (*accompanied by flashes of lightning and the crackling of electricity*) Admit it! Admit it! Admit it!

Pug I won't deny the way we danced. That much I will admit. (*He closes his eyes in bliss and sways back and forwards as he remembers.*)

Charlie (*afraid*) Pug, watch out, you're about to faint.

Pug (*severely, sits up straight*) Everything's as it should be.

Great crash from outside, a thundering noise as though a wall was collapsing and stones crashing down. Everyone takes cover, cowering.

Charlie (*who has rushed under the table to hide*) I thought the house was falling down.

Pug My bet – it's Olmo.

Charlie (*looks out of the window*)
I only see what's always there
No change however hard I stare.

Pug Disturbing the peace as usual.

Charlie (*from the window*) It's all quiet outside, I can hear the buzz of a bumble-bee.

SCENE TEN

The man with the carbuncle enters, dragging a great chunk of wall.

Man And what might this be?

Pug It's difficult to tell.

Man (*shouts*) It's my balcony!

Fizzipizzi Is everything falling down?

Man From the second floor!

Pug It's highly regrettable and also a bit of a worry that stonework shoud be so crumbly these days, but . . .

Man Crumbly? My house! The monster took a great bite out of it!

Charlie From the second floor, impossible! How could he reach it.

Fizzipizzi He must be gigantic. And imagine the teeth!

Man I won't stand for it any longer. That's it! Where's that old slag?

Pug You mustn't say slag to the lady, Monsieur.

Man Oh mustn't I? Then I'll say: you old rat-bag, you messy-muck, you tatty-bogle, you plague-pustule, you wart-hog – oh my carbuncle's well supplied with lovely words for the likes of her!

Pug Please calm yourself, we can pay all we owe and for all the damage as well.

Man Piss-pumpkin! Carbuncle's just come up with that word.

Pug Madame has already left in order to sell the aforesaid valuable.

Man Then I'll sit on this chair and I'll stay here till she gets back with the money.

*He sits down. They wait in silence for a long time.
Each in his/her own way tries to pass the time. Finally
Pug speaks up.*

Pug It won't be long now.

SCENE ELEVEN

*Antunes o Rei, a tall, slim, dark-skinned man, comes
in smiling and without saying a word. He acts as if
he's completely at home in the space, leaps on to the
table, where he crouches motionless, making a long
drawn-out trilling sound. Everyone stares at him in
astonishment.*

Charlie (*astonished*) Are you a bird?

Antunes (*laughs*) Yes.

Man That's all we were needing. A black man as well.
Is he one of you lot?

Pug When he's presented his visiting card and
introduced himself, I dare say we'll have nothing
against his company.

Antunes You're the pug.

Pug Yes.

Antunes You're the pug in the snappy clothes.

Pug You've guessed it.

Antunes All that's missing is the cigar.

Pug Well noticed.

Charlie How do you know that?

Antunes Someone once told me. (*He laughs.*)

*Antunes o Rei produces a cigar from his jacket, gives
it to Pug.*

Fizzipizzi *I've* got a light.

*Fizzipizzi gives Pug a light. Pug smokes the cigar.
Antunes crouches next to Pug.*

Antunes Give me a puff. (*He takes the cigar from Pug's mouth, puffs on it and hands it back.*)

Charlie Are you a dog?

Antunes (*laughs*) Yes.

Man He's not a bird or a dog, he's a black man.

Antunes (*laughs*) I think, at the moment, I'm a dog.

Pug (*sniffs him*) You don't smell like a dog.

Man He smells like a black man.

Fizzipizzi (*raging at the man with the carbuncle*) And you stink like a whitie! I can smell you from here. Even when I'm holding my nose.

Man The black man's got to go. Within six minutes he's got to be out of here. I'm watching the clock.

Pug What do you want, are you looking for someone?

Antunes I'm looking for the woman who lives here.

Charlie Oh, it's Granmaha you're looking for, she's not here. She's away. She'll be back soon.

Antunes Good, then I'll wait.

Man (*clock-watching*) Four minutes.

Now they're all waiting. The man with the carbuncle, who's concentrating on the clock. Antunes o Rei, who sits smiling, in complete calm. Pug, who puffs out great clouds of smoke. Charlie, who is staring in fascination at the black man. Fizzipizzi, who's rolling her eyes out of sheer boredom.

Charlie (*to Antunes o Rei*) Can you do that warbling again?

Antunes warbles, cocks his head from side to side and imitates some characteristically rapid movements of a bird.

(*enthusiastically*) Just like a bird.

Antunes (*laughs*) And this? (*He imitates a monkey.*)

Charlie A monkey! A monkey!

Antunes And this? (*He imitates a frog, lying in wait for a fly, and who finally shoots out his tongue with deadly accuracy.*)

Charlie, Fizzipizzi and Pug A frog! Frog! Frog! Frog!

Antunes takes up a majestic pose, like a king on a throne.

Are you a king on his throne?

Antunes (*quickly stands on his head*) I'm the king standing on his head!

Pug (*taking the cigar out of his mouth*) I used to be able to do headstands too.

Antunes takes the watering can, blows down the spout, a wonderful trumpet solo results.

Fizzipizzi (*applauds, hops with joy, imitates the trumpet too*) Can I have a go?

Antunes (*with one bound he's right next to the man with the carbuncle, who has been watching him in fascination and quite forgetting to look at the clock*) What's the time now?

Man (*angrily, clutching his head*) Shove off, you charred piece of charcoal, you. Get out of my house and never come back!

Charlie, Fizzipizzi and Pug Stay where you are. Stay where you are.

Antunes Is the carbuncle giving you gyp, old man?

Man It's all my pent-up rage against you, it wants to get out.

Antunes Your carbuncle's full of something quite different, I can tell you. The rage is in your mind.

Man (*pushes Antunes o Rei*) Off to the station! Away with you!

Antunes (*cheerfully*) Kids, I'm away to have a cup of coffee.

Man You're not away for a cup of coffee, you're just AWAY.

He shoves Antunes o Rei out, follows him and continues to abuse him

And I'm going right to the station with you. I'll see you right on to the train – right into the cattle-truck.

SCENE TWELVE

Pug, Fizzipizzi and little Charlie remain behind.

Pug (*smoking away*) This cigar matches up to my highest expectations.

Fizzipizzi (*stamping her feet, emitting rays and showers of sparks*) What a mean thing to do! What a mean thing to do!

Because they liked Antunes o Rei so much, they all want to imitate his feats.

Charlie I can blow a tune on the watering-can *too*. (*He tries, he squeezes out a pitiful sound.*)

Fizzipizzi I'm going to do the frog. (*She tries to copy what Antunes o Rei did as the frog, but can't.*)

Charlie (*laughs, is pleased*) Won't work. Won't work. Won't work!

Pug You need a lot of practice for that trick.

Fizzipizzi I haven't got the patience. I'd rather do the monkey. (*She tries the monkey, but she can't.*)

Charlie I can do a handstand. (*Tries to do a handstand, but falls straight over.*)

Granmaha (*returning*) Who's puffing away like a chimney here in the living-room?

Pug (*proudly*) Me.

Granmaha Oh yes, I'm sure. A dog with a cigar!

Pug Yes.

Granmaha Puffing like a chimney and filling the whole place full of smoke.

Pug I'm not puffing like a chimney, I'm savouring it.

Granmaha Wherever did you get that fire-stick?

Pug It was a present from a visitor.

Granmaha Just listen to him! Of course we frequently get visitors who hand out expensive cigars all the time.

Pug Only on special occasions.

Charlie (*to Granmaha*) Have you sold the crown, Granmaha?

Granmaha (*doesn't engage with the question*) What kind of special occasion do you mean? So we've something to celebrate then?

Charlie Yes.

Granmaha Well?

Charlie Because I didn't grow. And Olmo didn't eat me up.

Fizzipizzi (*leaps up and down, glowing*) Fizzipizzi hiss and glow!

Granmaha That's all we're needing. A short-circuit.

Fizzipizzi I gave him a light.

Granmaha (*to Pug*) Will you stop all that puffing.

Charlie Did you sell the crown?

Granmaha Don't ask, just don't ask. When I look at the state of this place and the smoke. The mess! A real pigsty. Other people manage to sit down together as a family decently at the table, one of them will even say grace, to stop all the bawling. If I said grace now, it would make no difference. Pug would go on puffing away. And Olmo outside is behaving like . . . like . . . I don't know what. He's growing and growing and eating away at the beautiful balcony. And I'm liable for it all. Is he still human, I ask myself?

Charlie Och, Granmaha, I was looking forward to the trampoline.

Granmaha Is it still really your brother Olmo? (*She tears the window open.*) Olmo! Come down here at once! Come in here, and I'll clip your ears for you.

Charlie He won't fit any more.

Granmaha As for you lot, I'm chucking you out, lock, stock and barrel.

Pug No, no.

Granmaha Out with everything, so I can get a chance to breathe. And if I can breathe, I'll make a nice cup of nescaf, smoke a fag and put my feet up.

Charlie (*sadly*) Why are you so angry with us?

Granmaha Don't ask, just don't ask.

Pug But we'd really like to know.

Granmaha (*in a rage and in despair*) Because I just can't go on like this.

Fizzipizzi We saved Charlie.

Granmaha And you, you're still here too!

SCENE THIRTEEN

The man with the carbuncle returns.

Man He won't be back.

Granmaha Who?

Man Off from the station! Gone! To the jungle where he belongs. And you're going to pay for all the damage you've caused.

Granmaha What with?

Man You should know. You've sold the crown and it's meant to be worth something.

Granmaha Yes, it's got its worth.

Man How much did you get for it?

Granmaha It's worth more than your house with its balcony and all its lovely furnishings, including the piano.

Charlie But the piano's ours!

Man Well, hand over the money. (*He brandishes the bill.*)

Granmaha I just couldn't bring myself to . . .

Man What's that, Madame?

Granmaha I didn't sell it.

Man Have I cottonwool in my ears? I didn't get that.

Granmaha (*shouting*) I didn't sell the crown!

Man (*yelling*) So there isn't any money!

Granmaha (*shouting*) No!

Man My carbuncle's giving me gyp, that's a sign it's telling me I'm going to commit a criminal act. I'll go to the police and make a statement that I have killed you and all the others along with you. That you're lying in your own blood. Killed by me. Cut down. For all the world to see.

Pug Watch out! Watch out! (*He creeps under the table.*)

Charlie I'm glad you've still got the crown, Granmaha.

Fizzipizzi (*emitting sparks and glowing*) Fizzipizzikizzi-hizzi, glow!

The man with the carbuncle attacks Charlie. Fizzipizzi attacks the man. He shrinks away.

Man Don't you touch me. You're electric. (*When he's touched by Fizzipizzi, he jerks as though he's got an electric shock.*) Immediate notice to quit! Cheats and rogues the lot of you. Get out of here! (*He throws a chair, a coffee-pot, a frying pan out of the window.*)

Pug yelps.

And that mutt is violent.

Pug It was only a slight cough.

Granmaha I *can't* sell the crown. Not for all the money in the world.

Man Because you stole it! Thief! I'll see that you go to jail.

SCENE FOURTEEN

Antunes o Rei returns. He has the frying pan that was flung out in one hand and the chair slung over the other arm.

Antunes Who's been throwing frying pans around?

Man Me. (*He throws other objects out of the window without noticing Antunes.*)

Charlie and Fizzipizzi He's come back! He's come back!

Granmaha stares at Antunes as though he were an apparition.

Antunes (*beaming*) I missed the train.

Granmaha (*almost speechless*) My king has returned!

Pug How wise that we kept the crown.

Antunes (*to Granmaha*) And I'm going to miss the next train and the next again.

Man (*goes to snatch the crown out of Granmaha's hand*) Give it here.

Charlie (*with the courage of a lion*) Hands off. That's his crown. He is the king.

Fizzipizzi (*emitting sparks*) I'm super-charged with electricity.

Man The money or the crown!

Antunes Sing for me, Granmaha. I want to hear you sing. That's why I came back.

Man Oh, my head. My carbuncle's so painful, I can't bear it. (*He screams, holds his head and at the same time tries to hold on to the crown.*)

271

Pug (*to Antunes o Rei*) We've got debts that
unfortunately we can't pay at the moment.

*Charlie tears the crown away from the moaning man
with the carbuncle and gives it to Antunes, who puts
it on his head.*

Antunes How big are the debts? (*He hands money to
the man with the carbuncle.*)

Man That's not enough. (*moans*) Oh, my carbuncle.

Antunes gives him more money.

That's not enough. (*moans*) Oh, how my carbuncle
throbs and aches.

*He holds his head, at the same time he takes the
money that Antunes o Rei gives him.*

That might be enough. But my carbuncle's still aching
and giving me gyp.

Fizzipizzi Serves him right.

Granmaha Goodness gracious, such a lot of money!
Wherever did you get so much?

Antunes But I'm Antunes o Rei.

Pug I've got it! He's the famous Antunes o Rei, King of
Musicians. Antunes o Rei from Brazil. He gets crowds
and crowds wherever he performs.

Charlie (*runs to the window and shouts out excitedly*)
Olmo! Olmo! Come quickly. Granmaha's king is here.

Pug (*severely*) Olmo's not one of us any longer.

Charlie That's a shame.

Pug Not at all.

Fizzipizzi He was going to eat you up.

Charlie (*shouts outside*) If only you weren't so huge and
such a greedy guts.

Olmo moans outside.

I can hear him moaning. (*Calls out to Olmo.*) Then you
wouldn't be so lonely.

Pug No, no. He must stay outside. He's much too big.

Man (*moaning*) Oh, how it throbs and aches!

Antunes Let me look and see what is in it, and wants to
get out. (*Puts a hand on the carbuncle.*) A bird. Look
a tiny bird!

Charlie (*enthusiastically*) A real bird!

*Indeed a tiny, brightly coloured bird has emerged and
is perched on Antunes' hand and they converse
through twitters. The man with the carbuncle has sat
down to one side, a hankie laid over his bald patch,
and he remains like this until the end of the play,
counting his money and recounting it again and again.*

Antunes Listen to what the bright bird says.

Granmaha I'm all a-dither, all a-daze. No, I really can't
believe –

Antunes Oh, my queen, I'll never leave.

Charlie He's the king. So handsome, proud.

Granmaha Hold, my hand, if that's allowed.

Antunes I'm the king. It's truth, not lies.
You're my queen, that's no surprise.

Pug The crown's our one big, bonus prize.

Antunes As a couple we're delightful?

All Super, duper, wonderful.

Antunes It would be nice . . .

Pug . . . oh, yes, I'm sure . . .

Antunes To go with you

The others clamour to be included.

And you and you,
On a great big world-wide tour.

All Yes, oh yes!

Fizzipizzi (*emitting sparks*) Fizzipizzikizzihizzi glow
See the sparks a-flying so.

273

Bird Trrrrriiiiiiii!

Charlie For now it is a well known fact
We're really something as an act.

*Fizzipizzi takes the funeral wreath down from the
hook, tears off the black ribbon and bows and hangs
it round Antunes o Rei and Granmaha.*

Fizzipizzi I award the victor's wreath.

Pug Here and there you're going to roam
Old pug at heart's a stay-at-home.
Yet I feel a love so strong
So I know I'll go along.

All Oh that makes us really happy

Pug And the pug, and the pug whose clothes are snappy.

*And finally Olmo has appeared at the window, he has
to bend right down in order to see in, the music and
the noise have aroused his curiosity, so that he gradually becomes smaller and smaller, and finally runs in
the door and is just as he was at the beginning.
Granmaha sings, Antunes o Rei flutes on the crutch,
Charlie trumpets away on the watering can, Olmo
drums on the kitchen pots, Fizzipizzi leaps about and
glows, so that there's a real firework display and the
pug throws away his tin whistle, because he can't get
a note out of it. To contribute to the festivities he
stands on his head. And Charlie comes to the front of
the stage and says:*

Charlie And I *have* grown a tiny little bit.

End.

Write in the Morning and the Rest is Adventure

Ella Wildridge interviewed by Jim Mulligan

Breakfast in a cluttered kitchen with the family jostling for attention and Granmaha torn between keeping the peace, seeing that everyone is fed and getting off to work: this is the opening of *Don't Eat Little Charlie*. In this play Tankred Dorst explores how far a theatre can go to fulfil our childish need for illusion. Translator Ella Wildridge says:

> Tankred Dorst is a fantastic man of the theatre. Each play I read in the early days was very different but very exciting in its form. Tankred constantly surprises audiences by making a temporal collage, not being scared to shift time frames or to play with size and dreams. His plays combine intellect, imagination and a sense of spectacle.

Tankred Dorst was brought up in a village where his father operated a tool factory. He read whatever was on his father's bookshelf and by the age of eleven or twelve was determined to be a playwright. The war intervened and he served in the army, was a prisoner of war in England and America and returned to find his family property confiscated. Throughout his adult life he has studied, lived and created theatre in Munich. Much of his work is co-written with his wife Ursula Ehler. As a dramatist he has never been directly involved in actual political problems of his country although many of his plays are basically political. The main question in nearly all his plays is: How can we live?

> When I was a student in the fifties some friends and I founded a puppet theatre and I wrote surrealistic

275

plays for audiences that were for students and adults,
not for children. I am not a specialist in writing plays
for young people. I don't think it is any different from
writing for old people, blue, green, rich or poor
people. My main concern is always to write a good
play with interesting characters. Ursula and I have
been living and working together for many years now.
We usually work from 10.00 in the morning till two
in the afternoon. Then we go somewhere to eat. The
rest is adventure.

From the chaotic start the characters operate realistically
in a world of magic-realism. Accept for a theatrical
moment that Granmaha has collected her family from
the detritus left at the railway station, that Olmo has an
insatiable appetite and wants to eat his little brother, that
Fizzipizzi is a super-charged electrified girl and that there
is a talking dog under the table. After that everything
becomes logical and sensible and, furthermore, can give
the audience an insight into society and our relationships. Olmo is a totalitarian tyrant who consumes
everything while the owner is another kind of tyrant
who has control of people at a micro-level. He is the
man with a head full of poison controlling your house,
furniture and payment of rent. He is the despot that
people come into contact with in their everyday lives.
Pug is the aristocrat who has come down in the world.
He is the devious survivor, the smooth operator, the
person who will negotiate with tyrants, will sacrifice
others and then crawl under the table to save himself.
He is literal, pompous and censorious. Granmaha is the
ordinary woman, the survivor who cannot bear to see
others in want and yet gets fed up when she is left
responsible for them. However, she has her crown and
her dreams and in this magical fairy story her king
comes to get her, Antunes being the creative person

without whom tyrants and despots would have their way over ordinary people. Fizzipizzi is the impulsive energiser, the one who makes people happy or angry or prone to falling in love while Charlie is naïve, the innocent child who cares about his brother despite the threat he poses and who laughs at everything.

The dark moments of the play come when the man with the carbuncle speaks. His language is vile and some lines jolt us out of our comfort-zones. 'Right, into the cattle truck' needs little elaboration. 'Shove off you charred piece of charcoal' is a truly offensive line spoken by a truly horrible character. But Tankred Dorst is able to soothe the offence by suggesting that the carbuncle can be lanced, the poison can be replaced by a bird, and music can transform us all.

The language in *Don't Eat Little Charlie* is subtle and complex. To some it might appear to be a chaos of conflicting rhythms but Tankred Dorst is great wordsmith. There is an arc of energy in the language as it moves through a series of dislocations, antiphonal exchanges, fairy-tale narrative and extended poetic interludes to a harmonious resolution. Using language in this way Tankred Dorst shows how all is change and haphazard. Our society is one where nothing stays intact, almost everything is in the wrong place and the contents of the house come from a railway station, itself a metaphor for change and movement. He is also able to reflect on family life. Amidst the boredom and turmoil of domestic interactions the need to be ordinary is set against the need for the poetic and beautiful. Hence the symbolism of the crown that, if sold, would pay off all the debts. In the world of Tankred Dorst the crown is too precious to be sold and the only way out of the sordid preoccupations of domesticity is through the King of Song and his magic. If he can produce a bird from the vile carbuncle, he can surely show us the beauty of ordinary experiences.

I have in my mind the most beautiful, poetic, imaginative performance. But undoubtedly there are some technical problems to be solved. I hope everyone involved will enjoy acting and looking at the actions of others. This play is more than an entertainment. I hope they will learn from the experience and will be able to say, like Charlie at the end of the play, 'I have grown a tiny little bit.'

Production Notes

Don't Eat Little Charlie is set in Granmaha's house,
which she rents from a man with a carbuncle on his
head. Charlie, Olmo and Pug live with her. Charlie is
small and shrinks as the play progresses, his brother
Olmo is greedy and will eat anything. When Granmaha
leaves to go to work in the station café he threatens to
eat Charlie – but Pug tricks him into leaving the house
so that he can eat and grow to his heart's content.
Meanwhile, Granmaha has picked up another refugee,
Fizzipizzi the electric girl, who suddenly appears and
begins to seduce Charlie. Olmo has grown to giant
proportions by now; having eaten part of the house, his
giant fist breaks through the window. He tries to get
through the door but is too big and breaks down the
wall. The landlord wants them to pay for the damage
with the only thing they have of value, a golden crown
given to Granmaha by a king she met at the railway
station. She is reluctant to part with it because it is her
only reminder of him. Suddenly Antunes o Rei appears.
He settles their debts. A bird flies out of the landlord's
carbuncle, Olmo returns to normal size and Charlie
begins to grow.

The smaller and more intimate your performance
space, the easier it will be to manufacture the sense of
Olmo bursting out of it. Granmaha's house is chaotic.
We know that it is stuffed with objects that have been
abandoned at the railway station. You might create the
effect of the changing size of Olmo and Charlie by
experimenting with size and proportion of the room and
the things they use. Objects become extraordinary in the

story. Plates get eaten, a watering can becomes a trumpet, a sofa becomes a honeymoon hotel and the fridge has a crown in it. The set should contain a window (big enough for a chair to be thrown through) and a door that works. You might want to tell the story of *Don't Eat Little Charlie* combining actors with puppetry. The simpler the environment is, the more a high-energy performance will convey a lot of the design necessities for you.

LIGHTING

should suggest the exterior and interior of the house. It is morning at the start of the play and the action probably takes place over the course of the day. Fizzipizzi sparkles, crackles and glows with electricity, she appears with tongues of lightning licking around her as if beamed in through the television. There is a firework display at the end.

SOUND

The play begins very noisily with sound from the TV and radio. If prerecorded sound is used it needs to be tightly cued to avoid the beginning seeming like random chaos as a lot of important plot points need to be heard. Olmo's voice increases to giant proportions in contrast to Charlie's which shrinks to the size of 'a grain of corn'. Sound will help add the spark and crackle to Fizzipizzi and convey the window breaking and the thundering noise of a wall collapsing and stones crashing down. There are music and songs.

CASTING

There are seven speaking parts, all of fairly equal weight. Although there are male and female roles, the style of the play allows for cross-casting. Whoever plays Antunes o Rei, a Brazilian King of Musicians, should appear musical and agile and able to stand on his head easily. Pug, a dog with human characteristics, is dapper and upper class. The man with the large carbuncle on his head is seemingly guided by the grey matter it contains. Charlie is little, but not necessarily young and wears glasses. Olmo needs to be able to carry a conversation and find a way to eat inanimate objects without breaking the flow. Fizzipizzi (pronounced Fitzipitzi) we assume to be adolescent and sparkles with electricity. Don't confuse 'Granmaha' with 'Grandmother'. She needs to be old enough to work in a bar and has a terrific singing voice. The characters inhabit an absurdist world which seems completely normal to them. Nothing seems to surprise them greatly at any point.

EXERCISES

Run the opening of the play. Have the actors create the sound of the TV and radio, as described in the stage directions, with their own voices. Granmaha's long speech has to float over the din and be heard by the audience. At first sight it may appear whimsical but it isn't – she has a lot of back-history to convey. Because no one is listening to each other in this opening section, make sure the actors don't anticipate the line before theirs or pick up on one another's speech patterns as they might in normal conversation. The lack of connection is an integral part of the fractured rhythm of the opening scene. Notice how Pug's line, 'Do you mind, that was the news', is comic when it comes out of the silence after the din. How could he possibly have been listening to it?

Notice the contrasts in temperament between Charlie and Olmo. Charlie is sweet tempered and undemanding. Olmo blocks Granmaha's stories all the time: 'A king travels by car (not train)', whereas Charlie accepts and encourages the story: 'And what did you do then?'. Play the 'Yes, But . . . accept-and-block' game as described in Keith Johnstone's book *Impro*: discover how this might apply to Charlie who always goes with the flow and doesn't appear to have any 'wants' of his own. Olmo is just one big want – more food. Greed is always punished in fairytales, but avoid having the actor play Olmo as a villain or as a pantomime character.

Explore different ways the characters might move.

- Have the group look at a point across the room and walk towards it without losing focus. Have them imagine that they have a bullet in their forehead leading them.
- Use the same exercise but imagining that they have a sponge full of syrup in the seat of their pants leading them.
- Do the same exercise led by eyebrows, then one eyebrow at a time.
- Do the same exercise being led this time by a fluffy chicken in the hollow of the neck.
- Use the same exercise, this time allowing the actors to be led by a boil which is throbbing. Have the actors imagine that the boil is growing in size. Have them attempt activities such as tying shoelaces, getting out of the bath, hoovering etc. with a boil the size of a

large carbuncle. Discover how the functions change when the carbuncle takes on a life of its own and starts ordering them around.

Ask the whole group to sit on chairs facing in a different direction to everyone else. Have them imagine that everything they are surrounded by is edible. Encourage them slowly to start tasting a thing or two and begin to notice more they would like to try. Have them eat more and more, imagining that the food is going through their bodies and filling them from their feet up through the hollow spaces of their legs. Have them keep eating and start to repeat the mantra, 'What more can I eat?' Allow them to eat still more so that they must now loosen their trousers and try to get up off their chairs in search of more to eat if they can move. Have them imagine that their fingers have swelled up like fat sausages. Have them become more desperate so that they begin to eat the furniture and one another.

Ask the group to

- Lie down with their eyes closed and picture a specific type of dog in detail.
- Try and pick up on the dog's breathing patterns and itches (avoid hyperventilating).
- Drop the dog breathing patterns to a minimum and return to your own rhythm while deciding what sort of temperament you might have. Are you excitable? Lazy? Mean?
- Enjoy the different sounds your dog might make. Slowly build up aspects that might work for you. How do you react to the postman? To other dogs?

Set up improvisations based on two or three doggy characteristics that the group have discovered, transferred to slightly more human situations. E.g., in an Art Gallery, Dog A is the guard, Dog B is examining the exhibits. Emphasise how important it is not to think that you are a human playing a dog, but a dog playing a human. See how different pairs hold a dialogue, how little/much do they need to do to appear doglike? Look at Pug's lines, he is a sharp rhythmic barker. Make sure the lines are delivered quickly and precisely.

Have two or three of the group wear a pair of shoes and a hat that might be appropriate for Antunes. Hot seat each actor in turn and question them about what else Antunes might be wearing, likes doing, etc. Give one a watering can or another object. Have them use it as an instrument or to mystical effect. Ask them to perform the legendary monkey and frog impersonations. Have the rest of the group choose a hat and a pair of shoes that represent a character in the play for them and pose for a group photo. Have Antunes lead them in a glorious conga-type dance.

Suzy Graham-Adriani
February 1999

EARLY MAN

Hannah Vincent

Characters

Sam

Bog Boy

Becky

Dan

Louise

Lucy

Liam

Jamie

Wesley

Terry

Patrick

Luke

Timbo

Mr Museum (a voice)

Setting: the play is set in a local museum,
and might be performed as a promenade piece.
The action should flow smoothly between
the different rooms in the museum,
sometimes simultaneously, so that there
are very few actual scene 'endings'.
For rehearsal purposes, scenes are demarcated
according to any exit or entrance
which marks a shift in tone or atmosphere.

SCENE ONE

A large group of pupils are gathered in the 'Early Man' Exhibition area. There is a TV screen in one corner. Cabinets display various artefacts, but the class clusters tightly around a case housing the body of a Bog Boy – so tightly in fact, that at first perhaps the Bog Boy isn't visible to the audience.

Lucy (*reading from a display card*) . . . between 170 BC and AD 230. His remains have been perfectly preserved by the peat content in the soil

Liam Is he dead then?

Becky Duh, no – he's alive and he's two hundred years old!

Lucy More like two thousand.

Dan Shut up, Boffin, it's a dead body innit. That's what counts.

Liam (*transfixed*) Yeah.

Louise (*breaking away from the group*) You lot are disgusting, all staring at a dead body.

Dan It's in a museum isn't it? That's what you're meant to do.

Wesley Yeah, what else is there to do in a poxy museum?

Dan clouts Wesley, who cowers, doesn't retaliate. Suddenly the TV flickers into life and a voice booms out:

Mr Museum Welcome to Bogborough Museum!

Cheesey music.

We hope you enjoy your visit!

Dan Who switched that on?

Mr Museum The museum has two main galleries,
comprising Ancient History and Archaeology, and
Twentieth-Century Design Classics and Popular
Culture.

Liam Sounds like the bloke off *Blind Date*!

Mr Museum In addition, there is a permanent exhibition
devoted to Local Interest . . .

Dan (*to Lucy*) Give us it.

Lucy What?

Dan The controls – give us them.

Lucy I haven't got any.

Mr Museum Toilets are located on the first floor . . .
And why not visit the Museum Shop before you leave!

Dan Here –

*He stands underneath the TV screen, gesturing to Terry,
who climbs up on his shoulders and turns the TV off.*

Lucy You'll get into trouble for that.

Dan shrugs.

Dan With who? I can't see anyone, can you?

Liam She'll grass you up – you wait.

Lucy (*tuts*) I don't care what you do.

Terry (*hostile*) Good – it's not as if you're the teacher or
anything.

Lucy (*defensive*) I never said I was.

Sam Acting like you are.

Louise Yeah. What have you got them for then? (*She
gestures to the pile of printed exercise books Lucy
is holding.*)

Lucy Miss Stringer said I have to hand them out.

*Lucy hands out the workbooks. Some of the pupils
look at them, but mostly they are secreted in the*

depths of rucksacks, or else rolled up and used as weapons.

Dan One of us should go on lookout.
Becky I will.
Dan Go on then.

Becky goes to stand at the door.

Becky Lookout for what?
Dan Stringer. Tell us when she's coming.
Jamie There's a sofa in the other room. And a telly.
Liam Bet it's the same as that – just some museum video.

Wesley wanders off.

Louise Where are you going?
Wesley Have a look . . .

The group divides into two as some of the pupils enter the Twentieth-Century Design room. There is a TV screen in here as well, which starts up as soon as the pupils enter.

Mr Museum Twentieth-Century Design Classics! (*music*) In this room you will see examples of the work of some of the most celebrated designers of our time . . .

Mr Museum burbles on while the students remain oblivious. The video commentary is accompanied by pictures of the artefacts on display. Meanwhile, Sam, Becky, Louise and Lucy loiter aimlessly in the Early Man Exhibition.

Becky (*to Sam*) Can I go around with you?

Sam looks at Louise, who scowls and turns away.

Sam Why d'you always have to follow us around?
Becky Please.

Sam tuts and stalks off after Louise who is wandering into the Twentieth-Century Design room. Becky follows them at a distance.

Sam His hair looks nice. (*Slight pause.*) Daniel's hair . . . he's had it cut. Marks out of ten?
Louise Is she coming around with us?
Sam I can't help it, can I. Are you in a mood?

Louise shrugs, sulky.

Louise This is boring.
Sam Marks out of ten?
Louise None. I'm bunking off this afternoon.

In the Twentieth-Century Design room stands a sofa in the shape of a pair of lips. The pupils bundle onto it, testing to see how many of them can fit on. A nearby notice reads 'Please do not touch'.

Becky (*reading the display card*) Designed by the Surr . . . sur-real –
Sam (*reading over her shoulder*) Surrealist, divvy. Salvador Dali, the sofa is modelled on the lips of the actress Mae West and commissioned by blah blah blah – boring!

Mr Museum takes up her commentary:

Mr Museum (*pompous*) Salvador Dali's sofa 'Mae West's Lips' was designed in 1936, and was donated to the Museum by Edward James, for whom it was made.
Louise (*admiring the sofa*) I like it. That would look cool in my bedroom, don't you reckon?
Sam Not as good as that inflatable one you're getting for your birthday.
Becky You lot shouldn't be sitting on that.
Dan Duh! It's a sofa!

Sam No it's not, it's Art. (*indicating the notice*) It says
don't touch.
Dan Don't say don't sit though, does it?

*He sits heavily on someone else and pats his lap,
inviting Becky to sit on him.*

Come on.
Becky (*embarrassed*) Get lost!
Louise (*fast*) I will.

*She jumps on top of Dan. Groans and shrieks of
agony from the pupils on the bottom.*

Becky And me!

Becky jumps on top of Louise, who throws her off.

Louise Fat cow!
Dan You're meant to be on lookout anyhow!
Becky Someone else's turn.
Dan Wes? Lookout – now.

Wesley goes to stand in the doorway.

Timbo I can't breathe!

They all tumble off the sofa.

Mr Museum On page three of your Museum Workbook
you will find a reproduction of a painting by the artist
David Hockney. A dress designed by the man in the
picture is also housed in the museum – can you find it
and draw it?
Liam (*cheeky*) No.
Louise (*scornful*) Treating us like a load of kids!

Sam grabs Louise and marches her off a little way.

Sam You sat on his lap!
Louise He put his arms around me.
Sam I saw!

Dan joins them, remarking on the contents of one of the display cabinets for want of conversation.

Dan What have they got a pair of platforms in there for? It's not as if they're old or nothing.

Louise Crap, innit.

Sam Better than school.

Louise This room's the best – more modern an' that. None of that old rubbish you normally get in museums.

Dan I don't mind that dead body . . .

Louise Eurr, I do – gives me the creeps.

Sam (*to Dan*) Have you ever seen one before? I have.

Louise Only your dog's.

Sam Still a dead body, wasn't it.

Dan (*to Louise*) I fancy you.

Louise (*laughing*) Shut up!

Dan I do.

Louise (*to Sam*) Marks out of ten?

Louise and Sam Ten!

Dan What?

Sam It's a code.

Dan What – secret?

Sam Kind of.

Louise Not really.

Dan (*to Louise*) I fancy you.

Louise (*laughing*) So you keep sayin'!

Dan Well?

Louise Well she – (*indicating Sam*) – fancies you.

Sam gasps aloud: horrified. If Louise regrets her indiscretion she doesn't let it show, remaining calm.

(*to Sam*) What? You do, don't you?

Sam runs out. Dan looks on, bemused. He puts his arm around Louise. She affects not to notice, shouting across the room at Becky.

Louise Oi, Becky! Come here.

Becky comes running

Go and get Sam. Tell her I didn't mean it.
Becky Why can't you tell her yourself?
Dan She's busy, that's why.

He kisses Louise. Becky watches, fascinated.

Louise *(aggressively, to Becky)* Get!
Mr Museum The museum's collection doesn't simply
focus on objects of material value. Artefacts may often
have been of personal value to their one-time owner,
but sometimes not even that . . . Objects and things
around us that we might consider trivial, or
unimportant, might one day be studied by future
historians, as evidence of how we lived our lives.

*Wesley looks at the bag of crisps he's just consumed,
and slides the empty packet into one of the display
cabinets.*

SCENE TWO

*After their antics on the sofa, some of the other pupils
have drifted back into the Early Man Exhibition where
Lucy is seated in front of one of the display cabinets,
drawing. Several pupils are trying to draw the Bog Boy.
Sam lingers miserably at the back of the room.*

Jamie How do you draw hands?

Terry looks at Jamie's drawing and laughs.

Jamie I'm crap at Art.
Terry You can say that again.
Jamie Let's see yours then.

There's a struggle during which Jamie's drawing gets torn.

(*shredding the remains of his picture*) I don't care anyway.

He scatters the pieces like confetti over the others, rubbing fragments into Terry's hair before escaping into the Twentieth-Century Room. Becky enters and approaches Sam.

Becky (*conspiratorial*) That Louise is a right cow . . .

Silence. Sam doesn't respond.

What's 'marks out of ten' mean? Is it a club you two are in?

Sam ignores her.

Is it true what she said?

Sam continues to ignore her.

About Dan?

Getting nowhere, Becky wanders over to Lucy.

What are you doing?
Lucy What's it look like?
Becky I don't know.
Lucy It says (*flapping her workbook*) in here we have to choose an exhibit and draw it.

Becky hangs around watching Lucy as she draws. She looks across at a small group of pupils gathered around the Bog Boy, drawing him.

Terry Do you think he's got a knob under that bit of cloth?

He draws a penis on Liam's sketch and a scuffle breaks out, resulting in a chase back to the Twentieth-

294

Century Design Room. Only Patrick, Lucy, Sam and Becky remain.

Patrick (*to Sam*) How *do* you draw hands? You're good at Art.
Sam No I ain't.
Becky (*to Lucy*) What's it meant to be?
Lucy Number forty-five.

Becky squints at the numbered objects in the display case.

Becky (*reads*) Pre-Iron Age brooch.
Lucy In the shape of a boar.
Becky Looks more like a pig.
Lucy (*scornful*) A boar is a pig. Kind of.
Becky (*reads display card*) The boar represented fearlessness and fertility. Do you think he wore it?
Lucy Who?

The TV comes on again.

Mr Museum (*suspenseful*) Early Man. The light levels in this gallery are kept low to protect the delicate materials on display. Exhibits include Roman, Bronze and Iron Age artefacts. Items such as cooking pots, spindles, tools and buttons tell us a lot about how people lived.

Patrick screws up his picture and wanders out. Sam stands in front of the Bog Boy, staring at him. He winks at her. Sam thinks she is seeing things, stares closer. Becky joins her.

Sam He just winked at me.

Becky looks at her.

I mean it! I saw his eye . . . open and close.
Becky Do you really fancy him?

Sam is aghast, thinking for a moment Becky means the Bog Boy.

Sam Who?

Becky Dan . . . you never told me.

Sam I don't tell you everything, you know. (*intent on the Bog Boy*) Watch and see if he does it again.

Becky I tell you everything.

Sam Shut up and watch.

Silence. They both stare at the Bog Boy. Louise enters.

Louise I didn't mean to tell him like that – it just came out.

Sam Sshh!

Louise Don't tell me to ssh! I'm only trying to apologise! I won't bother then!

Becky (*explaining Sam's distracted air to Louise*) She saw it move.

Louise (*to Sam*) I can't help it if he likes me, not you, can I! Can I? What am I going to say to him? (*'prissy' voice*) 'Sorry but I can't go out with you 'cos my best friend fancies you?'

Becky (*to Louise*) Are you two going out?

Louise (*to Sam*) I like him an' all you know!

She prods Sam, who stares intently at the Bog Boy, hardly hearing what Louise is saying.

Are you listening? I said I like him an' all! Anyway, we're going out now. Me and Dan.

She stalks out of the room, and it's only now that Sam understands what Louise has said.

Sam What's she say about her and Daniel?

Becky They're going out.

Sam Dan?

Becky And Louise. (*Slight pause.*) Do you like him?

Lucy has been answering questions in her workbook, referring to the material on display. Now she turns to Sam and Becky.

Lucy Where's that sofa everyone was talking about earlier?

Becky In the other room.

Lucy (*as she leaves*) The answers to 10a, 10b and 10c are in that case over there.

Becky (*sneers*) Like we care!

Lucy notices that Sam appears upset.

Lucy (*to Becky*) What's the matter with her?

Becky Nothing. Leave her alone.

Lucy leaves.

(*conspiratorial*) Is it Louise?

Sam wipes her eyes, banishing the tears which threaten. She looks at the Bog Boy, laughing nervously.

Sam I think I might be going a bit mad.

Becky Are you upset? About him and her?

Sam (*hardly listening*) I definitely saw him wink at me.

Becky (*reads the display card*) A boy aged between twelve and fourteen years, arch – arch . . .

Sam (*reading*) Archaeologists.

Becky Believe he may have died as part of a right . . . rightual –

Sam (*reading*) Ritual.

Becky Ritual sacrifice. I'm starving – come to the shop with me?

Sam I might stay – see if he does it again.

Becky I'll come back and tell you what Dan and the slag are doing. (*Becky leaves, cheerful.*)

Mr Museum There is some evidence that Iron Age
peoples believed in human sacrifice as a means of
appeasing their gods. Victims of such beliefs were
frequently buried with their possessions – presumably
for use in the afterlife – weaponry is often found
alongside the men, and jewellery with women –

Bog Boy I'm on in a minute.

Sam gasps, leaps away from the Bog Boy's case.

Bog Boy Here I am, this is me – look.

Mr Museum The boy whose body is displayed here is
believed to have lived around two thousand years
ago –

Bog Boy Two thousand one hundred and nineteen years
ago, actually.

Mr Museum – and was probably between twelve and
fourteen years old when he died.

Bog Boy I'm fifteen.

Mr Museum His body has been perfectly preserved
on account of the properties of the peat in which
he was found. He wears a cloak and hood made
from hessian, which show evidence of crude repair
work . . .

Bog Boy It's not my fault I can't sew, is it? I hate that!
'Crude repair work'! (*He aims a remote control at the
TV and silences it.*) That's shut him up! I'm fifteen,
anyway. That geezer on the video always says I'm
twelve or fourteen. I'm not, I'm fifteen.

Sam I . . . you can speak!

Bog Boy None of it's true, what they say about me.
I know it off by heart now. Every day, ten times a day
it plays. (*Shows her the remote.*) See this? They don't
know I've got it. Left it next to my case one day and
I swiped it.

Sam How come . . . how come you can talk?

Bog Boy (*rude*) How come you can?

Sam Yes but I'm . . . you're –
Bog Boy What?
Sam (*embarrassed*) Nothing.

Becky enters, eating a bar of chocolate.

Becky She's wearing his jumper and Laura saw them kissing.

Pause. Sam doesn't react, standing in shock.

Sam?
Sam I . . .
Becky (*offering the chocolate*) Want some?

Sam shakes her head, mute.

Are you going to be sick?

Sam nods.

Shall I come with you to the toilet?

Sam shakes her head.

He's not worth it, Sam.
Sam He's fifteen.
Becky I think he's a prat. We can go round together if you like – just you and me, yeah? You don't need Louise – what kind of friend goes out with a boy she knows you like?
Sam He's not twelve or fourteen, he's fifteen.
Becky No he's not. (*Thinks.*) Or maybe he is, and he's so thick they kept him in year eight.
Sam (*dazed*) He's got the remote . . .
Becky Remote?
Sam (*absent-mindedly*) For the video . . .
Becky Shall I go and see what they're doing now? I'll come back and tell you.

Becky leaves. When she is gone, the Bog Boy sits up.

Bog Boy See that brooch over there? In that case? Go and have a look for me – is it still there? There's a little kind of brooch thing with a pin . . . in the shape of a dog. Tell me if it's still in there.

Sam walks over to the display case, as if in a trance.

See it?

Sam There's a thing that looks a bit like . . . (*She reads the display card.*) It's a boar. The thing says it's a brooch in the shape of a boar.

Bog Boy It's a dog! Anyone can see that! It's mine. They've put the wrong date on it and they've got it all wrong, but it's mine! Can you get it for me? I want it back.

Sam It's all locked up.

Bog Boy There must be a key somewhere.

Sam Yes but I don't know where.

Bog Boy (*impatient*) It's really important – it was a present.

Sam We're in a museum – you can't go around taking things!

Bog Boy It was mine in the first place! What are you doing here anyhow?

Sam It's a residency, we're resident here for a day.

Bog Boy I'm the only resident here, and I'm here every boggo day.

Sam Are you dead?

The Bog Boy snorts, scornful.

Well – are you?

Bog Boy What do you think?

Sam How can I hear you if you're dead?

Bog Boy I did die . . .

Sam Were you a sacrifice?

Bog Boy goes quiet again as Lucy enters.

Lucy Talking to yourself? That's the first sign of madness.

Sam I wasn't talking to myself, I –

Lucy gives her a funny look and settles down with a computer game. Becky comes in.

Becky I heard them saying they're going to the rec after. She's still wearing his jumper.

Sam is silent, staring at Bog Boy.

Sam?

Sam He talks to me. You two . . . he talks to me.

Lucy Who?

Sam (*indicating Bog Boy*) Him.

Lucy (*incredulous*) Him?

Sam He told me to get his brooch for him – it's that one.

Lucy It can't be. The bog boy lived in a different century. (*pointing at the brooch in its display case*) See? The date on the brooch . . .

Sam (*annoyed*) You don't understand! He told me! Watch. (*She approaches Bog Boy.*) Hello? Can you speak again please? (*speaking clearly, as if to a foreigner*) This – is – my – cousin – her – name – is – Becky. My – name – is – Sam.

Bog Boy remains silent. Lucy raises her eyebrows and Becky turns on her.

Becky Don't look at her like that! What d'you make that face for?

Lucy What face?

Becky Like she's a nutter or something.

Sam He really did speak!

Lucy Yeah, right!

Becky shoves Lucy.

Becky If she says he did, he did – right?

Lucy Alright! (*She pulls a face as she leaves the room.*)

Becky (*calling out after her*) I saw that! (*to Sam*) Don't worry, I'll look after you.

Sam He said that brooch is his.

Becky I thought you were just saying that to wind her up.

A commotion erupts in the Twentieth-Century Room as Dan and Louise kiss on the sofa in front of all the other pupils, who stand around counting how long the kiss lasts.

Pupils (*chanting*) 1, 2, 3, 4 . . . (*etc*)

Sam What's that noise?

Becky I'll go and see.

She runs out.

SCENE THREE

Sam approaches the Bog Boy, closer.

Sam Are you real?

Bog Boy 'Course I'm real.

Sam How did you get here?

Bog Boy They brought me, didn't they.

Sam Who?

Bog Boy The Museum People. Dig dig dig. Load of rustling and shuffling. Stamping. Voices, then quiet. Gently – ever so gentle, but even the tiniest movement felt like thunder. My arms . . . my legs . . . carried me like a baby and brought me here.

Sam I don't understand . . . where were you?

Bog Boy Not far from here. It's a place . . . we used to call it Willow Walk.

Sam I know Willow Walk! I live just round the corner!

Bog Boy It was our special place. That's what we called
it. There was a willow tree . . .
Sam Not any more there ain't. It's all houses.

Silence.

What was it like before they dug you up?
Bog Boy Like being asleep. Nice. Nice and warm.
Sam Miss Stringer tells us off if we say nice. Says it's not
a proper word.
Bog Boy 'Course it's a proper word – what's not proper
about it?

Sam shrugs.

Sam My dog died. When I buried him I put his blanket
in to keep him warm.
Bog Boy Was he yours?

Sam nods.

Sam Got him when I was little.
Bog Boy The dogs in our village just ran about . . . they
were everyone's, no one really owned them. (*suddenly*)
Hang on!
Sam What is it?
Bog Boy The dogs . . . I haven't thought about them
for – for a long time. I'm trying to remember, see. It's
been so long, I forget, and I don't want to – I want to
try and remember.

Silence.

Sam Dad chose him for me, but he was mine. For my
birthday when I was seven. I decided his name and fed
him and everything.
Bog Boy He had a name?
Sam 'Course. Had it written on his collar.
Bog Boy What was it?
Sam It's embarrassing.

Bog Boy Tell me.

Sam No, you might laugh.

Bog Boy I could do with a laugh, come on.

Sam Smelly – his name was Smelly.

Bog Boy What's wrong with that?

Sam Most people think it's stupid.

Silence.

How come you talk like normal? How come you don't
    sound like Shakespeare or someone?

Bog Boy Who's Shakespeare?

Sam How come you don't say thee and thou and speak
    all ancient?

Bog Boy You're not the only school to come here, you
    know. Day in, day out they come tramping through
    here, staring at me, putting finger marks all over my
    case so I can't see out – here, can you rub that bit,
    look? That was you, that was – rub it so it's clean, ta.
    (*Slight pause.*) I hear it and I pick it up I s'pose . . .
    the language. Your language. Completely forgotten
    how I used to speak.

Sam Do you talk to any of the others?

Bog Boy I did once, but he told me to stop – something
    about voices in his head.

Sam Who gave it to you?

Bog Boy What?

Sam The brooch – you said it was a present.

Bog Boy Bran.

Sam Bran?

Becky comes running in, breathless.

Becky They're kissing on the sofa – in front of
    everybody. Come and watch.

Sam I don't want to.

Becky Come on!

Sam I want to stay here.

Becky (*dragging Sam away*) You're the only one who's not in there – she'll think she's won otherwise.

Sam and Becky join the others in the Twentieth-Century Room, where Sam is appalled to see Louise and Dan kissing. Most of the other pupils simply stand and watch, although some have become bored and are splintering off from the main group. Lucy plays her computer game in a corner.

Jamie (*laughing, to Sam*) It's better than a film, this!
Sam You know that bog boy? He can speak.
Becky (*embarrassed*) Sam, shut up going on about it!
Wesley Is it electronic?
Sam He's alive! Come and listen to him.

Wesley is ready to follow her, and she calls out to the rest of the pupils as they leave.

Oi! Come and hear the bog boy – he can speak!

A couple of the others follow Sam and Wesley into Bog Boy's room. Aware that they have lost their audience, Louise and Dan finally separate, massaging their jaws.

Dan (*to one of the pupils who was timing them*) How long was that?
Luke Four minutes, forty.
Dan Think I've got lock-jaw.

SCENE FOUR

Mr Museum The maps on display show the location of the bog in which the boy was discovered, during the preparation of nearby land for the building of a housing estate.

Sam stands in front of the Bog Boy's case, surrounded by the other pupils. She addresses Bog Boy.

Sam Er – hello. These are some other people in my class who want to meet you.

Silence. Dan and Louise join the rest.

Bog Boy?
Wesley Don't you have to press a button or something?
Sam It's not mechanical, he's real.

Terry pulls a face at the others, raising his eyebrows.

Louise Don't seem like he's got much to say for himself, does it?
Sam He did a minute ago – he told me to get his brooch out of there for him.

She indicates the display cabinet. Liam examines it.

Liam It's locked.
Louise (*scornful*) 'Course it's locked, divvy.
Lucy It's not his.
Sam Yes it is and he wants it back.
Louise (*nasty*) He told you this, did he?
Sam (*simply*) Yes.
Louise (*snidely*) Is he your boyfriend then?
Sam Don't be stupid.
Liam Fancy him, do you?
Sam No.
Louise What about marks out of ten, Sam? (*to the others*) She gives everyone marks out of ten, depending on how much she fancies them!
Sam I don't!
Louise She does!
Sam So do you!
Louise (*to Liam*) You were an eight –
Jamie What about me?

306

Dan And me!

Louise (*to Dan, glancing maliciously at Sam*) Ten, of course.

Sam Shut up!

Louise But she can't get a real boyfriend so she's got a bog boyfriend instead!

Sam He *is* real!

Liam Kiss him then! Go on!

Jamie Yeah, come on bog girl!

Louise (*sniggers*) Bog girl!

Liam and Jamie try to force Sam to kiss Bog Boy.

Sam Don't! You're making the glass all mucky! He doesn't like it!

Liam Kiss him!

The volume on the TV suddenly increases – it is deafening.

Mr Museum Whereas marshland is alkaline, the content of a bog is acid. Low oxygen supply and stagnant water means that decomposition is slow and dead matter gathers. Typical bog plants include sphagnum moss, bladderwort, rushes . . .

Louise (*shouting at the TV*) Boring!

Sam takes advantage of the distraction to escape into the Twentieth-Century Room and almost immediately Mr Museum's commentary returns to its normal volume again.

Dan Thought she was your mate.

Louise She's jealous. Of me and you. Fancies you big time, she does. That's why she got everyone to come in here – she couldn't stand to see us kissing.

Liam Here, boffin? Let's see your answers . . .

Lucy No way.

Liam Come on!

As negotiations start for the loan of Lucy's workbook, Becky joins Sam on the lips sofa in the Twentieth-Century Room.

SCENE FIVE

Becky I wish you wouldn't say all that stuff.
Sam What stuff?
Becky About him coming alive and talking to you.
Sam He did talk to me!
Becky It makes me look funny an' all, you know.
Sam Funny?
Becky With me being your cousin an' that. They think I'm mad like you.
Sam I'm not mad!

Louise enters.

Louise Show off.
Sam I'm not showing off.
Louise Yes you are! Trying to get Dan to fancy you. Think I don't know you? I know you!
Sam What have I ever done to you?
Louise Nothing – I just got sick of you always going on, that's all. 'Dan did this . . . Dan did that. Dan looked at me . . .' I liked him an' all, you know.
Sam Good! You're going out with him!
Louise Yeah I am.
Sam Good!
Louise You're jealous.
Becky So?
Louise Keep out of this, you.
Sam (*to Louise*) So?

Louise You should try and grow up, you should. Such a baby! Marks out of ten and everything – it's embarrassing! We're not kids any more. At least I ain't.

Sam Nor am I.

Louise You are. I ain't being mean or nothing, but you're still crying about your dog! (*disparaging*) It's only a dog.

Sam bursts into tears.

Becky (*to Louise*) Satisfied?

Louise leaves.

Sam I used to tell her everything!

Becky She's a complete bitch.

Sam (*crying*) She was my best friend!

Becky Not any more she ain't!

Pause.

Sam (*resolved*) I'm going to make him speak – ask him to speak in front of everybody.

Becky Don't be a mong. Forget it – forget everything, it's lunchtime.

Sam He wants to remember – Bog Boy does. He's been here so long he's forgotten things.

Becky stands, ready to go.

Becky (*losing patience*) Coming?

Sam *They'll* be there.

Becky Who?

Sam Kissing and holding hands.

Becky Don't let it get to you. And specially don't let her *see* it get to you.

Sam You go.

Becky goes to the door.

Becky (*turning back*) Sam? Come to lunch like everyone else . . .

> *Sam shakes her head. Becky leaves. After a few minutes of sitting on the sofa, Sam returns to Bog Boy's Room.*

SCENE SIX

Sam settles down next to Bog Boy's case.

Sam You know the girl with the long hair? The pretty one . . . she used to be my best friend.

> *Pause.*

Used to.

> *Silence.*

Are you listening?

> *Silence.*

She was kissing Dan – that's what all the noise was about earlier. On the sofa in front of everyone.

> *Silence. Sam tuts.*

Come on then.

> *Silence.*

(*irritated*) Come on!
Bog Boy What?
Sam (*surprised*) Oh –
Bog Boy Come on what?
Sam (*meek*) Say something.
Bog Boy Like what?

Sam (*annoyed*) How come you never speak when the others are here?

Bog Boy You're special.

Sam (*embarrassed*) Shut up!

Pause.

Bog Boy I can't see what you like about him, anyway.

Sam Who?

Bog Boy That boyfriend of yours.

Sam He's not my boyfriend, is he.

Bog Boy What's so special about him?

Sam He's got nice eyes.

Bog Boy Girls always say that about boys – (*'girlie' voice*) 'He's got lovely eyes!'

Sam He has! And he's funny. Everyone likes him.

Bog Boy Marks out of ten?

Sam Ten, definitely. How do you know about marks out of ten?

Bog Boy I'm not deaf, am I. I might be dead, but I'm not deaf.

Sam Oh. (*Remembering how the others tried to make her kiss Bog Boy, Sam is embarrassed.*)

Bog Boy *Bran* had lovely eyes.

Sam What colour?

Bog Boy Blue.

Sam So are Dan's.

Bog Boy The rest of our village had brown eyes, but hers were blue.

Silence.

Sam Was she your girlfriend?

Bog Boy My true love.

Sam Oh. (*Pause.*) I don't love Dan. Like. A lot. But not love – I'm too young.

Bog Boy How can you be too young to love someone?

311

Sam shrugs.

Sam It's what my mum says. Says I'm lucky not to love – they'll only break your heart. (*Slight pause.*) My dad left us. He's got another family. (*Slight pause.*) Where is she?

Bog Boy Who?

Sam Bran. Funny name . . . All Bran's what Dad used to have for breakfast. Where is she?

Bog Boy Bran means 'raven'. Why did your lot have to separate us? They left her behind. It wouldn't be so bad for me if she was here too.

Sam Tell me what she was like.

Bog Boy Blue eyes.

Sam What else?

Bog Boy Black hair. Like a raven. (*Slight pause.*) I can't remember anything else! (*upset*) It's too long ago! I've forgotten everything! Everything except the end, what happened at the end.

Sam What did happen?

Bog Boy Stabbed.

Sam You were?

Bog Boy Fifteen times in the back and neck. They don't tell you that bit, do they? You can see all the holes in my cloak where the dagger went in.

Sam Who stabbed you?

Bog Boy Stabbed, then strangled, then drowned. But I still wasn't dead so they poisoned me.

Sam Did it hurt?

Bog Boy looks at her and pulls a face as if to say 'Stupid question'. There is a silence between them.

Bog Boy I knew it would. Sometimes pain's so – sharp, though . . . you can't feel it. You stop feeling. See Mother – crying. Can't look, can't stand. Falling. Both of us. See her cheek in the mud, others – Dad – help

her up. Bran, on the ground . . . hair, sticky. Her
blood and mine mingling, soaking in.

Sam (*hesitant*) Did Bran die too?

Bog Boy Didn't tell her I was scared. She knew it,
but she wasn't scared, so I couldn't say how I . . .
I couldn't tell her. We used to tell each other
everything. Her so strong it made me weak. I didn't
want to die. (*Pause.*) Must be why it took them so
long. (*He shivers.*) I'm cold.

Silence.

Poison was worst. Sick and sick, over and over. Hard
like iron through my whole body, tight, hard.
Tightening. (*He shudders.*) Like others before me . . .
every year when Spring comes. And one of the dogs
once, when it ate some white berries . . . the sounds it
made, coming out of my throat.

Sam (*whispers*) That's horrible.

Bog Boy After, when it was all over . . . (*He hesitates.*)

Sam What? Tell me.

Bog Boy All curled up soft in the dark at last. Like lying
amongst the dogs asleep. And Bran's there. Warm.
Can't feel where my body ends and the bog begins.
Have you had that feeling? It's to do with temperature
. . . when you're the same temperature as the stuff
around you. Now everything feels cold, the smallest
sound or movement makes me – (*He shivers.*)

Sam (*gentle*) Do you need me to talk quieter?

Bog Boy It's alright, I like your voice.

Silence.

(*quiet*) We were the sacrifice.

Sam You and Bran.

Silence.

313

Bog Boy Together. It was a noble death, they said. That's what they told us. (*grim*) Didn't feel very noble.

Sam doesn't notice Dan come in.

SCENE SEVEN

Dan Alright?

Sam is startled.

Sam Where's Louise?

Dan Coming. (*Slight pause.*) Thought you two were mates.

Sam (*grim*) We were.

Dan (*indicating Bog Boy*) Said much, this lunchtime, has he?

Sam (*angry*) Think you're so hard, you do, boys do.

Dan (*mock innocent*) Me?

Sam You don't know the meaning of the word.

Dan shrugs, with something approaching shame.

(*staring at Bog Boy*) He knows. He was scared when he died. It was horrible, what they did to him. They were from his village and he knew what was going to happen. He just didn't know how it would feel.

Silence.

Dan (*genuinely attempting a compliment*) You're good at making things up, you are.

Sam is wound up, her eyes bright, her whole being energised, somehow, by Bog Boy's story.

Sam I didn't make it up!

Dan Yeah, whatever. My mum used to be brilliant at telling stories when I was little.

Dan is attracted to her – he's never seen her like this before. Meanwhile, Louise, Becky and other pupils enter the Twentieth-Century Room.

I didn't know you, you know, liked me.

Sam (*defensive*) I don't – any more.

Dan (*slightly nervous*) Shame. (*Pause.*) I would have asked you out, not her, if I'd've known. I only asked her 'cos I knew she liked me.

Sam How?

Dan She wrote me a note.

Sam Louise did?

Dan Didn't she show you?

Sam shakes her head.

How many marks out of ten do you give her for being your best friend?

Sam Minus twenty.

Dan laughs. He pulls a hairslide out of his pocket and offers it to her.

Dan Want this?

Sam Where d'you get it?

Dan I got it lunchtime. From a shop. Do you want it or not? You can have it . . .

Sam Why don't you give it to Louise?

Dan Nah . . . you have it.

Sam takes the hairslide and puts it in her hair.

Looks alright.

Sam Thanks.

Dan wanders out again, joining the others in the Twentieth-Century Room.

Bog Boy He's mucking you about, watch it.

Sam How do you mean?

Bog Boy I know what boys are like . . . I am one, remember.

Sam Yeah, a two thousand-year-old boy!

Bog Boy Still a boy. Will you hold my hand?

Sam I . . . I don't want to.

An awkward pause.

Bog Boy I'm freezing.

Nervous, Sam puts her hand inside his case and gently takes the Bog Boy's hand in hers.

Aren't I?

Sam You do feel cold, yeah.

Bog Boy You're nice and warm. I'll give you . . . (*He studies her hand.*) Only nine 'cos your nails aren't very nice.

Sam I bite them.

They sit there in silence for a moment.

Bog Boy (*wry*) You know what makes me laugh?

Sam What?

Bog Boy This – look. (*He shows her a thermometer inside his case.*)

Sam What is it?

Bog Boy They call it a humidifier. Got this idea I have to be kept at the right temperature . . . I mean, what am I? A roast chicken? I wouldn't mind, but it's freezing in here! Feel my feet – they're like blocks of ice! Feel!

Sam You need some socks or something.

Bog Boy Wouldn't quite go with my image. ('*Mr. Museum' voice*) 'Come and see the boy from the bog – in his slippers!' (*Slight pause.*) I think they think I'm going to fall apart or something if they don't keep the temperature right. Why couldn't they leave me where I was? Nice and warm, with Bran – (*suddenly*) I remember something!

Sam What?

Bog Boy On her hand – here (*He shows Sam the place on her hand.*) She had a line running across – a scar from where the dog bit her!

Sam Bran?

Bog Boy speaks fast, pleased to remember.

Bog Boy One of the village dogs bit her and she had a scar – raised, like a ridge – and pale. I liked it, I used to stroke it. That's why she gave me the brooch! If I could have it in here with me I know I could remember more.

Sam You know in the shop? In the museum shop? They've got these copies of your brooch. I could buy you one if you want – I've got enough money.

Bog Boy I want the one she gave me.

Silence.

Sam You know the sacrifice? Did you have to do it? Couldn't you have said no?

Bog Boy Bran wanted to. So did our families. They thought it was an honour. (*grim*) Some honour! Bran thought we would meet again in the Afterlife. She believed in the Afterlife.

Sam Didn't you?

Bog Boy Looks like I was wrong though, doesn't it.

Sam Is this the Afterlife then?

Bog Boy What else is it?

Sam I thought it was just my normal life.

Bog Boy She believed in reincarnation. If I had to come back, I'd come back as a dog. What about you?

Sam A dog would be good, yeah.

Bog Boy Bran used to say she'd come back as a girl again.

Silence. Becky enters.

Becky Are you going to Louise's birthday?

Sam shrugs.

I'm going. She asked me.
Sam Bully for you!
Becky Do you know what she calls you?
Sam I don't care.
Becky Bog girl.
Sam (*indicating her hairslide*) See this?
Becky Is it new?
Sam He gave it to me.
Becky Sam . . .
Sam (*interrupting her*) Not him, stupid – Dan.
Becky Dan gave you that?

Sam nods.

Louise'll go mad.
Sam *If* she finds out.
Becky He was meant to get her a present, lunchtime. She told him to.
Sam 'What the eye don't see, the heart doesn't grieve over.'

Becky looks at her.

Becky?

Becky runs out.

(*calling after her*) Becky!
Mr Museum Do you have an artefact you'd like to see displayed in the Museum? It can be anything which is of personal significance for you. If so, you may be interested in attending one of our Saturday courses . . .

Becky fetches Louise from the Twentieth-Century Room and they return to confront Sam.

Louise (*tears the slide out of Sam's hair*) Where d'you
get it?
Sam Ow!
Mr Museum For more information, ask at the
admissions desk on your way out. See you again soon!

Music.

Louise (*screams*) Where d'you get it?
Sam (*screams*) Nowhere!
Louise (*smacks her, hard*) Tell me!

*The other pupils gather to watch what is happening
and start up a chant:*

Pupils Fight! Fight!

*Louise lays into Sam, who fights back. It gets vicious
very quickly. Everybody gathers around.*

Pupils Fight! Fight!
Louise Thief!
Sam He gave it to me!
Louise (*kicks her*) Why? It's not your birthday, is it?
Sam (*fighting her off*) Yours isn't till next week!
Louise (*pulling her hair*) Trying to nick my boyfriend!
Pupils Fight! Fight! Fight!

*Dan is the only one left in the Twentieth-Century
Room, but now he joins everyone else, and as he
comes in, he sees the Bog Boy – who has been
enjoying the spectacle, and now cannot help himself
from joining in:*

Bog Boy Fight! Fight!
Dan (*horrified*) Bog Boy!

*Dan screams, alerting the others to the Bog Boy: they
all scream, clutching each other, terrified. Louise hides
behind Sam, crying. Bog Boy swiftly lies down again.*

319

None of the pupils can speak, they're either sobbing hysterically or standing frozen in shock.

Sam (*exhausted, to Becky*) See? You saw him didn't you?

Wesley He sat up.

Lucy Didn't you hear him? He was shouting.

Terry See if he's got his eyes open.

Wesley No way am I going near that!

Calm, Sam approaches Bog Boy.

Sam He hasn't. They're closed again. Come and have a look.

Becky No way!

Sam He won't hurt you.

Wesley Is it real?

Lucy Is he a ghost?

Sam He says it's the Afterlife . . . I don't know what he is.

Silence.

He was stabbed.

Wesley How do you know?

Sam He told me. But he still wasn't dead so they strangled him.

Becky (*fearful*) How could he not be dead?

Sam He just wasn't. And when they strangled him he still wasn't dead.

Dan So what happened?

Sam They tried to drown him, but he wouldn't drown.

Wesley Why not?

Becky Magic?

Lucy Maybe he didn't want to.

Sam He didn't. Him and his girlfriend were the sacrifice, but the Bog Boy didn't want to die. They poisoned him in the end.

Lucy joins Sam next to Bog Boy's case, studies him.

He had a nice life, so why would he want to die? There
were dogs, and he had a mum and dad and a lovely
girlfriend called Bran, with black hair.

Dan What's he doing now?

Sam (*gazing at Bog Boy*) I don't know what he does.
Just lies there.

Lucy He's not sleeping because you can't see him
breathe.

Silence.

Sam I held his hand.

Becky What did it feel like?

Sam Like paper, a bit. All crinkly. (*Pause.*) He doesn't
want to be here, and the longer he lies here, the more
he forgets about things he doesn't want to forget
about. That's why he wanted his brooch back. His
girlfriend gave it to him, because of a scar she had
on her hand where a dog bit her. He used to stroke
it when they held hands.

*Dan approaches the cabinet containing the brooch,
gazes at it.*

Dan This one?

Sam It says it's a boar, but really it's a dog.

Dan (*to Terry*) You could get that open, couldn't you?

Terry Easy.

*Suddenly the TV comes on again, at the beginning of
Mr Museum's commentary once more.*

Mr Museum (*loud*) Welcome to Bogborough Museum!

Dan Turn it off!

Sam It's him! It's the Bog Boy doing it –

The TV switches itself off again.

Sam He's got the remote control for the video – (*to Bog Boy*) show them!

But Bog Boy remains still, silent.

It's his way of telling us to get his brooch. He's excited. (*excited herself*) Come on!

Dan (*fast, indicating her hairslide*) Give us that back.

Sam hands it to Dan, who gives it to Terry. Terry wiggles the hairslide in the lock of the cabinet containing the brooch . . . and opens it.

Jamie (*triumphant*) Yes!

Sam Bog Boy – here's your brooch!

She reaches inside the cabinet and removes the brooch . . . and the anti-theft device goes off – a deafening alarm bell rings. Sam and the others jump out of their skins, terrified. Some pupils, including Terry and Louise, leg it into the Twentieth-Century Room. Sam doesn't know what to do.

Dan (*shouting above the noise*) Put it back! Put it back!

Sam (*shouting*) No! It's his!

Dan (*shouting*) Put it back before Stringer comes!

Lucy (*who has run to the door on lookout*) Miss Stringer and that museum woman are coming!

Dan (*shouting*) Keep her talking!

Lucy runs out.

Becky (*shouting*) Sam! Put the brooch back!

She snatches the brooch off Sam and chucks it back into the cabinet. The alarm bell is still ringing, and now the TV comes on, loud.

Mr Museum (*going apeshit*) The museum has two main galleries . . . On page three of your Museum Workbook (*music*) Ancient History and Archaeology . . . a

painting by the artist David Hockney . . . sphagnum
moss – can you find it and draw it?

Wesley (*shouting to Becky*) Shut the door!

*Dan slams the cabinet door closed and the alarm
stops. Silence, apart from their panicky breathing.
Then Mr Museum's commentary resumes at normal
volume. Dan goes to the doorway and looks out.*

Dan Boffin's chatting up Miss Stringer. They're walking
away.

Sam He's never going to get his brooch back. (*to Bog
Boy*) We tried – we did try.

Dan Why doesn't he say something?

Sam He only talks when I'm on my own.

Becky What's wrong with the rest of us?

Sam shrugs.

Sam Maybe he's shy.

Silence.

Dan Better leave you two alone then. (*to Becky and
Wesley, and any others who have crept back in since
the alarm stopped*) Come on.

*Dan leads the others back into the Twentieth-Century
Room where they sit on the sofa marvelling at what
has happened. Becky is the last to leave.*

Becky (*to Sam*) Sorry I was . . . you know.

Sam It's alright.

Becky Sorry I didn't believe you. And everything.

Sam It's okay.

Sam is left alone.

SCENE EIGHT

Sam At least they believe me now. (*Pause.*) Bog Boy?
It's me. (*Silence.*) Are you upset about your brooch?
We did try and get it, but you saw what happened . . .
what about if I keep coming in and talking to you?
You might remember stuff that way. I can come every
day after school – I don't mind.

Silence.

Bog Boy? Why don't you say something?

*Louise emerges from behind one of the cabinets where
she has been hiding.*

Louise It's because I'm here.

Sam is startled.

He won't talk because he knows I'm here. (*She crosses
the room.*) I'm going now, so you can have your
precious Bog Boy all to yourself.

Sam watches her go.

Sam She's jealous! (*Silence. Sam stares at Bog Boy.*)
They're probably all jealous. It was good they saw
you, heard you shouting an' that . . . so they know
I'm not making it up. So they don't think I'm mad.
(*rubbing her arm*) Look where she scratched me. I've
never had a fight before, not a real one.

Silence.

Bog Boy? I'm going to get one of these postcards you can
get in the shop, with you on. Stick it next to my bed.
Bog Boy Bed.
Sam What?

Bog Boy Bed . . . I remember . . . we used to lie on the moss – soft like a bed.

Sam You remember!

Bog Boy Smells lovely – like perfume. On the bank opposite there's this kind of bush and when it's got flowers on and it's a bit dark, you know – in Winter . . . it looks like it's on fire. (*Slight pause.*) Can you come like you said? I remember things with you.

Sam Yes, but not if I've got exams an' that.

Bog Boy People come on Saturdays and bring their own things to put in the museum, I've seen them. They get all sorts. Kids always bring their toys to put in, and some of the old people bring funny stuff like hats and letters.

Mr Museum . . . Objects and things around us that we might consider trivial, or unimportant, might one day be studied by future historians, as evidence of how we lived our lives.

Sam I could bring something to do with Smelly! His collar! I'll bring his collar and ask to have it put in the case next to your brooch.

Bog Boy They'll only let you keep it in there for a day.

Sam A day's enough.

Bog Boy You're telling me.

Silence.

I could be your boyfriend, if you like.

Sam is embarrassed.

Don't you like me?

Sam Yes . . .

Bog Boy But not like that.

Sam Not like that, no.

Bog Boy Just come and talk then.

Sam Yes.

Bog Boy Where did your friend scratch you?

Sam shows him, and Bog Boy gently runs his fingers up and down her arm, slow.

Bog Boy Hold my hand, Bran.
Sam (*gentle*) I'm not Bran . . . It's Sam, remember? (*She takes his hand in hers.*)
Bog Boy Yes, Sam. Nice and warm.

Pause.
The light around them gradually fades, and his hand stroking her arm is the only movement.
A warm breeze murmurs, then gradually gathers speed until it is rushing through the museum.
Sounds of small chisels tapping away somewhere in the distance . . . muffled voices, earth falling, being shovelled.
End.

Reach Out across the Ages

Hannah Vincent interviewed by Jim Mulligan

Hannah Vincent is near enough to her school days to remember what it was like to star both academically and socially and yet feel the insecurities of adolescence. At her comprehensive school she loved the excitement and close relationships of the drama productions and she continued to be fully involved in drama when she was at university, writing her first play for the Student Theatre Company to take to Edinburgh. Afterwards, in between mundane jobs, she was writing and sharing her work with a small group of friends. Her second play was produced by the Royal Court as part of their Young Writers' Festival, followed by a residency at the National Theatre Studio. She now works as a script editor for the BBC.

In *Early Man* a group of boys and girls aged about thirteen spend a day at a museum, more or less unsupervised. There is a teacher off stage but she is a slacker, out for an easy day, and leaves the young people to their own boisterous devices. They are left to tease, disobey the rules, bundle on a Salvador Dali chair, break confidences, betray one another, set up a world record for a lock-jaw making kiss and egg on Sam and Louise to fight over who should go out with Dan. Except for Lucy the boffin, the last thing they want to do is learn about boring museum artefacts.

> People of that age are emotionally volatile. One minute they are best friends then they are breaking up. Adolescents are rather brutal in their loyalties and the shifts of allegiance they make within their peer group. Certainly that was the case when I was at school. As

adults we manage it in a more civilised way. When you're at school you're not interested in learning. You pick it up by osmosis. It seeps in through the semi-permeable learning membrane. I think school is as much about learning to be a social creature as it is about learning the curriculum.

The museum video is a device used for giving essential information about Bog Boy, the only exhibit in the museum both to attract and disgust the children. But, despite the authoritative backing of academics, teachers and the museum, the video is not to be trusted and is just plain wrong. Sam learns this when, in a highly charged emotional state after Louise has betrayed her and declared that she fancies Dan, she turns to look at Bog Boy and is astounded to see him wink at her. Bog Boy tells Sam about how he loved his girlfriend Bran, how they would lie under the willows and how they were sacrificed in order to protect the village.

I wanted to suggest that Bog Boy is a boy for all time. The amazing thing about bog-people is that you can touch their skin and see the detail – the stubble on the chin, the wrinkled hands. They take your breath away because they are an embodiment of our own humanity and they make us aware that we are essentially the same as them. Much of our adolescent struggle is taken up with concealing our vulnerability, our humanity. It is cool to be mean and harsh and brutal but as we get older we are able to reclaim something of our sympathy for others.

Sam is on the fringes of her group. She is there but she is not quite top dog. Louise is probably prettier and more socially confident than Sam. At one time she is Sam's best friend and she knows that Sam fancies Dan but she

writes a letter to Dan behind Sam's back and makes a
very public claim to being his girlfriend. She is even
prepared to fight Sam physically to establish her status.
Sam has to learn that she does not need the approval
of her peer group or teachers or family in order to be
herself and Bog Boy helps her to achieve this self-
awareness. As the play progresses Bog Boy talks about
his love for Bran, his fear about the death he was to
undergo and his longing to remember what it had been
like being with Bran.

> Bog Boy sees Sam as almost a reincarnation of Bran.
> At the end of the play he takes her hand and traces
> the scratch on her arm as he once traced the scar on
> Bran's hand. He calls her Bran and she gently reminds
> him that she is Sam. She is able to reach out across
> the ages and hold hands with this boy from a totally
> different world. In a sense he is her inner voice, her
> imaginary friend, and it is through him that she is able
> to strike out and be herself.

At first Bog Boy is convinced he will only be able to get
in touch with his past if he has the brooch that Bran
gave him. In the final scene, however, Bog Boy and Sam
confide in each other and Sam promises to visit him
regularly so that he will be able to remember without the
aid of the brooch. He offers her the unconditional love
that no one else is willing to offer and they embark on a
relationship that will continue after the play. Although
Louise never hears a conversation between Sam and Bog
Boy, she senses that her relationship with Dan is nothing
compared to their relationship.

> I hope young people will enjoy *Early Man*. It is
> intended to be a bit of a romp. I hope they experience
> the sense of community that comes from working on a

production and the poignancy when it ends. But more than that I hope their relationships will reflect the harmonious relationships that are at the centre of the play. Most of all I hope they will see the way Sam is able to forge ahead, confident in herself, relying on her inner life. We all have recourse to that.

Production Notes

The play is set in a museum. The action is divided
between two exhibition areas and should be as fluid as
possible. The Early Man Exhibition area features a glass
case containing Bog Boy. It might be the shape of a
coffin without a lid and stand vertically or horizontally.
It could be made out of perspex or be a simple frame
where Bog Boy demonstrates to the audience that he is
sealed in and they accept the convention that the glass is
imagined. There is at least one other display case which
contains a brooch. A TV screen in one corner plays a
continuous loop with information abut the exhibits and
activities the museum organises. The second space is the
Twentieth-Century Room. Here the main exhibit is a red
couch designed by Salvador Dali which is said to have
been inspired by the legendary Hollywood actress Mae
West's lips. It would be good to adapt a settee to
resemble the original as closely as possible. It will need
to be robust enough for the cast to sit on and move
easily. All the characters, except Bog Boy, are dressed in
school uniform, though how they wear it will say a lot
about their character. Bog Boy's skin needs to have the
texture of crinkly paper.

The voice of 'Museum Man' which comes out of the
TV can be live or prerecorded. Bog Boy appears to
control it at times and the volume fluctuates. An alarm
bell is activated when the pupils try to remove the
brooch from the display cabinet. There is the sound of
a warm breeze murmuring and gathering speed until it
rushes through the museum, sounds of small chisels
tapping away in the distance, muffled voices, earth

falling and being shovelled. These sounds at the end of the play are reminiscent of Bog Boy being discovered and removed from his peaty burial place.

If you are using perspex in the display cases beware of the lights reflecting uncomfortably on the audience and performers. Wall and floor projections will help to establish the museum interior.

CASTING

The play has been written for a cast of thirteen pupils. There is scope to increase the cast size if the company are able to work as a strong ensemble. We are told that they are aged between fifteen and sixteen but the playing age can be younger. The actor playing Bog Boy must be capable of real stillness.

EXERCISES

Visit a museum. Look at how the artefacts are displayed and lit and what sort of security is in place. Observe how the public view the exhibitions: do they move through quickly or do they linger over objects of specific interest? Take note of how a crowd gathers and what people do to get a better view. Spend some time in one exhibition area. Close your eyes and listen to the sounds around you: do people speak quietly? Is the space echoey? What sort of information is relayed or displayed? Decide what similarities this museum has to the museum in *Early Man*.

Imagine that you have been asked to provide a twentieth-century object of particular interest to yourself and that it is going to be on temporary display in the museum.

Choose your object carefully and show it to the rest of your group. Explain why it is so special. Allow the group to examine it carefully and ask detailed questions about it. Decide how it would best be displayed When Sam is asked what object she would display she decides it would be the dog collar her pet wore before he died. What objects do you imagine the other characters might choose?

Create your own twentieth-century exhibition area using the objects which have been shown to the rest of the group. Imagine that you are a class on a day's residency. In a group of five, improvise entering the area silently –

- as if you've been dragged in against your will
- becoming increasingly interested in some of the objects on display
- imagining that security is really tight and that a roving camera will pick up on you straying too close to certain exhibits. Make it clear where the camera is focused at any one time
- without discussion, decide as a body which display is the most interesting and move to it, making sure that you can get a good view of it. Gradually try and lift the object from the display. Improvise what happens when the alarm goes off.

Imagine you are the archaeologists who unearth Bog Boy. What instruments do you use and what precautions do you have to take so that you don't damage him? What does the site look like? What do you discover there which will give you a clue to his age and lifestyle? What part of him do you unearth first? What position do you find him in? Slowly lift Bog Boy and carry him into the exhibition area. Arrange the actor in a position he can hold for a very long time. Now that he is an exhibit, discover just how small a movement the actor can make:

perhaps the blink of an eye will communicate to the audience that he isn't an inanimate object. What can the rest of the ensemble do to make sure that the audience's attention is on him?

Work out the fight sequence between Sam and Louise in great detail. Draw a storyboard/comic strip where the action is visualised moment by moment. Decide at what point the group are aware that Bog Boy is part of the action for the first time and how their reaction can best be communicated. Silently rehearse in slow motion how an ugly fight grows, the group joins in and how Bog Boy's inability to resist being part of the action turns a nasty situation into a great comedy moment.

Take a pack of playing cards and remove the ace, jack, king and queen so that you are left with numbers two to ten. Place two chairs several yards apart, this will be the playing area. Have a volunteer choose at random a card from the pack. Number ten holds the highest status possible, say that of a Queen or a President. Two is the lowest status possible for the purposes of this exercise. Have the volunteer enter the space and demonstrate what status the card has given them. A ten will mean that they will 'own' the space, their body language will suggest that they have high authority; a nine will suggest great self-confidence; an eight will be confident in the space; a seven is comfortable; a six will be neutral; a five is ever so slightly hesitant; and so on. Have the rest of the group observe and guess what card the volunteers have chosen. Take a look at the beginning of the play and decide what status you would award to the different characters. Pinpoint the moments in the play where Sam's status (for instance) changes. Decide why this has happened.

Becky is Sam's cousin and more loyal to her than the rest of the group. Improvise a scene off-stage which might explain why they have a special bond.

Bog Boy picked up modern day language by listening to other members of the public. He mentions that Sam isn't the only other person he has chosen to reveal himself to. Improvise a scene where Bog Boy starts talking to another visitor to the museum.

Suzy Graham-Adriani
February 1999

FRIENDLY FIRE

Peter Gill

Characters

Adie

Dumb Dumb

Shelley

Gary

Kenny

Wally

Cheesey

Donna

Karen

A Statue of a Soldier

The play is set around a war memorial,
in a street, Karen's house, a changing room,
Shelley's house, and a field.

The stage is bare. Chairs can be used where necessary.
For example, the changing room can be suggested
by a row of chairs. But apart from the essential
properties, no other representation is required.

The statue is played by an actor. No attempt should
be made to indicate a real statue. This should be effected
by the actor's dress and stance. He should be dressed
in the full battle dress of a private soldier in the
First World War. The pose and look should be suggested
by the statues of Charles Sergeant Jagger, particularly
the Great Western Memorial in Paddington Station.

The War Memorial.
  *Gary, Adie, Cheesey, Dumb Dumb, Kenny and Wally
carry the statue onto the bare stage and put it into its
position. It is a statue of a young soldier commemorating
the First World War. He is reading a letter.*
  *Gary, Cheesey, Wally and Kenny leave Dumb Dumb
and Adie on the stage.*
  *Dumb Dumb looks up at the statue. Adie speaks to
the audience.*

Adie That statue is a memorial statue commemorating
  the fallen of the First World War. It's Dumb Dumb's
  favourite statue. It's the only statue he's ever seen,
  I think. That's Dumb Dumb looking at the statue now.
  I'm Adie. We go to the same school. (*He leaves the
  stage.*)
Dumb Dumb (*to the statue*) What does it say? Who's it
  from? What you reading? Is it from your mum? Who's
  it from then? Eh? Tell us. Go on. Eh? Go on. Can't,
  can you? No. You can't.

Adie comes on.

Adie You seen Gary, Dumb Dumb?

Dumb Dumb shakes his head.

You seen Shelley?

Dumb Dumb shakes his head.

339

You ain't seen either of them? I thought I was going to
be late. But I'm always on time. Always. But I always
think I'm going to be late. How about you?

Why don't you ever say *anything*, eh? I don't know
why I'm asking. I don't think I ever heard you speak
above a whisper. In class, on occasion, you say
something once in a blue moon. If you can be
persuaded. If they can be bothered. You do, don't
you? You're a chatterbox. Sometimes you are. A right
chatterbox. See, you cracked a smile, you did. If you
don't say nothing, that's why no one don't bother
with you, in it? I've told you. They ain't got time.
I got time. That's why I'm bothering. But they don't
have time. (*Adie looks at the statue.*) He don't say
much either. But then that's how he's made, in it?

(*to the statue*) Is that it? Is that how you're made?
Is that it, eh? Are you one of the fallen?

(*to Dumb Dumb*) You're not one of the fallen,
though, are you? Eh? You talk too much you do,
that's your trouble. Ha ha. No, though. You ought to
try more. That's why they picks on you. It's annoying.
You know it is. You could be interesting. You could
be. You could be East of Eden. You could be
cannonball out of the sky. I've heard you speak. You
spoke last week when Crackle made you. You did.
You said yes or something. You did. (*Indicates the
statue.*) Do you like him? I like him. Look at him. Do
you like him? My mum says every Christmas Eve he
comes alive and goes down Union Street to see his
mum. Straight. There's Shelley.

(*to the audience*) There's my friend Shelley. She's
late. They're always late. The pair of them. Shelley
and my other mate, Gary.

(*to Dumb Dumb*) There's Shelley.

Dumb Dumb Yes.

Adie What?

Dumb Dumb doesn't say anything.

You said something. You did. You did. You wanna
watch it. You're a chatterbox.

Shelley comes on.

Hello, Shell. Where you been?
Shelley Sorry.
Adie Dumb's been talking. Ain't you? He's been going
on and on. Specially when he seen you, he did. Ain't
you?
Shelley Hello, Dumbs.

Dumb Dumb waves and moves off.

Adie That means he's going. Bye.
Shelley Don't laugh at him.
Adie He's not stupid, Shelley. He's not fucking mental.
I ain't laughing. Am I? Am I?

Dumb Dumb agrees.

You see.

Dumb Dumb goes.

You seen Gary?
Shelley No, I ain't seen Gary.
Adie Oh dear. Sorry. He's coming out. He said. Where
you been then?
Shelley I been down the pet rescue centre.
Adie What you been down there for again? You're
always down there. You're getting awful girly, Shelley.
Shelley I'm going there full-time in the summer holidays.
Anyway, I'm not always down there, only weekends
and the one night. I went in 'cos they got a cat I told
them about was neglected.
    Well then, where's Mr Wonderful? Ain't he coming?
Adie He's coming. He's coming.

Shelley Where we going? We going up town?

Adie I don't know. Got any money?

Shelley No.

Adie Gary got money. He'll have money.

Shelley He won't put his hand in his pocket.

Adie He will. What do you say that for?

Shelley He's tight.

Adie He ain't.

Shelley Where we going then?

Adie Down the arcade. Outside Macdonald's. Stand outside places. Look at the pictures outside the pictures. Have some chips. Have a can, one can between three. Have a laugh. We're scallywags, Shell, we are. Go round ours. Or Gary's.

Shelley No, I wanna go up town. I want to look at them jackets.

Adie There's Gary. (*to the audience*) Here's Gary. He's our mate. That makes three. See. Her. Him. And me. (*to Shelley*) There's Gary.

Gary comes on.

Gary (*to Shelley*) I called for you.

Shelley What for?

Adie Where you been?

Gary Where was you?

Adie She been down the pet centre.

Gary You're always down there.

Adie I told her.

Shelley Animals are more worth it than people. Better than most of the people I know. That's true, that is.

Adie See, if you was a dog she'd be nicer to you. If you was a dog. And she's a veggy.

Shelley I always been a vegetarian. Nothing new about that.

Gary Where we going?

Adie Got any money, Gaz?

Gary Not much. Ain't you got none?

Adie No I ain't. Shelley ain't got none neither.

Gary Well, where we going then? There's nowhere to go.

Adie What you got on?

Gary What?

Adie You washed your hair.

Gary Yeah. So?

Adie You're a ponce.

Gary 'Cos I washed my hair? Shelley's washed her hair, haven't you?

Shelley Yeah.

Adie He've got moisturiser on.

Gary You got a necklace on.

Adie Good, in it? Shelley made it.

Gary Let's have a see. (*He examines the necklace.*) Will you make me one of them?

Shelley No. I won't.

Gary Oh.

Adie Go on. Make him one. Go on, he wants one.

Shelley Oh, get the beads then. I'll make you one.

Gary Go round my house?

Shelley No. Up town. I wanna look at them jackets.

Adie Here's the men in black. (*to the audience*) That's Wally and Kenny, that is. Kenny and Wally. They're in our class too. Well, Wally is. Kenny's always on holiday.

Enter Kenny and Wally.

Kenny Hello. Hello.

Wally Where you off?

Adie We're off to see the wizard.

Gary Gis a fag, Shell.

Shelley Honest, Gary.

Gary I'll buy some. I'll buy some.

Wally Where you going?

Shelley You're not coming.

Kenny We're not coming, Wally.

Wally Oh, ain't we? Dear. Dear. That's a bit of a choker.

Kenny Hey, Shell. Karen Loder's had her baby. You heard?

Shelley Oh yeah.

Kenny I thought she was a mate of yours.

Shelley She was.

Kenny Didn't you know?

Shelley 'Course I knew.

Wally Ooo, ooo.

Shelley What?

Kenny Ooo, dear. Fell out, did yer?

Wally Here's Cheesey.

Adie (*to the audience*) Cheesey. Oh dear. He's in our class too.

Gary Cheesey. Oh, blimey. Come on, Adie.

Adie OK.

Enter Cheesey.

Cheesey Hello.

Shelley So long.

Cheesey Where you going?

Wally They're not going anywhere, Cheesey.

Kenny And we're not going anywhere with them, Wally.

Shelley And you ain't coming neither, Cheesey.

Cheesey Shelley, you're a cow.

Kenny It's a hostile world, man. It's a hostile world.

Cheesey I don't wanna go nowhere with them. Where they going anyway?

Kenny They're not going nowhere, Cheesey. Are you, Shelley?

Gary Come on then, Shelley.

Gary, Adie and Shelley leave.

Cheesey Well then, what you two up to then?

Kenny What we up to, Wall?

344

Wally All sorts, Ken.

Dumb Dumb has come on when Gary, Shelley, and Adie leave.

Cheesey Hey, you. What you looking at – you spas. Go on. Fuck off. Hang round for eh? Well, say something. You're stupid, you are.

Kenny Leave it out Cheesey. What's the matter with you?

Cheesey Yeah. Yeah. What's the matter with you and all?

Cheesey strongarms Kenny.

Kenny Leave off. Don't start.

Cheesey Behave yourself then.

Wally You could be a soccer hooligan, Cheesey, if you wanted to be.

Kenny He is a soccer hooligan. Only he can't get organised.

Wally Only he can't play football.

Kenny Only he don't grasp the offside rule.

Wally Not when he plays, he don't.

Cheesey I ain't no soccer hooligan.

Kenny You are a soccer hooligan, only you ain't been given the chance. Have you, Cheese? If you had the brains you could walk through a storm with your head held high.

Cheesey strongarms him again.

Don't.

Cheesey Well, behave then. Yeah. I'd like to go over there – Italy and that. France, Spain. Few cans. Who? Kick his head in. England. England. Man United – poofs and girls. Ooo, ooo. (*He grunts and kicks an imaginary head in.*) Scum. You Irish scum. England. When my uncle was stabbed, remember, yeah? The

geezer only got five years. Five years he got. No fuss
then. No enquiry then. No. Then. That's 'cos he was
white and because he was English. Not getting off.
Hard done by. Not me. I'm different, I am. I'm
English. If I was like a cripple, I'd show them. I'd
prove that I could walk. I'd prove it to them. No.
No. I'll do what I like. Don't stop me. You watch me,
I will. England.

    (*to Dumb Dumb*) What you laughing at? Don't
laugh.

Kenny He ain't laughing. We ain't laughing.

Cheesey Wankers.

He strongarms him.

Kenny Don't.

Cheesey Behave then. Wanker.

Wally They should have that above the blackboard.
    They should have it above all the blackboards.

Kenny What?

Wally Everybody masturbates.

Cheesey What's that then?

Kenny Yeah? What if you don't masturbate?

Wally Then you're a wanker.

Kenny Are you a wanker, Wall?

Wally Are you, Ken?

Kenny I have a wank but I ain't a wanker, Wall. I bet
    Dumb Dumb has a sly wank. Don't you, eh? And
    Cheesey. Well Cheesey. He's a wanker who wanks.

Cheesey Shut up.

Kenny Yes, sir. Yes, sir.

Wally Yes, guv.

Kenny Yes, Your Honour.

Wally Yes, Your Majesty.

Kenny Yes, My Lord.

Wally Yes, mum.

Kenny Yes, Squire.

Wally Yes, cunt.

Kenny Yes, Your Highness.

Wally Yes, love.

Kenny Yes, madam.

Wally Yes, officer.

Kenny Yes, sergeant.

Wally Yes, miss.

Kenny Yes, miss, miss, miss, miss.

Wally Yes, yes. Mum, Mum.

Kenny Yes, yes.

Cheesey You're off it, you two.
     What you gonna do then? Got anything on you?

Wally I ain't got anything.

Kenny Got the makings of a spliff. Is that what you
     want, Cheesey? I ain't got nothing.

Cheesey Where can we get something from? Where can
     we get something to smoke? Get a speed on.

Wally Over Ganga land.

Cheesey I ain't going over there, nigger country. Chasing
     macaroons. That's the other side a town. I'm not
     going all the way over there. And I ain't got no
     money. Got any?

Wally Don't look at me and don't ask Dumb. He's a
     good boy.

Kenny My dad grows it where he lives now.

Wally He don't.

Kenny He do. My dad, not my dad, my dad.

Wally His real dad.

Cheesey He got a real dad?

Kenny Ho ho. He's a traveller.

Cheesey Don't be soft.

Kenny He's with the travelling people. That's why I ain't
     seen him. But I seen him. When I went down there.
     He says school's no good to anyone. No more it ain't.

Wally That's why they've excluded you, Ken. It's not
     good for you.

Kenny I'm a traveller.

Wally You're a time traveller.

Kenny Let's go in the woods. Stop them chopping that copse. That copse. That copse. Burleigh Copse. Sixty odd, hundreds of years old. I'm a travelling man. No. Them roads bad. Protest. No. I'm dangerous. Big man, me.

Cheesey What you on about?

Kenny Tcha.

Wally Chill, man.

Kenny I'm a travelling man. Ooo ooo. On a train. School trip. To the moon. School trip to nowhere. School trip to London. School trip to Edinburgh. School trip to Lego-Land. School trip to Disneyland. School trip to Hell. School trip to dull places. I'm bad. Bad man. My dad. My home dad. He, he says I'm a bad character.

Wally And quite right he is.

Kenny Your mother, Wall.

Wally Your mother, Ken.

Kenny He beats me up 'cos I'm bad.

Wally Well, you are bad.

Cheesey (*to Dumb Dumb*) What you laughing at? Don't laugh.

Kenny He ain't laughing.

Wally Leave it.

Cheesey No.

Kenny Come on.

Cheesey No.

   (*to Dumb Dumb*) What you laughing at? Say something. Go on.

Wally He's not speaking.

Kenny He don't have nothing to say.

Cheesey Say something, go on.

Dumb Dumb moves away.

348

Where you going? Let's do him. He annoys me. Don't
go. Where you going? You're annoying me.

He hurts Dumb Dumb.

Dumb Dumb Nowhere.
Cheesey See, it speaks. You're a freak. Let's do him.
Let's strip him. Get something to tie him up.
Kenny No.
Wally Come on. Let's go.
Cheesey (*to Dumb Dumb*) How much you got on you,
eh?
Wally Come on.
Cheesey Eh? Punch him, go on.
Kenny No.
Wally I'm going.
Cheesey Go on.
Kenny No. Don't be stupid.

Kenny and Wally go.

Cheesey Scum. Dumb. Ain't you got anything? Eh? I'll
have that though.

He takes a chocolate bar from Dumb Dumb.

Ooo. Crunchy. Thanks.

He twists his arm.

Don't talk to me, then. (*He points to the statue.*) Talk to
him.

SCENE TWO

Karen's house.
Donna is holding Karen's baby.

Adie (*to the audience*) This is Karen's house. That's
Donna holding Karen's baby. Karen's in our class and
Donna is too. Only we don't know if Karen's coming
back. It's a nice house. Her mum keeps it nice.
Council do it up every seven years. (*She goes.*)

Donna In she lovely?

Karen Don't wake her.

Donna I won't.

Karen Put her down, Donna.

Donna In a minute. In she lovely? Don't you wanna pick
her up all the time?

Karen No. I don't. She ain't a doll. Get enough of that
at night.

Donna In she gorgeous?

Karen Yeah. I know.

Donna puts the baby down.

Donna There we are, darling.
Do you wanna fag?

Karen Don't smoke. Give it up. Not good for the baby.

Donna lights up.

Don't smoke all over her.

Donna I won't.
When you coming back to school?

Karen I don't know.

Donna You're coming back though?

Karen Not yet.

Donna But you're coming back?

Karen Yeah. I am.

Donna How you gonna manage?

Karen I'll manage. My mum's giving up work.

Donna You still look tired, Karen.

Karen I am.

Donna You gotta look after yourself.
She get through the night yet?

Karen No. I been crying a lot. You cry easy. I get tired.
She'll wake in a minute. You see. I've got a bottle
made up.

Donna Why, ain't you breast feeding her?

Karen No. I don't want to. I did in the hospital. I ain't
got the patience now.

Donna What you calling her?

Karen I don't know yet. My mum wanted to call her
Diana and my Aunty Gloria. But my dad said it was
morbid.

Donna Lucky she wasn't a boy. They might have wanted
you to call her Dodi. Diana would have been nice
though.

Karen I know. I'd like to call her Danielle after Danny.

Donna You heard from him?

Karen Yeah. Letter there. Read it if you like.

Donna Thanks. Diana would have been nice, though.

Karen Yeah. Poor cow.

Donna She was done in, Diana. Definite. Murdered, she
was. The Queen and the Secret Service had her done
in. They put a contract out on her. They couldn't risk
it, she was going to marry Dodi. She was pregnant.
They couldn't have a Muslim and that. They had it
done.

Karen No, that's not right. I don't believe that. My
mother says she was seen leaving the tunnel. This
woman in the flats nearby saw a woman in white
leave the tunnel. She walked away. Then she done a
runner. They had it all planned. She's living in
America. Wills and Harry, Wills he's called, they

know. So they're alright. They know, of course. My
Aunty Gloria knows all about everything about
Diana. She've got pictures, she've got books, she've
got mugs, she've got plates, she've got a Diana doll
from America. Says she's keeping it for the baby. She
knows all about it. Or they say she went up in a
spaceship. They come for her. She blames the Queen
Mum. She says she's an evil bitch. She says they
ruined that other poor cow's life.

Donna Who?

Karen Princess Margaret.

Donna In she dead?

Karen No, she lives in Jamaica.

Donna Diana was only ordinary, see. She was only a
nanny. They saw her off. My grandmother says she
was more upset over that than when my grandfather
died.

Karen My granddad says shoot the lot. He wouldn't
have them on the telly. Only he don't have no say in
our house. Go home my mother says. He goes mad.
He goes around muttering.

Donna You couldn't call a baby Camilla, could you?

Karen No. Not now you couldn't.

Donna Nice name, though. (*indicating the letter*) It's a
lovely letter. I thought your mum didn't want you to
see him no more, Danny.

Karen I know. She don't like him. I don't see him much
anyway. Now he's on remand. Visits. He's gonna
phone later. They can on remand.

Donna Why don't she like him? Too much of the
smokey and the cokey?

Karen Well, I've always been a bit of a rebel. That's me.
They throw a brick. I throw one back.

Donna (*reading the letter*) 'I'll stand by you, Karen.'
That's nice.

Karen He's worried about his dog though.

Donna Why?

Karen Well, his mum's got it. She don't want to keep it. I can't have it here. My mum won't have it anyway. He got no friends, here.

Donna What?

Karen Well, he got other dogs there. Splash, he's called.

Donna Ask Shelley. She knows all about what to do with dogs and that.

Karen No. I'm not speaking to her. She thinks she's someone.

Donna You fall out? I've heard you're not speaking.

Karen I can't be asked. She never asks me round her house. She's always round here. I can't be asked. Shirley Thomas asked for her phone number. I rang her up from the hospital.

Donna Didn't she visit you?

Karen Oh yes. I said is it alright to give her your phone number? I'm not going round giving out phone numbers. She thought it was funny. I had a pair of shoes off of her for £15. The day I gave her the money I could see she was ready to have a go in case I never paid her. I can't be asked. She can be a very selfish person. But that's me, see. This is me and I ain't gonna change for no one. This is me. I don't want no false friends. They're no use to you. Gis a drag. (*Draws on cigarette.*) And she said things behind my back. Like, I was stupid and that, why didn't I take precautions.

Donna Oh!

Karen Anyway I think it was up to Danny. He said he was being careful and that.

Donna Don't you take the pill?

Karen No I don't. I don't take no pill.

Donna She was a good mate.

Karen I know. We was good mates. But we wasn't the fucking Supremes though, was we? She hangs round with that Adie, anyway, don't she.

Donna I fancy him.

Karen And Gary.

Donna You used to like him.

Karen She goes round with them, anyway. They're weird.

Donna We used to have laughs. In the field, remember? Where there was a big dip, where there was a bomb crater – from the Second World War. Where we used to make fires, throw aerosol cans.

Karen That one blew up.

Donna That was you.

Karen Singed all my hair. Coppers thought it was the bomb.

Donna I gotta go. (*She sneezes.*)

Karen What's the matter?

Donna I always get a summer cold.

Karen That's pollen, that is.

Donna Ooo, I forgot. I brought you this. (*Gives her a matinee jacket.*) My mum had it made.

Karen Oh, it's lovely.

Donna See you. When can you come out? Can you?

Karen I can come out. I can't stay in for ever, can I?

Donna Oh, we'll go out then.

Karen Not Shelley.

Donna No. Tara then. She's a lovely baby.

SCENE THREE

The street.

Adie (*to the audience*) We're up town. We been everywhere. She seen the jackets. She don't like 'em. Gary's gone to get us a drink.

354

Gary carries on two drinks.

Gary Here you are.

He gives Adie a drink.

Shelley Did you get me one?

Gary You said you didn't want one. I asked you.

Shelley I didn't.

Gary You did, Shelley. I said special. Did you want one?

Shelley I said after. Didn't I?

Gary Did she?

Adie Yeah. She did. She called after you.
   I'll get her one.

Gary No. I'll get her one. (*to Shelley*) Anyway, here's
   your fags. (*Gives her fags.*) You alright for a bit?

Shelley Don't bother.

Gary No, I'll get you one.

Adie You two. You two. Honest. Stop it. What's the
   matter with you? You got to stop this.

Gary You're bad tempered, Shelley. You're a difficult
   woman. She's moody, isn't she? Moody cow. (*He goes
   to get another drink.*)

Adie Why you so angry with him, Shell? You know
   what he's like about you.

Shelley That's not my fault.

Adie You used to like him.

Shelley I never. Not . . . I can't help it. Like you can't
   help it. Why did all this have to happen? We was OK.

Adie What?

Shelley You know what. Now he won't leave me alone.
   I can't help it any more than you. Anyway he likes you
   more than he likes me. It's just sex. He do. He do. He
   likes you more than you like him, only you can't see it.

Adie Behave yourself.

Shelley I'll do what I like. I know nothing won't work
   out, though. Will it?

Adie What?

Shelley Nothing. Have you seen Karen Loder's baby?

Adie I haven't.

Shelley Her baby? I have. She won't look after a baby. She'll say she will. She won't care for it. Poor babies. All these babies. I don't want a baby.

Adie Don't have a baby.

Shelley They do. They make you decide to have a baby. You have to decide, it's all a big thing, you have to plan. I don't want to have to decide. Karen Loder didn't decide. They make you make decisions. If you don't have a baby, well. Everyone has a baby. They don't do it with boys. You don't have to think.

Do you fancy him? Do you love him?

Adie Fuck off.

Shelley You in love with him?

Adie Don't, Shell.

Shelley Anyway. I know you are. He knows you are. He wouldn't know what to do without you. He wouldn't.

Adie What's he done to you? He's gone to get you a drink. He runs round after you.

Shelley Why when boys do something are they always so pleased with themselves? They always got to get noticed for it. You flatter him. You do. He likes you to flatter him. You do. Just the way you takes notice of him. He loves it. You can't wake boys up and when you do, you can't stop 'em. Like they're out of control. They're always so cool until something affects them, like a football match, or they got a mark on their clean shirt. Then they turn into old women. He's an old woman. He's vain.

Adie Don't you find them, like, well, sweet?

Shelley No, I don't. Look at them when they're doing press-ups. That's the only time they're awake, when they're playing the fool. Times like that. 'Come on.

Come on. You can do it. Once more. And another one
my son.'

Adie I like it when they're intent. Don't you see the
beauty of him when he's doing something? That's
when they become all interested and focused,
attentive, surprised. When they're doing something. I
like watching him mend his bike. His hands. Have
you noticed his hands? Don't matter.

Shelley Where you going?

Adie It's alright. It's alright. (*He goes off.*)

Shelley Adie.

Enter Gary with Shelley's drink.

Gary Where's Adie?

Shelley He's gone.

Gary He'll be back.

Shelley How do you know?

Gary Here's your drink.
    Don't you like me no more?

Shelley Give over, Gary.

Gary What you so narked for? What I do?

Shelley You ain't done nothing.

Gary I have – haven't I?

Shelley You ain't. Don't start moaning.

Gary Why won't you go out with me?

Shelley I am.

Gary No. Don't. Come on.

Shelley I don't go out with no one.

Gary What's the matter with you?

Shelley I don't want your big paws all over me. Alright?

Gary Come on.

Shelley No, get off, Gary. Go after someone else. Go
after Donna, or Karen Loder. She's mad about you.
Keep your hands off me, Gary.

Gary I'm used to birds following me. What's the matter
with you?

Shelley Yeah, well. I'm not following you.

Gary Who do you fancy then?

Shelley I don't fancy no one.

Gary Do you fancy Adie?

Shelley Why can't you shut up?

Gary Sorry. I like you, Shell.

Shelley I like you. You're a mate.

Gary Bloody Adie.

Shelley You like Adie. He's all over you.

Gary Is that why you hang round with us. Adie?

Shelley I don't hang round with no one. What do you mean? We've always hung round together anyway.

Gary You want some big flash bloke, then. Is that it? You waiting for someone who's older, like Karen? You're a snob.

Shelley I ain't. And look what happened to Karen. I can be a friend.

Gary I don't want a friend. I got a friend. I want a girlfriend. I got loads of friends.

Shelley I like you. You know, Gary.

Gary You makes a fool of me. You do. You leads me on.

Shelley I don't.

Gary You do. You do. You know you do. You know what you did.

Shelley You just want to get it on with me. Not me. You're not interested in me. Me.

Gary What do you mean? What do you want?

Shelley I don't want nothing off you.

Gary I'd worship you. I'd look after you.

Shelley I can look after myself. And you wouldn't.

Gary You can't say that.

Shelley You wouldn't. You're only talking about sex.

Gary You look down on people.

Shelley I don't. You and Adie do. You think you're clever. Oh, stop it. What's going on? There used to be just us. Not all this on top of it. Where's Adie?

Gary Adie. Adie. Don't go on about Adie.

Shelley Well, you're all Adie. You can't talk to no one else.

Gary I'm talking to you.

Shelley You're not talking to me.

Gary What you want to talk about then? Eh? Go on. Fuck off.

Shelley You don't have to be like that. Alright, be like that then. Who do you think you are? You can't get what you want, you're in a strop.

Gary I got feelings. Go on. Fuck off.

Shelley I will. (*She goes off.*)

Gary (*shouts after her*) What'll I tell Adie?

Shelley I don't care what you tell Adie.

Enter Adie.

Adie Where's Shelley?

Gary Gone.

Adie Where's she gone?

Gary I don't know and I don't care. She can go where she likes. I don't care. I can get a bird. She won't have me, so what? Fuck it. I feel . . . Fuck it.

Adie What?

Gary I can't do nothing about nothing. Here or in the world. I like being in control. I'm not in control of nothing. I want power. I want to be in charge of nothing more like. We can do nothing. We know we can't. I can't do nothing. What can we do?

Adie You're just angry.

Gary I can't do anything. What can we do? You got no joy of doing anything. Don't matter what I think. Don't matter, except for trainers. Except for can I have a mountain bike, Mum? You know, you're like that. No choice. No choice.

Adie You never know what might happen.

Gary I know what's going to happen. I know what's
going to happen. Nothing. Nowt. Turn you down.
Failed. Not picked for the seven-a-side. We're left out,
let down. Impotent. Get it up where? Cold water.
Drenched, pouring down. I'm not kicking in. Fuck up.
No marks. Doing my very best. Could try harder. I'm
not an individual. I don't want to be an individual.
Sometimes I'm me. Sometimes I'm you. Sometimes I'm
from our street. Sometimes I'm in the pictures.
Sometimes, sometimes, I don't know what they want,
sometimes, sometimes I'm a prisoner. Sometimes I'm
in school. Sometimes I'm in England. Sometimes I'm
in Britain. Sometimes I'm a girl. Sometimes I'm a boy.
Sometimes.

    I want to be in extreme situations. I want to be in
the condemned cell or I want to be in the gas chamber.
Beetle just off mother. I can't control thoughts or
think. Can't have no control over thoughts. Thinking.
Everyone seems to be trapped in the wrong bodies,
in the wrong place, in the wrong person. The wrong
house. Trapped in the wrong house. I've taken my
pictures down off my wall.

    I think at night in the dark, looking out the window
at all the houses that someone's going to turn it off.
Turn it off or on. It's not real. I think I'm in someone's
argument. I cannot believe I exist. I cannot believe
that it's all happening. I think that it's going to be
switched off. How can you bear to have to live? I live
in a TV set. I think of dying. How can we die,
anyway? I wish my mother was dead.

Adie What you say that for? What's the matter with
you?

Gary I want to die. That's all she says. Turn it off. Then
there wouldn't be nothing.

Adie You does too much E, mate. You do.

Gary I don't. Anyway, it don't do you no more harm than traffic. When I last take E? You knows everything I do. I was with you. Months. Safe sex and drugs, that's all you hear. I've had earfuls of it. (*Takes out a condom.*) Look, it's perished. Past its sell by date.

Adie Don't, Gaz.

Gary Look, I want a shag. I only got it for Shelley. For Roger Jenkin's party.

Adie Did you?

Gary You know very well I didn't. What you talking about? You know, Adie. You know I didn't. She don't. Kissed her and then pushed up her mini skirt. Snogged her. Never shagged her. I pushed her mini skirt up. (*He laughs.*)

Adie What you laughing at?

Gary I'm laughing all the way to a wank. She let you?

Adie No, don't.

Gary You seen her fanny?

Adie When we was about six. And you did. And when we went in the sea that night. Put it away. I don't like looking at it. I don't like looking at packets of rubber johnnies in the chemist.

Gary No?

Adie No.

Gary Shy. Scared?

Adie I thought so but no.

Gary Look. (*Shows him the condom.*)

Adie No. I don't like it.

Gary Shy. Scared.

Adie Yeah. Scared you're going to use it.

Gary I will use it. If not this, another one.

Adie I know.

Gary Are women heterosexual? I bet they are. They sound as if they are. What's a typical heterosexual?

Adie Mr Watkins.

Gary No. Brad Pitt. Sylvester Stallone.

Adie Tony Blair, more like.

Gary Mr Dorkin, more like.

Adie More like my dad.

Gary More like Chris de Burgh.

Adie More like.

Gary More like.

Have you got to beat girls up? If you hit her, like, would you hit her like you hit a boy?

Adie I don't know. My father chased my mother up the stairs and she hid in the front bedroom.

Gary I mean. Would you go bang? I'd hit the wall. I'm going to hit the wall. I wouldn't want to do it, hit a girl. I'd like to hit my mother. Do you, like, smash 'em? I'm worried about it. I'm worried all the time.

Adie Worry. Everyone worries, don't they? I worry about everything.

Gary Yes. Well, you're a worrier.

Adie Well, it's life, isn't it?

Gary Why? I'm going to do the hard stuff. I am. I can't be worrying.

Adie You're not.

Gary I'm not. I'm not. Goody goody. I'm not. I might. But I wouldn't.

Adie I'm not goody goody. Shut up Gary.

Gary No. You're my friend. My mate. You're my only one friend I've got. You can't do no wrong. Don't laugh. Don't laugh. She fancies you. She loves you. She does. Why not me? I'm sorry when I take it out on you.

Adie I've had a time you're just having now.

Gary I want love. Why can't I have love then?

Adie Oh. (*He moves away.*)

Gary Do you know what I'm saying? No. You know what I mean. I'd do anything for her if she loved me. The bitch.

Adie Where you going?

Gary I dunno, Adie. Leave me alone. Don't follow me about, Adie.

SCENE FOUR

The War Memorial.
The boys bring on the statue.

Adie (*to the audience*) Back to Dumb Dumb's statue. And Kenny and Wally and Donna and Karen. And, yeah, Cheesey, yeah. (*He goes off.*)
Kenny You alright, Wall?
Wally I'm alright, Ken.
Kenny How are you doing?
Wally How many cans you had?
Kenny How many you had?
Wally I've had many cans.
Kenny How are you doing?
Wally I'm alright.
Kenny No, no. You're not. You're nothing, mate. You're scum. Official.
Wally You're right. You're right.
Kenny Trash. Trash.

Donna and Karen come on giggling.

Karen Where are you? Kenny, Kenny?
Kenny Here they are.
Wally Where you been?
Donna Having a wee.
Karen Behind a bush.
Donna Sh. Sh. Don't tell everyone.
Kenny Ladies. Ladies.
Karen Shut up, Kenny.

Enter Cheesey, doing his flies up.

363

I've had a laugh tonight.
Donna And me.
Cheesey Where we going now?
Kenny Here. We're going here.

The girls laugh.

Cheesey Ha ha.
Kenny I'm a bit . . . Ooo . . .
Wally You OK, Kenny?
Kenny I'm OK.
Wally So, you're OK.
Kenny Are you OK?
Wally I'm very OK, thank you, Kenny.
Karen Girl power.
Donna Yeah.
Kenny I got her knickers in my pocket.
Wally You ain't.
Kenny The boy is good. (*showing a pair of knickers*)
   These yours, Karen? Are they?
Cheesey Are they, Karen?
Karen They are not. They're not. I got my knickers on.
   Look.

She shows them. Boys hoot.

They must be Donna's.
Donna They are not. Look.

Shows her knickers. Hoots from the others.

Cheesey Whose are they then?
Kenny That's how you get girls to show you their
   knickers. (*Puts them on his head.*)
Wally Don't put 'em on your head.
Kenny I always put them on my head, Wally. You know
   that. (*He wears them for the rest of the scene.*)
Karen Where you get them? You got 'em off our line.
   You perve, Kenny. I can't stop laughing. This is my

FRIENDLY FIRE

first time out on my own. It is. It's funny. I ought to
go home.
Kenny No, don't go home.
Donna I'll come with you, Karen, in a little while. Stay
out a bit longer.
Karen I can't.
Donna Why you crying?
Karen I got to go home. Danny's going to phone. His
case is up in court next week.
Donna When?
Karen Next week.
Donna You goin' to court?
Karen Yeah. I got to stand by him. Ain't I?
Donna You going to court?
Karen Yeah. I am.
Donna What about your mum?
Karen I know.
Kenny Come on. Come, Karen. Cheer up.
Cheesey Where we going?
Karen I got to go home.

Dumb Dumb comes.

Donna Look who's here.
Cheesey What you doing here? What you want?
Donna Oh, he's stupid, he is. Leave him. Shoo, stupid.
Go on. Go on.
Cheesey Yeah. Go on.
Kenny Leave him.
Donna He gets on my nerves. You do.
Kenny Come on, let's go. Wall?
Wally Yeah, let's go. Leave him alone.
Cheesey No. Let's get him.

Grabs him. Dumb Dumb escapes.

Donna He's escaped.

365

They chase Dumb Dumb around the stage until they catch him.

Cheesey Ho ho.
Donna You're stupid, you are.
Cheesey Say fucking something. He does sometimes.
Kenny Don't.
Donna Yeah.
Cheesey Say something.
Karen I want to go home.
Donna Make him say something.
Cheesey You want to get him to talk, like? I will. I will. My pleasure.

He twists Dumb Dumb's arm until he calls out.

Kenny Leave off, Cheesey.
Wally Come on, you two.
Donna Yeah, he's stupid.
Cheesey He's nothing. Are you? You're nothing.

Spits at him. Donna laughs.

Karen Come on. I'm going home. Danny might phone.
Cheesey Dumb Dumb, what you got to say? What you got to say? What you got to say? You're a fucking little wanker. You're a fucking little twister, you are.
Kenny Don't. What you doing?
Cheesey It's his fault. He should speak up. He's stupid. You're stupid, are you stupid? What's the matter with you? A little scared? You should be. What's the matter with you? Eh? What's the matter?

Enter Shelley.

Shelley Hey, you. Leave him. Hey. Leave him.
Cheesey (*to Shelley*) You shut up and all.
Kenny Come on, Cheesey.
Cheesey You shut up, Shelley.

Shelley What you doing to him?
Donna Go on, Cheesey.
Shelley I'll have your fucking head off.
Donna Ooo ooo.
Shelley And yours, Donna.
Cheesey Will you?
Shelley (*to Karen*) And yours.
Kenny You alright, Shell?
Wally OK, Shell?
Kenny It's alright, Shell. It's alright.
Cheesey Will you?
Wally Peace, love.
Cheesey Come on then.
Shelley (*to Karen*) You, what you looking at? I'll have you and all . . . I'll have the two of you.
Karen Yeah, will you? Why ain't I home with my baby? Is that it, Shelley?
Shelley That's your business. You said it.
Karen I'll kill her.
Shelley Will you? You won't. You won't.
Kenny See what you done, Cheesey.
Cheesey What? What?

Enter Adie.

Adie You alright, Shelley? What's the matter?
Karen Oh, here's her boyfriend.
Shelley You OK, Dumb Dumb?
Donna Oh Adie.
Shelley Shut up, you.
Karen You just think I'm a fucking Sharon, Shelley.
Adie Well, you are a Sharon, Karen. That's why you're called Karen. 'Cos you're a Sharon.
Kenny Come on.
Wally Come on. We'll buy you a coke.
Kenny Come on, Cheesey.

Cheesey Do you want me to do him? Eh? Come here then.

Enter Gary.

Donna Here's her big boyfriend.
Gary Alright, everybody. Are you, are you alright, Cheesey?
Karen Come on. Let's go, Donna.
Kenny Yeah. Come, come on. And you, Cheesey.
Karen Come on Donna. I'm never going to speak to you ever again, Shelley. Come on, Donna.

They exit.

Adie He's the cavalry.
Shelley We'd have managed.
Gary Oh thanks, Shelley.

SCENE FIVE

The changing room.
   Gary, Adie, Cheesey, Wally and Kenny have been playing football and have nearly finished changing and packing their kit.

Adie (*to the audience*) This is the changing room. We been playing football. It was a draw.
Kenny Can I put these in your bag?
Wally Where's my shoe?
Cheesey England. England.
Wally Why didn't you bring your own bag, Kenny?
Kenny Well, Wall. Can I have your foot powder? My mum always gives me a wet towel.
Wally Here.
Cheesey That was never a penalty.
Wally Shut up, Cheesey.

Kenny I'm good looking. I am. Gis your comb.

Wally Ain't you got nothing? Do you want my gel?

Kenny No thanks, Wall.

Cheesey Ooo, ooo.

Kenny Mohicans are back in.

Wally They never was out.

Adie (*to Gary, asking for a comb*) Can I have that?

Wally Not with Mohicans.

Adie Thanks.

Cheesey We was playing against twelve men.

Wally The ref was Mr Dorkin, Cheesey. Spas.

Cheesey That was never a penalty.

Wally Where's the ball?

Kenny I don't know, where is it?

Wally We'd better lock it up. Where is it?

Kenny I dunno.

Wally Oh, yeah. I know. You said you'd had your belly
button pierced.

Kenny I have. You don't wear a ring in a match.

Wally You ain't had it done.

Kenny I have. I ain't going in the shower with you
again, Wally. You got an offensive weapon.

Wally I'm going to have it reduced.

Cheesey I'm not going in the shower with Adie again.
I might drop the soap. Ooops.

Gary Shut up, Cheesey.

Cheesey Oh, Gary, you spoke. They're quiet, the
lovebirds.

Gary Shut up.

Cheesey (*calling off*) See you, Lenny. That was a
cracking goal. Catch you up.

Wally Theirs was a good goal. Wan' it?

Kenny Yeah.

Cheesey What, that schwarzer? No. Rubbish.

Wally Yeah. But that was never offside.

Kenny It was.

Wally No, no.

Kenny It was, Wall.

Cheesey (*calling off*) Hey, Skikey. I'll see you over
there. OK?
   We should have slaughtered them.

Kenny You're quiet, Gary.

Gary I am.

Kenny What's the matter?

Gary Nothing's the matter with me.

Kenny Ooo, dear.

Cheesey Girls. Girls.

Wally I'm starving.

Kenny We going for a burger?

Wally No, I'm going home for tea.

Kenny My mum give me the money for a burger.

Wally You're deprived.

Kenny I know. Someone should make a programme
about me.

Wally They should.

Kenny No. She was being nice. Or a take-away.

Wally Come round our house. Save the money.

Kenny Or have a burger and then go round your house
for tea as well, Wall.

Wally You ought to eat more fruit, that's my mum.

Kenny My shin.

Cheesey Are we playing soggy biscuit?

Wally Shut up.

Kenny Did you hear him?

Wally Cheesey's the only one who's ever eat the soggy
biscuit.

Cheesey I never.

Wally You did.

Kenny No one's ever eat the soggy biscuit.

Wally Cheesey have. He have.

Cheesey Shut up.

Kenny Cheesey, you're a youth.
Cheesey Why are them two so quiet? Why's he so quiet? Why you so quiet?
Kenny He's angry with Adie over Shelley. She won't go out with him.
Cheesey Ooo, lover boy.
Kenny She loves Adie.
Cheesey Won't do her much good. Will it, Gaz?
Gary No, it won't.
Kenny What?
Gary I said it won't. Will it, Adie?
Cheesey Ooo. Sparring up. Is he a bender then? Really? Are you, Adie? Is he?
Gary Yes. She's never going to get him.
Cheesey Is he?
Gary Yes. He wants to suck my cock. Queer cunt.

Adie leaves.

Wally Well?
Kenny Wall.

Adie comes back for his bag.

Cheesey Adie forgot his handbag.
Adie Fuck off.

Adie punches Gary. They fight.

Cheesey Fight, fight.

The others part them.

Kenny Come on.
Wally Come on, Gaz.
Cheesey Come on, Gaz.
Wally There's the ball. Lock it up.
Kenny No. To me.

They play with the ball.

What about him?
Wally He'll be alright. Come on. Leave him.

They leave Adie.

SCENE SIX

Karen's house.
Karen is giving the baby a bottle. Donna is smoking.

Adie (*to the audience*) Karen's house. She's having
trouble with her mum. (*He goes.*)
Karen (*calling off*) Mum.
Donna You're never going to court.
Karen (*calling off*) I am. 'Course I am. Who's going to
stop me?

Mum. Donna's here. Donna, Donna!
(*to Donna*) Do you wanna cup of tea?
Donna (*calling off*) Yes. Thank you, Mrs Loder.
Karen I gotta go. He's relying on me. I gotta be there
when he's in court, haven't I?
Donna But your mum don't want you to go.
Karen I can't help that.

(*calling off*) Can I have one too, Mum? What? I am
going, Mum. I am. I am. And I can wear what I like.
I can. What do you mean, I'll end up with my throat
cut in a ditch? I'm going. Mum. He might be put
away. I got to go. What, what?

(*to Donna*) How many sugars?
Donna Two, please.
Karen I'm going anyway.

(*to Donna*) How many sugars?
Donna (*calling*) Two please, Mrs Loder.

SCENE SEVEN

Shelley's house.
  Gary comes in to see Shelley.

Adie (*to the audience*) Gary goes to see Shelley in her
  house. (*He goes.*)
Shelley What do you want, Gary? I'm doing something.
Gary What you doing?
Shelley What do you want to know for?
Gary Alright, alright.
  I ain't seen you, have I?
Shelley I got a lot on my mind. I got other fish.
Gary Oh, yeah?
  Seen Adie?
Shelley I seen Adie. I don't know what happened. So
  don't tell me. I don't want to know. I had to shut
  Cheesey up.
Gary I haven't seen Adie.
Shelley Haven't you?
Gary I don't know. What am I supposed to do?
Shelley Nothing as far as I'm concerned, Gary.
Gary I want to see Adie.
Shelley See him.
Gary I can't. Will you see him?
Shelley I seen him.
Gary Will you speak to him for me? Say, you know . . .
  You can do it, Shell. Though he can fuck off if he's
  going to be like that, going to sulk much longer.
Shelley You speak to him.
Gary He won't speak to me.
Shelley Have you tried? You haven't tried.
Gary No. I can't do that.
Shelley Why not?

Gary No. Don't be daft. I can't go running after Adie.
I can't do that.

Shelley Why can't you?

Gary No. You go round, Shell.

Shelley No, you go round. Go on.

Gary Shell . . . Shell.

Shelley Yeah?

Gary I still want you to go out with me.

Shelley Gary. This is daft. What's the matter with you?

Gary You love Adie, don't you? That's it, see. He got
you.

Shelley Shut up, Gary.

Gary Adie likes you.

Shelley Yeah.

Gary You gets on with Adie, like, you gets on with him.
He'll listen to you.

Shelley So what?

Gary What am I going to do?

Shelley Don't ask me.

Gary I wants to talk to Adie.

Shelley Talk to him.

Gary No, no. Anyway, I don't care, see. You can fuck
off, you can. I can do without you and Adie and
anyone and him. You're a bitch, Shelley. I'm going
mad in my head.

Shelley See, you can't get what you want.

Gary No, I can't. Clever, ain't you? Fuck off, I'm in hell
here. In my head. I can't do it. I can't. I'm going.

Shelley Go then. I never asked you to come round.

Gary You're a hard bitch.

Shelley Am I?

Gary It's all since Roger Jenkin's party. I know innit?
That's it.

Shelley What you mean?

Gary It is. First you wanted to come upstairs. Then Adie
don't like it. Then you wouldn't. Then you did. Then

Adie does one. It was all that night. That night when
it went all over the fucking place. You fancies Adie.
You won't say it though.

Shelley That's my business. Isn't it?

Gary Fuck off then, Shelley. See, I can do without
anybody. I can.

SCENE EIGHT

A field.
Gary is sitting down. Adie comes on and talks to the
audience.

Adie This is the field near Karen's house where we used
to spend a lot of time. There's only a scrappy bit of it
left now. I've come looking for Gary.
(*to Gary*) You're here then.

Gary Go away, Adie. No don't, Ade. Don't, Ade. Don't,
Ade. Don't go.

Adie I wasn't gonna go.

Gary I'm sorry. I am. I was angry with you. Scared.
Wanted to get you. I'm ashamed. My mum wants to
know why you ain't been round.

Adie I seen your mum.

Gary When?

Adie Just now. Give us.

Gary What?

Adie Give us, Gary.

Gary What?

Adie Give 'em us.

Gary What's this?

Adie Give 'em us. (*Takes a bottle of pills from Gary's*
pocket.)
What you got these for?

Gary I dunno.

Adie You wasn't gonna take them?

Gary I dunno. Ain't many in there.

Adie Enough to do you no good. You took 'em out of your mum's bag – what's the matter with you?

Gary I dunno.

Adie What's the matter?

Gary I would have come to see you.

Adie Not if you took these.

Gary I wasn't going to take them.

Adie Why didn't you come then?

Gary I would have.

Adie Yeah? No, you wouldn't.

Gary I would. I would. You're always first. You can't wait for nothing.

Adie I can't wait for nothing, only you. You can't wait for nothing that you really want. Like Shelley.

Gary That's no good.

Adie What we going to do?

Gary I don't know. I don't know what we going to do. We used to play about, like. Didn't we? We did, Adie.

Adie I know. I know. What do you want to do?

Gary I dunno.

Adie Do you want to?

Gary No. No thanks. I couldn't.

Adie You want everything, you do.

Gary I don't.

Adie You want Shelley.

Gary It's only natural, isn't it?

Adie Oh, aye.

Gary Shelley, she's a tease.

Adie She's not.

Gary She can have it.

Adie She don't want it.

Gary She ain't going to get it.

Adie You're afraid when you ain't got power.

Gary You took Shelley.

Adie I never did.

Gary I'm so lonely.

Adie Oh, yeah.

Gary When was you like it?

Adie Last year.

Gary When you was in hospital?

Adie It was when I realised it was hopeless. That I was, that you was. The knowledge dropped like a stone. A thud. The knowledge that what I imagined could happen was false. I was falling, falling. The knowledge dropped into real knowledge. The feeling. The knowledge. Hopeless. But it can't be hopeless 'cos you're hoping. Lost all confidence. I ain't got any.

Gary You're my friend. My only one. I don't care about no one else. I don't. If only you was a girl, Adie.

Adie I don't want to be a girl, thanks.

Gary I know. But it would sort it.

Adie For you it would, mate. I've always forgiven you. You always get forgiven, you. I'll always . . .

Gary Shelley loves you.

Adie No.

Gary She do, Adie. She'll never say. But she do. Why can't you face that?

Adie I don't want to. It's Shelley. I can't.

Gary You don't like Shelley like I like you.

Adie I like her like I like her. Leave me alone.

Gary If we could divvy it all up, it would be alright.

Adie What we gonna do?

Gary Dunno.

Adie You're in charge. You are, Gary. You know that.

Gary Not of Shelley.

Adie Of me.

Gary We have to live. Live. Don't we? Best we can. Sort out what we can put up with, what we can't. Hope something comes out.

Adie Shelley won't.

Gary Shelley will have to go her own way.
Adie Don't be like that.
Gary But she will. You know that.
Adie Oh dear. Remember our field?
Gary It's nearly all gone.
Adie Our stream.
Gary Our tiddlers.
Adie And Shelley, and you, and me. Better tell your mum you're alright.
Gary Will you come with me?

SCENE NINE

The War Memorial.
  The boys bring on the statue.

Adie (*to the audience*) But we still sees Shelley. We still meets by the statue. Everyone do.
  (*to the statue*) There he is. Hello mate. Still there then, are you?

Karen and Donna come on.

Donna Don't worry Karen, he'll be out soon.
Karen How do I know? He ain't been sentenced yet.
Donna But they'll take all his time on remand off that.
Karen He might get two years. That's what he said. They found him guilty. What am I going to do?
Donna Sh. Sh. (*Sneezes.*) I always get a summer cold. See. Never in the winter.
Karen That's pollen, that is. That's hay fever.

Enter Cheesey.

Cheesey Hello, Karen. I hear Danny's going down.
Donna Shut up, Cheesey.
Cheesey Oh, sorry. What's the matter? You OK?

Donna Yes. I got . . .
Karen She got a summer cold.

Donna sneezes.
Enter Kenny and Wally.

Cheesey Hey, Wally. Where you been? I been over your house.
Wally I called for Kenny.

Enter Shelley.

Kenny Hello, Shelley.
Karen I'm not talking to her.
Cheesey She heard about Danny? You heard about Danny, Shelley?
Shelley Don't wanna hear. Mind my own business.

Enter Dumb Dumb.

Hello, Dumb.

He nods.

It's alright. It's alright.

Enter Gary and Adie.

Gary Hello, Shelley.
Shelley Hello.
Gary You OK?
Shelley Yeah.
Cheesey Where we going?
Shelley Hello, Adie.
Adie Shell. (*to the audience*) We still see each other. It's not like it was before. Gary and me, like. Yeah. That is. But we still see each other. The three of us. See how it goes, eh? See how it works out. Walk away from it. Live through it. Live with it. You can't dodge it. Can you? What you dodging? (*to Shelley*) Alright Shell?
Shelley Yeah. I'm OK.

Dumb Dumb is looking up at the statue.

Cheesey Why's he always looking at that? What is it?

Kenny War memorial.

Cheesey What's that then? What is it?

Kenny Soldier, in it.

Cheesey What is it then? What's he doing? What's he saying, then? What is he? What's he for? What's that he's reading? What's he doing? What's he for? Why is he there?

Gary It's a war memorial, Cheesey.

Cheesey What for?

Gary War.

Cheesey What war?

Shelley Men start wars.

Kenny Not in our house.

Shelley Who starts wars then?

Gary Who fights 'em?

Wally I ain't started no wars. I ain't no war starter.

Gary Who fights 'em, Shelley? Girls don't fight 'em, do they?

Adie Why did his mother let him go?

Karen Don't be stupid.

Kenny No. That's right.

Shelley Men start war.

Gary Then why don't women stop 'em, then?

Wally Yeah. Hang on, Shelley. Perhaps it's women.

Shelley How?

Wally Well, we don't know what men would be like if there wasn't no women.

Donna Don't be daft. There wouldn't be no men if there was no women.

Wally That's it then, in it?

Gary I am a boy, Shelley. I am a boy.

Shelley And I am a girl, Gary.

Kenny Peace and love. Peace and love.

Shelley Look at Adie, Gary. You got him on a piece of string.

Gary Just because you ain't got him on a piece of string, Shelley.

Shelley I don't want him on a piece of string. Do I, Adie? Do I?

The soldier has dropped his letter onto the ground.

Adie Look, he's dropped the letter.

Karen What? Get out.

Adie He has.

Karen I'm going. Come on, Donna.

Donna No.

Wally What's it say?

Shelley Give here.

    (*She reads the letter.*) 13 Union Street. February 12, 1915. Dear son, I got your letter and I'm glad to hear you are well.

Gary Gis here.

    (*He reads.*) Dear old chap, this is just a line to see how you are, you old devil, and to tell you by the time you read this I shall be joining you.

They hand the letter around and read from it.

Karen Dearest Tommy.

Cheesey Dear son.

Donna My own dearest boy.

Kenny Dear Charlie.

Wally Dear Jack.

Adie Dear Reg.

Gary Dear.

Karen Dear Harry.

Shelley I enclose some socks which I have knitted for you.

Gary I expect it is wet where you are.

Karen The baby is doing well.

Kenny Last year we thought it would be over by
    Christmas.
Donna Your father got a chest, but he's still working.
Karen Mother has asked me to write to you.
Shelley Next door send their love.
Cheesey I enclose some cigarettes and that.
Donna Wish you could come home.
Wally When this is all over.
Adie Till I see you, my dear.
Shelley Your loving mother.
Karen Your loving wife.
Donna Your sister, Nelly.
Wally Your brother.
Kenny Your old friend, Wilf.
Cheesey God bless.
Karen All the best.
Donna Your loving wife.
Shelley Mary.
Gary Ted.
Adie Arthur.

> *The statue creates a series of images suggesting front
> line action: firing, bayoneting, holding his rifle above
> his head, choking, being shot, etc. These are arbitrarily
> juxtaposed one after the other during which the
> following happens*
>
> *Shelley, Karen and Donna are shocked by what they
> see and make sounds expressing their feelings, while
> Adie, Gary, Kenny, Wally and Cheesey call out the
> following:*

Gary Take cover.
Wally Over the top.
Kenny Shoot the officer.
Cheesey Stick the hun.
Adie Gas!
Gary Gas!

Kenny He's in the mud.
Adie I'm choking.
Kenny Send me home.
Wally Kill me.
Gary It's the rain. Steady, men.
Cheesey It's a whizz-bang.
Adie It's a shell.
Wally Fire at will.
Gary Take cover.

At the end of this, the statue takes up his usual pose.

Shelley What'll we do with this? (*indicating the letter*)

Dumb Dumb gives it back to the statue.

Kenny Why don't he speak?
Wally Why don't you speak? Say something.
    Why can't he say something?
Gary He can't.
Shelley Why can't he? Why can't he?
Adie Are you a deserter? Did you run away? Why don't
    you speak?
Dumb Dumb If he could speak, I would say I ain't
    nothing. I'm nothing. I ain't nowhere. Nowhere.
    There's nothing to say. Nothing. I ain't got nothing in
    evidence against me, though it may harm my defence.
    I got the right to silence. But I must warn me.

Young Men Sent to War
as the Serpent Enters the Garden

Peter Gill interviewed by Jim Mulligan

Although he has written parts for young people in his other plays, Peter Gill had never written a play in which each character is about sixteen years old. Faced with this task, he worked with young people and his research showed him that only particulars have changed in the condition of adolescents.

> It wasn't very easy to be a working-class child in the 1950s unless you were a grammar school boy like me. I think the 1950s were very difficult and depressing times for young people to grow up in. The condition of being young and having to deal with what has meaning for you and who you are is much the same now as it was then. Probably the only differences are the availability of drugs and young people now being more sexually sophisticated. There was a small group of artistic boys in my thug-ridden school and there were some gifted teachers who gave us profound insights. I left school when I was sixteen, and went to The Castle, now the Welsh School of Music and Drama. I quickly learned it was not very good and left after a year to take a job as ASM on an Arts Council Tour.

The stage is bare in *Friendly Fire*. Nine young people apparently fritter away their time hanging round the statue of a soldier or chat inconsequentially in each other's houses. *Friendly Fire* is not a devised work. It is a written play which must be treated like a string ensemble. Only the words, pared down to minimalistic exchanges and then blossoming into bleak metaphysical solos, are important. It is written so that it is director-proof, the direction coming from the acting and the speaking of the words.

The young people in this play are half-excluded from society. There are children who are much worse off than they are, in care for example, but it is still not very easy for people like my characters. Despite that, I don't see their lives as full of despair. There is a view that young people are not having a life at all. Well the colour red is the same for these adolescents as it is for the children of the Prince of Wales. In my view young working-class people are hugely misunderstood. The range of their emotional experience is considerable and I have no doubt young actors will be able to cope with these parts.

At the centre of the play there is a triangle. Adie, Shelley and Gary have been friends for years and there has never been a need to talk about their love for each other. Shelley is a tough, clear-thinking young woman who knows exactly how far to go and who is dismissive of her friend Karen because she has been stupid enough to have a baby. Now it is dawning on Shelley that Adie, the boy she loves, is probably more interested in, if not in love with Gary. She, for her part, rejects Gary's heterosexual posing which became objectionably obvious at Roger Jenkin's party.

Shelley does not have much time for Gary partly because she cannot see the pain he is in. He can get any girl he wants but not the one he really wants. Shelley realises that Adie does not love her the way she loves him and she works out that most men are drawn to each other in a very particular way so that she feels excluded. The three of them love in an innocent way but now the serpent has entered the garden. It needn't be a problem but we make it one.

Sex has come into their lives and now they have to
deal with it. I think probably Shelley is going to
withdraw and Gary is going to find it hard to do
without Adie. But they are only sixteen. Next year it
could all be different.

From the time Peter Gill started coming to London from
Wales when he was seventeen he was fascinated by
Charles Sergeant Jagger's statue of a soldier on Paddington
Station. The soldier is reading a letter and *Friendly Fire*
starts with Dumb Dumb talking to a similar statue,
asking who the letter is from. 'Is it from your mum?' But
the statue cannot reply anymore than Dumb Dumb can
communicate with the others. In the last scene the young
people reflect on the causes of war and Adie asks, 'Why
did his mother let him go?'

> The boys in this play are not far off being people who
> would have been in the First World War. I believe that
> Europe has not come to terms with what it did with
> its young men in that war. It's fashionable to demonise
> young men now but, when it comes down to it, it's
> young men without choice who have had to pay the
> price at critical points in this century. Adie questions
> the common belief that women have no power to stop
> what was happening. It appears to me that they seemed
> to collude with sending those boys to war. There were
> plenty of intelligent women around. They could have
> shot them in the foot but they chose not to.

As the soldier comes to life the young women are
shocked but the young men act out the part of willing
combatants, Gary the officer and the rest cannon fodder.
Finally Dumb Dumb speaks. 'There's nothing to say.
I got the right to silence.'

> In my play I am trying to put young people in touch
> with the history they are not aware of. They have

been robbed of it. The poor don't have a history. Nationalism is a fantasy of the upper classes.

The sad, appalling ambiguity of *Friendly Fire* is that young men today do volunteer to be slaughtered in places like Kosovo, in the name of nationalism, and even the young men milling around the war memorial somewhere in Essex might still choose to become part of a deadly history.

Production Notes

STAGING AND SETTING

As stated in the script, *Friendly Fire* is set around a war memorial, in a street, Karen's house, a changing room, Shelley's house, and a field. The statue is played by an actor. No attempt should be made to indicate a real statue. This should be effected by the actor's dress and stance. He should be dressed in the full battle dress of a private in the First World War. The pose and look should be suggested by the statues by Charles Sergeant Jagger, particularly the Great Western Memorial in Paddington Station. The actor/statue should be carried on and off stage as required. The stage is bare. Chairs can be used where necessary. For example, the changing room can be suggested by a row of chairs. Only essential props should be used. Lighting should be simply achieved. The play benefits from a fluid production and offers outstanding roles: the emphasis should be on the skill of the actors.

CASTING

The play is for a cast of ten aged between fifteen and seventeen. The parts are fairly evenly distributed, though the statue is silent and Dumb Dumb barely speaks until the end. There are three female parts and seven male.

EXERCISES

The play began its development with Peter Gill working for a week with a group of young men from the

Chichester Youth Theatre and the National's Young Theatre Company. The main theme they worked on throughout that time was *war*. They explored how young men who would have been labelled by society as thugs and troublemakers were sent off with colours flying to fight courageously for the love of their country. They examined the irony and unfairness of the situation. Peter Gill observed that war was a catalyst for 'boys' turning into 'men', and wanted to find out what had taken its place now, in a time of comparative peace.

During the workshop Peter Gill spent a lot of time observing and taking note of the way in which the group used language and interacted when they were working and relaxing during breaks from the workshop. These are some of the exercises he introduced to the group which you might find useful.

- In pairs – you have conflicting feelings. A is happy, B is profoundly sad. Let your bodies merge together to create one person. Both actors need to dramatise the conflict within the one person. A must sustain being happy and content and hold up B – who wants to crumble. Freeze this image so that it could be seen to represent the war within ourselves.
- Observe a group of three to five actors create an image they associate with war. Have a series of observers transform the image subtly over a period of time by moving a limb or adjusting stance, facial expression etc. Compare the twentieth-century images of war one might find outside the UK – in Russia, Italy or Hungary for instance. Decide what the images have in common and what they have to say about the period.
- Have the whole group talk in some detail about themselves. Discuss where each individual was born, where their parents and grandparents originated and

what they do/did for a living. Have each member of
the group decide what role they might have had if
they were living at the time of the First World War.
Have them read the work of the war poets, talk to
veterans and watch documentaries of the time.
- Imagine life in the trenches. Create a scene where you
have no choice but to kill a fellow soldier.

Peter Gill was interested in finding out where young men
of today feel they belong in society. Gary's speech, which
starts when Shelly has walked off and he is alone with
Adie, and begins, 'I can't do nothing about nothing. I'm
not in control of nothing. I want power. I want to be in
charge of nothing more like' epitomises the conflict of
emotions this young man is experiencing about his
maleness, national identity and class, and other big issues
such as his sexuality and own mortality.

Place the actor playing Gary in the centre of the space.
Have the actors playing the other roles in *Friendly Fire*
place themselves around him in a position where their
body language and expression clearly represents their
relationship to him at this point in the play. Discuss how
Gary's relationship to other characters in the play might
be contributing to his conflicting emotions at this point.
What, if anything, can he do to control his own destiny?

Create a monologue for Shelley moments after she has
had the altercation with Gary. What might it say about
young women of today in society?

Imagine that National Service has been reinstated.
Decide whether it would include young women as well
as young men and what sort of training it would involve.
In role as the young people in the play, create a scene
where they have been called for National Service. What
effect would this have on each of them?

Build up the background history of the characters by creating a series of improvisations where they have met up with one another around the war memorial over the last ten years. Discover how their relationship to one another might have changed with the passage of time.

Suzy Graham-Adriani
February 1999

GIZMO

Alan Ayckbourn

Characters

Ben Mason, a barman

In the hospital:
Professor Raymond Barth
GIZMO Project Chief Administrator
Dr Bernice Mallow, GIZMO Project
David Best, a neurologist
Nerys Potter, a physiotherapist
Ted Wilkins, a nurse

In the park:
Rust, Dazer, Fritzo, Hezza, Dart, Tiz, gang members
Manny Rice, a businessman
Rudi, his bodyguard
Keith, another bodyguard

In the flat:
Cevril Teese, Manny's girlfriend
Lando, a hit man

Audience members, passers by, etc.

Note: Gizmo has been written with a flexible cast
in mind. With doubling, it can be done with 11 actors
(8m 3f). Alternatively, it can be performed by
17 speaking actors plus an infinite number of extras.

Scenes

Scene One A hospital lecture theatre

Scene Two Ben's hospital bedroom

Scene Three The same

Scene Four A park

Scene Five Manny's apartment

Scene Six A hospital lecture theatre

The sets should ideally be as simple as possible and must in any event be designed so as to keep the scenes flowing with the minimum of hold-up between them.

A large lecture theatre in a private hospital. A number of people stand around talking quietly amongst themselves. Doctors, administrators, business people.

In a moment, Professor Raymond Barth enters. With him Dr Bernice Mallow.

Barth Good morning, everybody. Would you please be seated.

A general settling down.

For anyone new, I'm Ray Barth. I'm currently the PCA, the Project Chief Administrator for GIZMO, here at the Chepthorne Medley Research Hospital. I know you're all busy people so I won't waste your time. May I remind you, though, those of you who haven't attended a GIZMO briefing session before, that all information given out today is highly confidential so please, accordingly, we request you to observe all standard Class A security procedures. No notes, photographs, filming or recordings, please. Thank you. Now I'd like to introduce Dr Bernice Mallow who will be updating us on recent developments over the past six months. Bernice.

Bernice Thank you, Ray. Good morning, everyone. Thank you for taking time to share with us. First, let me say that I see, much to my alarm, the GIZMO project is about to enter its fifteenth year. So far it has cost a little over 25 million pounds sterling and employed over 700 doctors, technicians and micro engineers. Although I have personally only been associated with the Project for a comparatively brief six years, I am extremely conscious that there is an understandable impatience for results. Not least, I feel sure, from our funders at Chepthorne Medley. I would like, once again, to take this opportunity to thank them for their patience, for their generosity and for their unshakeable faith in GIZMO. Fifteen years in pursuit of a dream, however great, is a long time to wait. Well, patience is sometimes rewarded. Today, at long last, I am delighted to announce that we do finally have something to show. Not the whole dream – not yet – but at least, ladies and gentlemen, a part of the dream. A substantial part. A major step, certainly, on the way to a complete realisation of that dream. The oasis is in sight, dawn approaches, there is light at the end of the tunnel. (*She pauses somewhat dramatically.*) I want you to meet, now, two remarkable and unique men. Ladies and gentlemen, may I introduce David Best and Ben Mason.

Applause. David enters followed by Ben. Ben is pushed on in a wheelchair by Ted.

Ben, if I may talk to you first, how come the wheelchair? Do you mind telling me?

Ben (*a somewhat prepared reply*) Well, Bernice, about a year ago I was unfortunate enough to be involved in an extremely violent series of events. As a result of that, I was left over ninety per cent paralysed.

Bernice Could you be more specific, Ben? Was that the result of an attack? If so, what were the extent of your injuries?

Ben There were no injuries.

Bernice None? You mean you had no physical injuries at all, Ben?

Ben None whatsoever, Bernice. Certainly not in the way you mean.

Bernice Then what did happen precisely? David, perhaps you could help to explain?

David Well, Bernice, what happened to Ben is not that uncommon. Ben was working as a cocktail barman. He was unlucky enough to witness an appalling act of violence in the bar where he worked. A customer and his girlfriend were gunned down only inches away from him. As a result of this brutal slaying, Ben experienced a form of post traumatic shock. If you like, he literally froze with fear. The result being as you see him now.

Bernice And he's been like this for how long, David?

David Just over fourteen months.

Bernice And let me just confirm this, his paralysis is in no way the result of any physical injury?

David Ben's so-called paralysis, Bernice, his inability to move, is purely a choice that his subconscious mind has chosen to make. At the time of the attack, he was so distressed, so terrified, that his whole nervous system instinctively shut down in an attempt to disassociate itself from what it perceived as life-threatening events. It's a natural instinct. It's in all of us. And incidentally in most mammals, too.

Bernice Like a rabbit frozen in a car's headlights?

David Precisely that.

Bernice And what happens once the danger has passed? Does the effect wear off?

David Generally instantaneously. As soon as the danger has passed. Sometimes it remains for a few seconds, or even minutes or hours. But occasionally, in a case like Ben's, it becomes semi-permanent.

Bernice And is there a cure?

David Until now, the cure has been mainly patience. Physiotherapy sometimes helps a little, at least to stop the muscles from atrophying completely, but in the end, Bernice, how can you persuade a person to move, even a person wanting to move, when there is something far stronger in their mind forbidding them to move?

Bernice Presumably, David, somehow we have to persuade them to take control of their own body again?

David Absolutely. But easier said than done, Bernice.

Bernice David, obviously you're a doctor –

David I'm a neurologist, yes . . .

Bernice And you've been working closely with the entire GIZMO team. How does Ben's case link in with GIZMO? Can GIZMO provide a cure for Ben's condition?

David We have great hopes that it might.

Bernice Can you explain how?

David Certainly, Bernice. (*producing something from his pocket*) With this. (*He holds something up the size of a micro-chip.*)

Bernice And that is what? I don't know if you can all see it, it's tiny. What is it? A micro-chip?

David It's a form of one, yes. It's effectively a tiny micro processor which can be surgically implanted into the brain. It is actually covered with thousands of tiny, invisible fibres which attach themselves to the neural circuits in the brain. What effectively occurs is that this tiny device assumes control of the human body. What you're looking at here, ladies and gentlemen, is one half of GIZMO itself.

Bernice And does Ben have one of those implanted?

David Currently he does.

Bernice How does it feel, Ben?

Ben I don't honestly notice it. It felt a little odd at first but I think that was just the knowledge that it was there in my head. But I have no physical sensation of it whatsoever.

Bernice So what happens, David? Can you now send signals directly to Ben's brain? To his neuro-muscular system?

David Not quite as simple as that I'm afraid, Bernice. As you explained at the start, this is GIZMO still in its very early stages. Yes, we can send signals, but they're still quite primitive. What we've managed to come up with so far is PMRS – positive movement replication synchronicity.

Bernice Let me get that right. Positive movement replication synchronicity. Hmm. Sounds complicated. How does that work?

David Allow me to demonstrate, Bernice. Here on my wrist you see what looks at first sight like a perfectly ordinary, if somewhat bulky wrist watch. (*He holds up his arm.*) However, this is one particularly smart watch. Not only does it tell the time pretty well – (*glancing at it*) – very well, in fact – it also, via a series of built in sensors, detects the movements made by my own body which are then transmitted virtually instantaneously to the GIZMO receiver in Ben's head. As a result of his own stimulated neural system, Ben's muscles should then move in direct synchronicity with my own. In other words his movements should precisely imitate mine.

Bernice Sounds good in theory, David. Can we give it a try?

David Why not? I'd be happy to, Bernice.

Bernice Ben?

Ben Sure.

David Before I switch on I'd better start from the same position Ben is starting from. So I'll take a chair – (*He does so.*) – and to prove there's no trickery here, folks – I intend to sit with my back to Ben so neither of us can see each other . . . (*He sits now, directly behind Ben.*) . . . like so. OK. You ready, Ben?

Ben Ready.

David (*touching the watch*) Switching on.

Ben's body convulses slightly.

From now on both men move almost exactly together.

David grips the arms of his chair; Ben involuntarily grips the arms of his wheelchair.

David rises slowly from his chair; Ben does likewise.

Ben (*a little uneasily*) Hey . . .

Bernice Ben?

David You OK, Ben?

Ben I'm OK. I'm still a little unused to standing . . .

David It's OK, Ben, you're going to be fine. Just do what I do.

Ben I don't have a lot of choice, David – (*as David starts walking*) – Whey!

The two men walk a few paces.

They turn together.

They wave almost simultaneously at the onlookers.

The audience applaud. David and Ben applaud back. They bow.

As the applause continues, they turn to face each other. They walk towards each other.

They shake hands.

Bernice moves forward. She shakes hands with David. Ben's hand goes up and down in unison with their handshake, though he is shaking empty air.

Bernice turns to Ben. She takes his hand. Ben looks towards David a little helplessly. David executes a handshake gesture which allows Ben to do likewise with Bernice.

David leans forward while this happens and executes a mid-air kiss. Ben mirrors this landing a kiss on Bernice's nose.

The men bow once more to the crowd who are still applauding.

The three then leave the platform together.
The assembly stop applauding and get up to leave,
chattering animatedly amongst themselves.
The lights fade and come up almost immediately on:

SCENE TWO

Ben's hospital bedroom.
Ben is lying motionless, in his track-suit, on the bed.
Ted is sitting reading. He is wearing the PMRS on his
wrist. It is apparently switched off since Ben is motion-
less. A silence.

Ben Are you going to be much longer?
Ted (*engrossed*) What?
Ben Reading that?
Ted Why?
Ben Because I want to get up. I want to walk about.
Ted Well, go on. Walk about, I don't mind.
Ben I can't, can I? You know that. I need you.

Pause.

Look, will you switch it on, please?
Ted You want to go to the toilet?
Ben No.
Ted That's the only reason I'm supposed to switch it on.
   To take you to the toilet.
Ben Oh, come on, Ted.
Ted Those are my instructions. Cheer up, the physio'll
   be here in a minute. She'll sort you out.
Ben Thanks very much. That's all I need.

In a moment, Nerys enters. She is fit, young and
hearty. She also has on a track-suit and wears the
PMRS on her wrist.

Nerys Good morning.

Ben groans.

Ted Morning.
Nerys Right! Ready, are we?
Ben No.
Ted I'll leave you to it. Have a nice time. (*He goes.*)
Nerys Alright. Cheer up, Ben. (*She lies on the floor.*)
  Here we go, then. Switching on. Ready?

*Nerys switches on the GIZMO on her wrist. Ben's
body twitches as contact is made with his nervous
system.*

Ben Ah!
Nerys Come on. It doesn't hurt.
Ben How do you know it doesn't?
Nerys (*ignoring him*) And – up we get!

*She springs lithely to her feet. Ben is reluctantly forced
to mimic her.*

Ben Ow! Steady on!
Nerys (*ploughing on regardless*) And – shake it all out.

She shakes her body loosely. Ben follows suit.

And – shake it all out. And – shake! And shake! And
now let the head roll like this. And roll – and roll –
and roll. And the other way. And roll – and roll – and
roll. Good! Feeling relaxed?
Ben No.
Nerys And now the shoulders. Roll the shoulders, that's
it. Roll them. Good. And roll and roll. Now, gentle
jogging on the spot, remember this? Gently to start
with. Keep the rest of the body relaxed. That's it,
relaxed!
Ben It is relaxed! I'm not doing anything.

Nerys And a little bit faster now. (*She picks up the pace slightly.*) Good. Feel it hurt a little. It ought to hurt.

Ben It does hurt.

Nerys And a little bit faster now. Sprinting, sprinting flat out. Fast as we can, come on.

She runs on the spot vigorously. Ben makes agonised sounds.
Nerys slows down to a walk.

Good! And walk a little, now. Breathing deeply, Ben. Breathe, breathe . . .

Ben Can we sit down?

Nerys Sure. You want to sit down, you can sit down. I'm not stopping you.

Ben Oh, come on! You know I can only sit down if you sit down.

Nerys Me? I don't want to sit down, I want to do some more exercise. You're the one who wants to sit down. And – ready? – running once again, here we go.

Another burst of concerted running.
Finally Nerys slows down again.

Ben (*wheezing, very out of breath*) I think I'm going to have a heart attack.

Nerys No, you're not, you're perfectly fit. There's nothing wrong with you at all.

Ben Then what am I doing in here if there's nothing wrong with me?

Nerys Perfectly healthy. It's all in your mind, that's all.

Ben I know it's all in my mind. That's the whole point, you stupid woman.

Nerys (*rather viciously*) And – bending and floor touching now. One – two, one – two . . .

Nerys goes into a vigorous floor-touching exercise.
Ben is again forced to follow suit.

Ben (*in agony*) Ah! Ah! I'm sorry – I didn't mean that!

Nerys (*remorselessly*) . . . one – two . . . one and two. And one and two! (*She continues for several seconds. Finally stopping*) And relax!

Ben That it, then?

Nerys Certainly not. We're just warming up, Ben. And – jogging again gently now . . . Here we go.

They jog.

Ben Oh, God! I'm dying. I think I'm dying . . .

David enters. He watches them both for a second. Nerys notices him and stops.

Nerys Oh, good morning, doctor.

David No, no, carry on, please. I'll come back later.

Ben No, no, stay! Please stay, this woman's trying to kill me!

Throughout the next, they talk to each other as if Ben wasn't there. Nerys continues to exercise, forcing Ben to do likewise.

David How's he doing? Any progress?

Nerys Well, he's going to be fit, anyway. Whether he likes it or not.

Ben Listen, I'm a barman, not an Olympic athlete.

David But he's not contributing anything of his own accord?

Nerys Nothing as far as I can tell.

David It's all via the GIZMO?

Nerys So far.

David Yes, that's a worry. He ought to be contributing by now.

Ben Listen, I am here, you know. You can talk to me if you want to.

David No, it's all up there somewhere. In that mind of his. We'll get there eventually. Don't worry. (*turning to Ben*) How are you feeling, old chap?

Ben Terrible.

David Feel like moving on your own yet, do you?

Ben I can't. I keep telling you, I can't.

David Perhaps you're not trying hard enough, old chap. Come on. Have a try.

Ben I'm telling you. I cannot move.

David Just try and walk to the bed. Stand still for a second, would you, Nerys?

Nerys does so.

Come on, Ben, have a nice sit down. Wouldn't you like to try that for me?

Ben (*a motionless, internal struggle as he tries*) I – I – can't!

Nerys Come on, Ben. Try. You're not trying. You can do it. Go. Go.

Nerys makes little encouraging arm movement, as she speaks, urging Ben towards the bed. Ben copies her gestures.

David (*seeing Ben's movement*) Ah, look! There was something then.

Nerys No, that was me. Sorry.

David Yes, of course. Could you switch it off a minute, Nerys. Just so he can try moving on his own?

Nerys (*doubtfully*) If you're sure.

Ben (*alarmed*) No, don't switch it – Aaah!

Nerys switches off the wrist controller. Ben loses all control of his body and collapses on the floor in a heap.

David (*not very concerned*) Whoops!

Nerys There. As you see . . .

David Not too clever. (*bending down to Ben, not unkindly*) You've got to be ready to help yourself, old chap. We're all here to help you, to get you better. We're all trying our best. But in the end, it's down to you, you see?

Ben (*through gritted teeth*) Shit!

David (*straightening up*) Keep at him, Nerys. Do all you can. This project is crucial. I hardly need to tell you how much is at stake here. They're getting impatient. There's a lot of time and love gone into this. And money. We badly need a result.

Nerys I'll do my best, doctor.

David GIZMO's far too important for this one to foul it up. Far too important . . . (*He goes.*)

Nerys There. Did you hear that? I hope you took note. Right. Since you're down there. Floor exercises. (*She lies down on the floor.*) Ready?

Ben Oh, no!

Nerys switches on the PMRS wrist controller again. Ben's body immediately readjusts itself so that it copies her own.

Nerys Legs up to ninety – and ready for cycling, away we go.

She and Ben start peddling the air furiously, Ben groaning with the effort. The lights fade but return almost at once to:

SCENE THREE

The same.
  Ben is standing looking out of the window.
  Ted, still wearing the PMRS wristwatch stands
watching him, rather bored.
  Ted shifts and scratches his chest. Ben is forced to do
likewise.
  A pause.
  Ted scratches his head.

Ben Don't do that.
Ted Sorry.

  Pause.
  After a moment Ted sniffs and involuntarily wipes
  his nose with the back of his hand.

Ben Look, will you stop it.
Ted Alright.
Ben I don't want all your disgusting habits.
Ted My nose was itching.
Ben Well, keep your hands to yourself.

  Silence.

Ted You want to sit down?
Ben In a minute.
Ted Only my feet are hurting.
Ben In a minute.
Ted It's alright for you. I've been up since six o'clock.
  I've been up and down the wards. Emptying the bed
  pans. Serving breakfasts. You're lucky I'm letting you
  stand up at all. I'm only supposed to take you to the
  toilet.
Ben Yes, I know, I know. Thank you. Incidentally, next
  time would you wait till I've finished, please.

Ted How do I know when you've finished? I'm not a urologist. (*indicating the watch*) Look, if you don't sit down soon, I'm switching this off –

Ben You'd better not. You switch that off, I'll fall over. And if I fall over and hurt myself, you're in trouble.

Ted Well, why can't you just sit down?

Ben Because I've been sitting down for fourteen months, that's why. Except when that lunatic is forcing me to exercise. Standing here is a very wonderful experience, I can tell you.

Ted Wish I could sit down for fourteen months.

Ben You can't imagine what it's like. Just being able to look out of the window again.

Ted Lovely day.

Ben Yes. The park looks beautiful.

Ted Might look beautiful. It's full of perverts and muggers.

Ben I can't see any.

Ted Well, you won't see them, will you? They'll be lurking.

Ben Who will?

Ted The muggers. In the bushes.

Ben Rubbish.

Ted Them bushes are full of muggers.

Pause.

Ben I feel like going for a walk.

Ted What?

Ben Come on. Let's go for a walk.

Ted (*alarmed*) We can't do that!

Ben Why not?

Ted We can't just go out for a walk.

Ben Why not?

Ted You're a patient. You're not allowed out for walks.

Ben Why not?

Ted Because.

Ben I'm a patient, not a prisoner.

Ted You go for a walk, they'll all start wanting to go for walks, won't they? Whole hospital'll be going for walks.

Ben Of course they won't.

Ted They might.

Ben Most of them can't walk, anyway.

Ted I can't let you go for a walk. What would Dr Best say. He'd – he'd have me.

Ben You could go for a walk.

Ted Eh?

Ben If you wanted. What if you went for a walk? I'd have to go for a walk too then, wouldn't I?

Ted Why should I go for a walk?

Ben Better than standing here. Come on. You must be due for a break. You have one every three minutes. It's a lovely day. No one'll know. Tell you what, you walk ahead of me. Then if we're caught you can say you didn't know I was following you.

Ted (*dubiously*) Don't know about that. Can I stop and have a fag?

Ben 'Course you can.

Ted (*considering*) I'll go first, right?

Ben You'll have to.

Ted You follow on.

Ben I've precious little choice . . .

Ted starts to leave cautiously. Copying him, Ben follows.

Ted And don't get lost.

Ben Not unless you do.

They both leave. Almost immediately, the lights change and we are in:

SCENE FOUR

The park.
  Occasional passers-by, etc.
  Ted enters, followed at a distance by Ben.

Ted (*stopping*) Just a minute.
Ben (*doing likewise*) What's the matter?
Ted Going to have my cigarette.
Ben Well, don't be too long.
Ted As long as it takes, mate. That was the deal. I'm on
  a break.

  Ted gets a cigarette out and lights it. Ben echoes his
  movements.
    Ted inhales gratefully. Ben does likewise.

Want one?
Ben I don't smoke.

  Pause. Ted smokes. Ben mimes.

Ted You do now. (*He drags.*) What happened, then?
Ben When?
Ted To you? What happened? How did you get like
  that, then?
Ben I was – I was working in this bar.
Ted Ah.
Ben There was this – young couple. Very flash, you
  know. Lots of jewellery. Good clothes.
Ted I know the sort.
Ben It was early on. They were the only ones in there.
  Both sitting at the bar. He was showing off a bit.
  Obviously just met her. Wanting to make an
  impression. Lot of drinks. Champagne cocktails,
  vodka stingers. She could hardly stay on her stool.
  Laughing away, they were.

Ted Had it coming.

Ben (*angrily*) What do you mean, had it coming?
Nobody has it coming. Not like that, anyway.

Ted Some do.

Ben Anyway. They're sitting there laughing and suddenly
this feller's in the doorway. I didn't even see him
come in. I'm down the other end of the bar, you see,
restocking the ginger ale. And he stands there this
bloke and he calls out, 'Johnny' or 'Gianni' – maybe
Gianni – anyway, this other bloke's name –

Ted The one at the bar?

Ben Right. And the one at the bar, he goes as white as a
sheet. And the one in the doorway says it again, 'Hey,
Gianni. Welcome home, Gianni.' And then he brings
out this gun from under his coat and he shoots him,
calmly as that. In his chest.

Ted What sort of gun?

Ben I don't know. I don't know anything about guns.

Ted Machine gun?

Ben No. A pistol.

Ted Oh.

Ben One that went bang, anyway. Right in the chest.
And this bloke's coughing and there's blood
everywhere and the girl's screaming and holding on to
him. I don't know why she didn't get out of the way, I
don't know why she had to hold on to him. Why did
she have to hang on to him – ? And this bloke starts
shooting again – and naturally he hits her as well,
though I don't think he meant to particularly – though
maybe he did – and all of a sudden they're both of
them lying there. And he's dead and she's – she's
making this terrible sort of whining. Like a dog – like
when my dog broke its leg . . . And I know she's dying
as well.

Ted And then? Then what happened?

Ben This bloke with the gun, he sort of looks down at them. And he smiles. It was the most frightening smile I've ever seen in my life. And then he turns and he looks straight at me. And he's still smiling. And he says, 'Okay, barman,' he says, 'drinks on the house, eh?' And he starts walking towards me and I know then he's going to kill me, too. I know he is. Because I'd seen it all happen, you see. And I'm frozen, just frozen. Like the rabbit.

Ted (*spellbound*) Why didn't he, then? Shoot you?

Ben Someone came in from the street. They'd heard the shots and the screaming.

Ted What happened to the bloke?

Ben He dived round the counter and got out through the back.

Ted Lucky escape. For you, I mean.

Ben All that blood. I've never seen so much blood.

Ted He could've killed you.

Ben I know.

Ted He might still, I suppose. If he finds you. Would you recognise him?

Ben Mmmm?

Ted The bloke with the gun. Would you recognise him again?

Ben I'm hardly likely to forget him, am I?

Ted He could be hiding in these bushes.

Ben Great.

Ted Well. You never know. We'd better go back.

Ben If you like.

Ted You didn't tell me you was a marked man. I'd never have come out with you if I'd known you was a marked man.

Ted grinds out his cigarette. Ben mimes the same.

Looks like it's clouding over, anyway.

They start to walk again, Ben following, as before.
  Ted has gone only a few paces before his way is
barred by Hezza, Tiz and Dart, three female gang
members.

Hezza Excuse me, mister, you got the price of a cup of
  tea?
Ted (*backing off*) No, sorry I haven't, no.
Dart Oh, come on, mister . . .
Tiz Mister . . .
Ted I got no money, get out of me way . . .
Hezza Mister . . . Come on, mister . . .
Tiz (*simultaneously, with her*) Mister . . . give her some
  money . . .
Dart (*simultaneously, with them*) Go on, don't be so
  mean, mister . . .

The three girls close in, cajoling him.

Ted (*nervously*) Look, get out of my way, do you hear?
  You're not getting no money, not from me. Now piss
  off, all of you . . .

Three boys, Rust, Dazer and Fritzo appear. The girls
stop their chanting. Rust is clearly their leader.

Rust (*politely*) Pardon me. Are you giving these young
  ladies aggravation?
Ted What?
Rust Have you been frightening them?
Ted 'Course I haven't.
Rust Has he been frightening you, girls?
Dart Yes, he has.
Ted I have not.
Hezza Look at Tiz, she's shaking.
Tiz I'm shaking, look.
Rust That's appalling. What's he been doing then, girls?
  Exposing himself?

Ted (*indignant*) I have not.

Dart Yeah, he was flashing at us, wasn't he, Hezz?

Hezza I was terrified. Never seen anything like it . . .

Ted What you talking about? I've done nothing . . .

Rust You disgusting old pervert . . .

Dazer You filth . . .

Fritzo You ought to be ashamed of yourself . . .

Rust . . . corrupting innocent young girls . . .

Ted Innocent? What, this lot? Don't make me laugh.

Hezza Oh, thanks very much, I'm sure.

Rust Hey, hey! What are you saying? Are you suggesting these girls are not pure . . .

Ted You're joking.

Rust (*indicating Hezza*) That happens to be my fiancée you're talking to.

Ted Ah, well. I didn't know that. Beg your pardon, mate . . .

Rust You want to be more careful. Going around flashing at other people's fiancées . . .

Ted Bollocks. Who're the other two, then?

Dart We're her bridesmaids.

Ted Oh, give over. Go on, get out of me way.

Ted tries to push past her.

Dart (*over-reacting*) Ow!

Fritzo Did you jostle her, then?

Dart He jostled me.

Tiz Alright, Dart?

Fritzo First he's flashing, now he's jostling . . .

Dazer What's he done to you, Dart?

Dart I think he's broke my arm.

Ted I did not. How could I?

Dazer Right you, I'm having you. That's *my* fiancée whose arm you just broke.

Ted I never broke her arm. What you talking about? Let go of me . . .

Ben (*in alarm*) Ted!

*Ted is surrounded and swamped by the gang. We lose
sight of him in the melee. We have a clear idea of
what's happening to him because, from a distance,
Ben copies Ted's fate.*

*He falls to the ground under an unseen hail of
blows. He curls up to protect himself and after a few
violent convulsions, lies still. The gang step back to
reveal Ted in an identical position.*

Rust (*as they do this*) That's enough! Stand back. What's
he carrying, Dart?

Dart starts to search Ted.

Tiz We all going to get a share this time?
Rust No. (*to Dart*) What you got?
Dart Ten quid.
Dazer That all?
Rust Give it here.
Dart (*finding some more*) No. Wait. Eleven. Here.

She hands the money to Rust, who pockets it.

Tiz Why don't we get a share?
Rust I need it.
Tiz What for?
Rust Overheads.
Tiz (*puzzled*) Overheads?
Dart (*who is still searching Ted's body*) Hey, Rust, look
at this! (*Pleased with herself she holds up the PMRS
controller.*) What about that then?
Fritzo Hey! Hey!
Hezza Look at that!
Dazer What is it?
Dart It's a wristwatch, genius.
Hezza Big wristwatch.
Dart It's heavy.

Rust Give it here, then.
Tiz You keeping that as well?
Rust Yes.
Tiz Overheads?
Rust No.
Tiz Why, then?
Rust Because I like it.

Fritzo, meanwhile, has discovered Ben and moves over to him.

Fritzo Oy, Rust! There's another one over here.

The others turn, somewhat surprised.

Look.
Rust Did you do that?
Fritzo I never touched him
Rust How'd he get like that?
Fritzo I dunno. He was just lying here.
Ben Hallo.

The others move over.

Rust What you doing there?
Ben Just – having a lie down . . . (*to the others*) Hallo. Afternoon.
Dart He's a loony.
Dazer He's a dosser.
Dart (*to Rust*) Shall I search him?
Rust Might as well. (*putting on the watch*) Don't mind her searching you, do you, mister?
Ben No, go ahead – (*seeing what Rust is doing*) Look, please don't play with that watch, it's a –

Ben springs abruptly to his feet as Rust puts on the watch. Dart, who was about to search Ben, springs back, somewhat startled.

Dart Hey!

Rust What you playing at?

Ben Excuse me, that watch. Could you give it to me, please?

Rust What?

Ben I need that watch. I must have that watch.

Dazer Cheeky!

Rust My watch? You want my watch?

Ben No, it's my watch.

Hezza It's not your watch. It's his watch.

Dazer That nice man over there give it him.

Ben No, you don't understand . . .

Dart For his birthday.

Ben . . . I must have that watch . . .

Fritzo Shall I hit him?

Rust Search him first.

Dart Right.

Dart frisks Ben somewhat expertly.

Ben (*as she does this*) Look, that watch is worth practically nothing to you, I promise. But it's vital to me. It's – it monitors my medical condition, you see . . . That man there was a nurse . . .

Dart finishes her search.

Rust Anything?

Dart Nothing. No ID. Nothing.

Rust Listen, you. (*indicating Fritzo*) I ought to get him to hit you. But I'm in a good mood. It's a sunny day, I've got a nice new watch. Take advantage. I'm walking away now. I suggest you do the same, eh?

Ben You don't understand . . .

Rust Bye, bye.

Rust turns away. The rest of the gang start to follow him. Ben, copying Rust, turns away and starts to walk off in the opposite direction.

Dazer (*as Ben goes*) That's a good lad.
Ben (*still walking away*) If you'd only listen to me . . .

> *Rust stops and takes a look back over his shoulder. So does Ben.*

Rust Go on, then. I said, get going.

> *He waits. So does Ben.*

Off you go. I won't tell you again.
Ben Look, that wristwatch you're wearing, it's not really a watch, it's a –
Rust (*turning to face Ben*) Hey! Do you hear me? Go!

> *Ben has turned to face Rust.*

(*pointing at Ben*) You – you're really asking for it.

> *Ben is pointing back at Rust.*

Right.

> *Rust starts to move menacingly towards Ben. Ben starts to move menacingly towards Rust.*

That's it. You've had your chance. That's it.
Hezza Get him, Rust.
Dazer Go for him, Rust.
Ben (*as he moves forward*) Listen, you must understand, this is not really me doing this. It's you doing this.

> *The two stop close, facing each other.*

Rust Yes, that's right. It's me doing this. (*He produces a knife.*) It's me doing this, as well.

> *Ben copies Rust's action. The only difference is, he has no knife. The two start to circle each other crouching slightly.*

(*slightly puzzled*) This is a knife, you know.
Ben (*alarmed*) I know it is. Please.

Rust feints. Ben does likewise. Rust steps back still mystified. So does Ben. The others have gathered round to watch.

Fritzo Kill him, Rust.
Dart Go for him, Rust.
Hezza He's mad. He hasn't even got a knife.
Tiz You're gonna get killed, Mister.
Rust (*springing forward*) Come on!
Ben (*springing forward*) No!

Rust, startled by Ben's leap forward, leaps back. So does Ben. He has ended up close to Tiz.

Tiz (*producing a second knife, to Ben*) Here! Take this. (*She places it into his hand.*)
Ben (*alarmed*) I don't want this.
Hezza What you doing, Tiz?
Tiz Even things up a bit.
Rust (*to Tiz*) I'll deal with you later.

The fight starts in earnest, though very little comes of it. The faster, more physically aggressive Rust gets, the more Ben does.

(*during this*) Ha! Yeah! Come on!

These noises, one suspects, are to cover up his own increasing insecurity rather than to unsettle his opponent.

Ben (*despite his aggressive actions*) Sorry . . . no, I didn't mean that . . . sorry, really . . .

As the fight continues, Manny Rice appears. He is a well-groomed, well-dressed thug, the Mr Big of the neighbourhood. He is accompanied by his regular bodyguards, Rudi and Keith. They watch for a second. Manny says something softly to Rudi.

Rudi (*yelling in a terrible voice*) Oy!

The fight stops.

Rust Shit!
Hezza It's Manny Rice.
Rudi Here! Come here.
Rust Me?
Rudi Yes, you. Here. Mr Rice wants a word with you.
Rust (*hastily handing his knife to Hezza*) Get rid of that.

Ben copies this by giving his knife to Tiz.
   Rust moves towards Manny. Ben comes with him, a few paces behind.

You wanted me, Mr Rice.
Manny What's your name, boy? I know you, don't I? Rusty, isn't it? Something like that?
Rust My name's Rust, Mr Rice.
Manny Well, Rusty, you listen to me, because I'm not telling you again. This park belongs to me. It comes within my turf. It falls within my personal remit. You understand that, do you, boy?
Rust Yes, Mr Rice.
Manny This is a peaceful park, Rusty, intended for peace-loving law-abiding people. For babies and their nannies in search of fresh air; for old age pensioners on a quest for peace and quiet; for poets and nature lovers; dog walkers and bird fanciers; pigeon feeders and squirrel strokers. You get me?
Rust Yes, Mr Rice.
Manny It is not intended for squalid little pus-ridden scumbags like you, Rusty. I will not have innocent people molested in my park, alright?
Rust We haven't been molesting.
Manny (*indicating Ted*) Then what's that gentleman doing lying on the ground there? Taking a nap?

Rust No – he had cramp. He was jogging and then he fell over. We rushed over to help him.

Manny Only in your rush your boot landed on his head.

Rust No . . .

Manny And I daresay you decided to loosen his clothing by relieving him of his wallet, didn't you?

Rust No . . .

Manny Search him, Keith.

Keith steps forward and starts to frisk Rust.

Rust What you doing?

Rudi (*to the rest of the gang*) Clear off you lot, you hear? Out the park.

The gang disperses and goes off. Meanwhile, Keith kicks Rust's legs apart and forces his arms above his head. Ben follows suit.

Manny (*startled at seeing this*) Who's that, then?

Rust I dunno.

Manny What's he doing?

Rust I dunno.

Manny What you doing?

Ben Sorry?

Manny Are you with him?

Ben No, I was just taking a stroll. That's my friend who was . . . who fell over. (*He continues to copy Rust's contortions.*)

Manny Something the matter with you?

Ben No, just taking some exercise. The point is, you see –

Manny (*to Rust*) Have your lot been troubling him as well?

Rust No.

Keith Let's have the watch, Rust.

Rust The what?

Keith You heard. Give us the watch.

423

Rust That's mine.
Keith (*threateningly*) Give it . . .
Ben No, that's what I wanted to talk to you about. That watch is actually a very sophisticated piece of equip –

He fails to finish the sentence, however. At that moment, Rust removes the watch and hands it to Keith.
Ben instantly collapses like a rag doll.

Manny What happened? Rudi, have a look at him.

Rudi steps forward and looks at Ben.

What's the matter with him?
Rudi I don't know, Mr Rice. Could be delayed concussion.
Ben No, I'm fine really. If you'd only just give me the –
Manny Don't try and talk. Keith, get him in the car.
Keith Right. (*He is still holding the watch.*) You want this, Mr Rice?
Manny Yes, give it here.

He takes the watch from Keith and stuffs it into his pocket.
Keith heaves Ben over his shoulder.

Ben (*as this happens*) Listen, all you need to do is to take that –
Manny Don't talk! Careful with him, Keith, careful.
Keith Sorry, Mr Rice.

Keith goes off with Ben.

Manny Rudi.
Rudi Mr Rice?
Manny See that one over there gets to a doctor.
Rudi Yes, Mr Rice.
Manny We can't have my park getting a bad name, can we?

Rudi moves to Ted and during the next lifts him up in similar fashion and carts him off in the opposite direction.

(*to Rust*) As for you, you are an aberration, boy. You know what that means?

Rust No, Mr Rice.

Manny It means you are human ballast, son. Mislaid luggage. Redundant footage. You are not wanted on life's voyage, alright?

Rust Yes, Mr Rice.

Manny So take your sordid little gang of genetic deviants and bugger off.

Rust Yes, Mr Rice.

Manny If I see you here again, come closing time they will discover your head impaled on the spikes of the main gates, is that clear?

Rust Yes, Mr Rice. (*He hurries off, relieved that the interview is over.*)

Manny (*to himself*) I don't know. What's the world coming to? I ask you? (*calling, as he goes*) Keith! Start the car.

He goes off. As he does so the lights rapidly cross fade to:

SCENE FIVE

Manny's apartment. A bar. Two doors.
  Cevril, an attractive young woman in a low-cut dress, is sitting on the sofa reading a magazine.
  Manny enters, followed immediately by Keith, who is still carrying Ben.

Manny (*to Cevril*) Come on, shift yourself!
Cevril (*sulkily*) Why?

Manny Because we need the sofa, that's why. Put him down here, Keith.

Keith puts Ben down on the sofa, narrowly missing Cevril as she springs up.

Cevril Careful!

Manny (*ignoring her, to Ben*) How you feeling?

Ben I'm perfectly fine. If you'd only let me explain . . .

Manny If you don't mind me saying so, son, you don't look fine to me. You can rest here. I feel responsible. Cevril will look after you.

Cevril I will?

Manny Yes, you will. Alright, Keith, that'll do for now. I'll be down again in a minute.

Keith Yes, Mr Rice. (*He goes out, under the next.*)

Manny Now listen – what's your name again –?

Ben Ben. You see, the point is –

Manny Listen, Ben, I want you to relax. Treat this place as your own. Take time to recover. I'm a hard man, Ben, but I'm a fair one – know what I mean? Person gets hurt on my turf, walking in my park through no fault of his own, then I owe him, you see.

Ben I didn't know it was your park, I thought it was St James's Park.

Manny I'm looking after it for him while he's away. No seriously, Ben. There's owners and then there's the real owners. There's people who think they own things and then the people who really own them. Know what I mean? Little lesson in life. I'll be back in a minute. Got a little business to do, then we'll have a drink together. Cevril, look after him. Give him anything he wants – within reason, eh? (*He smiles.*)

Cevril Looks as if he's past most things.

Manny You do as you're told.

Cevril Yes, Manny.

Manny Don't want to make daddy cross, do you?

Cevril No, Manny.

Manny Good girl. (*He kisses her.*) Here. (*He takes the watch out of his pocket.*) Look. Present for you.

Cevril What is it?

Manny What's it look like? It's a watch.

Cevril Lovely. Might as well strap Big Ben on my wrist.

Manny See you in a minute. Oh, I'm expecting Lando round here in a minute.

Cevril Oh, no . . .

Manny Yes! If he arrives before I'm back, offer him a drink and all.

Cevril Cyanide.

Manny Don't know what you've got against Lando, I'm sure.

Cevril Nothing at all. He's just a mad murdering psychopath but apart from that he's perfectly charming.

Manny has gone.
   Cevril turns her attention to Ben. She studies him disinterestedly. She tosses the watch from hand to hand. Ben looks at her rather apprehensively.

What happened to you, then? Been in a fight?

Ben It's – rather a long story.

Cevril (*shrugging*) I've got nothing else to do.

Ben I witnessed a fight. Or rather I witnessed a killing. Two killings.

Cevril (*not over-impressed*) I see.

Ben I – I was left paralysed.

Cevril What? A bullet, was it?

Ben No. Just in my mind. Do you understand?

Cevril studies him.

Cevril Yes, that can happen. My sister run over a rabbit once. She can't drive at all now. Hardly get her into a car.

Ben Yes. That sort of thing.

Cevril So where did he find you, then? Manny? I thought he said in the park. What happened, you fall out your pushchair?

Ben You're not going to believe this . . .

Cevril Yes, I've heard that one a lot of times, go on.

Ben That watch . . . the one in your hand . . .

Cevril What about it?

Ben It's not just a watch it's a – sort of remote controller.

Cevril (*examining it*) This?

Ben It's called a positive movement replication synchroniser . . .

Cevril (*unimpressed*) There now.

Ben PMRS for short.

Cevril That's handy.

Ben No, really.

Cevril Really? What you do then? You time travel with it, do you?

Ben Of course not, it –

Cevril (*speaking into it*) Beam me up, I am trapped here with a lunatic.

Ben Look, just put it on. Put it on and I'll show you.

Cevril stares at him suspiciously. Finally she puts on the PMRS. Nothing happens.

Cevril Now what?

Ben I don't know. I've never worn it –

Cevril Oh, look! Venus! How did we get here?

Ben It's not for me, you see. It's usually worn by someone else.

Cevril It is 1746 and I am Queen Victoria.

Ben It may be switched off. Has it got a switch on it or something?

Cevril No. Only this . . .

Cevril touches something on the watch which causes
Ben to spring up off the couch and stand, mimicking
her stance.

(*startled*) Hey –
Ben That's it!
Cevril What is?
Ben Through that you can now control my movements.
As you move, I move.
Cevril (*disbelieving*) What?
Ben Try it.
Cevril Get off!
Ben Try it!

Cevril moves her arm suddenly. Ben does the same.

There you are.
Cevril What are you talking about? Anyone can do that.
Ben Try it some more.

Cevril tries one or two more movements, which Ben
copies.

You see!
Cevril Well, you're good, I'll give you that.
Ben You believe me then?
Cevril 'Course I don't. I'm not an idiot. I wasn't born
yesterday dinner time. It's a trick, that's all.
Ben A trick?
Cevril 'Course it is.
Ben What would be the point of it?
Cevril I don't know.
Ben Well, then.
Cevril Good line in chat though, isn't it? I'm afraid
when you have to go to bed, I have to go to bed as
well . . .
Ben Oh, really . . .
Cevril When you have to go to the –

Ben Oh, come on! Really!
Cevril Well.

She starts to move away. Ben does likewise.

Stop it.
Ben What?
Cevril Copying me. Stop it!
Ben I can't help it.
Cevril 'Course you can. Someone at school did that to me once.
Ben Really?
Cevril Kept copying me. All day. I punched her head in.

She moves again. So does he.

(*half-convinced*) I can't believe this.
Ben It's the truth.
Cevril I need a drink.

She moves behind the bar. Ben follows her.

You going to follow me everywhere?
Ben Until you switch it off.
Cevril What happens when I do that?
Ben I'll fall over again.
Cevril You want one?
Ben I don't drink.
Cevril The rate you fall over you can't afford to risk it. Now, what shall I have? I never know what to have. (*She ponders.*)
Ben May I suggest something?
Cevril You?
Ben If I may . . . Do you drink gin?
Cevril I drink anything.
Ben Alright, then. Cocktail shaker . . .
Cevril I thought you didn't drink. (*proffering it to him*) Cocktail shaker.

Ben (*hesitating, unable to take it from her*) No, hang on. It's easier for you to do it. I'll tell you what to do, OK? Put in some ice.

During the next, whilst telling her what to do, Ben echoes her movements as she obeys him.

Cevril Ice. (*She puts some in the shaker.*) That enough?
Ben Perfect. Angostura bitters!
Cevril (*searching for them*) Er . . . Angostura bitters. Yes. Got them.
Ben Just two or three drops over the ice . . .

She shakes the bitters into the shaker.

Whoaa! That'll do! Lemon juice . . .
Cevril Lemon juice. Say when. (*She pours.*)
Ben That's enough. Cointreau.
Cevril Cointreau. I thought you didn't drink. Say when. (*She pours.*)
Ben I don't. That's it. Gin.
Cevril Gin. How do you know all this? Say when. (*She pours.*)
Ben Whoaa! I used to be a barman. Lid on!
Cevril Lid on! Do you treat all your customers like this?
Ben Only the special ones . . . And shake.

Cevril shakes the cocktail.

Cevril Say when.
Ben Keep going. A bit harder. What did you say your name was?
Cevril Cevril.
Ben What S – E – V – ?
Cevril No. C – E – V – R – I – L. That enough?
Ben Little bit longer. Unusual name.
Cevril Yes. The story goes that my father turned up at my christening pissed as usual and when the vicar

asked him whether they'd chosen a name for me, he said several.

Ben (*laughing*) That'll do.

Cevril (*stopping*) Not a word of truth in it. Whor! I'm knackered. All this for a drink. What next?

Ben You drink it.

Cevril What, out of this?

Ben Sour glass. Got a sour glass? One of those there. No, the other one. That's it. OK. Now strain it into the glass.

Cevril (*doing so*) I hope this is going to be worth it.

Ben I guarantee it.

Cevril Right. Well, cheers!

Ben Cheers!

Cevril sips the drink cautiously.

Cevril (*reacting*) Blimey!

Ben No?

Cevril Fantastic. What's it called?

Ben It's called A Maiden's Prayer.

Cevril Dead right. It's the answer to everything.

Quite suddenly, Lando enters. He stares at them.

Lando Good afternoon.

Ben Afternoon.

Cevril (*sourly*) Oh, hallo, Lando.

Lando What's all this?

Cevril All what?

Lando Sorry to interrupt, I'm sure.

Cevril Not as sorry as me. 'Specially when you're the interruption.

Lando (*smiling*) You'd better learn to keep that mouth of yours shut, girl. Else one day I'm going to shut it for you.

Cevril You touch me and Manny'll tear you apart. You're just an employee round here, you know,

Lando. Like the rest of us. Just in case you'd
forgotten. I could put in a word, easy as that.

Lando I can wait. You're cream cake, darling, that's all.
Once your cream goes off, he'll bin you. Won't last for
ever, girlie. I'll be waiting. Who's he?

Cevril A friend.

Lando Of yours?

Cevril Of Manny's.

Lando (*approaching Ben*) I've seen him before. Where
have I seen you?

Ben (*nervously*) Nowhere, never met.

Lando Yes. Recently. It'll come to me. (*to Cevril*)
Manny's out, I take it?

Cevril He's back in a minute.

Lando So am I. (*to Ben*) You, don't run away. It'll come
to me. It'll come to me. We've met somewhere.

Lando goes.
Ben is breathing deeply.

Cevril You alright?

Ben (*faintly*) Yes.

Cevril You're not having a turn, are you?

Ben Who is that man?

Cevril His name's Lando. He – does jobs for Manny.

Ben What sort of jobs.

Cevril Things that – Manny doesn't want to get involved
with. You keep away from Lando, he's seriously
dangerous. I don't frighten easy but he scares the shit
out of me. Why does he think he knows you?

Ben Because we've met before.

Cevril You sure?

Ben I'd never forget him.

Cevril Where? Where'd you meet him?

Ben In a bar.

Cevril (*incredulously*) You had a drink with him?

Ben I was working there. He came in – he shot two
people – he nearly shot me.

Cevril The Blue Parrot? That bar?

Ben Yes, how did you know?

Cevril You were the barman, of course you were . . .

Ben Yes, I've just said.

Cevril (*remembering*) Yes! Of course! You're Ben –?

Ben Mason. Ben Mason.

Cevril And you really recognise him? Lando?

Ben Yes. How many more times?

Cevril And could you do that in court?

Ben Yes. I suppose so. If I was asked.

Cevril Bingo!

Ben They never traced who it was. They never charged
him.

Cevril Of course they didn't. They couldn't. Because
Manny gave him an alibi the size of a football ground.
Come on, we'd better get you out of here. Wait! I
better get changed. I can't even walk properly in this
thing.

Ben What's happening?

Cevril I'll be ten seconds. Don't whatever you do move
from there. (*She goes to the bedroom door.*)

Ben (*as she goes*) I'll try not to.

*Despite himself, he is forced to follow her. Cevril
closes the door in his face.*

*Ben marches up and down on the spot against the
closed door. Then as Cevril, now unseen by us, starts
moving about in the bedroom changing her clothes,
Ben copies her offstage actions.*

*He undoes the imaginary dress and steps out of it.
He runs to an invisible chest of drawers, opens one
and, taking out a bra, puts it on. He grabs a pair of
invisible jeans from a chair and struggles into them.
They are tight. Finally, he wriggles his feet into*

loafers, whilst simultaneously pulling a tee-shirt over his head. He runs his fingers through his hair as he makes a brief check in an imaginary mirror.

He hurries back to the door. As he gets there, it opens and Cevril is standing in the doorway, now dressed as described.

Cevril What you doing?
Ben (*rather guiltily*) Waiting for you.
Cevril Well, come on then, out the way. (*realising he can't*) Oh. Sorry.

She steps to one side. Ben does likewise. Cevril moves into the room. Ben goes into the bedroom and disappears.

(*turning*) Where are you going?
Ben (*off*) Sorry. I can't help it. We seem to have got out of sync.
Cevril Well, you can't stay in there. We need to be out of here. Come on out.
Ben (*off*) I can't. Tell you what, walk towards me a bit. If you walk this way, then that'll cause me to walk that way.
Cevril Then I'll be in the bedroom.
Ben Give it a try.

Cevril walks towards the bedroom door. As she nears it, Ben comes out. They are now facing each other.

Cevril Now what do we do?
Ben You'll have to turn me round by hand. We both need to be facing the same way.
Cevril Right.

She grabs him by the shoulders. He grabs her. They wrestle.

(*struggling*) No, don't you – turn me – I'm supposed
to be turning you . . .

Ben (*also struggling*) I'm sorry, I can't – help it . . .

Cevril (*giving up the struggle*) This is ridiculous. (*As she
regains her breath, a sudden thought.*) Incidentally,
when I was in there just now, were you doing what
I was doing? You must have been.

Ben (*vaguely*) Only sort of.

Cevril Glad I didn't do anything else. Tell you what, I'll
go round the back of you, we'll try that.

*Cevril edges round the back of Ben as he edges round
the back of her.*

Good . . . good . . .

*Cevril, now back to back with Ben, swiftly turns to
him. Ben immediately turns to face her.*

Oh, gawd! This is hopeless. Look, Ben, I'm sorry to do
this to you, love, but there really isn't time.

Cevril switches off the PMRS. Ben collapses.

Ben Ah!

Cevril Sorry. This is the only way, I'm afraid. If Lando
comes back and recognises you, we're both dead.

*With an effort, she grabs him under the armpits and
starts to haul him towards the front door.*
　*As they reach it, the door opens and Manny comes
in.*
　Cevril drops Ben and steps back.

Hallo, Manny.

Manny What you doing?

Cevril I was –

Manny Eh?

Cevril I was – just giving him a move round.

Manny Why are you dressed like that?

Cevril I was just –

Manny You know I don't like you dressed like that. I hate it when you dress like that. Now go in there and get changed.

Cevril No, I need to go out, Manny, I need to –

Manny (*quietly*) You're not arguing with Daddy, are you, Cevril?

Cevril No, I wasn't. I don't argue with Daddy.

Manny Because that's naughty that is. And we always agreed good behaviour, didn't we?

Cevril (*meekly*) Yes, Manny.

Manny Naughty girl. Daddy gives you everything you want, doesn't he? Nice sports car, jewellery, lots of good clothes, two thousand bloody pairs of shoes, even that nice watch there –

Cevril Yes.

She has been nervously fingering the PMRS which she now activates. Unseen by Manny, Ben regains his feet so that he stands close behind him.

Manny But all that depends, Cevril, on you doing exactly what Daddy tells you, doesn't it?

Cevril Yes, Manny.

She swings her right arm to and fro in a gesture of apparent apology. Positioned behind Manny, Ben does the same.

Manny Now I've had to punish you once before, remember.

Cevril Yes, Manny.

Manny I don't want to have to do that again because it hurt me more than it hurt you, believe me. Now, you get back in that bedroom and –

Cevril swings her arm and chops the air with the edge of her hand.

Cevril Hah!

Ben mirrors this, only his blow connects with the back of Manny's neck. Manny goes down like a felled tree.

Ben (*alarmed*) Ah! Did I do that?
Cevril No, I did.
Ben Who the hell are you?
Cevril Detective Sergeant Turner. Undercover Vice Squad. Come on, let's move it!
Ben What about him? Is he dead?
Cevril He'll be fine.
Ben More than my hand will.

Cevril kneels by Manny's body.
Ben does likewise.

What are you doing?
Cevril Taking his gun. Just in case we meet Lando on the stairs.
Ben Oh, my God. I'm going to have a relapse in a minute.

Cevril finds the gun.

Cevril Got it! Right, off we go.

She stands. Ben stands.

Just check the coast is clear.
Ben Excuse me . . .
Cevril What?
Ben I'm still facing the wrong way.
Cevril Be with you in a minute. (*She moves cautiously to the door.*)
Ben Excuse me . . .
Cevril (*mildly irritated*) What now?
Ben What's your real name, then? Your first name.
Cevril Cevril. It's still Cevril.
Ben (*smiling*) Oh, good. I'm glad.

Cevril (*smiling in turn*) Honestly.

*She opens the door slowly, the gun in her other hand.
Lando is standing there.*

Lando (*smiling*) Back again.

*Cevril steps back involuntarily and brings the gun up
to point at him. But Lando is quicker. He steps into
the room and chops down on her wrist. Cevril drops
the gun somewhere in the middle of the room.*

Now, now, now . . .

*Cevril aims a blow at him which he blocks. They are
obviously evenly matched. Once again all Cevril's
moves are matched by Ben, albeit somewhat
ineffectually. Several more moves and then Lando has
her in an arm lock.*

Cevril (*in pain*) Ben . . . help me . . .

Lando No good asking your boyfriend, darling. He's not
going to help you. I've met him before. He's a rabbit,
a scared little rabbit . . .

*Cevril elbows him, twists and escapes into the bedroom.
Lando follows highly amused.*

No way out that way, darling. Not unless you fancy the
window.

*The fight now continues offstage. We hear it and see
some of it, thanks to Ben's one-sided re-enactment of
Cevril's side.*

 *Cevril initially gives as good as she takes but
eventually Lando apparently, judging from Ben's
reaction, catches her by the throat.*

 *Ben's hand gropes behind him as he chokes. His
fingers find some object which he swings up towards
his assailant's head.*

A cry from offstage as Lando is struck.
As a result of this Cevril, according to Ben, is
pushed backwards with some force. Flailing his arms,
he tries to keep his balance. A crash of broken glass
from the bedroom. A cry from Cevril.

Ben (*echoing her cry*) Cevril!

We see Ben apparently in mid air for a second. He
falls on his back. He lies there.
   Silence.
From the bedroom, the sound of someone crawling
with great effort along the floor.

Ben (*calling, softly*) Cevril!

Lando appears in the doorway. His face is covered in
blood from a deep cut in his head.

Lando (*talking with difficulty*) Gone out the window,
   barman. Not good for your health from the fifth floor.
   'Fraid she's passed on to that great cocktail lounge in
   the sky. Forget her now. We've got our own little bit
   of business to finish, haven't we, barman?

He starts to crawl painfully across the floor towards
the gun and Ben.

Here I come, Ben. On my way.

With a supreme effort Ben sits up. It is clear that he is
doing this on his own. He looks at the gun.

(*divining Ben's intention*) Come on, then. Come on, race
   you, Ben. Race you . . .

The two men crawl with difficulty towards the gun.
They are finally both within reach and make a
simultaneous grab for it.
   Blackout. A single shot. Swiftly, the lights change to:

SCENE SIX

The hospital lecture room as in Scene One.
*The audience is gathered as before. Amongst the
dignitaries on the platform are Professor Barth,
Dr Bernice Mallow, David Best, Nerys Potter and
Sir Trevor Perkins.*
Barth is in mid-flow.

Barth . . . and it is perhaps only fitting that this award
ceremony should take place here at the Chepthorne
Medley Research Hospital. If it were not for the
outstanding work by the GIZMO team, these
extraordinary strides forward in the history of
medicine would never have been made. We would not
be standing here today to celebrate this truly inspiring
display of human bravery and courage. I would
therefore like to call upon the Chief Constable, Sir
Trevor Perkins, to make the presentation.

Applause. Barth sits. Perkins steps forward.

Perkins Thank you. I'd just like to add that these actions
have made a considerable contribution towards our
constant and unceasing war against crime. Thanks to
this individual gallantry, together with some remarkable
back up police work by our Rapid Response Team,
we have struck a strong blow against the gangs that
terrorise and presume to own our cities. I have great
pleasure in giving this Fiberts Modular Plastics Award
for Outstanding Bravery in the Community to Ben
Mason.

*Applause. Ben steps on to the stage and accepts the
award. He is now moving normally under his own
steam.*

Ben Thank you very much. Thank you. I would just like to say firstly, how much I owe to the Institute and in particular to the GIZMO project which I'm pleased to say is now becoming widely accepted as an important treatment for a wide range of post trauma and remedial work. As regards this award, well, if it belongs to anyone it belongs to Detective Sergeant Cevril Turner who is quite simply one of the most remarkable, one of the bravest people I have ever been privileged to meet. Thank you.

Applause. He moves swiftly back to the side of the platform.

Perkins And so to our second award, and – here I think my work's already been done for me – the second Bravery Award to Detective Sergeant – Cervil – (*aside, to Barth*) – sorry, is that . . .?

Barth Cevril.

Perkins Cevril – sorry – Detective Sergeant Cevril Turner.

Cevril is pushed on in a wheelchair by Ted.
Applause and cheers.
She is presented with her award by Perkins who then sits down.

Cevril (*for once lost for words*) What can I say? Thank you. That's all. I'm very lucky to be alive, I suppose. Thanks to all these wonderful people. Thank you, everyone. Thank you, Ben. Thank you.

Applause. Barth rises, signalling for silence.

Barth There is a sort of footnote to today's events which may be of interest to you. As you probably know, Sergeant Turner received spinal injuries as a result of her fall. Injuries which have left her, for several months, totally paralysed. However, thanks to

442

GIZMO, our story does come more or less full circle –
(*looking over to Ben*) – Ben, would you mind?

*Ben reveals a PMRS on his wrist. He switches it on.
In her wheelchair, Cevril twitches. Ben rises slowly; so
does Cevril. Applause. Ben steps forward; she does the
same. They turn and walk towards each other. He
holds out his hand; she does the same. They turn to
face their audience and bow together. They turn back
to face each other, Cevril looking slightly startled. Ben
kisses her. Cevril, whether she likes it or not (and one
rather gathers she does), responds. On this the lights
fade to:*
    Blackout.

I Will Take the Boy for £3 a Week

Alan Ayckbourn interviewed by Jim Mulligan

Alan Ayckbourn has spent the whole of his working life in the theatre, starting at the age of seventeen, when he left school on a Friday and started working as an Assistant Stage Manager on the Monday. Since then he has been a sound technician, lighting technician, painter, prop maker, actor, director and above all inspirer and artistic director of the Stephen Joseph Theatre in Scarborough.

At my school we had a teacher who was a complete theatre nut. He had worked with Donald Wolfit and every year he would tour a Shakespeare play with his students. When I was seventeen we went to Canada and America with *Romeo and Juliet*. It was a fantastic experience having all the joy of a professional tour with none of the responsibility. I decided then that I wouldn't go to university and my teacher pulled the one theatrical string he had. He rang Donald Wolfit who happened to be taking *The Strong are Lonely* to Edinburgh and needed an ASM. I still have the letter Donald Wolfit wrote: 'I will take the boy for £3 a week.' So there I was polishing furniture and playing a soldier and I was hooked for life.

By the time he was nineteen Alan Ayckbourn was working for Stephen Joseph in a makeshift theatre-in-the-round in Scarborough. Stephen Joseph believed that writers belonged to the theatre company and, since he could not afford to employ many writers, he encouraged members of the company to write.

My mother was a short story writer and as a result I had an image of writing in the family but I never

444

identified writing as my primary talent. However,
I accepted the challenge and by the second season at
Scarborough I had written a play. After that I very
rapidly got the boot from acting and became much
more interested in directing. Now directing takes up
much more of my time but it feeds the writer in me.

Alan Ayckbourn has three basic jobs: administering the
Stephen Joseph Theatre, directing and writing. He has
written over fifty plays and, in the past year alone, he
has written an adaptation of *The Forest* by Ostrovsky for
the National Theatre, a full-length play, *Comic Potential*,
The Boy Who Fell into a Book, a revue – and *Gizmo*.

A lot of my writing happens around other things.
If I get up in the morning with an idea, I'll write;
if I have an hour or two at the end of a dull day
before a meeting I'll write. But when I'm working
on a full-length play, which I do once a year, I need
a month. I spend about three weeks circling round
the problem and then write quickly based on thoughts
and ideas accumulated over several months.

The post-traumatic shock described in *Gizmo* is not a
recognised syndrome but is something Alan Ayckbourn
made up. He has written many sci-fi plays and the idea
of positive movement replication synchronicity has been
in his imagination for some time. In *Gizmo* he uses it to
provide richly comic scenes that are entertaining and also
very demanding for the actors.

I thought it best to set *Gizmo* on neutral ground that
is neither the world of teenagers nor my world. I also
wanted to write something which offered convincing
dialogue and a degree of physicality that would be
fun. I don't want to be pretentious about the play but
I hope there is more to it than entertainment. I get
excited about scientific discoveries. But they can be

dangerous. We have these boxes of knowledge and we are like kids on Christmas Day. We unpack the box and then lose the instructions. Genetic engineering, for example, can be a boon or danger in the wrong hands with the wrong government at the wrong time. But in *Gizmo* I am more interested in the interconnected lives of people. The point I'm making is that, although we may not be connected by machines, we are all in some sense, responsible for each other.

Gizmo is a fast-moving thriller and love story combined. In the play there is a park full of muggers and perverts: Manny, who sees himself as the real owner of the park; a hired killer; and an undercover police woman who falls in love with Ben, and who ends up physically paralysed and totally dependent on him. The play is also about bullies, some of whom get their come-uppance. Nerys is a merciless physiotherapist. Rust and his gang intimidate Ted and kick him into unconsciousness yet they grovel in front of Manny. Lando, the ruthless killer, is himself killed. Manny is a bully and a small-time crook. He has some control over his area and likes to think he is a benevolent guardian whereas, in fact, he thinks nothing of organising a contract killing. By the end of the play a lot of his world is destroyed and he will probably end up being eaten by bigger fish.

I think the play is moral. After all, the chief constable says, 'We have struck a strong blow against gangs that terrorise and presume to own our cities.' It's a small battle, only just the beginning. The real triumph is the love story. I've written it in a style that is fast-moving and makes demands on the whole company, not just the actors but the sound and lighting technicians as well. They'll have to work on it and they will also have to reflect on the issues. There's enough of the preacher in me to want to have an effect on young people.

The final scene of *Gizmo* sees the story come full circle. Cevril is now in the wheelchair and Ben wearing the gizmo brings her to her feet. The stage directions bring the play to a satisfying conclusion.

They turn back to face each other, Cevril looking slightly startled. Ben kisses her. Cevril, whether she likes it or not (and one rather gathers she does) responds.

Production Notes

Settings include a hospital lecture room, a hospital bedroom, a park, and an apartment. All of these sets should be as simple as possible. See how little furniture can be used or doubled up to serve another purpose. There should be no hold-ups between scenes. Use lighting and sound to suggest the locations. Rely on the actors also to make the settings clear through mime and movement.

CASTING

Gizmo is for a flexible cast. With doubling it can be performed by eleven actors – three female and eight male. Alternatively it can be performed by seventeen speaking actors and an unlimited number of extras.

EXERCISES

The actors need to be sensitive to the varied pace and comic timing in *Gizmo*. The following exercises will help the group to find ways of allowing the action to flow:

- Have the group think about their entrances and exits. The scene changes are important and need as much consideration as the scenes themselves. They don't have to be hurried or rushed but it is vital that the actors are alert at all times.

- Place six chairs in the space and ask six people to enter and then exit the space with a contrasting code of behaviour, e.g. enter slowly – leave fast; enter confidently – leave embarrassed, etc.
- Divide the group into two. Group A are seated, Group B enter with energy. This energy is passed to Group A who exit the space in the same manner. Experiment with other ways of entering the space and exiting in the same or contrasting manner.

Have the group walk around the space in a determined manner. Have them meet one another and ask a question. When they have an answer get them to move on.

- Have the group continue to move around the space and at a given signal have them create the following environments: the lecture theatre, the park, Manny's apartment. Make the changing locations clear through changes to the space, sound and the manner in which they address one another.

Ask the group to walk around the space in pairs. Have the partners walk side by side. One is A and the other is B. It shouldn't be obvious who is leading.

- Give the signal for the pair to swap over. Now the partners are back to back, if B is leading A is following the movements willingly.
- Have the pairs swap over so that A is leading and carries out a function such as carrying a heavy object upstairs, being a model on the catwalk, conducting the Philharmonic Orchestra, etc. Have B copy the movements unwillingly.

Split the group into two: Group A is female, Group B male. Have Group A walk in the space while Group B listens to the movement and rhythm. Swap over. Next have Group B mime an activity while being closely observed. Swap over. Choose whichever mimed activity has the most comic potential. Choose a male and female actor to be partners and have them imagine they are linked by the gizmo. The gizmo might be functioning badly, or be in the hands of the wrong person – it could be that whoever is in control is unaware of their powers. Have the group decide on a setting: eg. at the Conservative Party Conference in Brighton, linking tube carriages, a TV newsroom etc. Now have the group look at the scene when Ben and Cevril are alone in Manny's apartment.

Experiment with ways of involving the audience. Take Scene One in the hospital lecture theatre, for instance. Scatter the actors through the audience so that it is clear that they are also the audience for the lecture. Give them lecture notes and turn the house lights up to include them so that they are in no doubt. Find ways of making them applaud when the gizmo's functions are demonstrated.

You need to make the characters in *Gizmo* as real as possible for the comedy to work. Have the actors look at the information they are given in the text to build up a fuller picture of their character.

Have the group create some of the 'missing' scenes.

- Improvise the conversation between Ben and the hospital authorities before the lecture at the start of the play. Discover why Ben agreed to take part.
- Imagine that Ted returns to the hospital having to admit that Ben and the gizmo have disappeared. Decide whether the authorities are more concerned about Ben or the gizmo.

Look at Ben's character and study his journey through the play scene by scene.

Decide how the paralysis affects his body – can he only move his eyes or has he mobility from the neck upwards? How does this affect communication with the other actors? Look at the relationship Ben has to the other characters that appear in the play no matter how briefly. Nerys, for instance: does she bully him? Is she behaving in a 'you've got to be cruel to be kind manner' or is she a sadist? Do you think she treats all her patients like this or is she having an 'off day'?

Suzy Graham-Adriani
February 1999

THE KING OF THE CASTLE

Christina Reid

for my uncle Jonathan Fulton
Dunkirk 1940. Aged 22

Characters

Children, aged ten to twelve

Eileen
Rose
Billy
Freddy
Roy

Jean, aged fourteen to fifteen

Additional children: any number, any age, to enact
street-games/rhymes/songs, fly kites, dance, sing . . .

Adults

May, Eileen's mother, early thirties
Cora, Eileen's great-aunt, elderly
Arthur, a childlike man, early thirties

Music

'Run Rabbit Run' (Flanagan and Allen)
'The Teddy Bears' Picnic' (Henry Hall and His Orchestra)
'When the Lights Go on Again' (Penny Lee)
'At the Hop' (Danny and the Juniors)

Note

In my head, this play is set in Belfast in the decade after the Second World War because that is the city and the time of my growing-up. But I would hope that the play could be set in any place where children play on land that has been made derelict by war.

The sense of the children playing on something beyond their experience is of more importance than struggling to perfect a Belfast accent. Any company choosing to relocate the play can alter the games/rhymes/songs accordingly.

Most of the action takes place on what is locally referred to as 'The Wasteground'. It is a piece of derelict land with a high mound of rubble and straggled grey/green weeds – the remains of a small shop and house destroyed by a bomb during 'The Belfast Blitz'. Years of clambering children have compacted the blasted bricks and mortar into a hard knobbled hill.

The mound and surrounding wasteground are at the end of the street where the children live. There is a pavement along the front which is used for games that require a less uneven surface. A bit of old wall is used for ball games that require a flat vertical surface.

The indoor scenes in Eileen's house and the current shop/dwelling do not necessarily require a naturalistic setting – i.e., go for basic props and suggestion/lighting rather than elaborate structure or complicated scene changes that might hold up the action. Scenes between the set locations should be fast, fluid, without breaks in the movement and dialogue. Mostly, the whole set should be seen/lit, regardless of where the action is happening on stage, except where major lighting changes required by the storyline are specified in the script.

Lighting and sound effects can also create the illusion of kites and birds, although it would be magic if the kites could really fly – and even more so, the pigeons . . . Over to the creative imaginations of technicians, designers and the new generation of children who've grown up with C.D.T. on the National Curriculum.

A cold, grey, end-of-winter afternoon.
    *Characters on The Wasteground, in Eileen's House
and in the Shop seen simultaneously.*
    *Music: heard softly in the background from the large
old radio on the shop counter – Flanagan and Allen
singing 'Run Rabbit Run'.*

IN THE SHOP

*Jean is behind the counter, listening to the radio, reading
a film magazine. Jean is mad about the movies. When
she isn't directly involved in scenes in the play, she can
be seen in the shop fantasising about what she's reading,
or doing her face, hair, nails according to the latest fad.*

ON THE WASTEGROUND

Pigeons cooing, huddled together for warmth.
    *Arthur is sitting with his back against the mound of
rubble. He is an old young man of thirty something,
slow of speech and movement. He is wearing an army
greatcoat from the Second World War.*
    *Some boys are crawling stealthily, like soldiers,
towards the pigeons.*
    *The pigeons fly away, up and out of reach. The boys
wander off, looking bored, fed-up and a bit foolish.*
    *This is a cold, still scene. Throughout, the only noise,
apart from the radio, is the sound of pigeons cooing/*

flying, with perhaps some whispered mutterings among the boys. The boys pay no attention to Arthur, and if he looks towards them, towards anything, his eyes have a curious lack of focus or reaction.

The pigeons fly back down when the boys have gone. Like the boys, they behave as if Arthur is not there.

IN EILEEN'S HOUSE

Eileen's mother (May) and her great aunt (Cora) are keeping watch over an open coffin. May is noticeably pregnant.

As the music fades, Eileen enters with two cups of tea; stands hesitant, scared of approaching the coffin, having to see the body close-to.

Cora (*to May, about the deceased*) I knew she wouldn't last the weekend. You can always tell when they're ready to go by the faraway look in the eyes. (*to Eileen*) Have you kissed your granny goodbye yet?

Eileen stands rooted to the spot. May goes to her, takes the teacups from her.

May You don't have to if you don't want to, Eileen.
Eileen Thanks, Mammy.

Cora sniffs with disapproval as Eileen leaves the room and goes outside.

Cora In my day, it was customary, and no excuses.
May Times change, Aunt Cora. And no child of mine is goin' to be frightened by custom, or anything else that I have a say in.
Cora (*to the body in the coffin*) It's well seeing who your May takes after. (*to May*) Your mother'll never be dead as long as you're alive.

458

May I'll take that as a compliment to me and to her,
Aunt Cora.

*Another sniff from Cora. May goes to Eileen who is
now sitting on the step outside her house, looking at
Arthur on The Wasteground.*

Eileen You know what Aunt Cora said about my
granny? About the way her eyes went all faraway and
funny for a while before she died? Well . . . Arthur's
eyes look like that all the time, so they do.

May (*with a compassionate look at Arthur as he gets up
and walks away*) Aye, God help him. He wasn't
always that way. The war was a terrible time. Be
thankful you're too young to remember it. Now, don't
you be loiterin' long out here and catchin' your death
of cold, Eileen.

Eileen I hate the winter.

May Remember what your granny always said about
the seasons of the year.

*May goes back into the house. Eileen thinks for a
moment, remembers, smiles.*

Eileen A bad winter makes for a good summer.

THE WASTEGROUND

*An immediate change to summer – a complete contrast
to the opening scene: light, life, noise, as lots of children
run on to The Wasteground, scattering the pigeons. A
few, with pennies and half-pennies to spend on sweets
or small toys, invade the shop, disturbing Jean's movie
daydreams.*

Eileen runs into the pandemonium.

*In general, the boys run around a lot, kicking a
football and each other; playing games that involve*

*shooting with imaginary guns: The girls play throw/
catch/bounce ball games and skipping games that are
accompanied by chants/songs.*

*On the pavement, the boys play marbles, the girls play
hopscotch.*

*Shared games between boys and girls are not usual,
except where a small boy is being looked after by an
older sister (a parental arrangement that both siblings
hate). An example of a game exception, enjoyed by all
ages and both sexes, is 'Pirrie and Whip'. This is played
by placing a rubber screw-top from an old lemonade
bottle in a crack between the paving stones; winding a
whip (a leather bootlace) round the screw, then sharply
pulling the whip to make the bottle top spin across the
pavement. The winner is the one whose top spins for
longest. (The rubber tops are decorated with chalk
patterns which fluctuate as the top spins.)*

*'Pirrie and Whip', like most of the games, utilises
everyday items from the home. In the early 1950s, there
was still post-war rationing; working-class income was
low; children, like adults, had to 'make-do'. Any bikes
around were old battered hand-me-downs. It was more
common for children to share 'a guider' – a go-cart
cobbled out of bits of wood, orange crates, old pram
wheels.*

*This street-games scene should be fast/overlapping,
colourful, noisy – and should last for as long as it's good
fun to do and watch. (A selection of Belfast street-songs/
rhymes/games to choose from, is appended to the script.)*

*Eileen joins in with her best friend Rose and other
girls on The Wasteground who are chanting/singing as
they play skipping games, the two tallest girls turning the
ends of an old piece of rope, while others jump in and
out as the rhyme requires (two or three children can skip
together if the rope is long enough). Eileen jumps into
the rope when her turn comes round, and after a few*

*moments she is joined by a boy (Roy) who, like her, is a
brilliant skipper.*

*Great giggles and admiration about Roy's comedy
skipping from Eileen and the girls. Roy having the time
of his life; totally unabashed by the jeers of 'Big Cissy'
from some of the other boys. There's more envy than
malice in the jeering – they don't have his skill, or his
nerve to join in what is essentially a girls' game. And
Roy is essentially 'a disturber'. He enjoys being
different/stirring it.*

*Arthur wanders in, stands on the periphery of the
children's games, like an uncertain, lonely child.*

*Then Billy enters, his sycophantic side-kick Freddy
swaggering importantly behind him.*

*Billy pauses, waits for the other children to notice
that he has arrived, and that he is holding a large shop-
bought kite. He has the demeanour of a child on the
edge of a too early transition to adulthood – he could be
bigger than the rest of the children, but it's more to do
with attitude than size – perhaps copying/affecting the
behaviour of his father or an older brother or the tough-
silent-guy in the war or cowboy movies. The other
children are mostly wary of Billy; the youngest/smallest
maybe a bit scared; the more humorous or daring are
given to pulling faces at him, mostly behind his back.*

Freddy Hey everybody! Look what Billy got for his
  birthday! Show them, Billy . . .
Billy Who asked you to open your mouth, birdbrain?
Freddy Nobody, Billy . . .
Billy Well, shut it then. Okay, Freddy?
Freddy No problem, Billy. No problem. (*as Billy walks
  away towards the mound*) Wait'll youse all see this.
  Billy's brilliant at it, so he is. He's been practisin' all
  mornin' on the yard wall, so he has . . .

He stops, silenced by the murderous look Billy gives him, before climbing to the top of the mound.

Unseen by Billy and Freddy, Roy is causing concealed mirth among some of the children by doing John Wayne parodies of Billy's walk. He stops very quickly as Freddy almost spots him; pretends to be imitating Arthur.

Billy reaches the top of the mound; holds his kite aloft; stands for a moment looking down at the up-turned faces of Arthur and the children. Then he jumps to the ground, releasing the string on the kite. The kite soars/sails briefly as Billy jumps/runs, before it falls to the ground.

There is a moment's impressed silence from the other children.

Freddy Didn't I tell yous it was brilliant?!

Even though it's not the greatest bit of kite-flying in the world, it immediately acquires the stature of the-thing-that-every-child-wants-to-own-more-than-anything-else-in-the-entire-universe-ever-right-now.

All the other games are abandoned as the children run off shouting – a chaotic chorus of 'Mammy! . . . Daddy! . . . Can I get a kite like Billy's? . . . Can I? . . . Can I? . . . Aw, go on Mammy! . . . Please Daddy! . . . Please!!! . . . Everbody's got a kite but me!!!! . . . Please!!!!! Can I get a kite the day? Can I get a kite the marra? Can I? . . . etc., etc., etc. . . .

Arthur is left alone on The Wasteground with Billy and Freddy. He is staring, mesmerised by the kite, as Billy re-winds the string.

Freddy What are you lookin' at, daftie?
Arthur Kite . . . I had a kite . . . nice . . . pretty . . .
Freddy (*imitating/mocking Arthur's soft slow speech*)
   Nice kite, pretty kite . . . See you, Arthur? You're

wired to the friggin' moon. He is, isn't he, Billy?
(*Turns to discover that Billy and his kite have walked
off without him.*) Billy? . . . Billy? Hey Billy! Wait for
me! (*Runs off in pursuit of Billy.*)
Arthur I had a kite . . . we had a kite . . .

Arthur sits down at the base of the mound.
  The pigeons return to The Wasteground.
  *Cora walks past, pushing May's new baby in a
pram. Cora is wearing a coat with a large ostentatious
black mourning armband sewn on to one sleeve, and
is carrying a shopping bag. She looks at Arthur and
the pigeons; sniffs; walks on towards Eileen's house.*
  *Lights down on the Wasteground area as Cora
exits.*

IN THE SHOP

Jean puts kites on display for sale.

IN EILEEN'S HOUSE

*Eileen is standing on a chair, while May sews the torn
hem of her dress.*

May Will you stand at peace, Eileen! And stop your
sulkin' . . . if you weren't so hard on your clothes, I
wouldn't have to be constantly doing runnin' repairs.

*She turns to the baby, as Cora enters, pushing the
pram.*

Ach, God love him, is he still sleepin'?
Cora Good as gold. You don't know you're born with
that wee lad, May.

May has finished her sewing, bites the last bit of thread off the hem. Eileen climbs down from the chair, pulling a face at May and Cora fussing over her baby brother.

Cora Who licked the cream off *her* bun?

May She's sulkin' because I won't give her the money for a shop-bought kite.

Eileen Everybody's got one but me, so they have.

May Funny . . . that's what the kids next door are claimin' as well. Do yous all think your mothers were born yesterday and never compare notes, or what?

Cora I thought it was her own skippin' rope she was pinin' for? With wooden handles, if I remember the plea correctly.

May That was last week's fad. This week, it's kites-on-the-brain. It'll be something else by the weekend.

Eileen It won't . . .

May It will. And with God's Grace it'll be something that doesn't involve fallin' over and tearin' your frocks.

Cora takes a new skipping rope with wooden handles out of her shopping bag, hands it to Eileen.

Cora Here, take this back to the shop and see if they'll swop it for a kite.

Eileen (*overcome by the gift, even more so by the offer to swap it*) Aw . . . thanks, Aunt Cora . . .

In response to an eye-signal from May, Eileen plants an awkward kiss on Cora's cheek, before running out to swop the skipping rope for a kite.
May smiles at Cora who is as overwhelmed as Eileen about the awkward kiss.

May You're too good to her. She wouldn't have got either as easy from me.

Cora (*brusquely, without sentiment*) I've none of my own. Who else would I indulge?

Lights up on:

THE WASTEGROUND

Children, all holding kites (a mixture of shop-bought and rag-and-paper home-made) are looking up at Eileen who is standing at the top of the mound, proudly holding her shop-bought kite aloft.

Other children coming out of the shop with kites: Jean, glad to see the back of them, returns to her movie magazine.

There is now only one kite left in the shop.

Arthur stands on the edge of The Wasteground, watching.

Eileen I'm the King of the Castle! And nobody can knock me down!!

She jumps, releasing the string on the kite; lands on the ground; falls over.

The children cheer as the kite soars, then jeer as it falls to the ground.

Eileen checks her dress for damage, then sticks her tongue out at Billy as he confidently climbs the mound with his shop-bought kite, which is bigger and better than all the others.

Freddy leads a chant, which is taken up by some of the children – 'Billy! Billy! Billy!'

As Eileen re-winds the string on her kite, her attention is caught by Arthur who is moving from the edge of The Wasteground towards Billy climbing the mound. He is talking to himself, but glances in his curious blank way towards Eileen as he passes.

Arthur Nice kite . . . pretty kite . . . we had kites . . .
flew high . . . in the sky . . .
Freddy (*jeers*) Flew high . . . in the sky . . .
Roy Hey! Arthur's a poet and doesn't know it!
Freddy Arthur doesn't know nuthin'!
Eileen Leave him alone, you.
Freddy He's a frigging head-the-ball.
Eileen Takes one to know one.
Children (*laugh/jeer at Freddy*) Na-nah, na-na-nah . . .

*Freddy, embarrassed/furious, pushes Eileen towards
Arthur.*

Freddy Fancy him, do ye?
Billy (*from the top of the mound, angry, at Freddy*)
Leave her alone!
Rose (*giggling/sing-songs quietly in Eileen's ear*) Billy
fancies Eileen, Billy fancies Eileen . . .
Eileen He does not! (*But the suggestion makes her giggle
too.*)

*The two girls move off together, pulling faces that
suggest a mixture of being repelled and intrigued by
the notion of being 'fancied' by any boy; then sit
down on the shop step to unravel the strings of their
kites.*

Billy (*at Arthur*) Move yourself, moon-man!
Freddy Land on his soft head, Billy! Knock a bit of sense
into him!
Billy (*at Arthur, increasingly angry and loud*) I said,
move it! So do it!! Now!!
Arthur (*salutes*) Yes sir.

*Arthur salutes like the soldier he was, but wanders
away like the man/child he has become.*

Freddy (*to Roy*) Billy gets that from his da. Billy's da
was a commando in the war, so he was.

Roy Away on! He was a cook in the caterin' corps. My
  da peeled mountains of spuds for his rotten stew.
Freddy I'll tell Billy you said that!
Roy (*chants*) Tell-tale tit . . .
Children (*taking up Roy's chant*) . . . your Mammy
  can't knit . . . your Daddy can't go to bed without a
  dummy-tit . . .
Billy Geronimo!!!

> *The children scatter as Billy jumps off the mound,
> then run after him, following the flight of his kite
> offstage.*
>
> *Arthur is now sitting on the ground near to Eileen
> and Rose.*
>
> *Rose notices that Eileen is peering at Arthur,
> angling her head in different directions towards him,
> trying to focus his eyes on hers.*

Rose What you looking at him like that for?
Eileen You know his eyes? They're like the other way
  round of that picture-book our teacher showed us.
  The one with *The Laughin' Cavalier* and the *Mona
  Lisa* in it.
Rose That oul teacher was daft. And her oul book was
  rotten.
Eileen She said that pictures like that are called portraits.
  And when you look at them, the eyes sort of follow
  you. No matter what way you move, when you look
  at them, they're always lookin' back at you . . .
Rose I know. It would give you the creeps, so it would.
Eileen Arthur's eyes are creepy, only the other way
  round . . . you *can't* make Arthur look straight at you,
  no matter what way you turn your head . . . it's like
  he's always lookin' over your shoulder at somebody
  else . . .
Rose My ma says the army should of kept him in the
  looney-bin, and not let him out to roam the streets.

Eileen My mammy says he's more to be pitied than laughed at.

Rose Bet you a penny I can make him look at me.

Goes closer to Arthur, stares, turns her head, pulls faces at him. No response from Arthur.

Eileen See? I told you. You owe me a penny.

Rose He *did* look at me

Eileen He did not, Rose.

Rose He did so.

Eileen He never.

Rose He did.

Eileen Do it again, then. Double or quits.

Small pause.

Rose Have you *got* a penny?

Eileen No.

Rose Me neither.

Another small pause. They don't notice that Cora is passing by, not close enough to hear, but close enough to see. She slows down, watches.

Arthur I got a penny . . . (*Rummages in the pocket of his greatcoat, holds out his hand, palm up.*) . . . Lend us your kite . . .

Rose peers into Arthur's palm.

Rose Away on, bap-head. (*to Eileen, laughing*) It's an oul tap-washer.

Arthur Lend us your kite . . .

Rose (*as Eileen hesitates, as if thinking about it*) Don't be soft, Eileen! He'll only break it.

Eileen (*not wanting to lose face*) I wasn't going to, so I wasn't . . . get your own kite, moon man . . .

Arthur nods, gets to his feet, begins to walk away.
    Cora sees Arthur leaving and walks on towards Eileen's house.
    Freddy, Billy and Roy pass by at the far side of The Wasteground.
    Arthur turns towards the girls.

Arthur Get my own kite . . . me . . .
Rose Get a brain while you're at it!
Eileen Rose!
Rose What!?

Freddy nudges/makes faces to Roy about the two girls with Arthur.

Freddy (*yells at Eileen and Rose*) Show him your knickers!!
Rose (*yells at Freddy*) Away home and wash your legs, Freddy Cosgrove!!

The two girls walk off, arm in arm, heads in the air.
    Roy makes a strategic retreat as Billy thumps Freddy.

Billy Don't you talk dirty to Eileen! Okay?!
Freddy Okay, Billy. Okay . . . (*trailing after Billy*) It was only a wee joke, like.

IN EILEEN'S HOUSE

May is winding wool into a ball from the skein held by Cora between her thumb and forefinger. The baby is asleep in the pram which has a small teddy bear on a ribbon dangling from the hood.

Cora I took some flowers to the graves the day. You know there's more of our family lyin' up in the cemetery than living on the road now?

May It's being so cheerful keeps you goin', Aunt Cora. (*to Eileen, as she enters*) The wanderer returns. Where have you been all day?

Eileen I was just playin' . . . with Rose . . .

Cora The pair of them were hangin' around that wasteground with that Arthur one. What was he saying to yous?

May (*as Eileen hesitates*) Speak when you're spoken to.

Eileen He wanted the lend of a kite.

May Ach, God help him. Did you give him a go? (*as Eileen hesitates again, knowing her mother has a soft spot for Arthur*) Well? Did you?

Cora I didn't buy her a kite for sharin' with a grown man.

May Arthur's hardly what you'd call a man, Aunt Cora.

Cora That's what bothers me. If she was *my* child, I wouldn't be encouragin' her to fraternise with the likes of that.

May There's no harm in him. And people who go around sayin' different should know better. God knows what happened to that lad in France.

Cora He come back, didn't he? There was many as didn't, in both the great wars . . . (*She suddenly looks vulnerable, less fierce; speaks quietly.*) God rest them all . . . whatever soil they died on . . .

A small silence. A compassionate look/gesture from May to Cora.
   Eileen's barely concealed pleasure at hearing Cora being told off for a change turns to curiosity.

Eileen Why do you call them the *great* wars, if they make you want to cry?

May Instead of ear-wiggin' on adult conversations, away and take the wee lad out for a breath of fresh air 'til I put the dinner on.

Eileen Ach, Mammy . . .

May Don't you ach Mammy me, madam! (*as Eileen, miffed, pushes the pram out of the room*) And no tuttin'!!

Eileen bumps the pram down the step out of the house; is joined by Rose, who peers into the pram.

Rose Ach, isn't he lovely. (*jiggling the teddy bear on the pram hood*) And look at his lovely wee teddy bear. I wish I had a baby brother.

Eileen You can have *him* if you want.

Rose Come on and we'll go to the shop. I've got a sixpence. My da was that drunk when he got home, he never even noticed he'd dropped it.

They push the pram across The Wasteground towards the shop.

IN EILEEN'S HOUSE

The next scenes should be fluid, overlapping between the house and the shop as Eileen and Rose cross The Wasteground.
    May and Cora a bit awkward with each other.

May I'm sorry, Aunt Cora. I forgot she was there . . . and I didn't mean to re-open old wounds . . .

Cora No matter. I'll be getting on home.

May You'll do no such thing. You'll stay for your dinner.

Cora Your man'll be home soon. He won't want me around.

May He's on the late shift this week.

Cora Well, if you need the company . . .

May (*more in irritated affection than anger*) Whatever you do, don't strain yourself, will ye?

IN THE SHOP

Arthur is pointing to the last kite. Jean is more concerned about her appearance.

Jean No can do, Arthur. We've only got the one kite left. And anyway, you've no money.

Eileen and Rose have now pushed the pram to the shop door.

Eileen My mammy always says you should always ask if you wanta know. But she only ever answers you when it suits her.

Rose Sure they never tell you anythin'. When I asked my ma why my da makes her cry all the time, she give me a thump as if it was my fault.

Eileen I asked my daddy why he always makes himself scarce when Aunt Cora comes to our house, an' he said . . . (*lowering her voice in admiration at her father's daring*) . . . because she's an oul bat, that's why.

Rose What are you whisperin' for? That's what everybody calls your Aunt Cora.

They park the pram outside the shop. Go in.

Jean (*to Arthur*) My granny said if you come in, you could have a couple of lemon sherbets . . . (*as Arthur shakes his head*) For the last time, no money, no kite, Arthur. (*to Eileen and Rose as they enter*) See him? He'd do your head in. (*to Arthur as he points to some iced buns*) Help yourself. (*to Eileen and Rose*) They're for the pig-swill man the marra. They're that stale they're like cardboard boxes.

The girls giggle together as Arthur pays with the tap-washer, takes a piece of newspaper out of his pocket, carefully wraps the stale buns, puts the parcel in his pocket.

Jean (*aside to Eileen and Rose*) See him? See tapwashers? If they were poun' notes, I'd be livin' in Beverly Hills by now.

Arthur (*as he leaves the shop*) Thanks, Mrs Matchett.

Arthur pauses for a moment outside, looks at the pram, pats the covers or the hood, walks on back to The Wasteground.

Eileen He'll get the runs eatin' mouldy iced buns, so he will.

Rose Why did he call you Mrs Matchett? Who's she when she's at home?

Jean He calls anybody behind the counter Mrs Matchett. She was the woman owned the old shop. The one that got bombed where The Wasteground is now.

Rose My ma told me that bomb fell there because the woman picked the May blossom and brought it into her house.

Eileen My mammy says that's just an old wives' tale.

Rose Carry May blossom in, carry a coffin out. Everybody knows that.

Eileen My Aunt Cora says Mrs Matchett died because she considered herself too grand to go into the air-raid shelter.

Jean No matter what killed her, mad Arthur thinks she's still alive and the oul shop's still standin'. I wish he was right.

Rose What for? Aren't you dead lucky living in a sweet shop?

Jean It's rotten, so it is. You can have my job the day you leave school, if you want.

Rose Aw, thanks, Jean.

Jean Thanks for nuthin'. It's diabolical livin' above a
shop. My granny's forever in bed with her pains and
I'm forever stuck behind the counter. I haven't been to
a dance for a fortnight *and* Diana Dors is on at the
pictures this week.

Eileen You look awful like her, Jean, so you do.

Jean I know. (*Small pause.*) My boyfriend says if I dye
my hair ash blonde, he'll buy me an engagement ring.

*The boyfriend and engagement ring are closer to
movie fantasy than real life, but as Jean intended,
Eileen and Rose are very impressed.*

Eileen You have a real boyfriend?

Rose What's he like? Did he get down on one knee
when he asked you?

Eileen I wish I lived with a granny who'd let you get
your hair dyed and get engaged when you're fourteen.

Jean Fifteen, next month. And we're having a secret
engagement. You wear the ring round your neck,
under your clothes, next to your heart.

Eileen I seen that in the pictures one time. And they got
found out and they climbed down a ladder in the dark
and everybody was ragin' that they'd loped off.

Jean *E*-loped. It's American for when the heiress to a
secret fortune has to be rescued from her cruel relations.

Eileen Do you have to be an heiress to get eloped?

Jean Only if your lover is poor and handsome. If he's rich
and handsome you can be a penniless orphan . . . like
me . . . (*dreamy, re-imagining the movie scenario in
her head*) . . . unless my granny dies, an' then I'll be
the heiress of the shop . . .

Rose I wish I was an orphan.

Eileen Are you and your boyfriend gonna elope now, or
wait 'til your granny dies?

Jean We haven't decided yet. Don't yous two go telling
nobody. Swear you won't. They put you in a home if

474

you get caught, so they do. And they send your lover
to the Colonies.

Rose What's the Colonies?

Jean It's all full of jungles. And if people from here get
sent there, they get fevers and they die of a broken
heart. So swear yous'll never tell.

Eileen Cross my heart an' hope to die.

Rose Me too.

Eileen Is he *mad* about you, Jean?

Rose Does he kiss you an' all?

Eileen What's he called?

Jean (*a small hesitation as she chooses a movie name*)
Tyrone . . . you wouldn't know him, he's not from
round here . . . He bought me a fantastic lipstick.
Holywood Nights it's called. Do yous want a try?

ON THE WASTEGROUND

Arthur has sat down with his back against the mound.
He takes the iced buns out of his pocket.

IN EILEEN'S HOUSE

May with two cups of tea, handing one to Cora.

May I put a drop of whiskey in it.

Cora Whiskey? On a Wednesday? Is it a birth, death or
marriage we're celebrating?

May Just get it down ye.

Cora You're going to the dogs, our May. Just as well
your man doesn't work the late shift every week of the
year . . . (*But she takes a good sip and enjoys the tea
with whiskey.*)

475

May (*taking a sip, sharing a contented smile with* Cora)
Is that you and me declarin' a truce, then?

Cora I only said what I said because I'm fond of Eileen.
I wouldn't want her to come to no harm.

May Wouldn't I defend her with my own life if I
thought anybody was even *thinkin'* of doing bad by
her?

Cora Who knows for sure what *he's* thinkin'.

May I've known Arthur since the day we started
primary school. And I'm tellin' you he's harmless.

ON THE WASTEGROUND

*Arthur is slowly, carefully removing the iced buns from
the newspaper wrapping.*

OUTSIDE THE SHOP

*Eileen, Rose and Jean are now sitting on the step,
alongside the baby in the pram. Jean is putting make-up
on Rose's face. Eileen is splashing herself liberally with
Jean's perfume, and looking across at Arthur on The
Wasteground.*

Jean (*at* Eileen) Hey! Easy on, you! That's Ashes of
Roses, not bog water!

Rose Did Tyrone buy you that too?

Jean He's always buyin' me presents. He's dead scared
I'll take up with somebody else. He's dead soft on me,
so he is.

Eileen My mammy's dead soft about everybody. Mad
Arthur, my daddy, Aunt Cora (*gesturing at the pram*)
Him . . . everybody in the world she thinks needs

lookin' out for . . . except me . . . it's not fair, so it's
not.

Jean You're lucky. My granny doesn't like nobody.

Rose Except Arthur.

Jean Only 'cause he's not right in the head and can't
argue with her.

Rose My ma and da yell at each other all the time. An'
next thing they're tellin' me I have to go to bed early
an' slobberin' all over themselves like they're not right
in the head.

Eileen What do you think's wrong with Arthur's head?

Jean My granny says he was brought home from France
in the middle of the night. With an army blanket
draped all over him. And he was screeching like a
baby.

Eileen Why?

Jean I don't know.

Rose My ma says he was a craven coward.

Eileen What's a craven coward?

Rose I don't know.

Jean Will you sit still 'til it dries, or it'll all smudge?

IN EILEEN'S HOUSE

Cora He got a dishonorable discharge.

May Says who?

Cora It's common knowledge.

May He got sent home because he was war wounded.

Cora Tell that to the Marines. There's not a mark on
him.

May Not one that can be seen.

Cora He got scared and wouldn't fight no more. If that's
not dishonorable, I don't know what is.

OUTSIDE THE SHOP

Rose is admiring herself in the mirror of Jean's compact.
Jean is painting Eileen's nails, and noticing how she
keeps glancing towards Arthur.

Jean See him? See the Second World War? My granny
 says the First World War was the worst. There's an
 old soldier from it, still alive, on the next road, and
 he's got no legs and only one arm with no fingers.
 And he never speaks at all.

Eileen Are his eyes all funny?

Jean I don't know. He lives in a back room above the
 butcher's shop. And nobody's *ever* seen him.

Rose How do they know what he looks like, then?

Jean It's common knowledge.

Eileen Do you ever get scared there might be a Third
 World War?

Rose Sure, didn't they kill all the baddies with an atom
 bomb?

Eileen My mammy says it was ordinary people like us
 they killed. Just people who just happened to be livin'
 there. They weren't even soldiers or nuthin'.

Jean They weren't people like us. They talked funny and
 they had weirdo slanty eyes.

Rose Hey! Maybe that's what happened to Arthur!
 Maybe they captured him and drunk his blood and
 turned him into one of them.

Rose puts her forefingers to the sides of her eyes, pulls
them into a slant, does Boris Karloff zombie acting.
  Jean, not interested in movie fantasy that isn't about
romance, picks up the make-up and goes back into the
shop. Turns the radio on, fiddles with the knobs to
find a music station.
  Eileen glances uneasily towards Arthur who is now

breaking the iced buns into pieces.

Rose bumps into the baby's pram. The baby starts to cry. Rose makes baby noises, jiggles the teddy bear. The baby howls louder.

Eileen Stop shakin' that stupid teddy! You're scarin' him! (*rummaging in the pram*) Where's his dummy? I can't find his stupid dummy . . .

Rose You've dropped it . . . (*picking the dummy up from the ground, holding it out to Eileen*) . . . here . . .

Eileen looks at the dummy, shakes the dust off it, sucks it to clean the worst of the dust off it, puts it in the baby's mouth. The baby stops crying.

Eileen He'll want a feed now he's wakened. I'll have to take him home. See you Rose?!

Eileen, fed-up, pushes the pram away towards The Wasteground, where Arthur is now carefully placing bits of iced bun in a semi-circle, about a foot or so out from the base of the mound.
  Music: Henry Hall and His Orchestra playing/ singing 'The Teddy Bears' Picnic', from the shop radio.

Rose (*calls after Eileen, about Arthur*) Watch out the King of the Zombies doesn't get ye!

Rose goes into the shop, where Jean is dancing to the music. They begin to dance together, Jean teaching Rose the steps.
  Eileen looks even more fed-up when she sees this; walks on; then pauses, curious about Arthur's behaviour.
  He is now making another semi-circle of iced bun bits, a little further out from the first.
  He looks towards Eileen, holds out a piece of iced bun to her. She shakes her head, more uneasy now than curious; quickly pushes the pram off-stage.

479

Arthur goes on making the second semi-circle.
The lights go down on the whole set, the music
increases in volume as May's exasperated voice is
heard berating Eileen.

May I don't want to hear why his dummy and his poor
wee face is covered in dirt like a street urchin! Just
you get yourself upstairs to your bed, madam!

Lights up on:

EILEEN'S DREAM SEQUENCE

The sky is illuminated by two large suspended kites –
one with a moon face, one with a sun face, smiling down
rather sinisterly on The Wasteground.

Eileen, barefoot, in a nightgown, is at one side of the
stage watching as the children enter, dancing in time to
the music. The dance should be a mixture of Hollywood-
movie-cute and enjoyable-but-scary-fairytale.

The children all have teddy bear noses and ears,
except for Rose and Jean who are dancing together in
the shop – Fred Astaire in a top hat and Ginger Rogers
with a feather boa. An elopement ladder is propped up
against the shop.

Cora is standing in an upright coffin, arms folded
across her chest, miming the words of Henry Hall
singing 'The Teddy Bears' Picnic'.

May is standing alongside the baby in the pram,
conducting the music, smiling at everybody except
Eileen.

Arthur is lifting bits of iced buns, offering them to the
teddy bear children as they perform their dance routine,
moving closer to where Eileen stands, as he circulates.
He reaches her during the verse with the words 'At six
o'clock their mummys and daddies will take them home

to bed because they're tired little teddy bears'.

By this time, May is conducting the teddy bear children offstage. The last four are carrying the empty coffin with Cora walking behind, followed by Rose and Jean carrying the ladder. Eileen makes a movement/gesture towards her mother, but all May's smiles and attention are for the baby as she pushes the pram off-stage.

Eileen is left alone with Arthur. He takes her hands in his. She steps up on to his feet, as if in a trance. They dance.

Darkness descends slowly as the moon and sun kites move out of the sky during the last verse – 'If you go down in the woods today, you'd better not go alone, it's lovely down in the woods today, but safer to stay at home . . .'

Eileen comes out of her trance; steps down off Arthur's feet; runs away as the final sinister notes of the music end the song.

Blackout on the final note. Lights up on:

EILEEN'S HOUSE

The following morning.
May is settling the baby into the pram, whispering terms of endearment. Eileen comes in, scowls at her mother and brother. Picks up her shoes, puts them on.

May (*to the baby*) See you? See your sister? See if she dies with that look on her face? Nobody'll bury her.

Eileen I had a rotten dream last night, so I did. Aunt Cora was in my granny's coffin.

May (*a knowing/amused smile, points/wags her finger at Eileen*) That'll learn ye not to fall asleep wishful thinkin' about your poor oul aunt replacin' your granny in the family plot.

Eileen I wasn't . . . an' it wasn't funny . . . you were in the dream too, only you went away an' left me all on my own with Arthur. An' he had iced buns an' he made me dance on him in my bare feet, so he did, an' it was all wrong an' I didn't like it, so I didn't, so I just run away from him . . . (*Goes back to putting on her shoes.*)

May is very still for a moment, looks at Eileen's bowed head as she laces/buckles her shoes, then speaks very carefully.

May Eileen . . . Arthur has never . . . has he ever done anything . . . not in a dream . . . I mean, for real . . . that's not . . . that doesn't lie comfortable with ye?

Eileen (*genuinely puzzled by May's choice of words*) What do you mean?

May (*relieved that Eileen has no idea what she's on about*) Nuthin'. I should have known better than to let the thought even enter my head. You see Aunt Cora? She could cause a disturbance between two breast bones when the mood takes her. Here, give this to Arthur when you see him. (*Hands Eileen a newspaper, rag, wool concoction.*)

Eileen What's that supposed to be?

May (*miffed at this slight on her handiwork*) It's a kite.

Eileen It's all wrong. It'll never fly.

May Sure it'll please him anyway. Didn't you say he wanted one?

Eileen Ach Mammy. If I take that to the wasteground, Billy and Freddy'll laugh their leg off, so they will.

May You see if I ever catch you makin' mock of Arthur the way that skittery pair do . . .!

Eileen I don't . . .

May People should be thankful that their own didn't come back from the wars like that. That they come back at all. Now you take that kite and you give it to that poor crater Arthur, or I'll know the reason why, madam.

Eileen takes the kite, picks up her own kite, pauses . . .

Eileen Mammy . . .

May What?

Eileen Does my daddy not know what happened in the war that made Arthur's eyes go all funny?

May Arthur was in a different battalion from the rest of them that come back. Him and his best friend Stanley Porter joined up first and they got sent overseas together ahead of everybody else. First in and they nearly made it to the very end. Stanley even made a joke about it in his last letter home to his mother. 'Still here and not a scratch. The devil looks after his own, eh ma?' Stanley was a great one for the jokes, God rest him.

Eileen What happened to him?

May The day before Stanley's last letter arrived, his mother got the Telegram. We all used to watch the Telegram Man comin' into the street. Fingers crossed, hardly darin' to breathe. Gettin' the Telegram meant that the man of the house, be it father or son, was dead. Because Stanley's letter arrived after the Telegram, his mother thought they'd made a mistake and he was still alive. But he wasn't. The bad news travels faster than the good, in a war. Stanley's mother died still hopin'. (*dispelling the bad memories with happier memories*) Stanley was a lovely big lad, so he was. (*crossing her index and middle fingers*) Him and Arthur were like that. All the girls round here fancied them rotten.

Eileen Did you?

May (*loving this memory*) I went out with the both of them one time . . . to the pictures . . . sat between them, like no goat's toe . . . (*sharing a smile/giggle*

with Eileen, who is dead impressed) Oh, I was the
quare girl in my time, before I settled down . . . only
don't you be tellin' your father I said that . . . he
thinks I never fancied nobody but him . . .

They giggle some more, stop as Cora comes in.

Cora Private joke is it, or can anybody join in?
May I was just tellin' Eileen about Arthur an' Stanley
Porter . . . *(a sly wink in Eileen's direction)* About
how him and Arthur were more interested in their oul
racin' pigeons than they were in goin' out with the
girls . . . *(all innocence)* . . . isn't that right love?

*Eileen nods, smiles, loving that her mother has shared
a secret with her and not told Cora what they were
really laughing about.*

Cora Don't talk to me about them pigeons. They should
have been shot after the war, instead of bein' let go
wild to breed like rabbits. Flyin' vermin. My yard
wall's destroyed with them.
Eileen *(shares a grin with her mother as May mimes/
mouths Cora's oft repeated moan; moves towards the
door with her kite)* See yous later . . .
May *(picking up Arthur's kite)* 'Scuse me?

Eileen sighs, takes the Arthur kite, goes outside.

ON THE WASTEGROUND

*Most of the children are sitting around waiting for
enough wind to fly their kites. Some have given up and
gone back to other games. The sky has the leaden look
of impending thunder.*

*Jean is giving the shop counter a perfunctory dusting.
Gets bored, wanders off into the back room.*

Freddy is standing on the top of the mound, wetting his finger and testing the air.
Eileen sits down beside Rose.

Rose It's hopeless the day. There's no wind at all. Not even a breeze . . . (*spotting the Arthur kite*) What is that?
Eileen My mammy made it for Arthur.
Rose It's wick.
Eileen I know.
Rose Dump it before he gets here.
Eileen She'll kill me.
Rose Sure she'll never know.
Eileen My mammy knows everything. My daddy says she comes from a long line of women that were born with eyes in the back of their head.
Freddy (*testing the wind again*) No joy, Billy! (*peering offstage*) Hey! Daft Arthur's comin' (*jumping down from the mound as Arthur enters*) an' he's got somethin' up his coat . . . look . . .
Billy Whatcha got, moon-man?

Arthur has one hand inside his coat, the other hand and arm held protectively across his chest. His eyes are still remote; his speech and movements slow, but there is a new air of pride/excitement about him.

Arthur I got a kite . . . my own . . .
Billy Up your coat?! It'll be all crumpled you dafy looney.
Arthur No . . . it's not . . . See?

He slowly, carefully brings his hand out from inside the army greatcoat and produces a live pigeon.
The children gather round, amazed.

Billy Frig, he caught one.

Freddy How'd you do it, Arthur? Every time we ever get anywhere near them they fly away, don't they, Billy . . .?

Billy Shut up!

Eileen (*to Rose*) Iced buns . . . that's how he done it . . .

Rose What?

Billy It's only a dozy oul pigeon, Arthur. I'll swop you my kite for it.

Roy I'll swop you mine.

Freddy I'll swop you mine.

Billy Bog off. Mine's the biggest and best kite in the street, Arthur.

Arthur My kite can fly the highest.

Billy It's a friggin' bird. If you let go of it, you'll never see it again.

Eileen (*scared/uneasy, having spotted what the others have missed*) He's got a string round it's neck . . . take it off . . . let it go, Arthur . . .

Arthur My kite . . . Mine . . . fly high . . .

He puts the pigeon back inside his coat, climbs to the top of the mound. Stands, takes the pigeon out from his coat again, holds it out.

Arthur The King of the Castle!

Roy (*imitating Arthur's speech/walk*) Arthur's the King of the Castle . . . The King's a dirty rascal . . .

Some of the other children join in. Others watch as Arthur raises the pigeon above his head. Eileen is frightened without quite knowing why.

Eileen Arthur, don't!!

Arthur jumps off the mound, flinging the pigeon high above his head. As the bird soars, Arthur lands on the ground, pulling the string taut. The pigeon plummets, hits the ground with a soft thud. There is a short silent pause.

Billy Frig's sake! You've killed it, you daft eejit.

Arthur drops to his knees in front of the dying, twitching pigeon.

Rose It's not proper dead, so it's not. (*repeating what she has heard adults say about injured animals*) You have to put it out of its misery, so you do . . .

Arthur No.

Freddy It's more cruel if you don't, isn't it Billy?

Arthur (*slightly louder*) No.

Rose You can't just leave it to suffer. You hafta wring it's neck or somethin', Arthur . . .

Arthur (*howls*) No!!

His face contorts in a terrible scream. He beats the ground with his fists and howls.
The children panic, run towards the safety of the street, screaming for their mothers, calling out that Arthur has gone mad.
Eileen has to force her eyes away from Arthur and is the last to run. She trips and falls, grazing her leg, tearing her dress. Her terror about what is happening to Arthur is replaced by the more commonplace fear of her mother's wrath when she sees the torn dress.

Eileen Aw, no . . . my mammy'll kill me, so she will . . .

She stands up, alone now on The Wasteground with Arthur, looks warily across at him. Arthur has stopped howling. He is now weeping, kneeling in front of the dying pigeon. Eileen walks slowly towards him as he speaks.

Arthur Stanley . . . Stanley . . . get up . . . please, Stanley . . . Oh dear God . . . sweet Jesus . . . help me . . . send somebody . . . somebody help me . . . (*Looks at the twitching pigeon, listens.*) I can't, Stanley . . . I can't . . . don't ask me to do that . . . don't.

(*shaking his head as if in reply*) There *isn't* anybody
else . . . just you and me . . . and the dead . . . all
dead, Stanley . . . don't say that . . . you know I
wouldn't let you suffer . . .

*As Eileen comes close, Arthur puts his hands together,
his lips moving in a barely audible prayer.*

Arthur For thine is The Kingdom . . . The Power . . .
The Glory . . . for ever . . . for ever . . . God forgive
me . . . God forgive me . . .

*He leans down, kisses the pigeon. Leans back. Puts
his hand into the greatcoat pocket, takes his hand out
again. His hand is now clenched with the forefinger
pointing at the pigeon. He puts his other hand around
the clenched part to stop it shaking, makes a sound in
the back of his throat like a child firing an imaginary
gun.*
　　The pigeon lies still.
　　*Arthur weeps, takes off the army greatcoat, spreads
it over the bird. Sits, in his tattered old army underwear,
his head bowed, sobbing.*
　　Eileen bursts into tears.
　　*Arthur looks up, looks directly into her eyes,
touches her face. He speaks in an ordinary voice,
gentle, puzzled, concerned.*

What are you doin' here, child? (*as Eileen just stares,
overcome that he's looking right into her eyes*) Don't
be frightened. Are you lost? Do you not speak English?
I'm from Belfast . . . Don't cry . . . (*wiping her tears
with his fingertips*) You'll be alright, now . . . the
battle's over . . . I think we won . . .

May runs on to The Wasteground, followed by Cora.

May Eileen! Eileen!

Cora I warned you. I warned everybody. But does anybody ever heed a word I say?

Eileen turns away from Arthur when she hears her mother shouting. When she turns her head back to him, his eyes are blank again.

Eileen No. Look at me . . . Let Mammy see too . . . look at Mammy too . . .

May What do you mean? (*to Cora*) What does she mean?

Cora Did he touch you, Eileen?

Eileen (*dazed*) He looked at me . . . he looked at me.

Eileen is angling her head, trying to lock Arthur's eyes on hers again. May grabs hold of her.

May What way looked at you?

Eileen In my eyes . . . an' he stroked my face . . .

May What way? What else? I want the truth of it madam! An' I want it this minute! Do you hear me?

Eileen (*misunderstanding, blurting out the terrible truth*) My dress got tore.

May (*misunderstanding*) Oh dear God . . .

Eileen (*looking for sympathy*) And my leg's all cut Mammy . . . look . . . (*pulling the torn dress apart to show the graze*)

Cora Harmless, you said. Harmless. Aren't they all 'til they go too far?

May is horrified, frightened into panic by Cora, frightened for Eileen. She hits Arthur with her fists. Screams.

May If you touched her, I'll kill you! Kill you! Do you hear me?

She stops. Shocked at herself. Stares for a moment at Arthur who has not reacted to the blows, then grabs hold of Eileen who is speechless at her mother's behaviour.

Don't you look at me like that, madam. Home! Now!

Eileen runs off towards home. May follows, leaving Cora alone on The Wasteground with Arthur. She looks at him with a mixture of contempt and triumph that she's been proved right. Sniffs.

Cora Cover yourself.
Arthur (*blank, quiet*) Yes . . . sir.

Arthur lifts his coat off the dead pigeon, puts the coat on. Cora backs away in distaste as he lifts the pigeon, gently unties the bloody string from round its neck. Sets the pigeon down again. He salutes; holds the string out towards Cora.

You'll be wantin' Stanley's dog-tags, sir . . . he said . . . he asked if they might be sent home . . . to his sweetheart . . . after . . .

Cora stands rigid, then makes a small scared, stricken gesture/sound, as Arthur moves towards her. She backs away, stumbles away towards Eileen's house.
Arthur sits down on the ground beside the pigeon.
During this the sky has darkened, clouds casting shadows over The Wasteground. Perhaps a distant rumble of thunder is heard.
The deepening cloud shadows on The Wasteground suggest the shapes of the bodies of dead soldiers lying on the ground all round where Arthur watches over Stanley's body. He stares blankly ahead, at nothingness. It is as if he is the only live person in a dead world.
Jean comes back into the shop, turns the radio on. Opens a film magazine.

Music: Penny Lee singing 'When the Lights Go on Again'.

IN EILEEN'S HOUSE

Eileen looking tearful/cross is sitting with her back to May and Cora who are whispering together, glancing towards her.

May Eileen . . .

Eileen I don't want to talk about it no more, so I don't. I've already told yous, he didn't do nuthin' . . . you never believe what I say, so you don't . . .

May I do believe you . . . (*a look at Cora, seeking her confirmation*)

Cora I believe you too . . . I still have my reservations, but . . . (*Stops, silenced by May's look.*) I'll head on home then . . . see you the marra . . .

May Aye.

Cora (*to Eileen*) See you the marra . . .

Eileen doesn't respond. Cora leaves the house, passes The Wasteground, glances at Arthur, hurries on past. She looks diminished, forlorn, alone.

There is a small pause after Cora leaves May and Eileen alone together. Their following conversation is a bit awkward, but straightforward, without sentiment.

Eileen (*quietly, almost as soon as Cora is out the door*) I hate her.

May Don't ever say bad about your own.

Eileen Nobody likes her. My daddy goes out every time she comes round. She's always here, so she is.

May She's lonely. She has nobody. No man, no chick nor child to call her own.

491

Eileen No wonder. Who'd want to marry *her*?

May Half the men in Belfast, accordin' to your granny. Cora was lovely lookin' when she was a girl. Always laughin'. Laughed all the men away, except for the one. Nuthin' to look at, from his photos, but he won her heart.

Eileen So why's she an oul maid then?

May She's nothin' of the sort. She was married for a week. His commandin' officer came personal to give Cora his medal after the war. What use is a tin medal when you have no body to bury, no grave to tend, no nothin'. Poor Cora just had to find her own way to get through that hard day's night . . . you're too young yet to understand the way of these things . . .

Eileen I'm not. I'm eleven, so I am. And you'd think what happened to Aunt Cora would make her more nice to other people who got hurted in wars like Arthur . . .

May (*sighs*) Oh, child. If the world worked that way, there'd never be no more wars ever. Sometimes it's the ones who get hurt the most who go on to hurt back the most, in their turn.

Eileen Why?

May I don't know, love. I've never been hurt that bad. And neither have you. So think on . . . (*angry and ashamed about hitting Arthur, but also becoming well fed up with Eileen's sulky superiority*) . . . an' climb down off your high horse. I'm sorry for actin' hasty. But enough's enough. Alright, madam?

Eileen Alright.

A small pause. A hesitant smile/touch. A truce.

ON THE WASTEGROUND

*The soldier-like shadows on the ground have slowly
shifted towards and around Arthur, so that most of his
body is enveloped in the shadows of the dead. He looks
up as a pigeon lands on top of the mound. He makes a
very deep sigh sound; closes his eyes.*

*As the shadows engulf Arthur, the lights darken
around Eileen and May. Their voices are heard as the
light fades.*

Eileen You see kites? I don't like them no more.
May Every fad lasts a fortnight. There'll be another one
on the way and more to follow. I wish you enjoyment
of them all, darlin' . . . even though I shudder to think
what it might be when you're a teenager . . .

*Immediate music: Danny and the Juniors, 'At the Hop'.
Lights up on:*

1957/58

*Children, five years on, jive on to the pavement. Lots of
ponytails among the girls; boys with oiled, slicked hair.
Billy and Freddy have Bill Haley kiss-curls. Roy, the star
jiver, has the flashiest cheap suit. One or two of the
smaller children have hula-hoops.*

*Behind the children, The Wasteground is roped-off, a
builder's sign warning 'Danger. Keep Out.'*

*The music is very loud, blaring out from a transistor
radio on the shop counter. Rose, her hair now in a ponytail, is playing the transistor radio while she works behind
the shop counter. She is doing the hand-jive in time to
the music. Jean is still there, still reading magazines.
Although she is now only nineteen or twenty years old,*

*she looks old-fashioned compared to the younger
teenage children. Everything about Jean – clothes, hair,
make-up, etc., hasn't moved on; is still locked in a
notion, an image created by the movie magazines of the
forties/early fifties. If she has gone ash-blonde, the
glamour is dated rather than modern.*

*The children dance, hula-hoop their way offstage to
the music.*

*Eileen, in teenage clothes, her hair in a ponytail, walks
down the street, waves to Rose, walks on past the roped-
off wasteground, towards her house.*

*In the house, May is sewing lace on the hem of a rock
and roll petticoat for Eileen. Cora is dozing in a chair,
knitting fallen in her lap.*

*Eileen pauses, looks for a moment at a pigeon on top
of the mound, walks on home.*

Sound of pigeons cooing as the lights dim.

The End.

Belfast Street Games, Songs, Skipping Rhymes

*while skipping or standing in line, performed with
actions to suit the words*

I'm Diana Dors.
I'm a movie star.
I've got a cute figure.
And a flashy motor car.

I've got the hips.
I've got the lips.
I'm Diana Dors.
I'm a movie star.

Jelly on a plate.
Jelly on a plate.
Wibbly wobbly, wibbly wobbly.
Jelly on a plate.

Keep the kettle boiling.
Miss the rope you're out.
If you'd a been where I'd a been,
You wouldn't a been put out.

Ingle angle silver bangle.
Ingle angle out.
If you'd a been where I'd a been,
You wouldn't have been out out.

Cinderella dressed in yella,
Went upstairs to see her fella.
How many kisses did she get?
One, two, three, four . . . (*etc.*)

Whistle while you work.
Hitler is a squirt.
Goering's barmy. So's his army.
Bury them in the dirt.

Will you come to our wee party, will you come.
Bring your own cup and saucer and a bun.
You can bring a cup of tea.
You can come along with me.
Will you come to our wee party, will you come.

Will you come to Abyssinia, will you come.
Bring your own ammunition and a gun.
Mussolini will be there, firing bullets in the air.
Will you come to Abyssinia, will you come.

Christmas is coming and the herald angels sing.
Mrs Simpson stole our King.

Our Queen can birl her leg, birl her leg, birl her leg.
Our Queen can birl her leg. Birl her leg leg leg.

Our Queen can ate a hard bap, ate a hard bap, ate a
    hard bap.
Our Queen can ate a hard bap. Ate a hard bap bap bap.

*'The Queen' referred to here was 'The May Queen' or
'The Queen of The May'.*

Barney Hughes's bread.
Barney Hughes's bread.
Sticks to your belly like a big lump of lead.
Not a bit of wonder you fart like thunder.
Barney Hughes's bread. Barney Hughes's bread.

Skinnymalink melodian legs, big banana feet.
Went to the pictures and couldn't get a seat.
When he got a seat, he fell fast asleep.
Skinnymalink melodian legs, big banana feet.

There was a wee man and he had a wee gun.
Over the mountains he did run.
He had a cocked hat and a belly full of fat.
And a pancake stuck to his bum bum bum.

Over the garden wall.
I let the baby fall.
My ma come out and give me a clout.
Over the garden wall.

Over the garden wall.
I let the baby fall.
My ma come and give me a clout.
She gave me another to match the other.
Over the garden wall.

Holy Mary Mother of God.
Pray for me and Tommy Todd.
For he's a Fenian and I'm a Prod.
Holy Mary Mother of God.

Granny granny Grey, will you let me out to play.
I won't go near the water and chase the ducks away.

Granny in the kitchen.
Doin' a bit of stitchin'.
In comes the Bogey Man and out runs she.
Ach, says granny, that's not fair.
Ach, says the Bogey Man, I don't care.

Ah Ma will you buy me a, will you buy me a, will you
    buy me a.
Ah Ma will you buy me a, will you buy me a banana.

Ah Ma will you peel the skin, will you peel the skin, will
    you peel the skin.
Ah Ma will you peel the skin, the skin of my banana.

Ah Ma do you want a bite, do you want a bite, do you
    want a bite.
Ah Ma do you want a bite, a bite of my banana.

Ah Ma you ate it all, you ate it all, you ate it all.
Ah Ma you ate it all, will you buy me a banana.

Charlie Chaplin went to France.
To teach the cannibals how to dance.
Heel. Toe. A burlio.
Miss the rope and out you go.

Vote, vote, vote for Winston Churchill.
In comes Paddy at the door, aye-o.
For Paddy is the one that'll have a bit of fun.
And we don't want Churchill anymore, aye-o.

*This one is also done with the names of other politicians
and/or the names of the children who are skipping in
and out of the rope.*

Tramp tramp tramp the boys are marching.
In come the bailiffs at the door aye-o.
If you will not let them in, they will bust your belly in.
And you'll never see your daddy anymore aye-o.

Good morning to you sir.
Where have you been sir.
To the North Pole sir.
What were you doing there sir.
Catching polar bears sir.
How many did you catch sir.
One, two, three, four . . . (*etc.*)

I know a lady.
Her name is Miss.
And all of a sudden.
She went like this . . . (*straddle the rope on 'this'*)

On the hill there stands a lady.
Who she is I do not know.
All she wants is gold and silver.
All she wants is a nice young man.
Lady lady touch the ground.
Lady lady birl right round.
Lady lady show your shoe.
Lady lady run right through.

Apple jelly, blackcurrant jam.
Tell me the name of your young man.
A, B, C, D, E, F, G . . . (*etc*)

I love coffee. I love tea.
I love the boys and the boys love me.
I wish my mother would hold her tongue.
For she had a boy when she was young.

I had a dress and it was green.
I didn't like it so I give it to the queen.
The queen didn't like it so she give it to the king.
Shut your eyes and count sixteen . . . one, two . . . (*etc.*)

Pink bluebells. Cockle shells.
Evie ivy overhead.
Mammy does the washing.
Daddy cuts the meat.
How many hours does the baby sleep?
One, two, three, four . . . (*etc.*)

House to let. Apply within.
They put the lady out for drinkin' gin.
Her ma was fat. Her da was thin.
The baby had a boil on its chin chin chin.

One two three. My mother caught a flea.
She roasted it. She toasted it.
We had it for our tea.

If you weren't so Ballymena.
With your Ballymoney.
You could buy a Ballycastle.
For your Ballyholme.

Are you Hungary. Yes Siam.
Russia to the table for Turkey and ham.
Germany was Hungary. Took a bite of Turkey.
Dipped it into Greece. And fried it in Japan.

Dublin on the Liffey.
Yorkshire on the Ooze.
Belfast on the Lagan.
And daddy on the booze.

There was a wee man and you called him Dan.
He washed his face in the fryin' pan.
He combed his hair with a donkey's tail.
And scratched his belly with his big toe nail.

Hot cross buns. Hot cross buns.
One a penny. Two a penny. Hot cross buns.
If you haven't got a daughter, give them to your sons.
One a penny. Two a penny. Hot cross buns.

Long. Tall. Thin and yella.
See me? That's my fella.

Here comes the bride.
Forty inches wide.
See how she wobbles her big backside.

Mrs D. Mrs I. Mrs F.F.I.
Mrs C. Mrs U. Mrs L.T.Y.

Mrs M. Mrs I. Mrs S.S.I.
Mrs S.S.I. Mrs P.P.I.

There was an old woman who lived in a lamp.
She had no room to beetle her champ.
So she up with the beetle and broke the lamp.
And now she's got room to beetle her champ.

BALL GAME RHYMES

*The ball is bounced on the ground and/or against a wall,
with actions to suit the words. Some skipping rhymes
and ball game rhymes are interchangeable.*

One two three O'Leary.
Four five six O'Leary.
Seven eight nine O'Leary.
Ten O'Leary. Over it.

One two three O'Leary.
Four five six O'Leary.
I saw Da O'Leary.
Sittin' on his bumbaleary.

Desperate Dan thinks he's grand.
But he can't do bouncy.
He can't do upsy.
He can't do catchy.
He can't do dropsy.

Bounce ball. Bounce ball.
One two three.
Underneath my right leg.
And over my knee.
Underneath my left leg. Up against a tree.
Bounce ball. Bounce ball. One two three.

Upsy Mother Brown. Upsy Mother Brown.
Upsy. Upsy. Double upsy. Upsy Mother Brown.

Bouncy Mother Brown. Bouncy Mother Brown.
Bouncy. Bouncy. Double bouncy. Bouncy Mother Brown.

Queen-eo. Queen-eo.
Who's got the ball-eo.
I haven't got it in my pocket.

*This is chanted when one child stands with her back to
the others, tosses the ball over her head, then turns and
guesses who caught it. If she guesses correctly, she is still
Queen. If she doesn't, the girl who did catch the ball
takes her place.*

'Names': *another ball game for a group of children.
One player bounces and catches two balls alternately
against the wall while the other children take it in turn
to chant one thing she has to name, then two, then three,
then four . . . etc. If the player can't think of the right
thing to reply and/or breaks the rhythm of the ball or the
chant, another child takes over. Example:*

FIRST CHANTER One girl you must know.
EVERYBODY Wish you luck and away you go.
PLAYER Eileen!

SECOND CHANTER Two boys you must know.
EVERYBODY Wish you luck and away you go.
PLAYER Billy! Freddy!
THIRD CHANTER Three streets you must know.
EVERYBODY Wish you luck and away you go.

And so on. The things to be named can be anything –
shops, cities, countries, fruit, animals, birds, fish . . .

'Jumpy over the Ball': *a fast group ball game*

Children stand in a queue facing a wall. The first player
throws the ball against the wall, jumps to let it bounce
back under her feet, the next player catches it, throws it
against the wall . . . etc. Each player runs to the back of
the queue to wait for another turn.

'Dusty Bluebells': *a singing game*

Children make a circle, holding their clasped hands in
the air. One child weaves in and out through and under
their arms as they sing:

In and out go the dusty bluebells
In and out go the dusty bluebells
In and out go the dusty bluebells
I'll be your master.

At the end of the verse, the child stops behind the player
she has reached; taps her on the shoulder; sings with the
others.

Tapper rapper rapper on the left hand shoulder
Tapper rapper rapper on the left hand shoulder
Tapper rapper rapper on the left hand shoulder
I'll be your master.

At the end of this verse, the child whose shoulder has been tapped, steps out of the circle, goes behind the first child, holds on either to her shoulders or her hips, and they both weave in and out as the circle rejoins and the first verse is sung again. The two verses and the actions are repeated over and over, the circle decreasing as the weaving line increases, until everybody is in the line.

'Bangor Boats': *a game for two children*

They sit facing each other, the soles of their feet touching, their hands clasped. They pull each other back and forward (like a swingboat) as they sing:

Bangor boats away.
We have no time to stay.
Give it a kick. Make it go quick.
Bangor boats away.

Sometimes, a smaller child sits between the two singers, straddling their legs or feet up on a lap.

Most of these games/songs/chants were carried from one generation to the next by word of mouth and imitation. There are different versions/variations of many of them, not only in Belfast and the whole of Ireland, but in other cities and townlands in Scotland, Wales, England and in other countries worldwide. If you're more familiar with another version, or know something that's very similar or interchangeable, use it. (But be careful that it's not a later version with names or references that evolved after the time-scale of this play.)

If you're not sure, ask your granny or someone else who remembers and knows the way of it.

Secrets of a Five-Year Diary Unlocked

Christina Reid interviewed by Jim Mulligan

Christina Reid left school when she was fifteen. Twenty-five years later she abandoned her studies as a mature student when she was awarded a Thames Television theatre bursary for her first stage play and then became Writer in Residence at Belfast's Lyric Theatre. Her stage, screen and radio plays stem mostly from her Belfast working-class background, particularly its women who were her first inspiration.

> I come from a long line of women who tell stories. There were lots of respectable Belfast women in my mother's family. From a tiny child I remember them dressing up and telling stories that were a mixture of fact and fiction. I wrote down stories, they acted them out. I remember, when I was eleven I was given a five-year diary, one of those lock-and-key things. After a week I got bored with writing what had actually happened to me and started making up fantastic tales about myself. So I've always written things down but it wasn't until I was married with children that I won a competition for a TV play written by an Irish writer, for Irish actors and for an Irish audience. That play was staged later on.

The King of the Castle is based upon a short story written in the early 1980s but set in the early 1950s. The war is not long over and the children play on a piece of waste-ground, the result of one of the bombs in the Belfast Blitz. The wasteground is also the haunt of Arthur, a soldier who has come back from the war traumatised, unable to speak about what happened to him and

reduced superficially to the level of a child. At best he
is treated as if he is not there or else is derided and
tormented by the children and feared by the adults.
Eileen's mother knew Arthur before he went to fight and
remembers him as someone whom she was fond of and
even went out with on a date. She understands and
sympathises with him and tries to make Eileen see that
he must be treated gently. However, Eileen's great aunt
seems to see him as a danger allowed to roam the street.

When I was a child in the City of Belfast there were
some soldiers like Arthur who roamed the streets.
I was always curious about them because my grandfather fought in the First World War and my mother's
nineteen-year-old brother died from wounds received
at Dunkirk so we had photographs of heroic soldiers
in my grandmother's house. We didn't know anything
about post-traumatic shock syndrome in those days.
We called it shell-shock. I don't know what happened
to these soldiers but we were afraid of them and
fascinated. While doing some research for another
play I learned that over a million combatants of all
nationalities died in the first week of the Battle of the
Somme. That is simply unimaginable.

There are two crucial scenes in *The King of the Castle*.
The first is Eileen's dream sequence when she dances
with Arthur to 'The Teddy Bears' Picnic' with the
ominous words, 'You'd better not go alone . . . It's safer
to stay at home.' The second scene is triggered when the
children insist that Arthur should finish off the pigeon he
has almost throttled. In an instant he is re-living the
traumatic event that drove him into silence. He re-enacts
the mercy shooting of his friend Stanley. Eileen has
panicked, fallen over, torn her dress and grazed her knee.
She stares transfixed as Arthur gently wipes away her
tears – at which point her mother and great aunt burst

in. Their shocked cries silence Arthur and it is apparent
that he will now go back deeper into his trauma and
never come out of it again.

> May and Cora see Eileen with her leg cut and her
> dress torn and there is total wild panic. When Arthur
> holds out his dog-tags to Cora she is faced with what
> might have happened to her man who never came
> back from the war. Up to now she has only seen
> Arthur as a coward. Now she sees him as just one of
> thousands who were lost in some way. It frightens her.
> She knows she has done something wrong to lead this
> campaign against Arthur and she is diminished,
> forlorn and alone.

The King of the Castle may be about Arthur, but deeper
than that is the relationship between May and her
daughter Eileen.

> That relationship is very close to me and my mum.
> I didn't realise until I was older how hard she worked
> and how good she was. When I was a child she was
> hard on me and indulged my brothers and she would
> lose her temper. Like me she was a mixture of the fey
> and the very practical. But even as a child, I sensed
> that she would have died for me.

Throughout *The King of the Castle* the children play
street games and sing songs which Christina Reid
believes are still going strong in Belfast even if their
powerful hold has lessened for children in other cities
where they no longer play out in the streets. The short
story ended with Arthur kneeling down alone on the
wasteground, but Christina Reid wanted to give her play
an upbeat ending so she moved the action on five years.
The craze is now hula-hoops, the music rock-n-roll.
Developers have moved in and Eileen, in teenage clothes
and her hair in a ponytail, walks down the street.

I think the young people will enjoy the dream sequence, the street games and the rock-n-roll. They will also reflect on the story. One young person said she was devastated and ashamed at the way Arthur was treated. I hope theatre has the power to make people think. Children remember things vividly and, if this play moves them, they may re-think their attitudes to people who are different and to the victims of war.

Production Notes

STAGING AND SETTING

The play is set in Belfast in the early 1950s, the decade
just after World War Two. The action can be shifted to
another city where children play on land that has been
made derelict by war but the period must remain the
same. The play opens on a cold, grey wintry afternoon
and moves swiftly onto summer of the same year. In the
last scene the action fast forwards five years. There are
three acting areas, the wasteland, the shop and Eileen's
family's living room. The wasteland was a bomb site and
is full of blasted bricks and mortar. There are no trees or
greenery, any grass would be grey and dusty. It contains
a high mound of rubble which has been compacted into
a hard knobbled hill by children clambering over it:
different levels may be created by introducing
scaffolding, ramps and rostra. It needs to be sturdy
enough to walk on. Very little was thrown out in the
1950s because of post-war rationing, so the space should
not resemble a scrap-yard. Any junk would have been
put to good use – pram wheels, for instance, might have
been used to make a 'guider' or 'go-cart'. Props or
furniture such as the radio and pram should suggest the
period in which the play is set. The paving area in front
of the wasteground may be indicated by having a hop
scotch playing area marked in chalk. The wall might
have goal posts chalked on it. The shop is Jean's
Grannie's front room. It might be suggested very simply
by a shop bell and a light bulb being dropped in to
suggest an indoor scene. Colours in both the shop and
Eileen's house would be faded and chosen because they
don't show up the dirt. Scraps of wallpaper can be used

to indicate the remaining walls of the house or an interior scene if used on an adjacent wall. There is a coffin in Eileen's sitting room at the start of the play The mourning period might be indicated further by a mirror being covered. The cover should be removed when we return to the same location to indicate the passage of time.

The pigeons can be created in several ways. You can have enormous fun experimenting with the use of projection, shadow play or flapping books. Perhaps the simplest and most effective way is using a combination of sound and actors' response. The audience will respond to the story being told clearly and don't necessarily need special effects to help them keep up with the action. The sequence with Arthur and the pigeon is described in the dialogue. Decide how little the audience needs to see of the bird still to follow the story. The kite flying can also be achieved simply. The kites (make most of them look as home-made as possible) could be suspended from the rig or suggested by mime.

LIGHTING

can be used to differentiate the boundaries between the three acting spaces. It needs to indicate the passage from winter to summer, noisy and colourful to chilling and still moments, interior and exterior scenes. The dream sequence might be colourful and strange or turned on its head and be designed to be naturalistic with other scenes appearing to be more fantastic. Towards the end of the play soldier-like shadows shift towards and around Arthur, so that most of his body is enveloped in the shadows of the dead.

SOUND

needs to suggest pigeons cooing, landing and taking flight, a baby crying and kites fluttering in the breeze. Jean is listening to Flanagan and Allen singing 'Run Rabbit Run' on the large old radio on the shop counter. The script makes specific reference to several other songs and children's rhymes which may be live or prerecorded according to taste. Any mood music should be of the period. In the last scene the radio is blaring out music of the late-1950s, it could be Bill Haley, which Rose is hand-jiving to.

CASTING

There are nine speaking roles, five female and four male, three of whom are adults, with scope for any number of additional children to join in the games which make up a large proportion of the play, the dream sequence or to become the shadows of the dead. The children are all aged between ten and twelve apart from Jean who is fifteen. Arthur and May are in their early thirties and Cora is middle-aged.

EXERCISES

Look at films, newsreels, early TV programmes and magazines of the period. Talk to adults who were 'war babies' born during the Second World War and growing up in the 1950s. Ask them to recall and demonstrate the games they played as children. See if they recognise the chants that went with them and can recall the rhythms and ways in which they were used in the games.

- Choose any of the games which the script provides. Have half the group play the games while the other half observes them. Note who abides by the rules, who cheats, who is passive, dominant etc.
- Swap over. The group who were observing now choose one of the characters from the play (not Arthur). The script provides a lot of information about the characters – Billy affects the mannerisms of an adult, Cora sniffs a lot, Roy enjoys mimicking people. Have the group take up the game where the others broke off in role. Have the observers note how the characters interact and guess who they are.

The characters talk a lot about their lives off-stage. For instance, Rose tells Jean and Eileen that 'My ma and da yell at each other all the time. An' next thing they're tellin' me I have to go to bed early an' slobberin' all over themselves like they're not right in the head.' Build up a clearer picture of the characters by improvising scenes that they refer to outside the action of the play.

Look at what the characters say about one another in the script. People hold strong views about Cora and Arthur in particular: decide what is biased and what is accurate information.

Make a kite using newspaper, doweling, rags and twine for the tail. Choose a windy day and a good hilly location to fly it or to observe other kites being flown. Note how they move and how they are controlled. As a group, mime flying kites using the reel as a prop. Watch one of the group manipulate the kite. Take your lead from one member of the group when observing how the kite dips and ascends. Create the illusion that you are all watching the same event.

As a group, move stealthily towards an imagined flock of stationary pigeons. Without discussion, choose the right moment to try and capture them. Watch them take flight and follow their progress with your body. Make these movements as clear and concentrated as possible. Repeat the exercise with the sound tape.

Look at Eileen's Dream Sequence. Eileen appears strong and grounded but is clearly having disturbed thoughts which she is good at concealing. Dreams conjure up images, metaphors and symbolism which the waking brain normally filters out.

Break the dream sequence into the following headings and images:

> Two large suspended kites
> Hollywood movie/scary dance sequence
> Children/teddies dancing
> Rose and Jean/Ginger Rogers and Fred Astaire dancing
> Elopement ladder
> Cora in a coffin
> May being friendly to everyone except Eileen
> Arthur giving bits of iced buns to children/teddies
> Eileen left alone with Arthur

Using evidence from the play, decide what has prompted these thoughts and what they represent.

Arthur is an ex-soldier and a war casualty. His mind is damaged and he sees the world as it was before the Belfast Blitz. He believes, for instance, that Mrs Matchett is still managing the shop but we know she was killed in an air raid. Improvise one of the scenes which involves Arthur. Play the scene through his eyes. Gather material together on the effects of shell-shock and see how the symptoms relate to him.

Suzy Graham-Adriani
February 1999

THE PILGRIMAGE

Paul Goetzee

Characters

Granpa Grimm, Gregor's father, a shepherd
Mermer, Clove's mother
Clove, wife of Gregor
Gregor, a shepherd
Brag, a shepherd, brother to Gregor
Butt, eldest son of Clove and Gregor, shepherd
Lena, wife of Butt
Chaff, daughter of Clove and Gregor
Mendel, daughter of Clove and Gregor,
Chaff's twin sister
Josef, a goatherd
Sylvian, the man who lives in the trees
Virgin of the Shepherds
Virgin of the Goatherds

The Chorus

The Pilgrimage is set in a fictitious,
possibly Eastern European country,
in a wild and rugged landscape that can only
support sheep and goats. The music is the music
of Turkey, Armenia and the Balkans.

The time is the past, the present,
but hopefully not the future.

Music: a wild and haunting theme, ominous and
threatening, which breaks into something more
rhythmic, against which the Chorus say their lines:

Chorus
This is the mountain
These are the valleys where
Sheep and goats tear thistles
And dry grass
From the dust and stones

Clove I never thought it would happen to our family.
Gregor Things like this only happen to other people.
Chaff and Mendel Not to us.

Chorus
One hundred years ago
A woman appeared on the mountain
To three shepherd girls
Minding their flocks
She touched the twisted foot
Of one of them and made it straight
She told them terrible secrets
And vanished

Mermer People have long memories.
Grimm As long as time.
Butt People's memories are short.
Lena It all depends on what you want to remember.

Chorus
The people of these hills
Made a shrine on the mountain
It became

A place of pilgrimage
To this shrine came a group
Of pilgrims
Clothed in shame

Brag Nobody is innocent. All blood must be paid for.
Mermer It is that simple.
Brag A family must stand by its own.
Grimm Or it will destroy itself.
Chorus
Hear their story

The family take their positions: Mermer is carried on Clove's back. Clove has two stirrups hanging from her waist into which Mermer puts her feet. Gregor carries Grandpa Grimm in the same way. Mendel and Chaff are bound together at the wrist by a red cord. Brag wears an axe or machete in his belt. Butt wears spectacles and always carries a book, which he sometimes rests on Lena's back to read.

Chorus
Take the seedling memory
Plant it in anger
Water it with bitter tears
Nurse it with fear
And watch it
Blossom into hatred

The family breaks up and brings on a rough wooden table to which are fastened plates. Stools and/or benches are brought on for them to sit down.

Clove Food! Grandpa Grimm! Mendel, Chaff, Butt, Lena, Gregor, Brag!
Mermer Come and eat now. Or starve!
Chorus The family that eats together
Will not eat each other

So goes the proverb
In these mountains

Gregor (*entering with Grimm on his back*) I could eat a horse.

Clove Horse is off. It's mutton.

Gregor It's always mutton.

Mermer Mutton is good. Sheep is good.

Butt and Lena enter. He is reading a book using her as a reading stand.

Lena Haven't you finished that book yet?

Butt Last chapter, my sweet.

Lena Why do you read such big books?

Butt Because I like them. Books are knowledge. Knowledge is power. Power is an aphrodisiac. An aphrodisiac is an aid to sexual enjoyment. Ergo, books are sexy!

Mermer You are about as sexy as a whelk, Butt. Now, put that book down before I throw it on the fire!

Butt Yes, Mermer.

Mermer I was just saying.

Lena What were you just saying, Mermer?

Grimm She was just saying that sheep is good.

Brag (*entering in a bloodstained apron*) Sheep is life.

Butt If you say so, Brag.

Clove Wait! Where are the twins?

Brag On the slopes watching my sheep.

Mermer Plotting insolence and making mischief, more like.

Gregor Double trouble.

Butt Trouble squared to be precise. Their trouble-making increases exponentially by a factor of the sum of their number, that is to say . . . two.

A pause as they look at Butt.

Mermer Butt, eat your mutton before your head explodes.

Butt Yes, Mermer.

Mendel and Chaff enter.

Clove Where have you been?

Mendel Half a dozen of Uncle Brag's ewes went charging up the southern pass.

Chaff It took us ages to get them back.

Brag You didn't lose any, did you?

Chaff Of course not.

Mendel What do you think we are, stupid goatherds?

Chaff Sybil just had two beautiful lambs.

Clove I know, they're hanging in the larder.

Chaff Oh mother! They're only babies.

Grimm Babies make the tenderest meat.

Gregor May the Lord make us truly thankful for that which gives us our food and clothing: the blessed sheep.

All Amen.

Mendel Sylvian the treeman says he's seen goats on the western slopes.

Grimm Ignore him. He's as mad as my trousers.

Clove You shouldn't be talking to him.

Chaff He says he saw a herd passing by only yesterday.

Gregor We will have no goatherds here!

Clove Gregor, calm down.

Brag If he's right, we will have to drive them out. They will ruin us.

Mermer Remember the last time goats came to the valleys.

There is a long pause.

Chaff Of course we don't remember. We're not old like you.

Gregor Then listen. Let your grandmother pour vintage
wine into fresh gourds. (*He taps the twins on the
head.*)

Mendel and Chaff Ow!

Mermer The last time goatherds came to our mountains,
I was a little girl of seven. They came and drove out
all the sheep.

Chorus
Drove them out.

Mermer They rounded them up, slaughtered them and
burnt them in huge fires.

Chorus
Fire!

Grimm I was ten. I remember them taking my father's
sheep and hacking them to pieces.

Chorus
Hacked them to pieces.

Grimm They gave me and my brothers roast kid to eat.
They forced us to eat unclean meat.

Chorus
Unclean!

Grimm I wouldn't, so they beat me. I ran away from
them. They burned down my father's farm.

Chorus
Burning.

Grimm Slaughtered his flocks.

Chorus
Slaughter!

Mermer We have our memories. Now they are yours.

Grimm Memory is a gift to pass on to your children.

Lena Memory is a curse too.

Gregor Quiet!

Butt But, didn't we go into their mountains and burn all
their goats in revenge?

Grimm Of course we did. It's expected.

Mermer They started it.
Butt But . . .
Gregor But but but! Your head is full of buts.
Mendel That's why we call him Butt!
Butt But . . . but . . .

Mendel and Chaff start head-butting each other.

Mendel and Chaff But but but but but but! Ow!
Butt But!
Clove But what Butt?
Butt All I was going to say was that before the goatherds came to our mountains, we went to theirs and slaughtered all their goats.
Mermer That was a crusade!
Butt Against goats?
Gregor Against the unclean.
Butt So they didn't start it. We did.
Mermer No. Before that they came here and killed all our sheep.
Gregor Why are you saying all this anyway, Butt?
Lena Butt likes to study history.
Brag From books? What use are books? People who read books shouldn't keep sheep.
Lena Butt is a good shepherd – even if he does wear glasses.
Butt What?
Brag So how come he lost that ram down a gully the other week? Good breeding stock too. Balls on him like church bells. The ram I mean, not Butt.
Mermer Ram's balls in a dill sauce. That was a treat when I was a girl.
Gregor History is one thing, Butt. Memory another. You can say anything in a book. Tell lies, twist the truth. And because it's written down people will believe it. But it's what we hold inside our heads that matters.

That is pure and unchanging. We pass on our
memories in our songs and our stories.

Chaff So what do we do when the goatherds come?

Mermer We defend ourselves!

Grimm To the death!

All (*stabbing their knives into the table, Butt, Lena and
Chaff not too sure*) To the death!

Grimm Now carve that mutton, Gregor, before we all
die of hunger!

Chorus (*during which the cast clear the table and seating*)
This is our family
Our happy family
Bound together in common purpose
Tied with ropes of love
Sharp words are spoken
But wounds soon healed
Blows exchanged for
Kindness and embraces

Chorus
Nothing is a secret in our family
Nothing so dark it cannot be spoken
All wrongs can be forgiven
All hurt soothed

Chaff and Mendel are minding the sheep.
*Sylvian, the man who lives in trees, swings down
from branches overhead, hanging upside down as he
talks to them. He begins by throwing acorns at them.
At first, the girls ignore him, then it gets too much.*

Mendel Ow! Stop that, you freak!

Sylvian Make me.

Chaff Stop acting the goat, Sylvian. We shouldn't even
be talking to you.

Sylvian No, Sylvian is the bogie man, isn't he? The loon
in the laburnum.

Mendel That's not a laburnum.

Sylvian How would you know? It hasn't got four legs
and a fleece, so you wouldn't have a clue.

Chaff Get lost, treeman.

Sylvian Tell me something –

Mendel No.

Sylvian Why are you two always joined together?

Mendel Because we're twins.

Chaff We were born this way.

Mendel Blood flows along this cord.

Chaff And back again. Anyway, what's it to you?

Sylvian The goatherds are coming.

Mendel So you said.

Chaff We still don't believe you.

Sylvian I'm glad I don't herd sheep any more.

Chaff You don't do anything any more.

Mendel You just live in a tree and talk goat-shit.

Sylvian My mother always said: Sylvian, make sure you
keep both feet on the ground.

Mendel But you don't keep your feet on the ground.

Sylvian My father always said: never listen to your
mother.

Chaff Have you never come down?

Sylvian Never.

Mendel Isn't it uncomfortable?

Sylvian Not any more. I got used to it. Besides I can be
above the everyday. Think my own thoughts.

Chaff Eat leaves.

Sylvian To suck the meat from a warm thrush's egg –
paradise! It's not a bad life.

Mendel Our grandma said you were put up there as a
punishment.

Sylvian Well, maybe your dear old gran is right. I'm a
criminal. That's why I live in a tree. This is my prison.
My hell. My heaven. There's going to be more
burning and slaughtering soon. But it won't concern

me. Up here. I shall just witness all and weep.
(*Laughs.*) See you later! (*He swings back into the tree
and disappears.*)

Mendel Mad.

Chaff Completely mental.

*Josef, a goatherd, enters. He is carrying a kid in his
arms.*

Josef Hello.

Mendel Who are you?

Chaff You're not from round here.

Josef No. I'm lost. Have you anything to eat? I can pay.

Mendel We don't share food with strangers.

Chaff Until we know why they're here.

Josef I'm a herdsman.

Chaff We're all herdspeople.

Mendel Where are your sheep?

Josef I don't herd sheep.

Mendel What do you herd then, chickens?

Josef Goats.

Chaff and Mendel Goats!

Chaff Are you a bit retarded? Don't you know what we
do to goatherds round here?

Josef Yes . . . but I'm hungry.

Chaff Stay there. (*She takes Mendel to one side.*) Mendel,
what should we do?

Mendel Right. I know. We give him some food and some
water. Have a laugh and a joke, wait till he falls
asleep, then pick up a really big stone and drop it on
his head.

Chaff Then what?

Mendel Kill all his goats.

Chaff He looks quite nice . . .

Mendel He's a goatherd, a monster.

Chaff He doesn't look like a monster.

Mendel So what? He's dangerous.

Josef I can let you have this newborn kid for some food and something to drink. Look. (*He shows them the kid.*)

Chaff Ah, isn't it cute? I've never seen a kid before.

Mendel Ugh, it's horrible! Look at its eyes. Like the devil. Don't touch it, Chaff, it's unclean.

Chaff picks up the kid.

Chaff! It's wrong!

Chaff What do you call him?

Josef I don't call him anything.

Chaff That's not very imaginative.

Mendel Goatherds aren't, it's well known. They're stupid. They fall asleep as soon as it goes dark and they have to write L and R on their boots so they know which way to put them on.

Josef We have sheep-people jokes like that.

Chaff He hasn't got L and R on his boots.

Josef That's because it's worn off.

Mendel See!

Chaff I think he's joking. Aren't you?

Mendel Goatherds don't joke. They haven't got a sense of humour like us.

Chaff Where do you come from?

Josef From the south.

Chaff What's it like? In the south.

Mendel Chaff, why are you talking to him?

Chaff Mendel, shut up will you?

Mendel I'm going back to tell our dad. Then you're dead, goatboy.

Chaff You can't go back without me.

Mendel Exactly. At least one of us knows the right thing to do. You've got to come with me.

Chaff No, I want to talk to him. I want to know about the south.

Mendel I'm going without you then.

Chaff No, I'm staying!
Mendel Ow! You'll get a beating.

They start to pull backwards and forwards on the cord.

Chaff That's my problem. I want to stay!
Mendel We've always done everything together.
Chaff Maybe it's time for a change.
Mendel (*pulling out her knife*) Alright! If you won't come with me, I'll cut the cord. I mean it. I will!
Chaff You wouldn't dare!
Mendel I'm not going to stay with this unclean.
Chaff He's not unclean.
Mendel I'll cut it, Chaff. See if I don't.
Chaff Go on, I dare you.
Mendel What?
Chaff I dare you. Well, what are you waiting for?
Josef Please, there's no need for this –
Mendel Stay out of this, goatface! You've got to the count of three, Chaff. One –
Chaff Mendel, think –
Mendel Two –
Chaff You'll regret it.
Mendel Come back with me.
Chaff No!
Mendel Three!

Mendel cuts the cord. They both scream, then look at each other in horror. Mendel says nothing but runs away. Exit.

Chorus
  The cord has been cut
  The bond of family broken
  Blood spilled
  The bitter truth is spoken:
  Things can never be the same again.
Chaff What have I done?

The family reassembles. At the centre, Gregor holds up the arms of Chaff and Mendel.

Gregor What have you done?
Clove Chaff, Mendel. Answer your father. What have you done?
Mendel She wanted to stay with the goatherd.
Mermer Wicked child! Consorting with the unclean!
Chaff He wasn't unclean.
Grimm He stank of goats. It never leaves them.
Chaff We stink of sheep.
Gregor Shut up, the lot of you!

Brag enters still in his bloodstained apron, but this time holding a bloodstained cleaver in his hand.

Brag There! It's done.
Mermer Did you slaughter every last one?
Brag Every last one.
Grimm And are they burning?
Brag You can see the smoke for miles.
Chaff What about the goatboy? What have you done to him?
Brag He's been taken care of.
Chaff What have you done with him!
Brag He wouldn't tell us where the other herders were.
Chorus
  So we tied him to a tree
  And gutted and jointed him
  With our knives and axes
  His screams filled the quiet valley
  And echoed off the mountain
  The crows pluck at his eyes
  The fox sniffs the bloody entrails
  Flies hum a death-song
  Above his lips
  Murder!

528

Chaff You killed him!

Brag And if I did? So what?

Gregor Listen to me, Chaff. You are in serious trouble already. That mad treefreak, Sylvian, lost the use of his legs after he traded with goatherds. They were smashed with stones. That is why he lives in trees swinging by his arms like an ape. If anyone finds out you spoke to a goatherd, the same will happen to you.

Chaff Then let it! Anything is better than living another day in this place!

Chaff runs out. Exit.
The Chorus gasps and it divides into two. The family also divides: Butt, Lena, Clove on one side; Grimm, Gregor, Brag, Mermer on the other.

Chorus
The bond is cut
The family split
The strong chain snaps
Outrage follows hard upon
Outrage

Mountainside.
A body lies covered with a bloodstained sheet.
Chaff enters carrying the kid.

When black clouds fill the oceans
And the sun pours down freezing rain
When the lightning fork strikes upward
Then will end all pain

If this is done as a song, Chaff would join in.
Sylvian appears from the branches.

Sylvian I saw them do it, you know. Here. Against this tree. I covered him with the sheet.

Chaff Treeman, what can I do?

Sylvian Oh, it's 'Treeman what can I do', now is it? Not 'Get lost you loony leaf-eater'?

Chaff I'm in trouble and I've never felt so bad before. I feel as if I've cut off a part of my own body.

Sylvian Join the club. No one likes people to act on their own. It makes them look sheepish.

Chaff They told me about you. About what they did to you.

Sylvian Did you feel sorry for me?

Chaff A bit.

Sylvian I tell you what I did.

Chaff What?

Sylvian Prayed to the Virgin for a miracle. A new set of legs.

Chaff Did it work?

Sylvian No. But this is where the Virgin appears.

Chaff A hundred years ago.

Sylvian I see her every day picking daisies.

Chaff Don't lie.

Sylvian It's true, I swear. Pray to her. Ask her to bring your goatboy back to life. It's worth a try.

Chaff He didn't look like a bad person.

Sylvian What did you expect: cloven feet and long curly horns?

Chaff He came from mountains just like ours. He would have seen the same sunrise, the same stars, breathed the same air. Virgin, if you are here and you can hear me. Help me. Bring the goatherd back to life. I'll do anything if I can see him whole again. (*Pause, she waits.*) There: nothing.

Sylvian Wait!

Music: the Chorus parts and the Virgin emerges from them carried on high. They set her down.

Chorus
She appears not as a lady

530

But as a peasant girl
Her flesh and bones
The ragged yearnings
Of the desperate and the poor
She is made out of wishes
And needs and desires
Gossamer as daydream
Mountainous as prayer
Healer and carer
Open our hearts
Touch the stricken
Breathe life into
The lifeless

Chaff It's her!

Virgin Your name's Chaff, isn't it?

Chaff How did you know?

Virgin Did you expect me not to know? I'd be something of a disappointment if I didn't know your name. What can I do for you?

Chaff Can you bring the goatboy back to life? He's dead.

Virgin (*looking under the sheet*) And in more than one piece by the look of it. You're looking at a big job, sunshine. It'll cost you.

Chaff How much?

Virgin More than you'll want to pay.

Chaff I'll pay it. Anything.

Virgin There is another problem.

Chaff What?

Virgin He's goat. I only do sheep.

Chaff But aren't you the Virgin for all people?

Virgin What books have you been reading? They've got their own Virgin.

Chaff But you'd be doing it for me. A sheep-person.

Virgin Hm. Bit of a theological nicety, but I can roll with that one. Just this once. OK, here goes. Let sinew

bond with bone, gristle with offal blah blah blah . . .
that should do it. Right, I'm off. Remember, there's a
price. There always is.

*The Virgin merges back into the Chorus and they
carry her away.*

    *There is movement beneath the sheet, then Josef
appears.*

Sylvian What did I tell you?

Chaff He's alive! You're alive! It was the Virgin. She did
it! She brought you back to life!

Josef Murderer! Murderers! Filthy sheep herders! All the
stories about you are true!

Chaff No, you've got it wrong. The Virgin brought you
back to life!

Josef The Virgin of the goatpeople?

Chaff No . . . not exactly . . . our Virgin . . . but she did
a good job.

Josef Blasphemy! No phoney saint of yours could do
anything for me.

Chaff But you're alive. You were dead.

Josef Who says?

Sylvian Look, goatsbrains, your head was six feet away
from your body and your guts were all over the slopes
before I tidied you up. Not many people survive that
kind of minor injury, do you know what I'm saying?

Josef Goatpeople are tough. Indestructible.

Sylvian Do you ever get the feeling you're on to a loser
with some people?

Josef Give me that kid. It is all that is left of my herd.
I am returning to my people and I will tell them what
you did to me and to my goats. Then we'll see.

Chaff No, don't go! This wasn't supposed to happen, oh
no!

Josef goes. Exit.

Sylvian What did you expect? Violins? A fairy-tale
ending? His eternal gratitude maybe?

Chaff But it was a miracle. You saw it. He just thinks he
survived. He must believe he's superhuman.

Sylvian Next thing, he'll be gathering a cult-following
and letting them kill themselves for him.

Chaff What do I do now, treeman?

Sylvian Suffer. It's the way.

Chaff Thanks.

Sylvian You're welcome. Cuckoo's egg? No? More for
me then. Cheerio.

Sylvian goes. Exit.

Chorus
  And the goatherd walked back
  Boldly through the valley
  Holding the bleating kid in his arms
  The shepherds stared at him
  In disbelief
  Mouths on hinges
  Children clutching at their mothers' skirts
  Men glowered over closed gates
  This was a dead man
  Breathing air, treading earth underfoot
  Smiling a crooked smile
  At the fear on their faces
  Devil's work
  The goatherd went back to his people
  And told his story.

The family sets up the table and seating over the
Chorus.
  Clove brings in a soup tureen. She carries Mermer
on her back. Gregor carries Granpa Grimm. Butt and
Lena enter, then Brag carrying Mendel, who looks
very ill.

Chorus
Home
Sheltering thatch
Four stone walls
Strong fences
A gate that locks
Wood burns in the hearth
The family gathers
But the house is unquiet
Like a disturbed graveyard.

Clove Mutton soup anyone? No? No one? Very well, I'll give it to the pigs.

Gregor I'm not hungry.

Butt Nor me.

Lena Me neither.

Mermer You don't know what it's like to starve! Give me the tureen.

Clove gives her the tureen and ladle and she drinks the soup from it as she speaks.

Mermer They say he walked down the valley bold as a horse's buttocks.

Grimm Dark magic.

Brag I saw him die.

Gregor With our own hands, we killed him.

Mermer This is the work of Satan.

Butt Mermer, he came back from the dead.

Mermer Exactly!

Butt If that had happened to a shepherd, we'd be calling it a miracle and declaring him our saviour.

Grimm But he isn't a shepherd, so it must be the work of the devil. Proof!

Mermer He will return with an army. There will be terrible slaughter.

Gregor It will be a proving ground.

Brag A test of honour and courage.

Mermer A second crusade.

Grimm A cleansing.

Clove Is it true that Chaff prayed to the Virgin to bring back the goatherd?

Grimm As true as these trousers. It's all over the market place.

Mermer Shame on her!

Gregor Tha's enough. She's still my daughter!

Mendel My sister . . . a traitor.

Clove Mendel, how dare you!

Mermer Death to all nonbelievers! Death to all the unclean herders of Satan's children! Victory to the pure! Is there any more soup?

Clove No.

Butt I think you're getting this a little out of perspective.

Lena Butt, don't –

Butt She had no choice. She only wanted to talk to the boy and for that she was punished. Call me a simpleton, but it seems a little extreme to me.

Brag Butt, you're a simpleton. Let me ask you something.

Butt If it's about borrowing my complete works of Shakespeare, the answer's no, Brag.

Brag Don't try to be funny, Butt. Are you part of this family?

Butt Of course I am.

Brag Do you believe we should stick together no matter what?

Butt That all depends, you see –

Brag Answer the question, Butt. Do you or don't you? I'm waiting for an answer, Butt. We're all waiting. Well?

Lena What is so bad about people who herd goats instead of sheep? They're poor, like us. They try to scratch a living, like us. Are they so different?

Mermer Blasphemy!

Grimm Outrage!

Mermer Send for the priest! Cut out her tongue!

Clove Mermer, Granpa. Please. This isn't helping anybody. My daughter has cut herself off from this family.

Mermer Then she must answer to the consequences.

Brag I'm still waiting for an answer, Butt.

Butt Lena is right. We are the same people. That is all there is to it.

Lena How can we change what we feel? What we know is right?

Brag Easy. Do as you're told.

Butt We will not. We will do as our hearts tell us.

Brag What your books tell you, you mean!
This is what I found in Butt's cottage. It's a book.

Butt Surprised you recognised it, Brag.

Brag (*holding up a book*) It's about a shepherd who is so corrupt he sells his sheep for twice as many goats and then disguises all the goats as sheep. Everyone believes he is the Good Shepherd and follows him.

Gregor Butt and Lena, leave this house immediately!

Butt It's only a story.

Gregor It's a slur on all good shepherds. Pack your things and leave this valley!

Mendel No! Mother, you can't let him do that!

Mermer You be quiet, or you'll join your sister!

Clove Mermer, don't say that!

Mermer I will say it, and you will listen, daughter! Do you hear me?

Clove I hear you. But I swear I will not be a burden to my daughters. When you die, Mermer, I will burn these stirrups.

Mermer (*digging in her heels hard*) Quiet! These stirrups are passed down through the family. I carried my mother on my back, as she did hers. I gave them to you on your wedding day.

Grimm Listen to your elders, Clove. They have eyes into the past. They can see a pattern which you cannot.

Chorus
The pattern is a deep-dyed red
And it streams through time
Like a fresh kill on the wind

Gregor Leave us, Butt and Lena. Before our anger gets the better of us. Your cottage and your herds are forfeit, as is all your property. You have transgressed all we believe in. My heart is broken, my family torn in two. Go!

Mermer, Brag, Grimm Go!

Chorus Once the wound is dealt
It never heals
The blood flows
In spate
Like a river after winter snow

Brag brings on a sack filled with books. He empties the books into a stone hearth.

Homes are pulled down
Livelihoods destroyed
Knowledge lost
In a dawn of scattered ashes

Lena and Butt are expelled from their home like Adam and Eve from paradise. They watch the red glow as the books burn.

Our only link with the past
The memories of old men and women
Whose aged minds preserve
Hate and fear and anger
Like wasps in vinegar

Clove goes to comfort Mendel, but Mermer pulls her arm away.

537

Brag stands with Grimm and Gregor as they
oversee Butt and Lena's expulsion.

Chorus
When the child asks:
Why so much hate?
Her elders answer:
It has always been so
She asks:
Will it always be so?
They answer:
The pattern is deep-dyed red
And it streams through time
Like a fresh kill on the wind

Music: fast, percussive, discordant.
Over the music, the Chorus move/dance, dividing
reuniting and dividing again, demonstrating the
content of the Chorus' speeches.

Chorus
Two sisters quarrel
The weight of centuries
On young shoulders
The bond breaks
And the crack spreads
Dividing brother against sister
Father against son
Mother against daughter
Bitterness erupts
Fear spreads like a virus
Peace is tossed like a fox
Among bloodhounds
Spades that planted roots
Now bury the dead
The sweet pain of desire
Once played as a game for innocents
Is now released like a wild beast

And all that's seen is taken
The screams of the dying are now as common
As the final lowing of a slaughtered calf
Or the last bleats and squeals
Of lamb or pig
The world becomes a slaughterhouse
Mothers, daughters, sons and fathers
Grandmothers, sisters, uncles, brothers
Families cleaved into single souls
Single souls carved into
A hundred warring fears

The Chorus builds to a huge crescendo: a scream synchronised with a thunderous crash, then everything goes quiet.

So turns the world
So turn the mills of hate

A hillside.
    Chaff, Butt and Lena sit around the remains of a fire.

Chaff I'm starving.

Lena We're all starving. The whole country's starving, thanks to you.

Butt Lena, it wasn't her fault.

Lena No, I know, but you have to have someone to blame.

Butt Why?

Lena It makes you feel better, that's why! Sometimes, Butt, I wonder if you know anything that isn't written in a book.

Butt Don't you start.

Josef enters. His head is covered. He is carrying a long knife and a sack of turnips.

Lena Who are you?

Butt We don't want any trouble. We wanted no part of this war.

Lena He's got a knife. He's going to kill us!

Josef That's right. I have a sharp knife and in this sack I have the heads of sheep-herders that I have slaughtered.

Lena Oh my God!

Josef empties the sack on the floor. The turnips roll out.

Turnips!

Josef Yes. Help yourself. (*He uncovers his head.*)

Chaff It's you, the goatboy who came back from the dead! What are you doing here?

Lena Why have you come here? To kill us?

Josef Yesterday I would have. Yesterday I was a hero, a saint.

Butt What happened?

Josef Word travelled. They found out I'd been brought back to life by the devil. Now I am a traitor, an outcast.

Chaff You're welcome to stay with us.

Josef Thanks. Help yourself to the turnips.

They eat the raw turnips.

Butt Have you heard how the war is going?

Josef Last time I heard we were winning.

Butt No, you must be mistaken. We were winning.

Chaff We?

Butt That is to say, our people, well OK, the sheep-people were winning.

Josef The last figures were twenty thousand sheep culled to your nineteen thousand six hundred goats.

Lena A clear-cut victory to the goat-people obviously.

Long pause.

Chaff You know what I think.

Lena What?

Chaff I think we should go and see the Virgin.

> *They stare at her perplexed.*
> *Crossfade to another part of the mountains.*
> *Mermer, Clove, Gregor, Grimm, Mendel and Brag*
> *are huddled together. They are arguing.*

Mermer . . . I won't do it! I won't eat goat!

Clove We have no choice, Mermer. Brag found a kid dead at the bottom of a gully. It's fresh. We are starving.

Grimm Goat meat shall not soil these lips.

Gregor Granpa is right.

Clove No, he isn't right, Gregor! We have no food. That kid is food!

Gregor Never!

Brag Don't be so stubborn, Gregor. We must eat.

Gregor You've changed your tune.

Brag I'm hungry.

Gregor Where are your principles?

Brag Where are your brains?

Gregor This is our way of life. This is what we are fighting for. Not to be contaminated by the unclean!

Mendel Mother, I want to see Chaff again.

Mermer Don't mention that one's name here!

Clove No, Mermer, we will mention her. I want to see my daughter again too. I'm sick of this war.

Gregor But we're winning.

Clove If this is winning, I can't imagine what it's like to lose. Mermer, I want you to get off my back.

Mermer What?

Clove You heard. Get down off my back. I've had enough. And if Gregor had any sense, he'd put you down too, Granpa. Both of you can walk for God's sake!

Grimm That's not the point. We've earned the right to sit on your backs.

Mermer This is how I carried you when you were a child. Besides it's tradition.

Clove Well, it's about time things changed. Get down. Now. Go on.

Mermer I won't.

Clove Yes you will. Or I'll just let you fall.

Mermer You wouldn't dare!

Clove Try me.

Mermer (*reluctantly getting down*) You'll regret this. This is against all our customs. Oh, I can't stand . . . I'm going to . . . fall!

They watch her fall and flail on the ground.

I can't walk! Clove, I've forgotten how to walk!

Clove You'll learn again. Now, Granpa, down you come. Gregor.

Gregor What will the priest say?

Clove I don't care what the priest says. We're not carrying these two if they're perfectly capable of walking. Granpa, down!

Grimm You wouldn't let her do this, son, would you?

Gregor I'm too weak to support you any more, father.

Gregor releases Grimm's feet from the stirrups and he goes crashing to the ground. He flails about with Mermer.

Grimm Aaaaaah! Help me, someone, I can't walk! We are being cruelly treated by our own children! There is no respect any more!

Gregor Clove, have we done the right thing?

Clove I don't know, but I certainly feel a lot better. Let's go.

Mendel Where are we going?

Clove To see the Virgin. Come on, Gregor, Mendel. Brag, bring the kid. Mermer and Grimm, follow on when you've got the hang of walking again.

Clove strides off with Mendel, Gregor following. Brag stares open-mouthed, while Mermer and Grimm flail about on the floor, trying to remember how to walk.

The Mount of the Virgin of the Sheep People.

Chorus

So they came in pilgrimage
To the Mount of the Virgin
A mother to see her daughter
Sister to be reunited with sister
A whisper stirs into
The thunder of peace

Two groups move towards the mountain: Butt, Lena, Josef, Chaff and Clove, Mendel, Gregor, Grimm, Mermer, Brag.

They reach a mid-point and stand looking at each other.

They cannot speak
Their mouths are stopped up
With old hate
Cold hurt
Dried insults
Spattered pride
They simply stand and stare
Unsure of why they are here
Or what they are supposed to do
How much do you want peace?
What would you sacrifice
To cradle the trembling dove
In your hands?

Both sides of the family extend their hands to each other, tentatively, then drop them. They hang their heads and turn away.

Peace is a foreign country
When war has been your home
For far too long

Mendel Mother, speak to them.

Clove I can't! They seem so strange to me now.

Mendel Granpa, you say something.

Grimm Words come into my throat, child, and then they choke me.

Mendel Mermer?

Mermer No.

Mendel Brag, what about you?

There is a long pause. Brag is fighting something within himself. Then:

Brag You turned against us!

Clove Brag, no!

Brag Yes. You took sides against your own. You broke up the family. You deserve to be punished!

Chaff You are the ones who deserve to be punished! You and your pig-headedness!

Chorus
So begin all peace talks
With a lot of shouting

Mendel Chaff, don't, please! We are supposed to be making peace.

Mermer We can't make peace. We are too old for that.

Grimm How can we talk to you when you have that goatherd with you!

Chaff Because you must. See, he's not a monster. He's the same as we are.

Josef I wouldn't say that.

Chaff What!

Josef Well, goatherds were here first. In the mountains. It's well-known. The sheep came much later.

Gregor You see! That's the kind of people we're dealing with. Arrogant. Wrong-headed. Dangerous.

544

Brag (*drawing his knife*) You won't survive a second
time, goatherd!

Josef That remains to be seen!

*Josef draws his knife and he and Brag circle each
other.*

Chorus
So begin all peace-talks
With violence

Clove We've come to talk peace, not to start fighting all
over again. Put those knives away! Both of you!

Brag No.

Josef No.

Lena Why not?

Brag The sheep-people cannot make concessions in an
ongoing conflict situation. It is unreasonable to make
these demands in an atmosphere of heightened tension
and the goat-people must acknowledge the status quo.

Gregor What's he talking about?

Josef Whilst not wishing to jeopardise the peace talks
in any way, the goat-people are not convinced that it
would be in their best interests to abrogate the use of
armed force.

Lena What?

Sylvian So begin all peace-talks. With a lot of bullshit.

Gregor They're not ready for peace.

Clove Neither are we. We have to make ourselves ready.

Gregor Why here? Why now?

Clove Why not?

Butt This is the usual pattern, you see. Studies prove it.
It's a cycle.

Lena But the cycle can be broken.

Gregor How?

Lena It must be, or we'll be condemned to go on living
like this for ever.

Clove Everyone seems to have forgotten this is a shrine. We are here to petition the Virgin for help.

The Virgin appears from the Chorus.

Virgin I wondered when I was going to get a look in.
Mermer Who are you?
Virgin The Virgin of the Mountains, if that's alright with you.
Mermer But you look so . . . ordinary.
Virgin What you see is what you get. I am what you made me. I thought you might want to meet my opposite number from the south.

A Second Virgin appears from the Chorus.

Chaff Who's that?
Josef That is our Virgin!
Second Virgin That's right. Hello, Josef. Bad news about your miracle, but that was strictly speaking out of my jurisdiction.
Mermer There can't be two Virgins!
Second Virgin Why not?
Mermer Because . . . because it's like saying there are two moons. Ours is the only Virgin.
Second Virgin Nope, sorry granma, but the goat-people have got one as well.
Josef There is only one Virgin and that is our Virgin. The other is an imposter!
Virgin Did you hear what he called me?
Second Virgin He must be a priest.
Both Virgins Look, Josef whatever your name is, pin your ears back and listen to me for a minute. Heaven is just full of angels and gods and prophets and saints and martyrs and holy animals and God knows what and there's more of them coming in every day. You wouldn't believe the things people pray to. So don't

come round here telling us who's genuine and who isn't because not even we know that, alright? You can fight about that amongst yourselves.

Second Virgin And they do.

Clove Can you help us find peace?

Virgin If you mean can I or my friend here find it for you, the answer is no.

Mermer So what do we light candles and say prayers to you for then?

Virgin Search me. You started all that business.

Clove Please. Tell us what we can do.

Second Virgin I think you'll find peace is about sacrifice, but that's all I can really say at the moment.

Grimm Sacrifice? You mean like offering the blood of a slaughtered lamb?

Second Virgin Come on grandad, don't you think we've had enough of that to last us a lifetime?

Virgin Good luck anyway. We'll be rooting for you.

The Virgins merge back into the Chorus.

Mermer Fat lot of use they were.

Clove No, she had a point. What would you give up for peace Mermer?

Mermer Haven't I made enough sacrifices?

Josef Well, I could do without this. There's too much blood on it.

Josef throws his knife into the ring of stones that serves as a hearth.

Chorus
    A naked eye stares down steel
    The dove challenges the hawk
    To do something outside its nature
    But the hawk cannot fly with the dove
    And the dove cannot fly with the hawk

All images falter
Bitter memories bear sweet fruit
Only when the thoughts of human minds
Transform them
And the hawk coos
The dove hovers
The gun barrel spouts pure water
Raking thirsty hearts with bullets of rain.

Clove What about you, Brag?

Brag How will I defend myself?

Chaff There can't be any peace until you throw it down.

Brag How do I know I can trust him?

Butt You don't. That's trust.

Brag I can't. There's too much history.

Chaff History is something you learn from, Brag. You look at the past and you change. You don't just carry on as before.

Brag They hate us. We hate them. It's how things are. How they've always been.

Clove Throw down your knife, Brag. Take a risk. You have the courage for that.

Brag I don't know . . .

Chaff Throw it down, Brag.

After a long struggle, Brag throws his knife in too. They cheer.

Chaff I just want to be with my sister again.

Mendel So do I. Will you join the cord again, Chaff?

Chaff No.

Mendel No?

Chaff No. We can still be together without being tied to each other.

Mendel How?

Chaff Like this. Together when we want to be. Apart when we want to be.

Mendel and Chaff hold hands.

Mendel What about Granpa and Mermer? They still can't walk.

Mermer Heartless children!

Clove We can't carry them any more. They can learn again how to stand.

Gregor And if they don't?

Clove It's downhill all the way home. We can roll them.

Mermer Did I give birth to such a monster! I won't walk! I'm staying here to die!

Chaff That's your choice, Mermer.

Grimm and Mermer beat their fists on the ground in frustration and try to stand, but find it very difficult.

Chorus
    Things that have been flung apart
    Now join again
    Peace enters the heart like a dream
    Filling every corner with its light
    Who can say how long this peace will last
    Who can say if its hard lesson
    Will need to be learned again and again
    Down the generations
    One thing is certain:
    The dream of peace
    Must be held like a butterfly
    In hands at once delicate and strong
All Peace!

Music and dance.
    Suddenly, Sylvian the treeman comes into view, hanging from his branch.

Sylvian Do you want the good news first or the bad news?

The good news is the war is over.
You can all go home.
The bad news is: cattle-herders are bringing cows through the northern pass.

Final music and end of play.

Held in the Hands Like a Butterfly

Paul Goetzee interviewed by Jim Mulligan

Paul Goetzee went to schools where drama wasn't something you did once your voice had broken. It was not until he was doing an MA in Drama and Theatre Studies at Leeds University that he wrote his first serious work for the theatre and had it produced. He then started to work for a theatre company writing, directing, producing and acting.

> I was twenty-two and I was thrown in at the deep end. I had to write plays for old people in residential homes and for youth groups. We did pub shows and lots of community theatre. Over the past fifteen years I have worked with theatre groups and written twelve full-length plays and numerous shorter plays.

The Pilgrimage is a fable or parable that explores family life, ritual, religion and war.

> I come from a Catholic background and that is something that never leaves you. The appearances of the Virgin Mary at Lourdes and Fatima were familiar to me as a child and, when there was a report of the Virgin appearing a couple of years ago in Yugoslavia it set me thinking. As a writer you draw on the imagery you grew up with because it is so strong. And in any case I have the feeling that religion and making rituals is part of the psyche. In a sense it's not a bad thing because it allows you to externalise your pain and suffering and anxieties in order to find some solace.

In *The Pilgrimage* there is a strong sense of ritual and the tyranny it can impose on people when it is misused but there is very little of the highly structured religions we are familiar with. Instead the family of shepherds and their rivals the goatherds are metaphors for religion. The conflict between the two cultures, Paul Goetzee implies, is the same as the rivalry between two religions leading to the same cruelty and conflict.

> Where we live we tend to think of war as something that happens in other places. I was interested in what was happening only 700 miles from us, in Bosnia. I started thinking about bigotry, religion, war, violence and hatred. The conflict in Bosnia is partly to do with religion and it has been simmering for decades. All that hatred must have been passed on in families just as it is in the play.

The family of shepherds is locked in a paralysing oral history. Their hatred of the goatherds is nurtured by the telling of stories. Their dependence on each other is strengthened by irrational conventions such as the twins being tied wrist to wrist and the grandparents being carried everywhere in stirrups that are passed on from parent to child. Memory is the gift that is passed on to children. Memory is the poison ensuring that, once the wound is dealt, it never heals.

> The family thinks it is warm and close whereas in fact it is totally held together by hatred. And that hatred will, one day break it apart. That's what happens when one member of the family comes in with a totally alien view. It is anathema to the family and they find they are not so close and loving any more.

In these circumstances the family finds it can be just as cruel to one of its own members as it is to any outsiders. Even in the tightest knit family there are those who question its values – sometimes intellectually, sometimes in response to a feeling that something is wrong. Butt, the reader of books, has a window on the world and is able to see that the family's oral history is no more than bigotry. Chaff is able to see that a young goatherd is not evil. With this startling insight she is given the strength to cut the bond holding her to her sister and to the family. Once the cord has been cut the break-up of the family is inevitable. They can justify slaughter because it is 'a crusade', they can say a miracle is the work of the devil because it happened to a goatherd, they can 'take care of' an innocent goatherd by butchering him but they cannot get Chaff to stay another day in such a merciless family. Once Chaff goes, others follow. Before long, the outsiders are joined by the Goatherd and then, in the face of overwhelming slaughter, both sides turn to religion in the sense that we know it. They appeal to the Virgins for help.

> I wanted to explore the idea that these apparitions are the creation of people who need them, support they turn to in times of trouble. The Virgins work miracles but when the people want them to solve all their problems the Virgins come on with attitude. They are dismissive, their language is flippant, they take no nonsense and their advice is practical. If you want peace make sacrifices. And by that they certainly do not mean shedding more blood.

In the end there is a glimmer of hope. History is something you learn from, the sisters can still be together without being tied to each other, weapons are handed in and the dream of peace is held in the hands like a butterfly. It is the best one can hope for.

> I didn't want this play to be too big and global. It's about one family and one savage death. It's a

microcosm of what's happening in Bosnia and
Rwanda and a dozen other countries. I think
ultimately, if we communicate we can break down
barriers. There's the cynical part of me that says it's
been tried and people have been trampled by those
who want power or land or money. But there is a
gleam of hope. There are people who oppose what is
anti-human. I'd love to think this play might change
people but let's be real. The best I can hope for is to
find a voice that is clear and unpompous saying: 'It's
up to you. Test this out.'

Production Notes

STAGING AND SETTING

The Pilgrimage is set in a fictitious, possibly Eastern
European country. The country is a wild and remote
landscape that only supports sheep and goats. This is a
witty and powerful fable. Its mythical quality allows
scope for an audience to read what they will of the situation. The less specific you are in setting the play the more
it will say. Try and avoid 'over explaining' your own
take on religious themes, the expulsion of Adam and Eve
from the garden of Eden, the Bosnian conflict or the
situation around *The Satanic Verses*, because all of these
issues may or may not be in the play. Keep the design
neutral, put emphasis on telling the tale, and leave room
for the audience to use its own creative imagination.

Keep lighting and sound simple. Rely on the actors to
tell the story and the text to speak for itself. Sylvian, for
instance, doesn't need a tree to make it clear that he
swings from it. This sort of thing can be achieved physically. The music is the music of Turkey, Armenia and the
Balkans. There are clear directions in the script about the
mood it needs to create.

The Pilgrimage is for a cast of thirteen and a chorus.
It is appropriate for any age range. Running time is
approximately 45 minutes.

EXERCISES

Have the whole group walk in a large uncluttered space.
Call a number and have them get into a group of the size
of the number. Those who are left out are eliminated and

should have a sense of being expelled. Have the group notice how they walk away.

- Continue, but this time at a given signal the group move into a predecided shape, a triangle, square or whatever but without speaking or touching. Have them be open to following whoever naturally takes on the role of the leader.
- Have the group imagine they are walking in a field, have them concentrate on the ground and picture the grass, thistles, cowpats, daisies, etc. At a given signal, have them think they are sheep moving into a shape. Repeat the exercise with the group imagining they are sheepdogs rounding up sheep.
- Now add a shepherd, notice how the group takes orders.

Have the group experiment with different ways of lifting one another in pairs. Have them take account of different sizes, injuries and strengths. See how far and how long a carry can be sustained, especially if dialogue is going on.

- Have the group demonstrate their range of lifts. Look at how they can be sustained and come to an end neatly. See which are more successful as a flash of movement and which can last longer.
- In pairs (not necessarily of the same build) A carries B and then decides to put down the load. B doesn't want to be put down. Once on the floor B cannot move and A walks away. See what interesting shape the Bs make when they are put down. Look at the scene where the younger generation refuse to carry the older generation any longer.

Practise choral response at intervals throughout the rehearsal process with the following simple exercise:

DIRECTOR TO WHOLE GROUP 'What's your name?'
ACTOR (*for example*) 'Wade.'
WHOLE GROUP 'Wade.'

- The group must respond immediately, without prompting and aim to imitate the quality of the individual's voice.
- If the group as a whole can hear that they have not properly imitated the individual's voice, they must, without discussion, repeat the name until they feel they have achieved the right quality.

Have the group sit in a circle and read a line each from the choral speech on page 538.

- Have them repeat the exercise reading a word each. The effect is probably wooden and disjointed.
- Now stand in the circle to increase the group's fluidity and energy. Have an actor pass a 'clap' to the next person and so it travels round the circle quickly, energetically and with focus. Let the 'clap' travel forwards and backward and across the circle.
- Have the group look at the same piece of text again. Have them read a word each but this time be aware of 'feeding' the word to the next person rather than leaving the words hanging in the air.
- Continue this exercise, but have the group take more than one word at a time.
- Have the group speak 'on top of' another actor's word or phrase if it will be more effective.

Have the group walk around the space silently in pairs. A leads and B is following, but this shouldn't be obvious to an observer. Let them swap over.

Two pairs join together to form a group of four and repeat the exercise. As the group turns a corner or moves

PAUL GOETZEE

in another direction a new leader automatically takes over.

Sustain the exercise with groups of eight. Make sure that they are ready to sense a new leader, or prepared to take the lead. Tell them if there is doubt anyone can take the lead. It should look like they've rehearsed for years.

If you can manage it, add some Balkan, perhaps Turkish or Armenian music.

Have the group work in pairs again. A leads, as if a five-year-old, B follows and imitates, A suddenly moves in the manner of a ninety-year-old and B follows.

Have the group break into fours and, without discussion, nominate a leader and move as ninety-year-olds.

Have the group expand to eight and move as before towards a shrine. On arrival they drink water which makes them young again. Let them experience short-lived jubilation before their bodies age once more.

Have the group get into pairs and discover how long it can take to hold hands.

A moves to hold B's hand and discovers it has a contagious disease – have the rest of the group note the hesitation and emotions at play.

Have the rest of the group hold their breath as they watch and let out a collective sigh of relief as the pair make contact.

Repeat the exercise with the observing group moving closer together, craning necks to see what's going on. Have them appoint a spokesperson. Make it clear that the spokesperson is different by having the group lower themselves physically and letting the spokesperson step forward to comment on the action.

Have the group take a section of the chorus in the script.

Divide the group in two.

Group A: Is a chorus speaking to a divorced couple
Group B: Is a child speaking to a child in a wheelchair.

The object of this exercise is to communicate to the
audience (i.e. the couple or the child) using text, voice
and group movement.

Suzy Graham-Adriani
February 1999

TAKING BREATH

Sarah Daniels

Characters

Alana, sixteen
Gemma, Alana's sister, fourteen
Elliot, seventeen
Steve, Elliot's step-brother, twenty
Rachel, Elliot's sister, nineteen
Lucy, fifteen
Jamie, sixteen
Cassie, seventeen
Tom, nineteen
Kelly, eighteen

SCENE ONE

Alana stares at the TV (the sound is switched off).
Gemma, carrying an old biscuit tin, comes in.

Alana What do you want?

Gemma Nothing.

Alana Piss off then.

Gemma Turn the sound up.

Alana (*she grabs the remote but doesn't turn the sound up*) It's the news.

Gemma Yeah.

Alana You must have such a sad life.

Gemma Don't you think it's appropriate to be sad today? She was your great-grandmother as well.

Alana Appropriate? What sort of word is that, for someone your age? Who do you think you are? You don't even wear a bra.

Gemma At least I made the effort to go to her funeral.

Alana I'm grounded, remember?

Gemma Not in the daytime.

Alana (*about the biscuit tin*) What's that?

Gemma It's some of her stuff, from the home. Mum and Dad thought it might be appropriate to my history course work.

Alana They gave it to you? What about Nanna?

Gemma Grandma didn't want it. She thought I'd appreciate it.

Alana Did she say anything about me not being there?

Gemma Only that perhaps it was for the best, in the circumstances. (*about the TV*) Please turn it up.

Alana What for?

Gemma (*about the television*) Quick. Please. It's that road protest.

Alana Those dirty hippies. Who cares. Someone should tell them if we had more roads then there'd be less asthmatics.

Gemma If I was you I'd go down there and point that out to them then?

Alana Yeah, really. What is their problem? So trees get cut down, so? Others get planted all the time but if a person stops breathing then you can't do nothing. (*Realises what she's said.*) No one can . . .

Beat.

Gemma Go on, turn it up. I want to hear it because Great-Grandma once worked in one of those houses they want to pull down you know . . .

Alana Just shut up. You don't know that.

Gemma She told me.

Alana She was so harpic she never knew what she was saying.

Gemma She told me she was in service.

Alana In the war you mean?

Gemma Not the armed services, you idiot. Like a live-in maid.

Alana Don't go writing about that in your stupid history assignment. We don't want all those stuck up arses in that bloody boffin snob school to think we're descended from servants.

Gemma She was also one of the first women to go to university even though they weren't allowed to –

Alana Yawn, yawn. I'm sure they didn't mean you to write about her. She's only just died.

Gemma History is not only the last millennium. It's last week, it's yesterday . . . it's the second just gone . . . from when I walked in here till now is history.

Alana I wish it was. What's the point of it though?
Doing a moronic little project.
Gemma So I don't end up like you.

Alana throws the remote at her. It misses.

(*picking it up*) Thank you.
Alana (*then seeing a photo of Elliot on the TV*) Go on
then. Turn it up.
Gemma I'm trying . . .
Alana You can say that again.
Gemma It's not working now.
Alana Look at him. Come on.
Gemma I can't. I think you've broken it. Who?
Alana Him. That tree protester bloke. (*teeth kissing
noise*) He's well fit.
Gemma That's just what he isn't. He's been in a coma
for a week.
Alana Oh. Has he?
Gemma Yep.
Alana How come?
Gemma Maybe at your age you should stop wasting all
your time thinking about yourself and start watching
the news.
Alana Give us the remote then . . .
Gemma No. Fuck off.
Alana What? Right, that's it. I'm telling Mum you said
that.
Gemma And who do you think she'll believe? (*making
sure she can get away*) After what you've done, she'll
never trust you again. Loser.

*Gemma, fearing Alana's reaction, leaves quickly but
Alana merely stares ahead at the silent TV.*

SCENE TWO

*Steve and Rachel look very upset but remain completely
frozen in their positions at Elliot's bedside. Elliot
suddenly sits up. Steve and Rachel remain as statues.*

Elliot Would you look at them? Look how upset they
are. This is revenge I've only ever been able to
fantasise about. They're sorry now. Yes! Even him.
Look at him. He's always hated me and now he's
paying for it. The times he's threatened to kill me. Ha,
ha. He's my step-brother. Thank God. If I'd had his
genes in me, I'd have killed myself. And her, my big
sister, Rachel. She's just like a cat. You know how evil
they are, swiping at a bird or a mouse, maiming it,
then playing around with it for the sheer pleasure of
being spiteful? Well, they most probably learnt how to
do that from her. Let me give you a for instance. The
first time I brought a girl to the house who, by the
way, Rachel insisted on referring to as 'Elliot's babe'.
Like if girls are sexist it doesn't count or what?
Anyway, I was weary because she was being a bit
too curly-lipped-okay-friendly. Then she produces it.
When I was eight Mum used to be an agent for Kays
Catalogue. I once drew over the underwear pages,
crudely embellishing the photos of the models with
the help of a felt tip pen by sketching in the rude bits
that the underwear was covering. And, unknown to
me, my sister, the sadistic pervert, had kept it for all
those years waiting for the perfect moment to expose
me, if you'll pardon the expression. She didn't actually
show it to the girl or anything but the threat was there
all evening. I hope she remembers that now and every
other humiliating little thing she's done and I hope
she's so sorry she's thinking suicidally. At least she and

me have the same dad. Did have. He died of cancer when I was two. (*about Steve*) But him. His mum just got pissed off and went. And I know, I know kids aren't meant to be blamed for that but there's got to be exceptions to every rule and he's one of them. His dad shacked up with Mum and then buggered off leaving him with her. She could hardly chuck him out. He's twenty now and the only job he could get was as a scab. The only thing he seems able to cook for himself is toast with brown sauce on. He can't seem to get the hang of any of the basics in life, like white things should be washed separately in the machine. Mum still has to do his ironing. Where is she, though? She should be here, shouldn't she, at my bedside? Mum? Oh no. Now, I remember. She's away. I hope they haven't dragged her back. It's the first time she's been away without us. Maybe it's me. Maybe I've been away years. No, I can't have. Those two look exactly the same. This is now. I am Elliot. I am here. I am here, now. How did I get here? Where was I to get here now? Try to remember Elliot. (*He shuts his eyes.*)

SCENE THREE

A week earlier. Night. Jamie, Cassie, Tom and Kelly are on a platform in a tree. Tom has a rope in his hand.

Jamie Right?

Tom (*making sure that the rope is secure*) Yeah, great. You?

Cassie (*switches her torch on*) Everyone got a torch?

Jamie I've got a couple of candles and a box of matches in my pocket –

Kelly (*groans*) Jamie . . .

Cassie Good thinking. We're stuck up a tree. One gust of wind and we'll all be burnt to a cinder.

Jamie I didn't have a torch and the shops were shut.

Kelly It'll be OK, Cassie. It's a clear night.

Cassie It is now.

Tom You know if all the stars in the Milky Way had names and it took a second to say each one it would take one person four thousand years.

Kelly Is that so, Patrick Moore?

Cassie Shame we don't let the trees in the world hang around that long.

Kelly At least this one is going to be saved.

Tom Thanks to toi, and toi and toi and moi.

Kelly, Cassie and Tom slap each other's hands.

Jamie So you reckon they'll be able to see us up here, yeah?

Cassie Aren't you supposed to be watching the rope? (*Calls.*) Are you alright, Elliot? (*Goes as near to the edge as she dares.*)

Tom Careful.

Cassie (*calls*) Elliot?

Elliot (*voice off, from behind her*) Over here. I could use a bit of help getting up to join you.

They lean over and pull Elliot, holding an enormous empty tub of margarine, up on to the platform. He puts the tub down and wipes his hands on his wrists and then on his trousers.

Jamie Everything lubed?

Elliot Yep, it's so well lubricated that the chain saws will slip out of their hands.

Cassie I only hope margarine isn't detrimental to bark.

Elliot No, and it didn't contain any animal fat either. I swear.

Cassie It's just that I don't want anything to undermine this protest.

Elliot And you think I do?

Tom Lighten up, Cassie. We wouldn't have been tipped off if it weren't for Elliot.

Cassie I know. I know. I guess I'm just . . . OK, positions everyone.

They all seem reluctant to move.

Jamie (*to Elliot*) You're sure that they're coming tonight?

Elliot Yes, they knew the protest was planned for tomorrow and so they want to do as much as they can tonight. They're even offering to pay time and a half.

Tom Which in itself is unheard of.

Jamie Yeah. You're positive you ain't been set up?

Elliot I was listening on the extension upstairs.

Kelly And you're sure he didn't know you were listening?

Elliot Yes. He thought I was out. Then as I left to come here I overheard him trying to bribe Rachel to iron his work clothes.

Kelly What? Does he polish his hard hat an all?

Elliot Believe me, Steve is a hat polisher of the first order.

Tom I'm convinced.

Kelly Come on then. We don't want to be caught unawares.

Cassie Ready?

They all nod and sit cross-legged on the platform. She takes five sets of handcuffs from her pocket and she handcuffs herself to Tom on her right and Jamie on her left and then ceremoniously throws the key away. Tom then handcuffs himself to Elliot. Elliot and Jamie go to handcuff themselves to Kelly. Each time both pairs of cuffs are locked in position the key is thrown away.

Kelly Wait up. I got to do that little bit extra . . .

Elliot Please, Kelly don't . . .

Kelly (*about the nail*) I saved it specially . . .

Cassie Just sit down can't you?

Kelly You want to make it easy for the bastards or what? (*She takes a ring out of her ear/nose/lip/ mouth/belly-button and starts to nail it to the tree.*)

Tom Don't do that! Please . . .

Jamie D'you think it's a good idea to put it in the tree?

Kelly (*about the nail*) It won't do no harm. It's not copper. I'm allergic to that meself.

Cassie This is one of the lungs of the planet! We're all risking our lives to protect it. You'll make a travesty out of the whole thing if you damage it.

Tom Actually, iron nails can't be used in oak because the acid in the wood corrodes the iron.

Jamie But this is a sycamore tree, ain't it?

Tom I was just saying.

Kelly (*pointing to the appropriate hole*) I'm very proud of this and I'm going to use it. I am allowed to pin it to the platform I take it . . .

Cassie It's up to you . . .

Kelly Ta. (*She starts to bang the nail, already in the orifice, to the platform.*) Did you ever used to see that programme . . . whatsit, *Ready Steady Cook?*

Tom I don't think you've quite put us in the mood for gory yarns about food.

Kelly This ain't about food. This is about when this guy's nose stud fell into some prawn sauce stuff and Fern had to fish it out and help him put it back.

Jamie Kelly, please . . .

But she's finished the task. With some manoeuvring Elliot and Jamie manage to cuff themselves to her.

Cassie You don't worry that piercing is a form of self-harm?

Jamie Only for the platform.

Kelly Shouldn't we ring a few more people on the mobie to alert them?

Elliot I wish you'd suggested that before we cuffed ourselves. Let's see if I can – (*He tries to put his hand in his pocket to get the mobile phone.*)

Tom I think we should save the battery in case of emergencies. People will get wind of what's happening soon enough.

Jamie We hope.

Cassie How much support do you think there'll be tomorrow?

Jamie Don't hold your breath, this isn't horse-riding country.

Tom The road does back onto a park.

Jamie I know where it is, pal. I used to play round here when I was a kid. That's why I'm up here now.

Elliot It might back onto a park, but the people who own the houses the other side of it never go in it. They call it mugger's country.

Cassie Let's just hope these houses aren't just piles of rubble by the time they realise what's happening.

Jamie But they can't start demolishing them with us in the tree right next to them, can they?

Tom They won't be rushing to do anything.

Elliot Don't underestimate them.

Tom But we've put a few delaying tactics in place.

Elliot Yeah?

Kelly Only sugar in tank stuff.

Elliot What in what?

Tom As in refined and petrol.

Kelly Not to mention a few nails in the tyres.
Jamie And snipped cables.
Elliot What?
Tom Just H.T. leads. Rotor arms. Mainly.
Jamie Yeah, that sort of stuff.
Elliot Whose?
Cassie Those things they got lined up and parked round the back. Don't worry, we wore gloves.
Elliot Not that the thickest Hard Hat wouldn't be able to make an accurate guess at who did it.
Jamie Need to prove it though.
Kelly It's just machinery.
Elliot (*hears something*) What was that?
Tom What?
Elliot Listen.

Silence.

I think I can hear someone . . .
Cassie Elliot stop it.
Elliot I'm not messing about.
Kelly I can't hear anything and no one can say I haven't got my ear to the ground.
Tom In the Arctic you know you can hear someone else's conversation from about three kilometres away.
Jamie We're not in the bloody Arctic. We're handcuffed in the dark to a tree which might be chopped down any minute and nobody will hear our screams until it's too late.
Cassie It's OK. After three. Three.

They start singing the verse which starts 'We'll walk hand in hand' from the Pete Seeger song, 'We Shall Overcome'. Elliot looks uncomfortable and Jamie is very embarrassed.

Jamie It's bad enough without having to sing this embarrassing old hippy shit.

Cassie It serves two purposes. While keeping our spirits up, it will alert them to our presence.

Jamie Yeah? Well, it's doing my head in.

Tom I didn't hear anything anyway . . .

Elliot Shush.

Kelly You know I think I can hear something . . .

Cassie The position you're in, I'm surprised you can even breathe, never mind hear.

Jamie Probably you only heard a bird or something scratching underneath the platform . . .

Elliot I heard footsteps . . .

Tom (*shouts*) Anyone there?

Silence.

Cassie (*starts to sing*) 'We are not afraid . . .'

Elliot suddenly manages to slide his hands out of his cuffs, climb from the platform and disappear from view.

What are you doing?

Tom Elliot . . .?

Kelly He's freaked.

There is a loud crack. It could be the sound of a branch snapping or a gun firing or a car back-firing.

Cassie What was that?

Tom Sounded like a branch snapping.

Jamie (*shouts*) You alright? Elliot?

Kelly He must have slipped . . .

Jamie Sounded more like a gun shot to me.

Cassie Jamie, please! Where's the mobie . . .

Kelly He had it. Elliot. (*Shouts.*) Elliot.

Tom It could have just been a car back-firing . . .

Cassie Move towards the edge. Let's see if we can see him.

Still handcuffed, obviously, they all shuffle as best they can towards the edge. Jamie is the one who has to lean over.

All Elliot!

Silence.

Jamie I can't see anything. He must have legged it.
Cassie He's not answering us. State the obvious, Cassie.
Jamie He wouldn't, would he? If he'd bottled out.
Kelly Suppose he's hurt?
Cassie Are you sure you can see?
Tom If we all slowly move up, we can lower Jamie over the edge so he can have a better look.
Jamie It's OK. I can see. I can see. And I can't see any broken branches or him. I'm telling you, he's gone.

SCENE FOUR

Elliot and Lucy, from 1913, have fallen on top of one another. They disentangle themselves.

Lucy (*frightened, tries to fight Elliot off, and drops her toffee hammer in the process*) Get away from me, you disgusting oaf.
Elliot I don't want to be anywhere near you.
Lucy Likewise.
Elliot What do you think you're doing?
Lucy What do you mean, what am I doing? I'm trying to get you off me.
Elliot I don't want to be on you. I think I must have slipped. I'm sorry. (*He stands up and backs away from her.*)
Lucy Who are you?
Elliot What's it to you? (*Beat.*) My name's Elliot if you must know. And yours?

574

Lucy Lucy.

Elliot Are you alright, Lucy?

Lucy I'll have to be won't I? And you?

Elliot I think so. Were you coming to join the protest?

Lucy And what business is it of yours, if I was?

Elliot There's no need to look so worried. I'm part of it. Was.

Lucy You? (*She starts looking on the ground for her hammer.*) Or has he sent you to spy on me?

Elliot Who? You dropped something?

Lucy Yes. It was in my hand. It's got to be here somewhere.

Elliot No one sent me to spy . . .

Lucy In my experience, if you don't mind me saying, it's very unusual to find men in the protest.

Elliot Then you can't have much experience, if you don't mind me saying, because it's not like Greenham. There's a lot of men now.

Lucy I don't mean to be rude but you're not making much sense. Are you sure your brains didn't take a scrambling?

Elliot Don't take it the wrong way, of course we owe a lot to women. It's still very female, the way we protest . . . nurturing, peaceful, respectful of mother earth . . .

Lucy That's ridiculously old-fashioned. Where have you been? We're not simpery Madonnas any more.

Elliot Funny, I never thought of Madonna as simpery . . . but then I was a bit too young to be into her . . .

Lucy We're more at home with a bomb than a bottle. Nurture ho. You are behind the times. We smash things now. (*finding and holding aloft her toffee hammer*) That's what these are for. Deeds not words.

Elliot I agree with direct action but it doesn't have to be violent. In fact it's important that it's never violent.

Lucy Then you can't care much about the cause. Emily is still seriously ill in hospital.

Elliot Who's she?

Lucy Don't you read the papers? Her what run out in front of His Majesty's horse.

Elliot I hope the horse wasn't hurt.

Lucy No, but she's not yet regained consciousness.

Elliot I don't agree with some of the methods of hunt saboteurs.

Lucy It was a horse race!

Elliot Like, as in Epsom Park?

Lucy That's exactly where it was! You was having me on, wasn't you? Just now. You know all about it. (*She feels faint.*) Ooh, I don't know what's happened to me.

Elliot I think you've fallen.

Lucy Are you a doctor now or what?

Elliot No.

Lucy Then don't say that. Please. Please don't let that be true.

Elliot It looks like you're OK though.

Lucy Like I'm what? What's that?

Elliot It's alright. I'll stay here with you. Make sure you're alright.

Lucy (*pinches herself*) I told him I had a gentleman friend looking out for me. Now, looks like I dreamt one up.

Elliot Let's just sit down for a bit and get our breath back.

Lucy Don't you start nothing.

Elliot Of course not.

Lucy No, of course you can't. If you're in my imagination, you'll do anything I want.

Elliot I don't know what you're on but I don't think you should be taking a trip like that, not on your own.

SCENE FIVE

The others still handcuffed together up the tree are beginning to feel cold, tired and hungry.

Kelly I reckon it was my piercing what sent him over the edge.

Cassie Don't blame yourself.

Tom No, we shouldn't have mentioned destroying the equipment. He doesn't agree with that.

Cassie I know. He's a fully paid up, dyed-in-the-wool fluffy.

Jamie I don't reckon it was nothing to do with that. I reckon he knew he was going to bottle it before he sat down.

Kelly Is that right, Miss Marple?

Jamie Did you see when he'd finished greasing the tree, he wiped his hands on his wrists? Believe me, he was leaving his options open right from the off.

Kelly I'm beginning to wish I'd done the same. At least not nailed myself down.

Cassie Bit Christian, the symbolism isn't it?

Jamie I don't like to say nothing but I think it's barbaric.

Tom As I recall Christ wasn't crucified through the ear.

Kelly Can someone try and help me with this?

Tom Not with my eyes open. It makes me too queasy.

Jamie Me too.

Kelly You're as gutless as Elliot you are –

Jamie Either that or he was a plant.

Tom A what?

Jamie Think about it. He could be working for them, like his brother.

Cassie But if he was, he wouldn't admit that his brother was, would he?

Tom I suppose it could be a double bluff.

Cassie Can we stop talking about him and do something else?

Tom Being handcuffed together hardly lends itself to a game of Scrabble.

Jamie Yeah, whose stupid idea was that?

Cassie See that? On the side of the house.

Kelly No, actually. I can't move my head in case you hadn't noticed.

Tom All it is, is a tiny window which has been bricked up.

Jamie So? The house was converted into flats.

Cassie Yes, in the eighties. But that window was blocked up years ago. You've only got to look at the discoloration of the bricks.

Tom And?

Cassie So why would you brick up a window?

Kelly Window tax?

Tom The house isn't that old. The window tax was in the eighteenth century. These were only built at the turn of the century.

Kelly If I'd wanted to be on *University Challenge* I'd have gone to university.

Cassie Alright, point taken.

Jamie Go on . . . why was it blocked up?

Cassie Apparently the daughter of the house had a boyfriend who used to climb up this tree and talk to her through the bedroom window but her father got to know about it. So one night the father goes out with a gun and lies in wait at the bottom of this very tree for the young man. He dozes off but sure enough, just past midnight he sees a figure up in the branch. It must have been that branch there. The father pulls the trigger and the figure falls and lies motionless at his feet. He then discovers that he's shot his beloved daughter who, unbeknownst to him, had planned to elope that very evening with her lover by climbing out of her bedroom window and down the tree. He then ordered that the window be bricked up.

Kelly How could they be lovers if she just talked to him through the window?

Cassie You know what I mean. They were obviously in love and he taught her how to climb out of her window and she was to meet him and run off . . .

Tom Each man kills the thing he loves the most . . .

Jamie Do what?

Tom Oscar Wilde . . .

Kelly Oh bloody hell.

Jamie How come he mistook his daughter for a bloke?

Cassie It was dark.

Jamie Even so.

Cassie Short-sighted?

Tom When someone starts to lose their sight, the brain lacks stimulus and it can make up images, like hallucinations . . .

Kelly Is that so, Dr Raj Persaud?

Cassie It's just a myth.

Jamie How come you knew it?

Cassie When I was trying to find out more about this place from the local history library . . .

Kelly You went in a tree tomb. You traitor.

Cassie Pardon?

Kelly What were the books made out of? Or were they the product of recycled lungs or what?

In the distance the others become aware of a flashing orange light. Silence.

I was only joking. No offence.

Tom Shush.

Kelly Don't you start – (*then realising*) This isn't an hallucination is it?

Cassie If it is, it's a collective one.

Jamie Here we go, here we go . . .

*The lights get brighter, the noise of engines becomes
louder as the vehicles get closer. The sound of men
tramping through the park, and of chainsaws being
started.*

SCENE SIX

*Elliot and Lucy are still underneath the tree. Elliot is
looking at the inscription on the hammer.*

Elliot And the S?

Lucy Guess who gave it to me?

Elliot I can't.

Lucy Guess.

Elliot I don't know anyone you know.

Lucy You might not know her personally but you'll have
heard of her.

Elliot Scary Spice?

Lucy Sylvia.

Elliot (*not understanding*) Oh Sylvia. Right.

Lucy Anyway. (*Takes the hammer.*) It's been very
pleasant talking to you but I must remind you I'm on
a mission.

Elliot Right you are, Scully.

Lucy Do you mind? I am the chamber maid. I have
nothing to do with the scullery.

Elliot Sounds kinky. How about I come with you and
then how about we go for a burger?

Lucy For who? You're sure he hasn't sent you?

Elliot Who?

Lucy Master George.

Elliot No, I told you. Where are you going now with
that little hammer?

Lucy None of your business.

Elliot You go then. I'll wait here for you to come back.

Lucy I'm not coming back here.

Elliot I thought you said you worked here.

Lucy I have decided to terminate my employment forthwith.

Elliot What will you do?

Lucy I have ambitions. Well, dreams . . .

Elliot Yeah and you think I'm one.

Lucy And a very amicable one you've proved to be. You know I've never told a living soul this but what I want more than anything is to go to university.

Elliot Why haven't you told anyone?

Lucy Because they'd laugh at me.

Elliot Why should they?

Lucy Well, me . . .

Elliot I know it's expensive but you could take out a loan.

Lucy I could study but they still wouldn't let me get a degree . . .

Elliot Why not?

Lucy Because I'm a woman.

Elliot (*laughs*) That's ridiculous.

Lucy Why, do you think I'm a man?

Elliot Of course you can go. Women can do anything now. That's the time we live in.

Lucy It's so easy for you to say.

Elliot This victim mentality isn't doing you any good.

Lucy I'm not quite sure what you mean but I'm quite sure I can't wait for further explanation. I'll keep you no longer.

Elliot Hang on just a bit. I don't feel well.

Lucy What is it?

Elliot My head hurts something chronic.

Lucy Shall I see if I can go and get help?

Elliot No, no. I'll be alright in a couple of minutes.

SCENE SEVEN

The tree top, which is now completely lit from below. There is a sense of a great many people underneath the tree.

Cassie We've just got to keep calm and let them know we're here.

Kelly That might not make us any safer.

Jamie They've got chainsaws.

Tom I don't think any police have arrived. They'll be able to do what they like. It'll be our word against theirs.

They start to sing 'We Shall Not Be Moved'. The noise from below stops but they are interrupted by a man using a loud hailer.

Man Oi! One of your lot is down here, hurt.

Cassie Elliot?

Jamie Take no notice. It's a trick.

Tom I thought you said you were sure he'd gone.

Jamie I was. I am.

Man He looks in a bad way. We'll need your help to know what happened.

Cassie They're bluffing.

Jamie How can you be so sure?

Cassie Elliot said his brother was working for them. If his brother is down there, his brother would say, 'Hey, this is my brother. His name is Elliot, etc., etc.,' wouldn't he? (*Shouts down.*) What's his name?

Man He's not got I.D. on him.

They look at each other.

Jamie Cassie's got a point.

Man For fuck's sake what's more important, him or the tree?

Tom What should we do?

Kelly What can we do?

Man We've got people down here coming up but it would be better if you came down . . .

Kelly It sounds like a ruse . . .

Cassie Call their bluff . . .

Sound of ambulance sirens.

Tom What bluff? Even they wouldn't risk dialling 999 as a hoax.

Cassie (*to Jamie*) I thought you said you definitely saw him run off.

Jamie I said I'd thought he'd run off. I couldn't see him.

Kelly You don't know the ambulance is coming here.

Cassie Maybe they've called in advance of cutting the tree down with us in it.

Tom You know what –

Kelly No, and what's more we don't want to. I vote we give ourselves up.

Cassie You don't know that Elliot is down there.

Tom But I'm not going to take that chance.

Jamie Me neither. (*Calls down.*) We're locked on up here but we're prepared to give up.

Kelly Please someone help me get the nail out before they get to us.

Cassie Elliot, you've ruined the whole thing. Because of you this tree will die. I just hope you can live with that.

SCENE EIGHT

Alana is alone. Gemma comes in wearing the toffee hammer from a key ring on her belt.

Alana Where have you been?

Gemma Grandma's.

Alana Where did you get that?

Gemma It was in that tin of Great-Grandma's stuff.

Alana Let's have a look.

Gemma (*takes it off and hands it to her*) It's got some engraving on the back.

Alana What's it say?

Gemma Nothing. It doesn't make sense.

Alana F.L.Y.I.T.C.S.

Gemma What do you reckon it means?

Alana F.L.Y. – Fly. I.T.C.S. Information training centres. Information training centres for flies?

Gemma (*about the hammer*) You can have it if you want.

Alana Na, I'm too old for this sort of thing. (*then*) You're being a bit nice all of a sudden. What do you want?

Gemma I'm stuck with my course work.

Alana I thought you'd just come back from interviewing Nanna.

Gemma I have.

Alana And?

Gemma Apart from saying that it was actually rather oppressive to have your mother alive for most of your life.

Alana Not nearly as oppressive as having your little sister alive all your life –

Gemma You better get yourself a job so you can save up for a contract killer 'cos if nature takes its course you'll be dead before me.

Alana Oh happy day.

Gemma Don't say that. Don't even joke about it.

Alana What's it to you? You know they want to switch the machine off for that tree boy.

Gemma It's like they said, don't dwell on it.

Alana They haven't though, only because they still haven't been able to get hold of his mum.

Gemma I wish our parents would go on holiday without us.

Alana Not much chance of that now. Go on say it. Thanks to me.

Gemma I wasn't going to say that. Grandma asked after you.

Alana What did she say, how oppressive it was knowing I was still alive?

Gemma No, she said she wants to see you –

Alana Did she? Did she tell you how Great Nanna went from being in service to university?

Gemma No, that's just it, she wouldn't.

Alana Oh my God, it must be something loathsome and odious.

Gemma Will you go and see her –?

Alana No way.

Gemma But she said she'd tell you.

Alana You mean I'm so low, I can't be corrupted any further.

Gemma Go on.

Alana She didn't ask to see me, did she?

Gemma Yes, she did and she said she'll only tell you.

Alana You've just made that up so I'll go round there. She was glad I didn't go to the funeral because I'd show everyone up. Her mother was so . . . whatever she was . . . Nanna can't even bring herself to tell you. Ha. It looks like it's genetic. I come from a long line of no-good-waste-of-space-fuck-up-losers.

SCENE NINE

Rachel and Steve by Elliot's bed. This time he is lifeless.

Rachel Elliot, I could kill you. Just come back, wake up.
Mum is on her way home –

Steve comes in.

Steve She's arriving at Heathrow this evening.

Rachel What time?

Steve She doesn't want us to meet her. She wants us to
stay here and talk to Elliot.

Rachel What did you tell her?

Steve Only that he'd had a fall and was in a coma.
Don't worry, I didn't mention that they were waiting
for her to arrive before they switched off the machine.

Rachel He probably wouldn't be in this state if someone
had called the ambulance sooner but I don't suppose
you mentioned that either.

Steve How many more times? Hundreds of us were told
to go to that site. It was like a military operation or
something. We were told to advance in rows and not
to break the line and get on with the job of demolishing
the houses. I had no idea he was there.

Rachel Someone must have called an ambulance.

Steve We knew they'd found a body.

Rachel And you're telling me, it never crossed your
mind that it could have been Elliot?

Steve I didn't think.

Rachel Come on. You must have seen the ambulance
arrive . . .

Steve Yeah.

Rachel And you must have seen who went in it. And
recognised him.

Steve I didn't get close enough.

Rachel Have you apologised to him?

Steve For what? I haven't done anything.

Rachel Except wind him up by getting a job as one of those pathetic bailiff's lackeys.

Steve He wound me up more like by getting involved in those daft tree-top protests. You seem to have conveniently forgotten that you also used to go into one when he started spouting that pretentious eco warrior, earth firster jargon.

Rachel At least his choice was one of principle.

Steve Oh yes, principle. That luxury afforded to the privileged few. He can take a year out of his studies. He has a place at university. They'll wait. Someone like him, they'll hold their breath. He's worth waiting for. People with principles never have to take jobs that pay three forty an hour. They're allowed principles but I'm not supposed to be allowed the dignity of taking the only job that I've been offered in a year. If I had choice maybe then I'd have principles.

Rachel Everyone has choice.

Steve Where d'you get that idea? Off *Songs of Praise*?

Rachel We shouldn't be doing this, not with his friends waiting outside. I'm sorry.

Steve Me too. No, I am.

Rachel (*going over to Kelly*) You can come in, now.

Kelly tentatively approaches. She has an enormous Elastoplast over her nose or ear, whichever place has had the nail removed from it.

Kelly Thanks . . . I'm not sure . . .

Rachel We'll wait over here . . .

Rachel and Steve stand back from the others.

Kelly Elliot . . . hi. They've said we should come and say goodbye . . . I wanted to show you the nail. It's still got a bit of my nose hanging on it – look. I thought it would make you laugh . . . or gag or something . . . Actually, I thought it might shock you enough to make you open your eyes . . . I really wish I had the power to do that.

Jamie comes in and goes over to Elliot.

Jamie Pal, you got to buck up or they are going to pull the plug. I really couldn't see you lying down the bottom there, you know that, don't you? (*then*) But also I was frightened, wasn't I, to lean over further . . . if I had . . . maybe I would have seen you . . . but I suddenly freaked being tied up there and was terrified I'd slip over, dragging the others on top of me. Please, mate, just come round, if only to tell me it's alright.

Tom comes in and goes over to Elliot.

Tom Elliot, you know that the human nervous system has a greater number of possible connections than a telephone exchange with a line to every person on earth. Mate, you just need to connect and pick up the receiver.

Cassie comes over to Elliot.

Cassie I think it's important that you know that because you're lying here, they don't dare cut down the tree. We don't even have to maintain a presence there. You can't get near it in fact for the flowers that surround it. And everyday there's been more. You're a national hero, Elliot. You and you alone saved it. Thank you.

Rachel sees them out. They smile appropriately at her but give Steve dirty looks. When they've gone and he's alone, Steve goes over to Elliot.

Steve Alright, I have always been jealous of you and her come to that but I didn't do it out of spite or jealousy. I did know it was you lying there and I pretended I didn't know you. They've located Mum, your mum, and she's on her way back. It would be brilliant if you weren't lying here now because, mate, I'm having a hard time of it here. It's hard to admit, it's just that some of those guys, the muppets with the chainsaws, they make *Reservoir Dogs* look like an advert for Pedigree Chum. I didn't want it to be you but I was afraid, in front of the others, to own up to knowing you. And scared that the bosses would think I'd tipped your lot off. I was ashamed, humiliated, I stood there doing nothing and feeling sick but it's nothing to how bad I feel now. Your mother's on her way back. Please, Elliot don't let me have to face her without you.

SCENE TEN

Elliot and Lucy.

Elliot My head feel loads better . . . I think I can sleep now. You go . . .
Lucy Come on, get up, go back to your friends . . .
Elliot I can't face them. I've been too much of a coward.
Lucy You can't sleep here . . .
Elliot I'm so tired I could sleep anywhere . . .
Lucy It's too cold . . .
Elliot (*very drowsy*) It's not. I'll be fine.

Lucy hears footsteps.

Lucy What was that?
Elliot What?
Lucy Someone's watching us.
Elliot (*mumbles*) You're imagining it.
Lucy (*shaking Elliot*) It's him! It's him!
Elliot (*unable to rouse himself*) There's no one there.
Lucy There is – look. I'm for it now.

Elliot Take a deep breath.
Lucy So will you be . . . please go . . . just go . . .
Elliot (*trying to rouse himself*) I can't. I can't see anyone.
Lucy Elliot, run . . . get away . . . get help . . .
Elliot (*with great effort rouses himself but is unable now to see her*) Lucy? What's happening? Where are you?

SCENE ELEVEN

Hospital. Steve and Elliot.
Elliot twitches.

Steve Do that again? And again? Elliot speak to me. Can you? Elliot? (*He moves towards the door, calls.*) Nurse?
Elliot Lucy?
Steve What? Did you say something?
Elliot Lucy.
Steve It's me, Steve . . .
Elliot Lucy.
Steve Who are you pissing well calling Lucy? Stop winding me up.
Elliot (*becoming distressed, calling out*) Where is she? What's happened to her?
Steve It's alright it's me – Steve. You're safe.
Elliot (*shouts*) Lucy?
Steve Hold on mate. I'm going to get someone. Just hold on.

SCENE TWELVE

Gemma sits alone. Alana bursts in.

Alana Lucy was Great-Nanna's name, wasn't it?
Gemma So?

Alana If I go round to see Nanna and get the info, will
you come to the hospital with me?
Gemma The hospital? Alana? You're not?
Alana Of course not. How could I be? I haven't been
out for weeks. No, you know they were waiting for
that bloke's mother to get back from holiday . . .
Gemma What?
Alana Before they could switch the life-support machine
off. The tree-top one. Elliot. He's come round. But
he's gone harpic. He keeps calling for someone called
Lucy.
Gemma How could that possibly have anything to do
with Great-Grandma?
Alana I don't know, do I, but they're asking for anyone
called Lucy who knows him to come forward to jog
his memory.
Gemma That'll be hard, or were you planning to take a
medium with you?
Alana Don't be sick. It might get me in to see him –
Gemma Do you really think that's such a good idea?
Alana I don't know.
Gemma Then . . .
Alana Don't you think it's worth a try?
Gemma Don't ask me.
Alana If I could help him somehow I wouldn't feel so
shit about –
Gemma Okay. Deal.

SCENE THIRTEEN

*Elliot is sitting up. Jamie, Kelly, Cassie and Tom are
visiting. Steve stands watching some way off.*

Kelly I used to know a Lucy.
Elliot Yeah?

Kelly But I don't think you ever met her. She was a dinner lady at my primary school.

Cassie Kelly!

Kelly At least I'm trying.

Elliot She was at the bottom of the tree.

Cassie So you keep saying.

Jamie She couldn't have been, pal. I'd have seen her.

Elliot You remember we heard footsteps?

Jamie I don't think I heard nothing until they all came swarming through the park.

Elliot Before. When we were on the platform. You heard them too, Kelly.

Kelly I can't say I did really. Having my ear squashed against the platform was a bit like having it against a shell. Sounds got distorted.

Tom You were unconscious, Elliot. If there had been someone with you when they found you, they'd have seen her as well.

Elliot Yeah, they took her. They took her somewhere. She didn't want to go.

The others look at each other and Jamie starts to hum the X-Files *theme music.*

Cassie Shut up, Jamie. Haven't you ever heard of post-traumatic stress disorder? I think we should go and let Elliot get some rest.

Alana and Gemma go up to Steve. The others go leaving Elliot alone.

Alana We're here to visit Elliot.

Steve (*looking at her suspiciously*) And you are?

Alana Er . . . Lucy.

Steve (*recognising her*) And the rest. What do you think my name is, Jack Arse, Jack Shit? I read the papers you know. Just get lost before I get you thrown out of here.

Alana I've come to see Elliot . . .

Steve He's getting all the drugs he needs.

Gemma Hang on –

Steve I don't know who you are but I know who she is. She was in the papers for selling E to that lad what dropped dead and she's just been excluded from school. You should be locked up, not allowed to roam around hospitals. How dare you turn up here?

Alana I think I might be able to help him.

Steve What is your problem? Not been in the limelight for a couple of weeks, is that it? You want me to call the police? You a publicity junkie or what?

Gemma She risked coming here to see if she could help your brother. If he was my brother I think I'd try it wouldn't you?

Steve And you are?

Gemma Her sister.

Steve Her real sister?

Alana Unfortunately. (*They both look at her.*) For her.

Steve How come you talk so different?

Alana She won a scholarship to a private school.

Gemma A snob school. Now are you going to let us talk to your brother or not?

Steve Whatever it is you got to say you can say it to me.

Alana Alright, I know it might sound weird but –

Gemma Don't tell him. If he won't let you see Elliot we'll go. Come on.

Steve Wait up. You can see him but I'll be sitting in. And I want you gone by the time my mother and sister get here.

They go up to Elliot.

Alana Hi.

Elliot (*wary*) Hello.

Alana I've come to talk to you about Lucy . . .

Elliot You're not her.

Alana No, but –

Elliot You do look a bit similar.

Alana I hope not. She was a hundred and one and totally harpic.

Elliot looks puzzled.

Gemma (*by way of explanation*) Clean round the bend.

Alana On top of which she's been buried a week.

Elliot Not the same one then. She was only about your age.

Alana This is all going to sound completely mad, right. She was in service in that house. You know what that means?

Elliot She was a maid who had to live in . . .

Alana Yeah. Anyway, she was a bit of a slapper by all accounts an' all.

Elliot Really.

Gemma She doesn't mean that.

Alana That's what Nanna told me.

Gemma Our great-grandmother's daughter.

Elliot She said that about her own mother?

Alana That's what she meant. Apparently she was used to entertaining men in her bedroom. One night the son of the house thought he heard someone breaking in and he went out and thinking he saw a burglar up the tree, he shot him. Only it was dark and it wasn't a bloke but our great-grandmother, Lucy, obviously Luce by name loose by nature, who had been climbing out to meet her lover.

Elliot But I thought you said that she only died last week?

Alana Because she wasn't shot dead. She survived. The family didn't want any trouble from the police so they gave her wads of money to be quiet.

Elliot Slapper is a rather sexually derogatory word to use about your own mother.

Gemma I think it's weird that she told her daughter about it.

Alana No, she didn't tell Nanna anything. But they moved back into this area when Nanna was a little girl, and she heard people talking about it. Lucy never talked about her time in service until the end of her life when it was like she didn't know whether she was talking out loud or not.

Elliot It's all so strange . . . it's like a dream now. She was a bit stunned and when I said I thought she must have fallen, she looked panic-stricken.

Alana She'd just fallen out of a tree from a great height after being shot. She'd have to be some cool babe to be serene about it.

Elliot No, I think the son of the house was sexually harassing her. That's what it was . . . I think she was worried that she might even be pregnant . . .

Gemma She told you all that?

Elliot I don't suppose she was inhibited as she might of been if she'd thought me real. She believed that she'd dreamt me up. To get him off her back.

Alana Off her front don't you mean?

Elliot Don't you see, she threatened him with a boyfriend. He must have been scared that the bloke would come and beat him up or something so he went out with the intention of shooting him and if caught he was going to say that he thought the boyfriend was a burglar. However, he shot her by mistake.

Gemma Then how come everyone thought she was a woman of very loose morals?

Elliot That was probably part of the deal with the family to protect their son. They'd give her money as long as she stuck to their version of the story. And once she'd taken the money and given her word she never went back on it.

Alana She sold out.

Elliot Did she go to university?
Gemma Yes.
Elliot Well, that's what she did with the money.

Silence.

Gemma Amazing.
Alana What a shame Gran and Mum never knew. They could have been proud of her.

Elliot sees the hammer hanging from Gemma's belt.

Elliot That's her hammer.
Gemma (*she takes it off her belt and shows it to Elliot*) It was, yeah.
Elliot Yes. Look, F.L.Y.I.T.C.S. Did she tell you what that stood for?
Gemma No. I only got this after she died.
Elliot For – Lucy. – Yours – In – The – Cause. – Sylvia.
Gemma No kidding. What, Sylvia, as in Pankhurst?
Elliot That's why she was so proud of it.

Silence.

Alana So when you get out of here, you want to go for a burger sometime or what?
Elliot I'm afraid I'm veggie.
Alana That's like 'Sorry I'm washing my hair,' right?
Elliot Thanks though . . .
Alana Actually, it's her you have to thank. She did all the work.
Gemma No, I never.
Alana (*shrugs*) I think I'll go for a Coke. (*Calls over her shoulder to Steve.*) Black liquid as opposed to white powder. (*to Gemma*) Meet you back at the canteen.

Steve follows Alana.

Steve Thanks. Hey, hold up. I just wanted to say thanks. I really do appreciate it.

Alana Yeah, right.

Steve Sorry he gave you the brush off.

Alana I don't mean to be offensive but I'd sort of gone off him the minute he opened his gob.

Steve Oh, yeah?

Alana Listen, if there's one thing I can't stand, it's boys who slap you down by politically correcting your fucking language.

Steve What can you stand then?

Alana Don't waste your breath asking.

Steve I know this much. You like shocking people.

Alana Everyone's supposed to be good at something, aren't they? (*She goes.*)

SCENE FOURTEEN

Elliot and Gemma at the bottom of the tree which is still surrounded by floral tributes.

Elliot This is too weird. It's like I've died.

Gemma I suppose you nearly did.

Elliot Yeah and in 1913 so did your great-grandmother.

Gemma If she had then she wouldn't have been my great-grandmother, if you see what I mean, and Grandma wouldn't have been born then neither would my mother or I –

Elliot Stop it. You're doing my head in. Why wouldn't your gran tell you the story about her?

Gemma At first I thought it was because it involved sex but I don't think it was that actually. I think she thought it would help Alana.

Elliot How?

Gemma (*shrugs*) Explaining that her great-grandmother survived a great trauma but was able to get on and make something of her life?

Elliot And has it had any effect?

Gemma Yeah, it seems to have worked. She spends less time in front of the TV and she's been a lot nicer to me.

Elliot That must be a relief.

Gemma Feels very strange. Not as strange as you having met my great-grandmother when she was only a girl. How do you explain that?

Elliot I don't know . . .

Gemma If I wrote any of this down, they'd probably send me to see the Ed. Psych. to have my head examined.

Elliot (*holding her head*) Ah, yes very unusual, descended from a matriarchal line of headstrong, intellectual and attractive women. (*He leans over to kiss her. Gemma turns away.*) Sorry . . . sorry . . .

Gemma I just had a horrible thought . . . that I might turn into a hundred-and-one-year-old woman . . . Did you kiss her?

Elliot No!

Gemma Oh, well, I guess that makes . . . it a bit better . . . but I also get the feeling that someone's watching us.

Elliot Not again. Keep still. (*He looks around.*) Oh yes. Over there.

Gemma What's he doing here?

Elliot I think he's following me . . .

Gemma Creepy.

Elliot Ever since I got well he's been very protective. It was much better when he wanted to kill me.

Gemma Do you think he's seen us?

Elliot Let's see if we can give him the slip. Come on.

SCENE FIFTEEN

Alana stands alone on the tree platform. Steve climbs up.

Alana (*jumps*) What are you doing here?

Steve Spying on my step-brother.

Alana They've gone.

Steve Do you do the same then?

Alana The same what?

Steve Making sure she's OK. Ever since it happened, I want to make sure Elliot's OK.

Alana Gemma will always be OK. No, I thought I'd come here to see if I could feel what my great-grandmother felt when she fell out of this thing. I didn't realise Gemma had a date with Elliot.

Steve You jealous?

Alana shakes her head.

I am.

Alana You're too bloody old for my sister.

Steve No, no. I mean of him. His belief in something, that it matters, that's he's prepared to put his life on hold for it, that he has friends who feel the same. Oh shit, I feel embarrassed now.

Alana It's easy to believe in something. Why don't we start the 'Give concrete and exhaust pipes a break' movement?

Steve (*laughs*) Yeah, you know the worst thing about all this environmental mania is that it will push up the price of cars and I can't ever see myself affording one as it is.

Alana Still, I suppose it's thanks to them that this park's still here. Imagine if poor people had nowhere to go but walk round and round the locked shopping centre of an evening, watching others stuffing their faces in restaurants where you can buy champagne by the glass and being able to spend more money on Pick-and-Mix sweets in the cinema than on the film.

Steve Are your parents hard up, then?

Alana Take no notice. I'm talking out of my arse.

Steve Do they know where you are?

Alana No.

Steve Will they be worried?

Alana If they find I'm not in my room, yeah. But making me stay in is, I think, more about their concern about someone beating me up than wanting to punish me.

Steve (*takes some money from his pocket*) You don't fancy . . .

Alana What you doing, trying to give me money for sex?

Steve No!

Alana I will if you want.

Steve I was going to say I've got money for a film and some Pick-and-Mix.

Alana No, thanks, I want to stay here, but you go ahead.

Steve I thought you knew how your great-grandmother fell.

Alana Suppose she didn't fall though? Suppose she jumped? Suppose she was pregnant and so ashamed she couldn't face it so she threw herself out of the window?

Steve Suppose she did, so what? (*Beat.*) No, don't even think about it. You don't have to do the same. Things are different these days.

Alana How?

Steve There are abortions for starters.

Alana I'm not pregnant. That would be easy . . . so much easier.

Steve Than what?

Alana Being me. Being the girl that sold the E that killed him. Whatever I do I will always be known as that girl and even if I'm not I'll always know it. There'll be days and days like this and months and years. But if I jumped out of this tree do you think I might be able to meet him and tell him not to take it and that he would then live until he was a hundred and one?

Steve No, I think that's barking.

Alana What, as in, up the wrong tree?

Steve Yeah.

Alana shrugs and turns away.

You have to move forward.

Alana I don't know how.

Steve What do you want?

Alana I want to be brave enough to jump.

Steve Sometimes the most courageous thing to do is to keep breathing.

The End.

The Most Courageous Thing is to Keep Breathing

When she was sixteen, a friend persuaded Sarah Daniels
to visit the local repertory theatre using free tickets that
the school had been given. The first grudging visit
developed into a passion that led, ten years later, to a
full-time career as a dramatist.

> In a way that wasn't even perceptible to me, I went
> from thinking what a dull boring thing the first play
> I went to was, to the point where I couldn't wait for
> the next one. When I left school I went to a lot of
> political and feminist fringe theatre. Inevitably, I saw
> some plays that were not very good and this gave me
> confidence to think that maybe I could write a play, so
> I got to work on one for eighteen months in my spare
> time without telling anyone. I sent this play to the
> Royal Court and, although it was rejected, I had an
> encouraging letter.

The Royal Court put on Sarah Daniels's second play and
then Anthony Minghella, script editor for the children's
drama series *Grange Hill* at the time, asked her to
submit a script. She has now been writing for *Grange
Hill* for ten years and has written for the BBC soap
opera, *East Enders*.

In *Taking Breath* five young people spend a night on a
tree platform to prevent the destruction of the trees and
some houses. One of the protestors, Elliot, tries to leave
the tree, falls and is left unconscious. As he is lying there
he encounters Lucy, a servant who in 1913 worked in
one of the houses that is to be demolished. The dramatic
thread weaves backwards and forwards in time. In the

opening scene we learn that Elliot has been in a coma for a week. We then have scenes on the tree platform interspersed with Lucy telling Elliot about the suffragettes, how she was sexually harassed, how she had tried to frighten off the son of the house by telling him she had a boyfriend. Finally we have scenes in the hospital where Alana and Steve meet and we see them on the tree platform.

Sarah Daniels had in mind a play about protest but also about cowardice and bravery. In *Taking Breath* Elliot loses his nerve and leaves the platform, Jamie is too scared to check if Elliot has fallen, Tom can't get down quickly enough, Kelly is obsessed about the damage to her ear and Cassie, in the face of danger, reverts to singing 'embarrassing old hippy shit'. Not exactly the stuff of eco-warriors.

> I wasn't writing about experienced eco-warriors. I know that seasoned campaigners take a lot of safety precautions. I didn't want my characters to be very good at it. They aren't old hands. They get this piece of news that the demolition is to begin a day early so, on impulse, they decide there and then, without thinking of the risk, to handcuff themselves to the tree. I have great admiration for anyone who has the courage to protest, even if cowardice may make them forget their principles in the heat of the moment.

In *Taking Breath*, Alana and Steve meet in the hospital. They are both abrasive characters and react angrily to each other. He is guilty about the way he has treated his half-brother and angry at the way his life has gone up to this point. Alana has her own guilt

> I have a lot of affection for Alana. At the start of the play she is depressed and rude. I think she is very frightened at what she has done. Part of her

depression is that she is afraid to face the outside world. And then she learns that Elliot has come out of his coma and is asking for someone called Lucy. By this time Alana has learned quite a bit about her great-grandmother and believes she might be the Lucy that Elliot is asking for. I believe it is very brave of her to go to the hospital with her sister to face the outside world, the hostility and the ridicule. It is fortunate that she meets Steve, one of the few people who can help her.

By the end of *Taking Breath*, Elliot has recovered from his coma, the tree is still standing and Alana and Steve are supporting each other in a tentative, ambiguous way. For all her bravado Alana is in no mood to contemplate a relationship with Steve. He, however, understands her because he has been unhappy, out of work, impoverished and has felt guilty. The question of protest is also somewhat ambiguous. The play examines the way protest has gone on throughout the century and how it has changed. Lucy the suffragette is at home with a bomb, she smashes windows with her toffee hammer and believes in deeds not words. She is incredulous at Elliot's way of protesting, which he sees as very female, nurturing, peaceful and respectful of mother earth. Steve refers to principle as the luxury afforded the privileged few.

> I think that everyone can have principles but, if you are poor and out of work as Steve is, you have to weigh the dignity of having a job against your principles. This is not an 'issues' play but most plays are political as much by what they don't say as what they deal with. I don't think theatre can revolutionise things but it can be one of many influences that can change people. I think if a play can engage your emotions, intellect and imagination then there is a chance that it will shift your attitudes.

Production Notes

STAGING AND SETTING

Settings for *Taking Breath* include a platform in a tree, a
living room and a special care room in a hospital. The
action between each location should be as fluid as
possible and happens in the course of a week. The tree
top needs to give a sense of height since action happens
below. The tree's spirituality and magic may be conveyed
by using a gobo or by lighting the branches from below.
Use sound to suggest the rustle of leaves, and the tree
whispering and breathing. The more successful you are
in creating the tree top in the quiet of a moonlit night
the more impact you will get from the noise of engines
approaching, the chainsaw being activated and the
ambulance siren. You will be able to create a sense of
distance between the protestors and the 'heavies' who
have come to remove them by having the man with the
loud hailer and the other voices off-stage. The hospital
room can be suggested very simply with a hospital bed
on casters and the sound of a life-support machine.
Avoid blackouts which fragment the story and allow the
cast to wheel on the bed, portable TV and settee, etc,
as part of the action. From Scene Ten onwards the
transitions from locations happen very quickly and are
emotionally charged. For example, you could tie together
neatly the woods and hospital scene, where Lucy enters
Elliot's time, by playing this scene in the hospital. Elliot
can stay in bed and the lighting can suggest the location.
When Elliot and Lucy meet it is important that they
don't realise that they are from different times so their
costumes will need to be thought through carefully.
Modern fashion is eclectic and influenced by the turn of

the century. The protesters are likely to be dressed in
'grunge style' clothing for example, long skirts, layers,
underclothes and boots. It would be quite plausible for
Lucy to be wearing something similar. Or her clothes
might be concealed by a cloak.

CASTING

The play is written for a central cast of ten. Their age
range is from thirteen to nineteen. There are five female
and male roles. Male voices are heard off-stage.

EXERCISES

Much appears in the press about teenage protestors and
'eco warriors'. Look at back issues of newspapers, articles
and photographs. Build up a picture of the sort of causes
young people are prepared to go to extremes to support.
Look at the group of protestors in *Taking Breath*. Discuss
to what degree each individual is committed to saving
the tree. Discover how their varying degrees of commit-
ment affect their actions.

Have half of the group look at Scene One and the other
half at Scene Five. 'Action' the text by working through
it and deciding, moment by moment, who is doing what
to whom in each line: e.g., shocking, shaming, prompting,
etc. Have the group observing Scene One stop the action
at intervals and guess which actions are being used.
Repeat the exercise for those observing Scene Five.

Distribute playing cards amongst the group so that each
has one card per scene. King is high and ace is as low as
it gets in this exercise. A high card means that the actor
must play the dominant emotion in each scene to highest

possible effect. A low card means keeping the effect minimal. Discover how highly-charged a scene should be by establishing which cards work best.

Have the whole group sit on the floor together with legs outstretched, knees and feet together and holding hands. The aim of this exercise is for everyone in the group to get into a standing position without bending their knees, moving their feet apart or letting go of the hands of the people either side of them. Now vary the exercise by getting the group to put coats on, have a drink, open a crisp packet etc. See how this exercise can be applied to the tree-top protestors when they are handcuffed together.

Improvise the scene which we hear but do not see – when the men come to knock down the tree. Experiment with building up the noise of their approach from a distance and the menacing sound of their vehicles approaching. Play the scene as if they are expecting to see the teenagers in the tree. Repeat it imagining that their presence takes them by surprise. 'Hotseat' the group of men and have them describe what they encountered.

Elliot and Lucy are brought together through the synchronicity of time and location. Lucy could have died the same moment that Elliot fell out of the tree and their subconscious met. At this moment they have a lot in common. They are both young protestors, they are terrified for their lives and they have fallen unconscious in the same place. We know what happened to Elliot moments before he fell but we can only speculate about what happened to Lucy. Using the information from the play, have the group create a back history for her by improvising the scene before she lands on the ground. Decide which of the theories about her is most likely to be true.

Have the group tell each other ghost stories and tales of the paranormal throughout the rehearsal period.

We know from the script that Lucy was involved in the suffragette movement in 1913. This is the year that the suffragettes became militant and Emily Davidson died after running across the race course and under the King's horse. The movement at this stage was underground and disguises were provided by the Actresses' Franchise League. The women protested by smashing windows, and this is what Lucy's toffee hammer is for. It has extra significance because it was the gift of Sylvia Pankhurst, a leading suffragette of the time. Find out what you can about the movement and how Lucy is likely to have been involved in it.

Look at the scene where Kelly, Cassie and Tom visit Elliot in hospital. Find different ways of staging the confessional speeches. These could be private moments, whispered individually to him, or they could be round the bedside talking openly. Play it so that the others are aware of what Jamie is about to say. Play this moment again when what he says comes as a complete revelation.

Suzy Graham-Adriani
February 1999

The following companies premièred the BT National Connections portfolio of new plays in Spring 1999.

1812 Youth Theatre, Helmesley, Yorkshire
Armagh Youth Drama Group, Belfast
Aylwin Girls School, London
Bangor Drama Club, Co. Down
Barbican Youth Theatre, Devon
Behind the Scenes Youth Theatre, Edinburgh
Bentley Wood High School, Middlesex
Bishop Luffa School, West Sussex
Blackbird Theatre, Belfast
Boilerhouse Youth Theatre, Huddersfield
Borders Youth Theatre, Scottish Borders
Bos Productions, Bristol
Brimsham Green School, South Gloucestershire
Brookfield High School, Merseyside
Brunton Youth Theatre, East Lothian
Cabinteely Youth Theatre, Co. Wicklow,
Caithness Youth Theatre, Thurso
Callington School and Community College, Cornwall
Cannock Chase High School, Staffs.
Cardiff High School
Central Buchan Youth Theatre, Aberdeenshire
Central Junior Television Workshop, Nottingham
Chelmsford County High School, Essex
Chichester Festival Youth Theatre
Christleton High School, Chester
City of Nottingham Education Theatre Company
Classworks Youth Theatre, Cambridge
Commotion North Ayrshire Youth Theatre
Connected Youth Theatre, Rugby
Contact Youth Theatre, Manchester
Cranleigh School, Surrey
Crawshaw School, Leeds
Crucible Youth Theatre, Sheffield

CRYPT: Warehouse Youth Theatre, London
Cumbernauld Youth Theatre
Dashers, Monmouth
Downend School, Bristol
Droichead Youth Theatre, Co. Louth, Ireland
Dulwich College Drama Department, London
Dumont High School, New Jersey, USA
Durrington High School, West Sussex
Eastbourne Youth Theatre
Eden Court Youth Theatre, Inverness
Elizabethan High School, Nottinghamshire
Fearnhill School, Herts.
Flies on the Wall, Gloucestershire
Fred Longworth High School, Manchester
Frome Community College, Somerset
Galway Youth Theatre, Ireland
Gordonstoun School, Scotland
Group 64 Youth Theatre, London
Half Moon Youth Theatre, London
Hall Green Little Theatre Youth Section, Birmingham
Harlington Upper School, Bedfordshire
Harlow College Community Arts Group, Essex
Harper Green School, Lancashire
Hasland Hall Community School, Chesterfield
Heatham House Youth Theatre, Twickenham
Heywood Community School, Gloucestershire
Hills Road Sixth Form College, Cambridge
Hillside School, Herts.
IMP Youth Theatre, Lincoln
Impington Village College, Cambridge
Integrierte Gesamtschule, Kandel, Germany
Interplay Youth Theatre Project, Leeds

Isle of Skye Youth Theatre
Ivybridge Community College, Devon
James Hornsey High School, Essex
Lagan College, Belfast
LBT Youth Theatre, Huddersfield
Leighton Buzzard Children's Theatre, Bedfordshire
Lochaber Youth Theatre, Kinlochleven
London Bubble Mega-Bytes, London
Looe Community School, Cornwall
MacRobert Youth Theatre, Stirling
Manningtree High School, Essex
Mansfield Palace Youth Theatre, Nottinghamshire
Medina High School, Isle of Wight
Methody Drama, Belfast
Milan University Youth Section, Italy
Minsthorpe Community College, West Yorkshire
Monaghan Youth Theatre, Ireland
New Peckham Varieties, London
Noadswood School, Hants.
North Down Youth Drama, Co. Down
Northern Theatre Company and School of Performing Arts, Hull
Our Lady and St. Patrick's College, Knock, Belfast
Penrice School, Cornwall
Petersfield Youth Theatre, Hampshire
Playback Youth Theatre, Exeter
Poole Grammar School, Dorset
Porthcawl Comprehensive School, Wales
Queen Elizabeth Maridunum School, Carmarthen
Rainbow Factory, Belfast
Rainsford High School Senior Youth Theatre, Essex
Raw Talent Youth Theatre, Birmingham
Red Lemon Youth Theatre, Dun Laoghaire
Redruth School, Cornwall
Sandbach School Theatre, Chesterfield
Scottish Youth Theatre, Glasgow
Scuola Media Statale "C.ALVARO", Torino, Italy
Scuola Media Statale "G.MARCONI", Torino, Italy
Shared Experience Youth Theatre, London

Shelley High School, Huddersfield
Shetland Youth Theatre
Shrewsbury Sixth Form College
South Ribble Youth Theatre
South West Youth Theatre, London
St. Cuthman's School, West Sussex
St. Edmund Arrowsmith High School, Wigan
St. Ives School, Cornwall
St. John Fisher School, Peterborough
St. Mary's Youth Theatre, Leeds
St. Monica's High School, Manchester
St. Osmund's Middle School, Dorset
St. Thomas High School, Devon
Stagedoor, Norwich
Stagerite Youth Theatre, York
Starfeis Ross-shire, Inverness
Strodes College Theatre Company, Surrey
The Blue School, Somerset
The Colfox School, Dorset
The College Youth Theatre, Blackburn
The Gantry Youth Theatre, Southampton
The Lakes School, Windermere
The Young Company, Plymouth
Theaterwerkstalt (Theater & Schule), Munich, Germany
Theatre Royal Bath Youth Theatre, Bath
Theatrebox, Essex
Thirsk School, North Yorkshire
Varndean College, East Sussex
Victims of Art, Leicester
Waterford Youth Drama, Ireland
Welwyn Hatfield Youth Theatre, Herts
West Lothian Youth Theatre
West Sussex County Youth Theatre
Woodlands School, Essex
Woolston High School, Cheshire
Wymondham College, Norfolk
Y Pant Comprehensive School, Wales
Young Octagon Theatre Company, Somerset
Young Tore, Devon
Youth Connection, Co. Durham
Youth Lyric, Belfast
Youth Theatre Yorkshire, York
Ysgol Morgan Llwyd, North Wales
Ysgol Y Creuddyn, Wales